PRE-COLUMBIAN ARCHAEOLOGY

Readings from
**SCIENTIFIC
AMERICAN**

PRE-COLUMBIAN ARCHAEOLOGY

With Introductions by
Gordon R. Willey
Harvard University

Jeremy A. Sabloff
University of New Mexico

W. H. Freeman and Company
San Francisco

Some of the *Scientific American* articles in *Pre-Columbian Archaeology* are available as separate Offprints. For a complete list of more than 1200 articles now available as Offprints, write to W. H. Freeman and Company, 660 Market Street, San Francisco, California 94104.

Library of Congress Cataloging in Publication Data

Main entry under title:

Pre-Columbian archaeology.

    Includes index.
    1. Indians—Antiquities—Addresses, essays, lectures.
2. America—Antiquities—Addresses, essays, lectures.
I. Willey, Gordon Randolph, 1913-   II. Sabloff,
Jeremy A.   III. Scientific American.
E61.P73   970.01'1   79–26329
ISBN 0–7167–1182–6
ISBN 0–7167–1183–4 pbk.

Printed in the United States of America

9 8 7 6 5 4 3 2 1

PREFACE

P re-Columbian archaeology, the study of the peoples and cultures of the New World before the first European contacts, has received increasing professional and public attention in recent years. Many exciting findings and interpretations are resulting from this attention, and SCIENTIFIC AMERICAN has often been the place where archaeologists have discussed their research in terms accessible to the interested reader who has little or no background in archaeology. This collection of articles has been compiled with both the general reader and introductory archaeology students in mind. It can be used in courses concerned with American archaeology or in world prehistory courses in conjunction with another SCIENTIFIC AMERICAN collection, *Hunters, Farmers, and Civilizations: Old World Archaeology* (with Introductions by C. C. Lamberg-Karlovsky). Although American archaeologists are also greatly interested in the methodological and theoretical development of their discipline, many introductory courses, or segments of these courses, are structured to offer students a perspective of what is currently known of the cultural history of the New World from the time of its initial human habitation until the start of European contacts more than 20,000 years later. This book is designed to offer useful background materials for such courses. Those interested in the theoretical and methodological development of American archaeology might wish to look at our *A History of American Archaeology*, Second Edition (also published by W. H. Freeman and Company, 1980).

We have chosen eighteen articles published in SCIENTIFIC AMERICAN over the past three decades. We have arranged these articles into three main geographical divisions, North America, Mesoamerica, and South America, and we have written short essays to introduce each of the three sections. These essays provide the reader with an overview of the cultural developments in these geographical areas and show how the specific data and interpretations in the articles fit into these more general developments. Maps have been included in the introductory essays so that the reader may locate the sites and regions discussed in the articles. We also have provided a general introductory overview of the evolution of prehistoric cultures in the Americas at the beginning of the book to give readers a feeling for the different kinds of cultures that appeared in the New World throughout the Pre-Columbian period.

A few additional words about the three main geographical divisions used here might be helpful. Actually, they are not strictly conventional geographical definitions but have been modified to meet archaeological convenience. The North American continent includes several culture areas—for example, the Great Plains, the Eastern United States, and the Southwest. Such culture areas were not immutable through time. Indeed, in very early times, Pleistocene environmental and cultural boundaries undoubtedly differed from later configurations; but, in the later Pre-Columbian periods, the culture area concept is a useful one, as are the area chronologies that pertain to them.

The Mesoamerican division is more a cultural definition than a geographical one. Mesoamerica subsumes the southern two-thirds of Mexico and the northern portions of Central America. Most archaeologists and ethnologists conceive of this as a single culture area. Its various regional cultures participated in a common interaction sphere for the interchange of goods and ideas for at least two or three millenia.

South America, which takes in the southern portions of Central America, the West Indies, and the South American continent, is, like North America, composed of several quite different culture areas. Some of these areas are discussed in the articles, and other areas are briefly referred to.

We hope this compilation of SCIENTIFIC AMERICAN articles imparts some of the excitement that currently pervades American archaeology as scholars continue to make great strides in understanding and giving meaning to the Pre-Columbian past of the Americas.

September 1979   Gordon R. Willey
                                                         Jeremy A. Sabloff

CONTENTS

General Introduction   1

I   NORTH AMERICA

II   MESOAMERICA

III   SOUTH AMERICA

Note on cross-references to SCIENTIFIC AMERICAN *articles:* Articles included in this book are referred to by title and page number; articles not included in this book but available as Offprints are referred to by title and offprint number; articles not included in this book and not available as Offprints are referred to by title and date of publication.

PRE-COLUMBIAN ARCHAEOLOGY

GENERAL INTRODUCTION

This collection of articles is intended to provide an overview of ancient human life on the American continents. The articles included here address the major archaeological problems of this prehistoric past. These problems, which are similar to those of Old World archaeology, may be summed up very briefly. *First*, who were the first representatives of humankind in the New World? Where did they come from, and when did they arrive? What kind of lives did they lead? *Second*, when, where, and how did the descendants of these first immigrants establish an agricultural mode of existence? *Third*, from these beginnings of farming and settled life, how were more complex societies and social orders fashioned? And, *fourth*, how did these societies produce the civilizations and Pre-Columbian American states that confronted the first European explorers when they landed on the shores of the New World?

There seems to be little question now that the earliest inhabitants of the Americas were Asiatics who arrived via the Bering Strait and Alaska in a remote Pleistocene (Ice Age) time. But the question of just how remote this time was has been a source of continuing controversy among American archaeologists. One school is of the opinion that the earliest human inhabitants arrived at a relatively recent time, perhaps as late as 10,000 B.C., or just prior to the onset of the late Pleistocene glaciation. At an extreme opposite end of the argument are those who believe that the first Americans may have crossed from Asia as far back as 40,000 years ago or more. An intermediate position, and one favored by perhaps the majority of the New World prehistorians, is that the first entries were most likely in the range from 30,000 to 20,000 years ago during an interglacial era, when the passage from Alaska into midcontinental North America was more feasible.

The first migrants were modern human beings (*Homo sapiens*) of a Mongoloid racial stock, from which the modern American Indian populations are derived. It is unlikely that these migrants had any particular geographical or territorial goal as they moved into the Americas. Rather, they were small family bands of hunters, gatherers, and fishers who were pursuing a livelihood in lands that had become open to them with the recession of the glacial ice fields. These pursuits took them across or along the land bridge then formed between the Northeast Asian (Siberian) and Alaskan mainlands. They would have traveled by foot or in small boats (kayaks). Clearly, there must have been many such migrations over several centuries and perhaps millenia. We do not know what language or languages these migrants spoke, although we can speculate that these early tongues were ancestral to the many diverse languages now spoken by the American Indian groups of the New World.

The tools and artifacts that were made and carried by the early American hunters provide archaeologists with their main source of information about the lifeways of these people. At the same time, these implements and the geological contexts in which they are found are the bases for interpretations—and arguments—concerning the time of arrival of these early immigrants into the New World and the cultural heritage they brought with them. Those who believe that the first human presence in this hemisphere dates back 40,000 years ago or more rest their case on extremely crude stone tools, which in their opinion resemble Middle and Lower Paleolithic forms in the Old World—chopping and scraping forms—and which are believed to come from early geological deposits in the western United States. Also, some human bones from this same general area not only have ancient geological contexts but also have been dated by physicochemical analyses to very remote periods. But the scattered nature of these putative early finds, the uncertainties of their geological associations, and the experimental nature of new laboratory dating techniques in the physical and chemical sciences have led many American archaeologists to adopt an attitude of caution regarding such early dating for human occupation of the New World. These skeptics, while admitting that technological crudity in stone artifacts might be indicative of great antiquity, also offer the counterargument that limitations in sampling and recovery of only partially complete artifact inventories might offer misleading evidence. Still, with the growing number of publications reporting on careful stratigraphic excavations of early sites, and with the accumulation of a significant body of radiocarbon datings of these discoveries, the majority of American archaeologists are now becoming convinced of man's presence in both North and South America between 30,000 and 20,000 B.C. The artifactual materials from these discoveries are, for the most part, crude chopping and scraping tools, however, some finds among them show resemblances in techniques of flint-chipping to the finer blade tool traditions of Europe and Asia—the Old World Middle and Upper Paleolithic stages—and these technological resemblances have suggested to some scholars the possible Old World origins of the more clearly defined New World artifacts.

These more clearly defined New World Early Man manifestations appear by 12,000 to 10,000 years ago (10,000 to 8000 B.C.), and they are characterized by a chipped flint blade and projectile point tradition that appears throughout much of the Americas. This is the well-known tradition of the Clovis and Folsom and related hunters who pursued and killed large Pleistocene animals (mammoth, mastodon, and early forms of bison). Although the emergence of this tradition is probably to be explained in part on the basis of Old World-derived advances in lithic technology of the preceding millennia, this development is not well understood. There is little doubt, however, that the Clovis-Folsom technology developed in the Americas from such prototypes. Indeed, the uniqueness and the suddenness of the Clovis-Folsom phenomena and the general vagueness of earlier American evidence had led some archaeologists to believe that this American Paleo-Indian horizon represented the very first peopling of the New World; but, as we have seen, finds of the last decade or so would now seem to indicate that the Clovis-Folsom or Paleo-Indian tradition is not the very earliest New World culture type, although it is certainly the most clearly defined.

With the end of the last glaciation (*ca.* 8000 B.C.) and the concomitant climatic and environmental changes that took place at that time, a wide variety of cultural adjustments and developments occurred throughout the New World. The late Pleistocene hunters and gatherers adapted to a great many new ecological niches, which came into being with the Post-Pleistocene. In many regions, subsistence continued to be heavily weighted toward hunting; in others, marine or littoral adaptations proved to be the most successful; in still others, adaptive subsistence strategies turned more and more toward

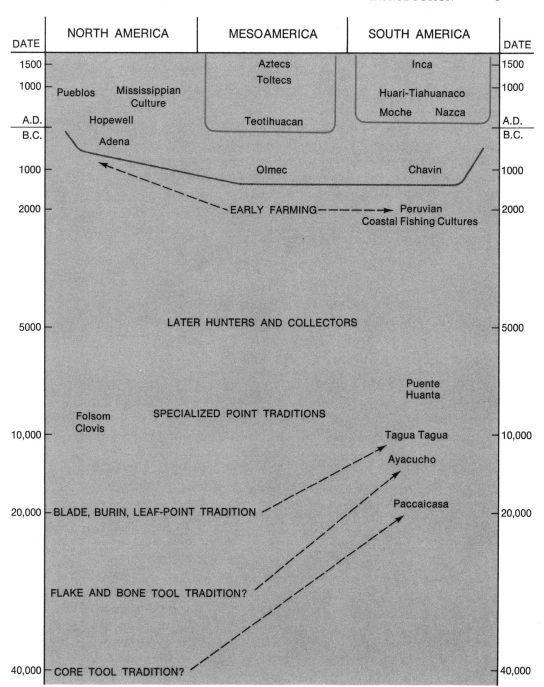

DATE	NORTH AMERICA	MESOAMERICA	SOUTH AMERICA	DATE

(chart labels)

DATE

1500
1000
A.D.
B.C.

1000

2000

5000

10,000

20,000

40,000

NORTH AMERICA

Pueblos   Mississippian Culture
Hopewell
Adena

Folsom
Clovis   SPECIALIZED POINT TRADITIONS

BLADE, BURIN, LEAF-POINT TRADITION

FLAKE AND BONE TOOL TRADITION?

CORE TOOL TRADITION?

LATER HUNTERS AND COLLECTORS

EARLY FARMING

MESOAMERICA

Aztecs
Toltecs

Teotihuacan

Olmec

SOUTH AMERICA

Inca

Huari-Tiahuanaco
Moche   Nazca

Chavin

Peruvian
Coastal Fishing Cultures

Puente
Huanta

Tagua Tagua

Ayacucho

Paccaicasa

DATE

1500
1000
A.D.
B.C.

1000

2000

5000

10,000

20,000

40,000

This chronological developmental chart of Pre-Columbian cultures refers to the lithic traditions associated with MacNeish's article "Early Man in the Andes." According to his interpretation, the Core Tool, Flake and Bone Tool, and Blade, Burin, and Leaf-Point traditions resulted from slow diffusions from Northeast Asia through North America and Mesoamerica, with eventual manifestations in South America as indicated. The gray line marks the beginnings of nonegalitarian or chiefdom societies; the blue line marks the development of the state in Mesoamerica and Peru. Various culture types or phases referred to in the accompanying introductions and articles are indicated on the chart.

plant gathering and toward experimentation (however casual or accidental at first) with the plant resources at their disposal.

Some of the most highly specialized of these Post-Pleistocene hunting and fishing cultures are those known from eastern North America, and the term *Archaic stage* cultures is often applied to them. They are found throughout the eastern part of the continent. Their hunting equipment included the *atlatl,* or throwing stick, which was armed with flint-tipped darts. The projectile tips of the stage are characteristically large, heavy-stemmed forms, well adapted to deer and smaller game. Other characteristic artifacts include ground and polished stone axes and boat-shaped or winged-shaped items, often very finely crafted, which were used as weights on the throwing-sticks. Polished stone ornaments were also common in many regional Archaic cultures. While the Archaic peoples of the eastern North American continent lived a seminomadic existence, with a seasonal shifting of residence to follow food resources, some of their sites are of considerable extent and depth. Most notable among these, for example, are the huge shell midden mounds of the Tennessee River and the St. Johns River in Florida. Such sites indicate sizable congregations of people, even if on only a periodic basis. Other generally similar shell-fishing stations, although pertaining to quite different Archaic stage cultures, are those of the California and the Brazilian coasts.

With regard to those Post-Pleistocene cultures whose harvesting of and experimentation with wild plants provided the context for the beginnings of agriculture, the best evidence to date of this important transition comes from a small highland valley in Mexico. Other records of the rise of agriculture have been found in the Andean area and to a lesser extent elsewhere. In general, in the tropical latitudes of the New World, wild plant resources offered a greater number of suitable food plants for domestication, and in these latitudes we find evidences of the earliest settled village life based upon farming. From these beginnings, plant cultivation appears to have spread rapidly and widely in the New World, so that large populations on both continents came to depend on this type of subsistence economy.

Unlike the Old World, the rise of native village life in the Americas relied essentially on plant foods. Except for certain regions in the central and southern Andes of South America, animal domestication never became an important part of agriculture or an economic alternative to plant cultivation in Pre-Columbian America.

This New World transformation from food gathering to food production was one of the most important thresholds of culture change for Pre-Columbian peoples and societies, and the causes of the change have intrigued archaeologists for decades. The causes were not simple. It was not a matter of the sudden discovery that maize (corn) seed would grow and improve with selective and continuous planting. On the contrary, the evidence indicates that such plant experimentation had been going on for a very long time—in some regions dating back perhaps as early as 7000 B.C. Rather, the key step in this course of domesticated plant development seems to have been a major reliance on such domesticated foods and a corresponding deemphasis of wild plant gathering. This decision had profound consequences, because the commitment of labor and resources to this new direction did not allow for an easy turning back. Some authorities have argued that this step was a directed attempt to provide food resources for growing populations; others see the sequence reversed—a random or fortuitous initial choice led to increased food supplies, from which the population increase followed. In either case, it seems obvious that the overall relationship between agricultural production and population growth was an interactive one; and, by the very nature of the data, the archaeologist is forced to investigate both lines of argument.

The consequences of the rise of agriculture are clear, no matter why or how it happened. The movement away from a shifting or seminomadic type of existence toward a settled life-style brought about a number of social and economic changes, especially the development of larger and more complex societies. Such complexity is reflected in the growth of social ranking, economic diversity within the community, and the beginnings of the organized apparatus of government. Whereas previous village communities were clusters of individual family or kin-built residential dwellings, the more complex societies are characterized by architectural and other settlement remains that indicate the existence of corporate labor organizations and centralized direction by rulers or chiefs.

The general anthropological term for this type of society, which is based on ranking over and above simple age and sex criteria, is a *chiefdom*. Although there is considerable variation in the social, political, and economic structuring of chiefdoms, an essential quality is ascribed leadership that depends on hereditary succession.

For America, the most detailed evidences for the chiefdom type of society came from ethnographical and early ethnohistorical accounts, which afford us some insight into how such societies worked. For example, the Natchez of the lower Mississippi Valley, when encountered by the French explorers at the end of the seventeenth century, had a rigid class structure divided into two lower classes and a class of nobles. Their ruler was all-powerful in his petty domain. In life, he was carried on a litter and otherwise revered by his subjects; his death was the occasion for great ritual mourning, with wives and retainers slain and placed in the burial with the departed leader.

There is rich archaeological evidence for the growth of such societies throughout the Americas. In the eastern United States, we see the first signs of such complexity with the rise of the Adena and Hopewellian communities (500 B.C.–A.D. 500) in the lower Ohio Valley. Large earthworks and specialized burial places for the elite mark the principal centers of these cultures. An extensive trade network among the elites of the eastern United States and peoples in widely scattered parts of North America allowed the Adena–Hopewell rulers to obtain exotic resources, which symbolized and probably bolstered their high status. Subsequently, the Mississippian cultures elaborated permanent politicoreligious centers, from which aristocratic rulers must have held sway over substantial territorial domains. The huge mound site and metropolis of Cahokia, in the vicinity of present-day East St. Louis, is an example of such a center. It is believed to date from about A.D. 900 to 1400.

In other parts of North America, we also see evidence of societies that probably were on a chiefdom level of development, in view of their labor-intensive constructions. In the Southwest, for example, the *kiva* constructions of the Puebloan (Anasazi) peoples at such sites as Pueblo Bonito in Chaco Canyon, New Mexico, clearly indicate such a political and religious centralization. There are also many archaeological evidences of similar societies in southern Central America, Colombia, Ecuador, and tropical-forest South America.

The chiefdom level of sociopolitical complexity was not always tied to a fully agricultural economy. The Adena–Hopewell development may have been only partially agricultural; however, other food resources, obtained through hunting, fishing, and plant collecting, supplemented the subsistence base in a way that allowed for such growth and complexity. On the Northwest Coast of North America, the ethnographically known tribes of that area had developed a class structure and large ritual centers based on an economy of salmon fishing and hunting. A comparable development, but one known only archaeologically, is seen in the Pacific coastal fishing cultures of Peru, where large public architecture dates as early as 2000 B.C. and essentially prior to a full agricultural economy. The key factor is, obviously, a guaranteed and reliable annual harvest, whether from hunting, fishing, or farming. Nevertheless, we think it significant that most of the American chiefdoms were agriculturally based, and we see in this kind of economy the evolutionary potential that led to the subsequent threshold of the state and civilization, which is achieved only from an agricultural subsistence base.

The states and civilizations of the later Pre-Columbian periods in Mesoamerica and Peru have agriculturally based chiefdom societies as their prototypes. For instance, the Olmec of ancient Mexico, who first arose about 1200 B.C. on the Gulf Coast of modern Veracruz and Tabasco, built large political and religious centers with temples and chiefly residences. They further commemorated their ruling class with monumental stone sculpture done in a highly sophisticated art style as well as with mortuary practices of a lavish sort. In Peru, several centuries of agricultural development, a characteristic associated with chiefdom societies, follow the early fishing chiefdoms of the littoral. The climax of this development comes with the Chavin culture, which is analogous to that of the Mesoamerican Olmecs in being representative of a high chiefdom social order.

The growth of cities, increasing social complexity, highly centralized political authority, and great economic diversification characterize the evolutionary developments beyond chiefdoms. These more complex entities frequently are associated with the political concept of the state. The state, according to most definitions, consists of highly formalized political institutions based upon legitimate coercive authority. Kin and kin-group sanctions have given way to more impersonalized laws and regulations. States possess police forces and standing armies. They regulate and organize manufacturing, trade, agriculture—in effect, all economic pursuits. The authority of the state is not entirely coercive, as religious persuasions and sanctions are an important part of it, but these sanctions are closely coordinated with centralized government force. The state is thus a further development in the general trend of increasing social complexity that is expressed in the chiefdom.

Archaeological evidence of state formation would include such things as insignia of office of multiple levels of political authority and central place establishments. Specialized manufacturing would be indicated by residential or settlement evidence of guild or craft institutions. Similarly, we would expect to find evidence of long distance trade carried out by a professional merchant class in the employ or direction of the state. Finally, history shows that states have tended to be highly aggressive and expansive. They have often come into being as a result of the expansion and aggrandizement of one chiefdom at the expense of its neighbors. Indeed, this dynamic of conquest and incorporation may be taken as a very fundamental quality of this sociopolitical form, and signs of organized militarism are to be expected in the archaeological record.

Early states appeared in two distinct areas of the New World—Mesoamerica and Peru-Bolivia. In each case, as we have said, they appear to be end products of long histories of increasing social complexity of the chiefdom level. Admittedly, the line between advanced chiefdoms and the state is an indefinite one, particularly when we attempt to mediate this definition through archeological data alone. However, the understanding of the processes of complex development is more crucial to archaeologists than the mere labeling of sociopolitical types.

In Mesoamerica, there is general consensus that the phenomenon of the state appeared in Central Mexico with the rise of the Teotihuacan civilization and the sudden and burgeoning growth of the city of Teotihuacan in the last century B.C. Previously, Teotihuacan had been one of several competing chiefdoms in the Basin of Mexico vying for economic and political control of the region. But in a single century, Teotihuacan's estimated population expanded from some 5,000 persons to over 30,000. Concomitant with this growth was the depletion or complete disappearance of rival Basin of Mexico centers and the clear domination of Teotihuacan over the region. Within a few more centuries, certainly by A.D. 500, the city of Teotihuacan had grown to the large urban proportions of 150,000 to 200,000 people living in a tightly nucleated single settlement. Along with this population growth came vast public construction projects of temple-pyramids, a royal palace complex, hundreds of elite class palaces or compounds, a huge formal market area, and thousands of closely packed apartment-like residences. Within this urban concentration, archaeologists have identified workshop and craft *barrio* areas for obsidian workers, figurine makers, potters, and other specialists. Beyond the perimeters of the city, which covered over 20 square kilometers, were some outlying communities. Most of these had been established by Teotihuacan power, and many were set up as resource extraction stations for various kinds of raw materials. Other places in this valley settlement pattern appear to have been subadministrative and lesser religious centers. All these outlying settlements were very small in comparison with the great metropolis.

From this urban base, Teotihuacan expanded its economic, political, and religious influence to distant parts of Mesoamerica. It was, without question, the greatest power of its time for the entire area. Its influence can be seen archaeologically in the distant trade of its pottery and obsidian as well as in the spread of its architectural and art styles to sites as distant as Tikal in the Maya lowlands and Kaminaljuyu in the Guatemalan highlands.

This tradition of Mesoamerican urbanism reached its climax in the great city of Tenochtitlan (at the site of modern Mexico City), which Cortes and his followers encountered in such a dramatic way in A.D. 1519. The early Spanish chronicles describe a "glittering city" on the islands in Lake Texcoco, which the Spaniards estimated to have contained some 60,000 houses as well as great central monuments. Tenochtitlan was both the political and economic capital of the Aztec empire, drawing vast quantities of tribute from subject peoples and extending from this urban base the armies that dominated its Meso-american rivals.

In Peru-Bolivia, the first appearance of the early state is not as precisely defined or generally agreed upon by archaeologists as the Teotihuacan example in Mesoamerica; however, most authorities would admit that the regional kingdoms of the latter part of the Early Intermediate Period (*ca.* A.D. 200–600) had achieved the complexity of state structures. A good example would be the Moche kingdom of the several valleys of the North Coast of Peru, from Jequetepeque in the north to Nepeña in the south. The apparent capital of this political entity was the huge site of Moche proper in the valley of the same name. For a long time, this site was known to archaeologists for its enormous adobe pyramid—one of the largest such Pre-Columbian structures in the Americas—and its immense palace complex. Now, more recent explorations have shown that Moche also had an extensive residential area of urban proportions. Moche mural paintings and a highly realistic depictive style of pottery painting give further evidence of Moche political achievements— rulers are shown seated on thrones surrounded by courtiers and interviewing bound prisoners who have been brought before them by their victorious military forces.

Other early Peruvian states comparable to Moche were probably those on the Central Coast (the Early Lima archaeological complex), the South Coast (the Nazca culture), and the various highland valley regions of the interior. In Peru, as time went on, the processes of state formation became, if anything, more intense than in Mesoamerica. Between about A.D. 600 and 1000, two political empires characterize the area, one based on Tiahuanaco in the Bolivian highlands and another on the central highland site of Huari. The Huari state, as indicated by ceramic styles and architectural forms, dominated virtually all highland and coastal Peru, overrunning and incorporating such earlier regional kingdoms as Moche and Nazca. After this period of empire building (the Middle Horizon), there was a reemergence of regional states once more. The most notable of these late kingdoms was the Chimu on the North Coast, with its mammoth capital at Chan Chan. These late states were then subjugated and welded into the famous Inca empire, the greatest conquest state of Pre-Columbian America. This state was governed from Cuzco, its major capital, and from a series of secondary capitals. The Inca empire extended from Central Ecuador into Central Chile and Northwest Argentina.

This cultural-historical review recapitulates, in a very general way, a cultural and social evolution that may be traced along many lines—including subsistence, demography, and social and political change—from earliest to latest Pre-Columbian times. This evolutionary process has parallels in the archaeological record in parts of the Old World, although the cultural contents and historical events are clearly different. Even though there is increasing evidence for limited contacts between the Old and New Worlds in ancient times, most archaeologists believe that the basic cultural developments in the two hemispheres were essentially separate; and, although archaeologists are now able to sketch broadly the growth of cultures throughout the Americas, the nature of specific processes of cultural change and growth remain open to further study and discussion.

Suggested Reading

The interested reader will want to consult these books as well as their bibliographies.

Adams, R. E. W. 1977. *Prehistoric Mesoamerica*. Little, Brown, Boston.

Adams, R. McC. 1966. *The Evolution of Urban Society*. Aldine, Chicago.

Baudez, C. F. 1970. *Central America*. Archaeologia Mundi, Geneva and London.

Coe, M. D. 1968. *America's First Civilization*. American Heritage, New York.

Coe, M. D. 1978. *Mexico*, second edition. Praeger, New York.

Culbert, T. P. 1974. *The Lost Civilization: The Story of the Classic Maya*. Harper & Row, New York.

Jennings, J. D. 1974. *Prehistory of North America*, second edition. McGraw-Hill, New York.

Jennings, J. D. (ed.). 1978. *The Ancient Native Americans*. W. H. Freeman and Company, San Francisco.

Lamberg-Karlovsky, C. C., and J. A. Sabloff. 1979. *Ancient Civilizations: The Near East and Mesoamerica*. Benjamin/Cummings, Menlo Park, Calif.

Lanning, E. P. 1963. *Peru Before the Incas*. Prentice-Hall, Englewood Cliffs, N.J.

Lathrap, D. W. 1970. *The Upper Amazon*. Thames and Hudson, London.

Lathrap, D. W. 1975. *Ancient Ecuador: Culture, Clay, and Creativity, 3000–300 B.C.* Field Museum of Natural History, Chicago.

Meggers, B. J. 1966. *Ecuador*. Thames and Hudson, London.

Reichel-Dolmatoff, G. 1965. *Colombia*. Thames and Hudson, London.

Rouse, I., and J. M. Cruxent. 1963. *Venezuelan Archaeology*. Yale University Caribbean Series, No. 6, New Haven, Conn.

Service, E. R. 1975. *The Origins of the State and Civilization: The Process of Cultural Evolution*. Norton, New York.

Steward, J. H. 1955. *Theory of Culture Change*. University of Illinois Press, Urbana.

Taylor, R. E., and C. W. Meighan (eds.). 1978. *Chronologies in New World Archaeology*. Academic Press, New York.

Weaver, M. P. 1974. *The Aztecs, Maya, and Their Predecessors*. Seminar Press, New York.

Willey, G. R. 1966–71. *An Introduction to American Archaeology* (2 Vols.). Prentice-Hall, Englewood Cliffs, N.J.

NORTH AMERICA

NORTH AMERICA

I

INTRODUCTION

In the 20,000 years (or possibly much more) since the first human beings set foot in North America, this great area has witnessed a huge variety of cultural evolutionary developments in its many different environments. During the earliest times of occupation, throughout the late Pleistocene Ice Age and into the early Post-Pleistocene periods, the human occupants of North America practiced a hunting and gathering way of life. In some regions, this hunting and gathering adaptation proved so successful that groups in these regions continued their hunting and gathering subsistence strategies even in the face of changing environmental conditions. In other regions, over long periods of time, some groups began to change to a more settled village agricultural existence. Population pressure, pressures from neighboring cultures, and environmental changes are some of the factors often cited by archaeologists to account for these changes.

The first four articles of this North American section discuss some of the evidence for early human occupation in the Americas and provide the foundation for discussions of later developments in North America. The article by William Haag, "The Bering Strait Land Bridge," discusses the geological evidence for the existence of the Bering land bridge, which large numbers of animals crossed from the Old World to the New, and vice versa. Eventually, human beings, almost certainly following some of the game animals, also entered the New World over this bridge. Although there is nearly unamimous agreement that the peopling of the New World occurred via a land bridge from Siberia to Alaska, the exact date of the initial human crossing remains a hotly debated subject in archaeology. Whatever the date, be it 20,000, 30,000, or 40,000 years ago or more, the first human migrants who entered Alaska would have been able to use a very broad bridge in their passage into the Americas. Haag cites evidence to show that a 150-foot drop in sea level would have formed a land bridge about 200 miles wide, whereas a 450-foot drop, which would have been reached at maximum glaciation, would have formed a land bridge 1,300 miles wide. Obviously, the newly arrived immigrants would have had no idea that they were entering a "New World" previously unoccupied by human beings.

Douglas Anderson's article, "A Stone Age Campsite at the Gateway to America," describes his excavations at the site of Onion Portage on the Kobuk River in Alaska. Anderson's discussion gives a good view of the nature of early hunting and gathering camps in Alaska. The site's location is such that both hunting and fishing would have been quite productive in certain seasons. Although Onion Portage does not represent a camp of the earliest settlers in the Alaskan area, it does show what a relatively early site looks like.

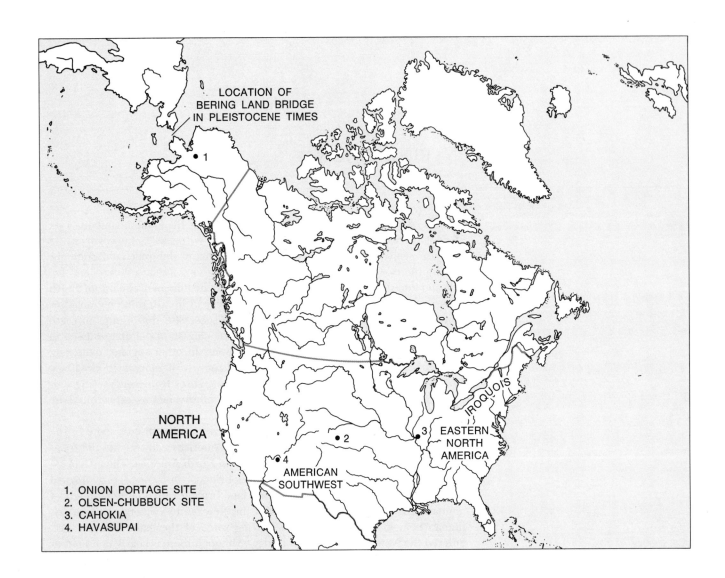

A map of North America showing the locations of the principal archaeological sites and regions discussed in the articles in this section.

The articles by Vance Haynes ("Elephant-Hunting in North America") and Joe Ben Wheat ("A Paleo-Indian Bison Kill") describe the archaeological manifestations of peoples who hunted ancient mammoths and bison near the close of and following the last period of Pleistocene glaciation in North America. The mammoth hunters used a distinctive fluted, chipped-stone projectile point known as a Clovis point. Most Clovis sites in western North America have been dated to a short time-span between 11,500 and 11,000 years ago (9500–9000 B.C.). Clovis sites are also known from eastern North America.

Peoples who used different projectile points to hunt big game appear to have concentrated their attention on bison in succeeding periods (from about 11,000 to 8,000 years ago), first hunting *Bison antiquus* and subsequently *Bison occidentalis*. Wheat's article describes one particular *Bison occidentalis* kill site in Colorado.

The ancient peoples who hunted the mammoth and bison have often been called the Big Game Hunters. However, although some of our best archaeological evidence concerning these peoples comes from the sites where large game was killed, many archeologists have come to believe that it may be a misnomer to characterize the cultural traditions between 11,500 and 8,000 years ago as Big Game Hunting, since this term implies that such hunting was their only subsistence activity. For many groups at this period, small game hunting as well as plant gathering may also have been quite important. Haynes' article contains well-supported arguments concerning the role of humans in the extinction of ancient mammoths and the southward migrations of peoples using Clovis points through an ice-free corridor in Canada approximately 12,000 years ago. However, these subjects are the focus of much controversy in the archaeological literature, and the arguments are still unresolved.

Wheat's article gives a good impression of how much cultural information the archaeologist can infer from the relatively sparse human remains and extensive animal remains of an early kill site. Recent analyses of such carefully excavated archaeological sites as the Olsen–Chubbuck site have given archaeologists a much clearer picture of the nature of ancient hunting patterns.

Unlike Mesoamerica, which we will discuss in the following section of this book, North America was not an integrated cultural system in Pre-Columbian times. Following the last retreat of the major Pleistocene glaciation (roughly 8000 B.C.) and the subsequent climatic and environmental changes that occurred in North America, varying adaptations were made in the different areas of North America. These differing adaptations resulted in widely varying cultural trajectories from Post-Pleistocene times until the period of European contacts. The articles included here concerning these later cultural developments pertain to two major areas—Eastern North America and the Southwest.

In the eastern sector of North America, peoples adapted their hunting and gathering strategies to the widely varying environments of the area, including the large river valleys and heavily wooded forests. The so-called Archaic Period (*ca.* 6000–700 B.C.) was a time of growing population in many regions, and, toward the end of the period, there were signs of increasing social complexity. Burials with various objects indicating status differences and the appearance of large earthen mounds are two of the archaeological indicators of growing complexity. Food plants were apparently cultivated by at least 3000 B.C., if not much earlier, according to recent discoveries at the important Koster site in southern Illinois, but agriculture seemingly did not play an important role in Eastern subsistence economies until well after the time of Christ.

The Woodland or Sedentary Period, which followed the Archaic Period, provides increasing evidence of year-round settlements dependent in part on agricultural produce. In the Ohio River Valley and adjacent regions, the ruling elite of a number of sites gained new power and wealth, as evidenced by the large burial mounds built to commemorate their deaths and by the extensive exchange network that linked these elites with distant resource areas. Olaf Prufer's article on the Hopewell Cult discusses the climax of this elite interaction sphere between about 100 B.C. and A.D. 600 and describes the goods and ideas that flowed through the system.

The Hopewell interaction sphere has been of great interest to archaeologists in recent years. It used to be thought of as the Hopewell "culture," a unified complex that diffused from Ohio to surrounding regions. However, in the past two decades, it has become evident that the interaction sphere was really an exchange network that supplied the elites of widely varying cultures or traditions with exotic materials and symbols of their authority and wealth.

In the Southeast, the Woodland or Sedentary Period was followed by the Mississippian or Late Prehistoric Period, which lasted virtually until the time of European contact. For the first time in Eastern North America, agriculture became the principal means of subsistence, particularly along the rich floodplains of many of the rivers. The most visible archaeological features of this time were the huge temple mounds found at such sites as Etowah in Georgia or Moundville in Alabama. Cahokia, the largest Mississippian site known to archaeologists, occupies, together with its satellites, a large section of the Mississippi Valley bottom around East St. Louis, Illinois. Melvin Fowler describes the results of recent investigations at Cahokia in his article "A Pre-Columbian Urban Center on the Mississippi." Although the modern construction of roads and housing developments has unfortunately destroyed much of Cahokia, archaeologists have been able to preserve some parts of the site. Ongoing research has enabled archaeologists to begin to obtain a picture of how complex and extensive this ancient city was. It is now believed, for example, that the site may have had up to 50,000 inhabitants at its peak.

James Tuck describes another Late Prehistoric development in the northeastern region of North America. Tuck discusses a political organization that has often been mentioned in history books and that played a crucial role in Colonial times—the Iroquois Confederacy. He summarizes recent data showing that the Iroquois culture of the Onondagas, Oneidas, Cayugas, Senacas, and Mohawks developed indigenously in the general upstate New York region sometime after A.D. 1000. Tuck also shows how archaeological evidence can be combined with historical information to give us a picture of the development and ultimately the decline of the Iroquois "Great League of Peace."

Unlike the Mississippian peoples, who had a complex politicoeconomic structure that integrated widespread but densely settled groups and featured a high degree of economic specialization, the Iroquois had a less complex system focusing on individual villages. Tuck shows how this relatively small group of Iroquois tribes (numbering about 12,000 people in total) with a village agricultural economy was able to form a political and military organization with important impact on precontact and postcontact events.

In the American Southwest, the varied environments of the area led to differing adaptations and cultural trajectories. After the end of the Pleistocene, the peoples of the Southwest hunted small game and gathered plants for a number of millennia. Like the East, domesticated plants appeared a very long time before agriculture emerged as a key subsistence strategy. Domesticated maize (corn), for example, was found in Bat Cave in New Mexico between 2000 and 3000 B.C. However, it was not until just before the time of Christ that settled villages based on an agricultural economy first began to emerge.

Beginning with the rise of agricultural villages, Southwestern archaeologists traditionally have divided the area into three principal cultures—the Mogollon in the mountains of South-Central New Mexico and Arizona, the Hohokam in the desert of Arizona, and the Anasazi centering on the mountains of northern New Mexico-Arizona and southern Colorado-Utah. One of the Mogollon groups, the Mimbres, produced some of the most aesthetically interesting pottery in North America. The Hohokam area witnessed the construction of sophisticated irrigation systems at such sites as Snaketown, which were a means of intensifying the agricultural possibilities of the desert environment. The Anasazi developed the well-known Pueblo architecture at such sites as Pueblo Bonito in Chaco Canyon as well as the amazing cliff dwellings at Mesa Verde.

Other cultural developments occurred near the borders of the Southwest. To the west of the main Anasazi centers, for example, the Grand Canyon region had a long history of prehistoric occupation. Douglas Schwartz reports in his article "Prehistoric Man in the Grand Canyon" on one aspect of his extensive archaeological research in the Grand Canyon. Like many Southwestern archaeologists, one of his interests lies in the linking of prehistoric archaeological sites with known historical and modern Indian tribal groups. Schwartz notes that, after a period of florescence between A.D. 900 and 1100 on the plateau dress above the Canyon, a people known as the Cohonina had a major decline. He argues that the remnants of the Cohonina migrated into the Canyon, where they became a group that is now known as the Havasupai. Other archaeologists have argued that the ancestors of the modern Havasupai, who live in a side canyon called Cataract Creek Canyon, were not the Cohonina but the Cerbet, who moved into the Canyon from the west. Whatever the eventual resolution of this argument, Schwartz's article indicates how archaeologists can use excavations and surveys to investigate the changing environmental adaptations of prehistoric peoples and to relate these changes to a variety of historical problems.

1

The Bering Strait Land Bridge

by William G. Haag
January 1962

It is widely thought to have been a narrow neck of land over which man first came to America. Actually it was 1,300 miles wide and was traveled by large numbers of plants and animals

The New World was already an old world to the Indians who were in residence when Europeans took possession of it in the 16th century. But the life story of the human species goes back a million years, and there is no doubt that man came only recently to the Western Hemisphere. None of the thousands of sites of aboriginal habitation uncovered in North and South America has antiquity comparable to that of Old World sites. Man's occupation of the New World may date back several tens of thousands of years, but no one rationally argues that he has been here even 100,000 years.

Speculation as to how man found his way to America was lively at the outset, and the proposed routes boxed the compass. With one or two notable exceptions, however, students of American anthropology soon settled for the plausible idea that the first immigrants came by way of a land bridge that had connected the northeast corner of Asia to the northwest corner of North America across the Bering Strait. Mariners were able to supply the reassuring information that the strait is not only narrow—it is 56 miles wide—but also shallow: a lowering of the sea level there by 100 feet or so would transform the strait into an isthmus. With little else in the way of evidence to sustain the Bering Strait land bridge, anthropologists embraced the idea that man walked dry-shod from Asia to America.

Toward the end of the last century, however, it became apparent that the Western Hemisphere was the New World not only for man but also for a host of animals and plants. Zoologists and botanists showed that numerous subjects of their respective kingdoms must have originated in Asia and spread to Amer-

ica. (There was evidence also for some movement in the other direction.) These findings were neither astonishing nor wholly unexpected. Such spread of populations is not to be envisioned as an exodus or mass migration, even in the case of animals. It is, rather, a spilling into new territory that accompanies increase in numbers, with movement in the direction of least population pressure and most favorable ecological conditions. But the immense traffic in plant and animal forms placed a heavy burden on the Bering Strait land bridge as the anthropologists had envisioned it. Whereas purposeful men could make their way across a narrow bridge (in the absence of a bridge, Eskimos sometimes cross the strait in skin boats), the slow diffusion of plants and animals would require an avenue as broad as a continent and available for ages at a stretch.

The expansion of the Bering Strait land bridge to meet these demands is a task that has intrigued geologists for many years. Although their efforts have not completely satisfied zoologists and botanists, it is apparent that the Old and New worlds were once one world, joined by a land mass that now lies submerged beneath the seas on each side of the Bering Strait. The clues to the appearance and disappearance of this land mass are to be found both on the bottom of these waters and in such faraway places as the coral atolls of the South Pacific and the delta of the Mississippi River.

Today the maximum depth in the Bering Strait is about 180 feet. On a clear day from the heights at Cape Prince of Wales in Alaska one can look across the strait and see land at Cape Dezhnev in Siberia. St. Lawrence Island, Big Diomede Island, Little Diomede Island and

smaller islands make steppingstones between. South of the strait is the Bering Sea. Its floor is one of the flattest and smoothest stretches of terrain on the entire globe. With a slope of no more than three or four inches to the mile, it reaches southward to a line that runs from Unimak Pass in the Aleutians to Cape Navarin on the Asiatic shore. Along this line—the edge of the continental shelf—the sea floor plunges steeply from a depth of about 450 feet down 15,000 feet to the bottom of the ocean. The floor of the Chukchi Sea, north of the Bering Strait, is not quite so smooth; the depth varies from 120 to 180 feet, and irregularities of the terrain bring shoals upward to depths of only 45 feet and lift the great granite outcrops of Wrangell and Herald islands above the surface of the sea. Along a line that runs several hundred miles north of the Bering Strait, from Point Barrow in Alaska to the Severnaya Zemlya off Siberia, the sea floor plunges over the northern edge of the continental shelf to the bottom of the Arctic Ocean.

Sounding of the Bering and Chukchi seas thus depicts a vast plain that is not deeply submerged. At its widest the plain reaches 1,300 miles north and south, 600 miles wider than the north-south distance across Alaska along the Canadian border. The granitic islands that rise above the water testify that the plain is made of the same rock as the continents.

David M. Hopkins of the U.S. Geological Survey has shown that this great plain sank beneath the seas somewhat more than a million years ago as a result of the down-warping of the crust in the Arctic region that began with the Pleistocene epoch. Before that, Hopkins calculates, most of the area was above sea level throughout most of the 50-million-year duration of the preceding Tertiary period.

The continuity of the land mass of Asia and North America during the Tertiary period helps to solve a major portion of the biologist's problem. The paleontological evidence indicates that numerous mammals, large and small, moved from Asia to America during that time. With the subsidence of the land, however, the flow must have stopped. Nor is there any chance that the land rose up again during the million-year Pleistocene period. It is true that the Pacific region along the Aleutian and Kurile island chains is geologically active. But by comparison the Bering Strait region is rather stable; studies of ancient beach terraces on the islands in the surrounding seas indicate that the vertical movement of the land could not have exceeded 30 feet in the course of the Pleistocene. The smoothness of the Bering Sea floor is another indication of prolonged submergence. Deep layers of marine sediment have smoothed out whatever hills and valleys it acquired when it was dry land and exposed to erosion.

Fossil evidence for the origin and geographic distribution of North Ameri-

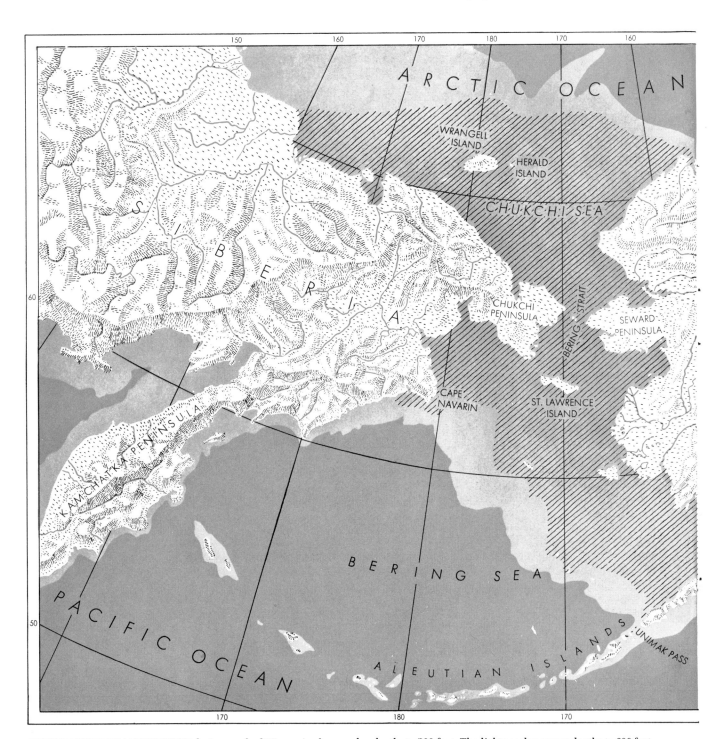

BERING STRAIT LAND BRIDGE during much of Wisconsin glaciation was at least as wide as hatched area, which marks present-day depths to 300 feet. The lighter color covers depths to 600 feet. The 600-foot contour roughly marks the margin of the continental

can mammals nonetheless shows that numerous animals, large and small, came from Asia during the Pleistocene. Beginning early in the Pleistocene, several genera of rodents arrived; such small mammals breed more rapidly than, say, elephants, and they spread far southward across North America, although not into South America. Later came the larger mammals: the mastodon and mammoth, musk oxen, bison, moose, elk,

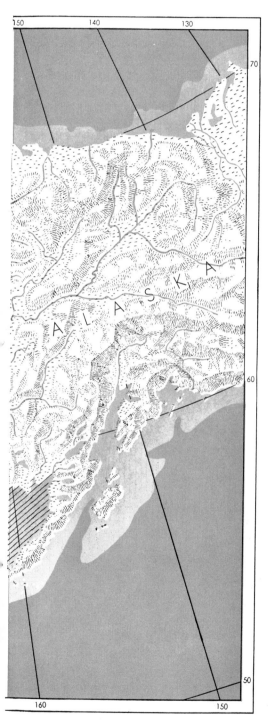

shelf, with its sharp drop to the bottom of the deep ocean, several thousand feet lower.

mountain sheep and goats, camels, foxes, bears, wolves and horses. (The horses flourished and then died out in North America; the genus was not seen again in the New World until the conquistadors brought their animals across the Atlantic.) Evidence from botany as well as from zoology requires a substantial dry-land connection between Asia and North America throughout the Pleistocene.

At this point it is well to remember that the sea level at any given place on the globe depends not only on the height of the land but also on the depth of the ocean. The depth of the ocean in this sense is a question of the volume of water in the ocean. With the Pleistocene began the ice age that has apparently not yet run its course. During this million-year period, for reasons subject to warm debate, at least four great ice sheets have built up, advanced and retreated on the Northern Hemisphere. That the ice can lock up considerable quantities of water on the land is evident even in the present interglacial period. The abrupt melting of the Greenland and Antarctic icecaps would, according to various estimates, raise the present world-wide sea level by as much as 300 feet.

To estimate the volume of water locked up on the land in the great continental glaciers of the Pleistocene one begins with the measurement of the land area covered by the glaciers. The great ice sheets gathered up sand, gravel and larger rubble and, when the ice proceeded to melt, deposited a mantle of this "till" on the exposed ground. From such evidence it is calculated that ice covered 30 per cent of the earth's land area during the glacial maxima of the Pleistocene.

To arrive at the volume of water in the glaciers, however, one must have some idea of the thickness of the ice as well as the area it covered. The Greenland icecap is more than a mile deep, and in Antarctica the rock lies as much as three miles below the surface of the ice. It is clear that the Pleistocene glaciers could have been thousands of feet thick. Multiplication of the area of the glaciers by thicknesses predicated on various assumptions has shown that the freezing of the water on the land may have reduced the ancient sea level by 125 to 800 feet. Such calculations are supported by evidence from coral atolls in tropical seas. Since the organisms that build these atolls do not live at depths greater than 300 feet, and since the limy struc-

tures of such islands go down several thousand feet, a lowering of the sea level by more than 300 feet is necessary to explain their existence.

By all odds the best evidence for the rise and fall of the ancient sea level is offered by the Mississippi Valley, its delta and the adjoining shores of the Gulf of Mexico. In Pleistocene times about a dozen major streams entered the Gulf. As ice accumulated in the north, lowering the level of the sea, the streams followed the retreating shore line downward. On the steeper gradient the water flowed faster, cutting deeper and straighter valleys. Then, as the ice retreated, the sea rose and again moved inland, reducing the velocity of the streams and making them deposit their burdens of gravel and silt at their mouths and farther inland. Consequently during the glacial minima the rivers built up great flood plains over which they wore meandering courses. Each glacial advance brought a withdrawal of the Gulf and quickened the rivers; each retreat raised the level of the Gulf and forced the rivers to build new flood plains.

Had the earth's crust in this region remained stable, all traces of the preceding flood plain would have been erased by the next cycle of cutting and building. But the rivers, particularly the Mississippi, deposited vast quantities of sediment in their lower valleys, building "crowfoot" deltas like that of the Mississippi today. (Many large rivers, such as the Amazon, have never built such deltas because coastwise currents distribute their sediments far and wide.) The accumulating burden of offshore sediments tilted the platform of the continent, pressing it downward under the Gulf and lifting it inland. In succeeding cycles, therefore, the build-up of the flood plain started farther downstream.

Evidence of the succession of flood plains remains today in the terraces that descend like a flight of steps down both flanks of the Mississippi Valley toward the river. Near Memphis, Tenn., the highest and oldest terrace lies about 350 feet above the plain of the present river and slopes toward the Gulf with a gradient of about eight feet per mile. The terrace below lies 200 feet above the plain and slopes about five feet per mile; the third terrace lies 100 feet above the plain, with a slope of about 18 inches; the fourth, only 40 feet above, with a slope of only six inches. The present flood plain has a gradient of about three inches per mile. Out in the Gulf, where the river has buried the older deposits

WILLIANA TERRACE

BENTLEY TERRACE

MONTGOMERY TERRACE

PRAIRIE TERRACE

PRESENT
FLOOD PLAIN

SUCCESSIVE TERRACES that formed in lower Mississippi Valley during the Pleistocene glaciations are shown in this highly schematic cross section. The terraces, with the oldest at the top, were flood plains laid down between glaciations. During each glacial period the river, rejuvenated by the fall in sea level and the consequent drop in its mouth, cut deeply into the preceding flood plain. The Prairie Terrace represents the flood plain that the river laid down between the early Wisconsin and the late Wisconsin glaciations.

under the younger, the successive slopes of the river bed are steeper.

In this setting geologists have been able to measure with great confidence the degree to which each of the glacial advances of the Pleistocene lowered the level of the sea. Borings along the axis of the old stream channels reveal the gradient of the bottom. The terraces show the slope of the alluvial plain associated with the successive streams. From these data the elevations of the earlier river mouths and consequently the sea level can be determined. The Rhine and Rhone rivers have yielded similar in-

formation, and on the Kamchatka Peninsula in Siberia it has been observed that the streams flowing into the Bering Sea are flanked by steeply sloping terraces.

The Mississippi-Gulf region has provided especially secure and precise information about the course of the last great Pleistocene glaciation, the so-called Wisconsin stage of the Pleistocene. In no other area of the globe have oil prospectors drilled so many test holes through the recent sediments into the Pleistocene; the number of holes runs into the thousands, and they dot the map

30 miles out into the Gulf. In accordance with the law, the records of these wells show the types of material brought up by the drills at fairly evenly spaced intervals. The undersea sediments that were uncovered by the retreat of the sea at the maximum advance of the Wisconsin glacier mark a horizon familiar to all well drillers. Where these sediments were exposed to the air long ago they became oxidized and show as a bright reddish-orange zone. From the examination of many well records one can tell where, geographically, these sediments were exposed to air and where

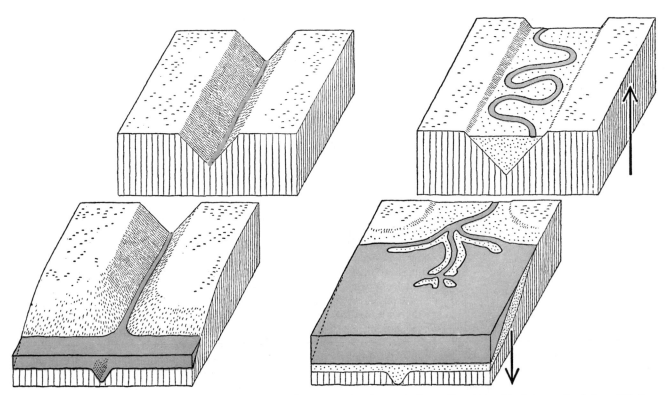

EFFECTS OF GLACIAL ADVANCE AND RETREAT on rivers entering Gulf of Mexico are shown in these diagrams. Upper block of each pair is river valley, lower block is mouth of river. At left, glaciers have lowered sea level. River flows faster and cuts a deep,

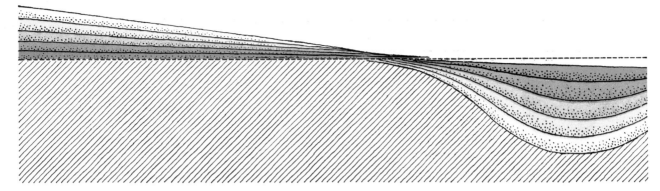

SLOPE OF TERRACES is illustrated in this schematic longitudinal section of lower Mississippi and Gulf region. The weight of the accumulated sediments (*right*), with the oldest deposit at the bottom, made the crustal rock sink and the adjacent land area rise like a great lever with the fulcrum near the coast. Because of this tilt the flood plains laid down during interglacial periods remained as terraces. The broken horizontal line marks present sea level. Hatched area is the older material of the continental crust.

they remained underwater, and so fix the coast line at the time the sea reached its lowest level. In addition, numerous samples of formerly living matter have been recovered from well borings at known depths and from archaeological sites. The dating of these by carbon-14 techniques permits accurate plotting of the course of events in time.

From this rich supply of evidence it has been determined that the Wisconsin glacier reached its maximum 40,000 years ago and lowered the sea level by as much as 460 feet. As the glacier grew and the oceans receded, an ever broader

highway was revealed at the Bering Strait. With a sea-level fall of only 150 feet, the bridge connecting the two continents must have been nearly 200 miles wide. Because the slope of the sea floor is so gentle, a further fall in the sea level uncovered much larger regions. At 450 feet the entire width of the undersea plain from one edge of the continental shelf to the other must have been exposed, providing a corridor 1,300 miles wide for the flow of biological commerce between the no longer separate continents. During the peak periods of the earlier glaciations the Bering Strait land

bridge would have presented much the same appearance.

Because the maximum exposure of the land bridge necessarily coincided with a maximum of glaciation, one might think the bridge would have been blocked by ice. Geological evidence shows, however, that neither the Chukchi Peninsula in Siberia nor the westward-reaching Seward Peninsula of Alaska were glaciated during the Wisconsin period. Even large areas of central Alaska remained ice-free throughout the period. As for the now submerged plain on the floor of the Bering Strait and

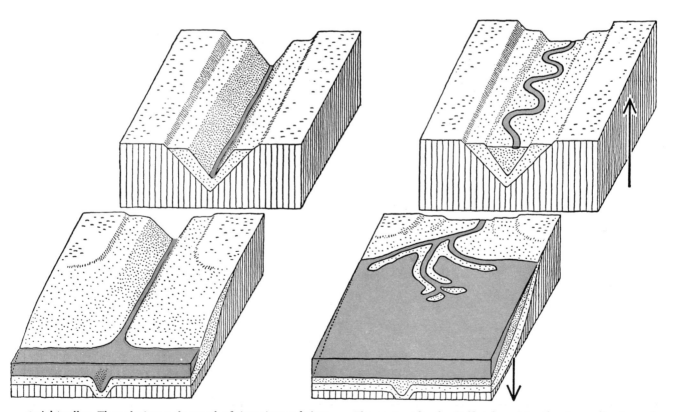

straight valley. Then glaciers melt, mouth of river rises and river deposits sediments to make flood plain in valley and delta at mouth.

The crust under the Gulf sinks, raising the river valley (*second from left*). The cycle is repeated at next glaciation and interglacial.

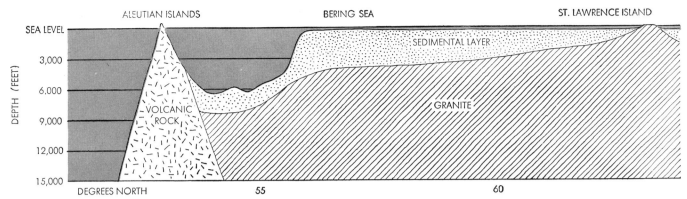

DEPTH (FEET)

ALEUTIAN ISLANDS BERING SEA ST. LAWRENCE ISLAND

SEA LEVEL

3,000

6,000

9,000

12,000

15,000

SEDIMENTAL LAYER

VOLCANIC ROCK

GRANITE

DEGREES NORTH 55 60

CROSS SECTION THROUGH BERING STRAIT along 169 degrees west latitude shows great breadth of shallow region. Earth's crust beneath strait is granitic and is part of continental shelf. Big Diomede Island lies in the narrowest part of the strait. The whole

the adjoining seas, it seems clear that the rocky rubble, found where currents clear away the silt, was "rafted" there by icebergs; no part of this accumulation is attributed to glacial till deposited by the melting of glacial ice on the surface.

Conditions are made the more propitious for life on the bridge by the latest theory on the causes of glaciation. Paradoxically, this demands a warm Arctic Ocean over which winds could become laden with moisture for subsequent precipitation as snow deep in the Hudson Bay area, where the glacier had its center of gravity. Western Alaska would have had little snowfall and no accumulation of ice. This deduction is supported by the finding of trees in the Pleistocene deposits on Seward Peninsula. It is not thought, however, that the land bridge was ever anything but tundra.

It must be admitted that the Bering Strait land bridge of the geologist, appearing only intermittently above sea

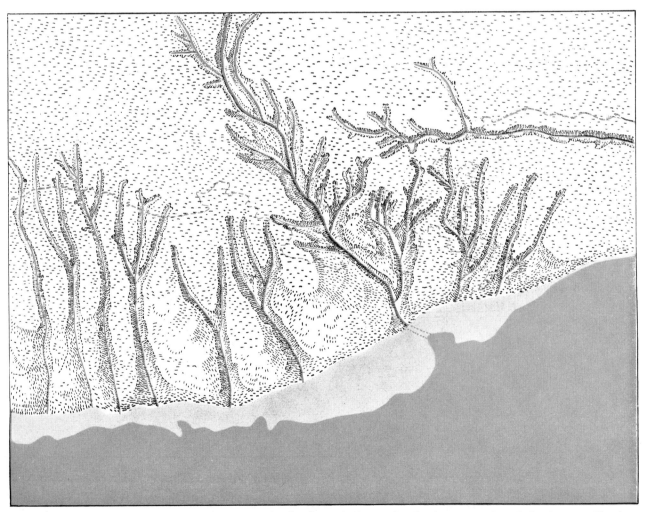

WITHDRAWAL OF WATER of the Gulf of Mexico at height of the Wisconsin glaciation exposed most of continental shelf. Edge of shelf is 600-foot-depth contour, where dark color starts. The rivers cut deep valleys and dumped their sediments in the deep water.

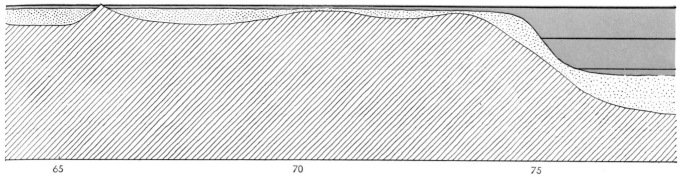

BIG DIOMEDE ISLAND HERALD SHOAL CHUKCHI SEA

65 70 75

shallow area has been tectonically stable for the past million years. Glaciations rather than local uplift exposed its surface. The thick-ness of the sedimental layer is actually not definitely established for much of the region. Pacific Ocean is at left, Arctic Ocean is at right.

level, does not fully serve the purposes of the zoologist and botanist. Most zoologists find no evidence in the movement of animals that requires alternate opening and closing of the passage between the continents, and they argue for a broad bridge available throughout nearly all of the Pleistocene. What is more, the animals that came across the bridge were not typically cold-climate animals (none of the true cold-climate animals, such as the woolly rhinoceros, ever reached America). On the contrary, the animals were the ones that would prefer the warmer interglacial times for their spread. They may, of course, have made the crossing just as the climate was warming up and conditions on the American side were increasingly favorable to population increase and diffusion.

The botanists find even more compelling evidence for a broad land bridge throughout most of the Pleistocene. Eric Hultén of the University of Lund

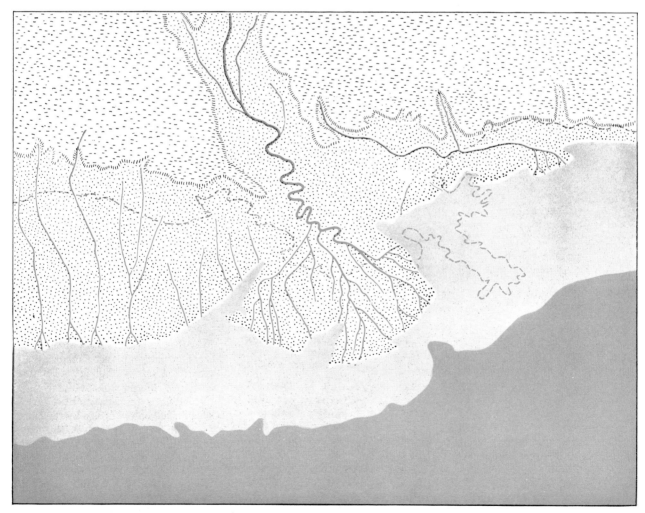

RISE IN WATER OF GULF at mouth of Mississippi accompanied retreat of glaciers. Sea level shown is only 100 feet lower than at present. Rivers flow slowly, building flood plains and deltas. Broken colored line marks today's coast and Mississippi delta.

LAST GREAT GLACIATION, the Wisconsin, at its maximum covered about 30 per cent of the earth's land area. The glaciers (1) and accompanying pack ice (2) locked up vast quantities of sea water, lowering sea level by 460 feet and exposing a 1,300-mile-wide, ice-free land bridge in the region of Bering Strait (3). The broken colored line marks present-day seacoasts and lake shores.

in Sweden recently calculated that a bridge 700 miles wide is necessary to account for the distribution of plants in Alaska and northeastern Siberia.

Giving full weight to the biological evidence, it seems amply demonstrated that a bridge wider than present-day Alaska joined the Old and New worlds during a large part of the Pleistocene. There is much to suggest that the land surface of this bridge was smooth and unbroken. And it appears that large animals moved freely across it during the 80,000 years of the Wisconsin stage and probably throughout much of the preceding interglacial stage.

Before the end of the Wisconsin period the first men must have crossed the bridge. It seems almost a truism that Asiatic man would have followed the slow spread of Asiatic animals into the New World. The men would most likely have come along the coastal margins and not across the interior that lies under the present-day strait. Their remains are covered, therefore, not only by 300 feet or more of water but also by as much as 100 feet of sediment laid down in the Recent period as the sea encroached on the continental shelf. Archaeologists need not be surprised in the future to discover evidence of man here and there in North America 50,000 years old and even older.

2

A Stone Age Campsite at the Gateway to America

by Douglas D. Anderson
June 1968

Onion Portage in Alaska is an unusual Arctic archaeological site. It provides a record of human habitation going back at least 8,500 years, when its occupants were not far removed from their forebears in Asia

It seems virtually certain that men first migrated to the New World from Asia by way of the Arctic, yet for some time this fact has presented archaeology with a problem. By 10,000 B.C. Stone Age hunters were killing mammoths on the Great Plains. There is evidence suggesting that man was present in Mexico even earlier, perhaps as early as 20,000 B.C. Until 1961, however, the Arctic gateway region had yielded few traces of man before 3000 B.C. In that year excavations were begun at a site in Alaska where the remains of human occupation are buried in distinct strata, affording the investigators a unique opportunity for reliable dating.

The site is Onion Portage, on the bank of the Kobuk River in northwestern Alaska. It has been intensively excavated from 1964 through 1967. The findings may eventually demonstrate that man was present in Alaska as long ago as 13,000 B.C. Already they show that men with strong Asian affinities were there by 6500 B.C.

Why is the stratified site of Onion Portage so unusual? Archaeological evidence concerning the hunters of sea mammals who lived on the shores of Alaska and northwestern Canada is quite abundant. North of the Aleutian Islands, however, no coastal site has been discovered that is more than 5,000 years old. The reason is that the sea, rising as the last great continental glaciers melted, reached a point close to its present level some 5,000 years ago, thereby drowning the former coastline together with whatever evidence of human habitation it harbored.

The change in sea level would not, of course, have affected early sites in the interior. Such sites are scarce and usually unrewarding for other reasons. One is that the environment of tundra and taiga (treeless barren land and northern forest) could not support as many hunting groups as the game-rich shore. Another reason is that campsites on interior rivers were likely to be washed away or buried as the river shifted its course. In fact, throughout the interior only places where the ground is elevated and dry offer much archaeological promise.

The remains of numerous hunting camps have in fact been found on elevations in the Alaskan interior. These camps were apparently established to enable the hunters to catch sight of caribou on the tundra. As the hunters waited they made or repaired weapons and other implements; the campsites are littered with broken stone projectile points and tools and with the waste chips of their manufacture.

Herein lies another problem. At a rocky site where little or no soil is forming a 6,000-year-old spearpoint may lie beside one discarded only a century ago. It is nearly impossible to prove which is the older or exactly how old either one is. Even where soil has developed and the artifacts have been buried, the Arctic environment plays tricks. The upper layers of soil, soaked with water and lying on top of permanently frozen lower layers, tend to flow and disarrange buried objects. As a result both absolute and relative dating of archaeological material from sites in the Arctic interior was rarely possible before the discovery at Onion Portage.

Some 125 miles upstream from where the Kobuk River enters the Chukchi Sea the course of the river is a lazy meander five miles long. Situated at the upper end of the meander, Onion Portage is bounded by steeply cut banks on the upstream side and by a long natural levee downstream. The terrain has not been radically altered by stream erosion for at least 8,000 years. The name Onion Portage comes from the wild onions that grow profusely along the gravelly shore and from the overland haul across the base of the point, which saves five miles of upstream paddling. Today the boundary between trees and tundra is only a few hundred yards north of Onion Portage. Beyond the trees the open tundra continues all the way to the Arctic Ocean, 270 miles farther north. To the south the terrain is open taiga, dotted with patches of spruce, willow and (in sheltered places) birch.

A sandy knoll dominates the wooded landscape at the site. Hunters both ancient and modern have used this vantage as a lookout for the thousands of caribou that cross the river at Onion Portage, moving north in the spring and south in the fall. From the knoll the approaching animals can be seen soon enough for men to be stationed for the kill at points where the herd is likely to cross the river. The fishing at Onion Portage is also good; several species of salmon migrate upstream during the summer. The prized sheefish, which is scarce in other Alaskan rivers, is also caught by the local Eskimos.

Over thousands of years the lower and flatter parts of Onion Portage have been buried several times under sand eroded from gullies in the knoll. In places the alluvial fans that spread out from the gullies have built up layers of sand as

much as three feet thick. Unusually high spring floods have also engulfed the site from time to time, leaving thin deposits of silt. Windstorms too have spread thin sheets of drifted sand across the site. Each such covering killed the turf buried under it; the new turf that formed on the fresh surface was separated from the dead turf below by a sterile layer of sand or silt. All the deposits combined make up the sequence of strata at Onion Portage. In places the sequence is 20 feet thick. More than 70 of the surfaces show evidence of human occupation. The layers of turf are concentrated in bands, each of which contains from three to 14 occupation levels. The bands have been given consecutive numbers, starting with Band 1 just below the surface and ending with Band 8, the deepest dated series of occupation levels at the site.

The Onion Portage site was discovered in 1941 by the late J. L. Giddings, Jr., of Brown University, who was traveling down the Kobuk on a raft. He stopped and excavated several 500-year-old Eskimo house pits to gather material for an Arctic tree-ring chronology he was then establishing. He returned to the site 20 years later; test digging that year revealed the stratified layers. Giddings began a full-scale excavation in 1964, with the support of Brown University and the National Science Foundation. In the same year he died. Recognizing the uniqueness of the site, both institutions urged that the work be continued the following season. Froelich G. Rainey, director of the University Museum at the University of Pennsylvania, an Arctic specialist and a longtime colleague of Giddings', and I, one of Giddings' former students, were invited to take over the excavation. In the 1966 and 1967 seasons the work at Onion Portage has continued with the same support under my direction.

Our study is by no means complete. Soil samples from various levels at the site, for instance, are still being analyzed at the University of Uppsala, the University of Alaska and the University of Arizona for their chemical constituents, pollen content and even for microscopic diatoms. Samples of charcoal from each of the eight bands have already yielded

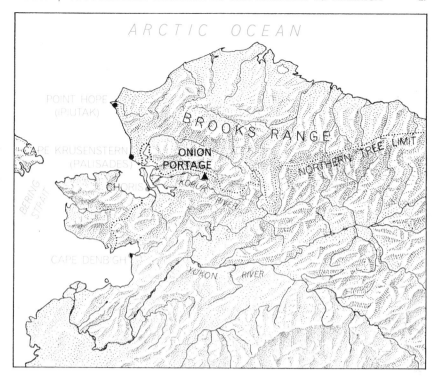

ALASKAN SITES at which artifacts have been found that resemble those unearthed at Onion Portage include the four located on this map. Onion Portage, the first known stratified site in the New World's Arctic interior, was discovered by J. L. Giddings, Jr., in 1941.

carbon-14 dates that will enable us to fit the expected biological and geological information into a sensitive chronology. The chronology now spans a minimum of 8,500 years and may eventually go back another 6,500. Even now a preliminary correlation of the carbon-14 dates with the stone tools, weapons and other remains unearthed at Onion Portage has produced some surprising results. One finding substantially alters assumptions about cultural developments in the New World Arctic.

In presenting our preliminary results I shall start with the earliest of the three main cultural traditions we have found at Onion Portage. American archaeologists use the word "tradition" to describe a continuity of cultural traits that persist over a considerable length of time and often occupy a broad geographical area. A single unifying tradition may be shared by several distinct cultures. The word "complex" is used to describe the distinctive remains of a culture. A tradition usually includes more than one culture complex. It is with the earliest culture complex of the earliest tradition at Onion Portage that I shall begin.

The complex has been named Akmak, after the northern-Alaskan Eskimo word for chert, the flintlike stone that the hunting people of this complex most commonly employed to make tools and

weapons. Most of the Akmak implements have been found on the sandy knoll at the site, between six inches and two feet below the surface. Some have been uncovered along the side of one of the gullies that cuts into the knoll and at the bottom of the gully's ancient channel, which is 10 feet below the bottom of the present channel. Others have been found below Band 8, where, having been carried down the gully, they had lain since before the first levels of Band 8 were formed. The fact that some of the material comes from below Band 8 indicates that the Akmak artifacts are at least 8,500 years old. They may be as much as 15,000 years old. Two fragments of excavated bone are being dated by carbon-14 analysis, but the sample is unfortunately too small to produce a reliable carbon-14 reading. We hope that future work at the site will produce material to settle the matter.

Most Akmak implements are of two classes. Comprising one class are large, wide "blades," the term for parallel-edged flakes of stone that were struck from a prepared "core." The other class consists of "bifaces," so named because the stone from which they were made was shaped by flaking surplus stone from both sides. From the blades the Akmak artisans produced a variety of tools. They include long end scrapers, curved implements with a sharp pro-

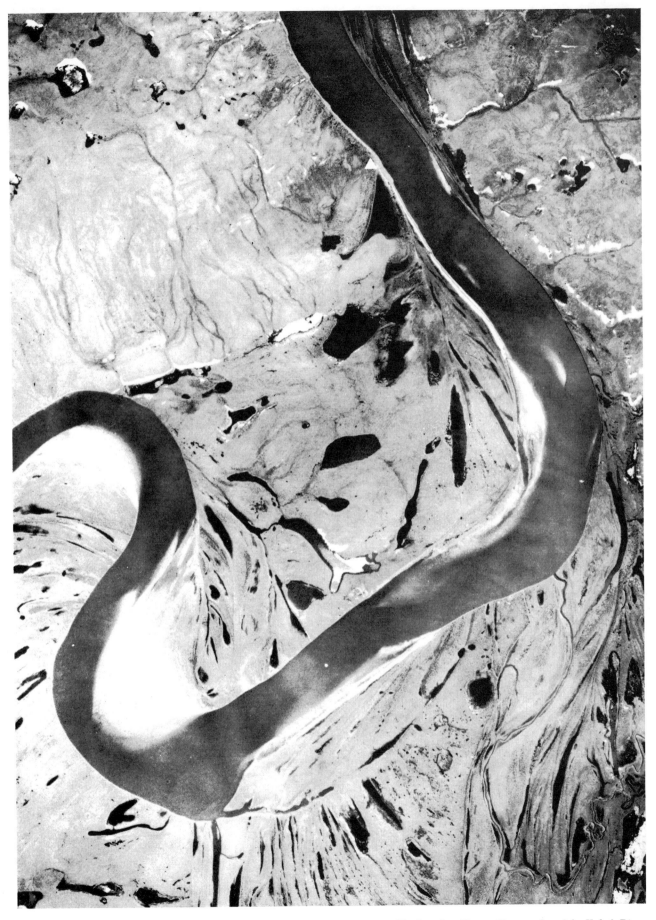

ONION PORTAGE SITE is located by the white triangle (*top center*) in this aerial photograph. The site lies on the upstream bank of a point of land enclosed by a wide meander of the Kobuk River, 125 miles from the sea in the interior of northwestern Alaska.

tuberance resembling a bird's beak and knives shaped by flaking one or both faces of a blade. The bifaces, which have the general form of a disk, were usually made by first striking the side of a slab-like core; the detached flakes left scars that end at the center of the disk. Numerous smaller flakes were then removed around the margin of the disk to give it a sharp edge. Nothing like these implements has been found in Alaska before. Indeed, the tools that most resemble Akmak disk bifaces come from the area around Lake Baikal in Siberia, where they are found at sites that are between 12,000 and 15,000 years old.

Using a technique similar to the one for producing large blades, Akmak artisans also made "microblades." Most microblades are about an inch long and quarter of an inch wide. They were struck from a small core prepared in a way that is characteristic of "campus-type microcores," so named because the first to be discovered in America were found at a site on the campus of the University of Alaska. Campus-type microcores have been found in many other parts of Alaska and also in Siberia, Mongolia and Japan. The oldest ones come from the island of Hokkaido in Japan and the Kamchatka Peninsula in the U.S.S.R.

Many Akmak microblades were made into rectangular chips by breaking off both ends of the blade. Prehistoric hunters set such chips in a groove cut in the side of a pointed shaft of wood, bone or antler. The razor-sharp bits of stone gave the pointed weapon a wicked cutting edge. Grooved shafts of antler associated with rectangular microblades have been found both in Siberia and in the Trail Creek caves in western Alaska. Although grooved shafts have not been found at Onion Portage, it is reasonable to assume that the Akmak rectangles were intended for mounting in them.

The Akmak artisans also made burins: specialized stone tools with a sharp corner particularly useful for making grooves in antler and bone. The Akmak technique for producing burins was to strike a blow that left a chisel-like point at the corner of a flake [see illustration on page 31]. Akmak burins show signs of wear both at the tip and along the edge,

TRADITION	CULTURE	DATES	STRATIGRAPHIC LOCATION	
ESKIMO	ARCTIC WOODLAND ESKIMO	A.D. 1000–1700	BAND 1	
?	NORTHERN INDIAN?	A.D. 400–800	BAND 2	
ARCTIC SMALL-TOOL TRADITION	NORTON/IPIUTAK			
?	CHORIS COMPLEX	1500–500 B.C.	BAND 3	
ARCTIC SMALL-TOOL TRADITION	DENBIGH FLINT COMPLEX	2200–1800 B.C.	BAND 4	
NORTHERN ARCHAIC TRADITION	PORTAGE COMPLEX	2600–2200 B.C.	BAND 5	
	PALISADES II COMPLEX	3900–2600 B.C.	BAND 6	
		4000–3900 B.C.	BAND 7	
HIATUS				
AMERICAN PALEO-ARCTIC TRADITION	KOBUK COMPLEX	6200–6000 B.C.	BAND 8	
	AKMAK COMPLEX	? 13,000–6500 B.C.	BELOW BAND 8	

FEET BELOW SURFACE

EIGHT MAIN BANDS in the stratigraphic column uncovered at Onion Portage are related in this chart to the evidence of human occupation they contain. Starting before 6500 B.C., and probably much earlier, three major cultural "traditions" succeed one another. The third tradition, interrupted about 1800 B.C., was initially represented at the site by the culture named the Denbigh Flint complex. It was evidently ancestral to the Eskimo tradition that appeared at Onion Portage about A.D. 1000 and continued thereafter.

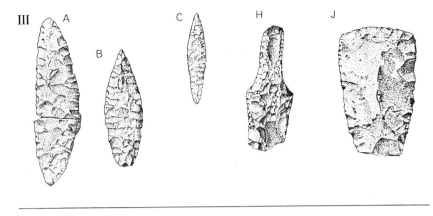

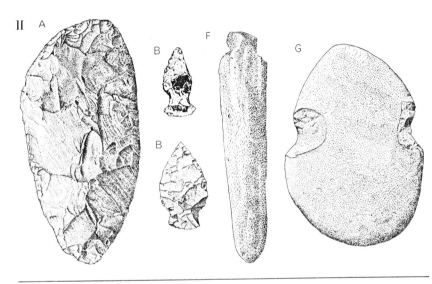

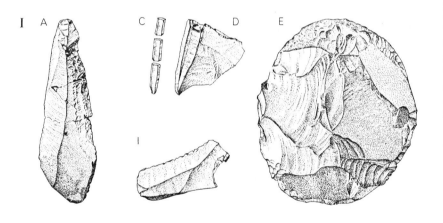

A — KNIFE   D — CAMPUS-TYPE MICROCORE   G — PEBBLE SINKER
B — PROJECTILE POINT   E — DISCOID BIFACE   H — BEAKED TOOL
C — EDGE INSET   F — NEEDLE SHARPENER   I — BURIN
     J — ADZE BLADE

ARTIFACTS OF THREE PERIODS at Onion Portage reveal the presence of three separate cultural traditions: the American Paleo-Arctic (I), the Northern Archaic (II) and the Arctic Small-Tool tradition (III). Knives (*A*) are present in all three traditions and stone projectile points (*B*) in the last two. Hunters of all three traditions had projectiles, but the two Arctic traditions favored points made from antler or ivory and inset with tiny stone blades (*C*). Unique to the earliest tradition are "campus-type microcores" (*D*) and disk-shaped bifaces (*E*). Characteristic of the non-Arctic Archaic tradition are stones for sharpening needles (*F*) and sinkers for nets (*G*). Burins appear in both of the Arctic traditions; the one shown (*I*) is Akmak. Unique to the later Arctic tradition are peculiar beaked tools (*H*) and small adze blades (*J*). All the implements are reproduced at one-half natural size.

indicating that they were used not only for grooving but also for cutting.

The Akmak tools suggest relationships between Onion Portage and Asia. Considering the changes in Arctic geography during the past 30,000 years, this is scarcely surprising. At the height of the last continental glaciation Asia and North America were connected across what is now the Bering Strait. The land area that the lowered sea level had exposed was more than a mere isthmus. At its maximum extent between 20,000 and 18,000 years ago it was virtually a subcontinent, a tundra-covered plain 1,300 miles wide that must have been populated by herds of game and hunters pursuing them. The great plain, which has been named Beringia, made Alaska an extension of northern Asia. At the same time two continental glaciers in North America effectively cut ice-free Alaska off from the rest of the New World. The isolation of Alaska did not end until sometime between 14,000 and 10,000 years ago, when the glaciers began to melt rapidly. By then Beringia had already been twice drowned and reexposed by fluctuations in the level of the sea. Then, about 10,000 years ago, Beringia began its final submergence, a process that was not completed until some 5,000 years ago.

To repeat, the Akmak period at Onion Portage ended about 6500 B.C. and may have begun as early as 13,000 B.C. Between these dates dry land connected ice-free Alaska with Siberia while glaciers forbade or at least inhibited contact with the rest of North America. The resemblances between the Akmak culture and Siberian cultures, and the lack of resemblances between the Akmak culture and Paleo-Indian cultures to the south, reflect this geographic history. At the same time there are significant differences between the Akmak culture and the Siberian cultures, suggesting that the Akmak complex resulted from a long period of isolated regional development. Because the tradition of which the Akmak complex is the earliest appears to have been an indigenous development, arising from earlier Arctic-adapted cultures, I have named it the American Paleo-Arctic tradition.

The next evidence of human habitation found at Onion Portage is in two levels of Band 8. Carbon-14 analysis of material from the higher level suggests that the people who camped there did so sometime between 6200 and 6000 B.C. I have termed the remains from Band 8 the Kobuk complex.

The limited variety of Kobuk-complex

artifacts suggests that the material found at Onion Portage represents only a part of a larger assemblage of stone tools. Fewer than 100 worked pieces of stone have been recovered from the two levels. Most of them are rectangles made from microblades. There are also two burins made from flakes, a few remnants of campus-type microcores, a single obsidian scraper and several flakes, some of which have notched edges. All the implements were found adjacent to hearths on deposits of silt. The silt suggests that Onion Portage was a wet and uncomfortable place when the Kobuk hunters camped there. The hearths are probably those of small groups that stayed only briefly.

At a number of surface sites in the Brooks Range I have collected stone implements that are almost identical with those of the Kobuk complex. The only major difference is that the Brooks Range tool assemblage includes biface knives, which are missing from the Kobuk levels at Onion Portage. I suspect that the difference is more apparent than real; if we had unearthed a larger Kobuk inventory at Onion Portage, it probably would have included biface knives. In any case, the presence in both the Akmak and the Kobuk assemblages of microblade rectangles and campus-type microcores suggests that, although the Kobuk complex represents a later period, it is nonetheless a part of the American Paleo-Arctic tradition.

Quite the opposite is true of the material we have unearthed in Band 7, Band 6 and Band 5. After a hiatus of some 2,000 years an entirely new cultural tradition arrived at Onion Portage. Its lowest levels are dated by carbon-14 analysis at around 4000 B.C. There are no microblades among its tools. Instead of using weapons with microblades inserted in them the newcomers hunted with projectiles tipped with crude stone points that had notched bases and were bifacially flaked. The new assemblage also includes large, irregular knives made from flakes, thin scrapers, notched stone sinkers and large crescent-shaped or oval bifaces. We also unearthed two heavy cobblestone choppers.

The tools from Band 7 and Band 6, which contain the early and middle phases of the new tradition, are nearly identical with a group of tools from a cliff site overlooking Cape Krusenstern on the Alaskan coast 115 miles west of Onion Portage. The cliff site is known as Palisades; the name "Palisades II complex" has been given to these phases of the new tradition at Onion Portage. The tools of the Palisades II complex reflect an uninterrupted continuity, marked only by gradual stylistic changes, for 1,400 years. One such change affected the hunters' projectile points. The notched base characteristic of the early phase gave way in the middle phase to a base with a projecting stem.

The contents of Band 5 indicate that around 2600 B.C. a period of rapid change began at Onion Portage and con-

tinued for 300 years. Several new types of tools appear; projectile points, for example, are neither notched nor stemmed but have a straight base. These and other differences in the assemblage indicate that the occupation levels in Band 5 belong to later phases of the new tradition. They warrant a label of their own, and I have named them collectively the Portage complex.

How is the arrival of the new tradition at Onion Portage to be explained? It is noteworthy that the duration of the new tradition coincides almost exactly with a major alteration in the climate of Alaska. About 10,000 years ago, as the region's last glacial period drew to a close, the Alaskan climate entered a warming phase that reached its maximum between 4000 and 2000 B.C. Throughout the period of milder weather the forest margin moved northward, steadily encroaching on the tundra. By the time of the maximum the boundary between tundra and taiga had probably advanced well beyond the position it occupies today. During the 2,000 years of the maximum it seems likely that Onion Portage lay well within the northern forest zone.

Far to the southeast, in the forests of the eastern U.S., an Indian population had pursued a woodland-oriented way of life beginning as early as 6000 B.C. Its weapons and tools reflect a forest adaptation; they belong to what is known as the Archaic tradition, as op-

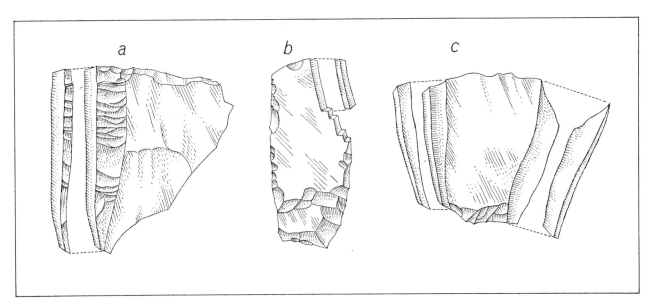

GROOVE-CUTTING TOOLS, or burins, were made by Akmak (a) and Denbigh (b) knappers at Onion Portage. The Akmak knappers chipped a notch into the edge of a prepared flake before striking a blow (arrow) that knocked off a long, narrow spall, giving the flake a sharp, chisel-like corner (color). The Denbigh knappers, using the same burin blow (arrow), knocked much smaller spalls off flakes carefully prepared in advance. They used the tiny spalls as tools for engraving. Choris knappers (c) used the burin blow to strike fine, regular spalls from flakes of irregular shape. This produced no burins; the knappers made tools from the spalls instead.

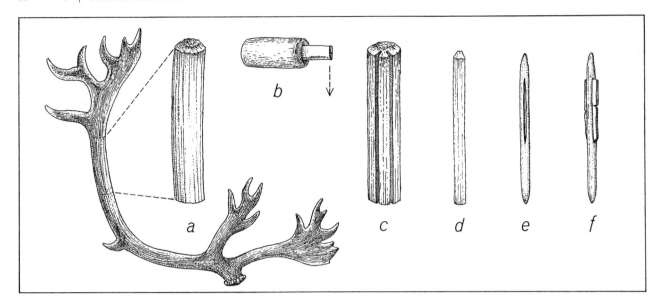

PROJECTILE POINTS can be made from antler and microblades as shown here. A length of antler (*a*) is deeply grooved (*c*) with a burin (*b*) mounted in a handle for easy use. The triangular antler segments (*d*) are then rounded and pointed, and grooves are made in one or both sides (*e*). Razor-edged bits of microblade are then set in the grooves (*f*) to form a cutting edge. The Akmak, Kobuk and Denbigh levels at Onion Portage contain edge insets. Akmak and Kobuk insets are rectangles; Denbigh insets are crescents.

posed to the older Paleo-Indian tradition. I find it significant that, during a time when the forest had shifted northward, an assemblage of tools with many resemblances to the Archaic tradition should appear at Onion Portage. Crescent-shaped bifaces, projectile points with notched and stemmed bases, heavy choppers and notched stones that the Indians of the Archaic tradition used as sinkers for nets are among the elements common to the two assemblages.

Up to now evidence for the early diffusion of the Archaic tradition northward and westward from the woodlands of the eastern U.S. does not go much beyond the Great Lakes region. Artifacts that resemble Archaic-tradition tools have been found in central and northwestern Canada and in central Alaska, but their age is undetermined. The fact that the tools are distributed throughout this area nonetheless suggests the possibility that Archaic peoples, or at least the art of making tools in the Archaic tradition, moved northward into the Arctic along with the advancing forest. The findings at Onion Portage seem to support this suggestion. I have therefore named the Palisades II complex and the Portage complex together the Northern Archaic tradition. The differences between the second tradition at Onion Portage and the American Paleo-Arctic tradition that preceded it seem great enough to suggest that they were the products of two different populations. They may have been respectively early Northern Indians and proto-Eskimos.

Almost immediately after 2300 B.C. there was a resurgence of Arctic culture at Onion Portage. The evidence in Band 4 marks the arrival of hunters representing the Arctic Small-Tool tradition. This tradition is well known from other Arctic sites. It is the culture of the earliest people in the New World Arctic who were equally at home on the coast and in the interior. The element of the tradition that is present at Onion Portage is the Denbigh Flint complex, first recognized at an Alaskan coastal site on Cape Denbigh [see "Early Man in the Arctic," by J. L. Giddings, Jr., SCIENTIFIC AMERICAN, June 1954].

The characteristic implements of the Denbigh people are burins and edge insets—the sharp stones shaped for insertion into grooved weapons. Some Denbigh edge insets were made from microblades, but all of them differ from the rectangular Akmak and Kobuk insets in that they are delicately flaked into half-moon shapes. The Denbigh people produced microblades for a variety of other uses. For greater efficiency they devised a new form of microcore. It is wider than the campus-type core, and it allowed them to strike off wider and more easily worked blades.

The people of the Denbigh Flint complex flourished widely in the Arctic between 2500 and 2000 B.C. Many students of Arctic archaeology consider them to be the direct ancestors of today's Eskimos, pointing out that the geographic distribution of Denbigh sites almost exactly coincides with the distribution

of Eskimos in historic times. Parallels between the Denbigh Flint complex and the American Paleo-Arctic tradition, including the use of microblades and edge-inset weapons, suggest that the Denbigh culture may well have descended from the Akmak and Kobuk cultures.

After 2000 B.C. the New World Arctic and coastal subarctic area supported a number of Eskimo regional groups, none of which developed along exactly the same lines. Choris is the name given to one regional people that inhabited the Alaskan coast near the mouth of the Kobuk River, hunting caribou and living in large oval houses. The Choris-complex people have an involved history that spans 1,000 years from 1500 to 500 B.C. At Onion Portage, Choris artifacts are found in Band 3.

The earliest known pottery in the New World Arctic comes from Choris sites. The pottery was well made, was decorated by stamping patterns on the surface and was fired at a reasonably high temperature. In the earliest phases of the Choris complex, evidence for which is found at sites on the coast but not at Onion Portage, the pots were decorated by striking the wet clay with a cord-wrapped paddle. The pots are too skillfully made for it to be likely that the Choris people were experimenting with clay for the first time. Instead a fully developed industry must have been introduced from the outside. Exact counterparts have not yet been found abroad, but the basic Choris pottery patterns suggest a source in Asia. This is apparently not the case for Choris-complex tools such as knife blades and skin scrapers. Some of the Choris edge insets for weapons resemble Denbigh types, but the other tools do not. If anything, they resemble Northern Archaic artifacts.

The Choris tool assemblage presents a puzzle in the form of large, regularly flaked projectile points that look very much like the Scottsbluff, Plainview and Angostura points made by the Paleo-Indian hunters of the Great Plains. The nearest Paleo-Indian sites, however, are removed from the Choris complex by some 2,500 miles and 3,000 years. What this likeness means in terms of a possible cultural relation between the Arctic and the Great Plains is a question to which I shall return.

From 500 B.C. to A.D. 500 the hunters who camped at Onion Portage left a record of steady Eskimo cultural evolution that includes evidence of increasing communication between the coast and the interior. Some of the artifacts recovered from the middle levels of Band 2, for example, are typical of those found at the seacoast site of Ipiutak, some 200 miles away on Point Hope. Regional variations nonetheless persist. Tools ground out of slabs of slate are found along with Ipiutak-complex tools at Onion Portage, but ground slate is unknown in the Ipiutak assemblage on Point Hope.

One final break in the continuity of Arctic-oriented cultures is apparent at Onion Portage. It is found in the upper occupation levels of Band 2, which were inhabited around A.D. 500 or 600. The artifacts in these levels are totally unlike those of contemporaneous Eskimo cultures along the coast. It seems logical to assume that forest Indians moving up from the south were responsible for the new cultural inventory. Whatever the identity of the newcomers, they did not stay long. Around A.D. 1000 Onion Portage was again in Eskimo hands.

Measured in terms of the number of artifacts and wealth of information, the modern period recorded in Band 1 is the best-known in the Onion Portage sequence. Our current studies, combined with Giddings' earlier ones, give a remarkably detailed picture of the Kobuk River Eskimos' gradual change from a part-time coastal economy to a full-time way of life adapted to tundra and taiga conditions, in which networks of trade maintained communication with the Eskimos of the coast.

Taken as a whole, the stratigraphic record at Onion Portage has cast much

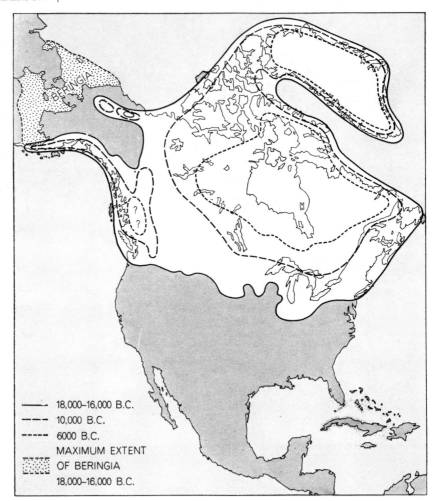

- — — — 18,000–16,000 B.C.
- – – – – 10,000 B.C.
- - - - - 6000 B.C.
          MAXIMUM EXTENT
          OF BERINGIA
          18,000–16,000 B.C.

ICE BARRIER, formed by union of two continental glaciers, cut off Alaska from the rest of North America for perhaps 8,000 years. The era's lowered seas exposed Beringia, a vast area that made Alaska into an extension of Siberia. Arctic and Temperate North America were not reunited until the final withdrawal of the two ice sheets had begun (broken lines).

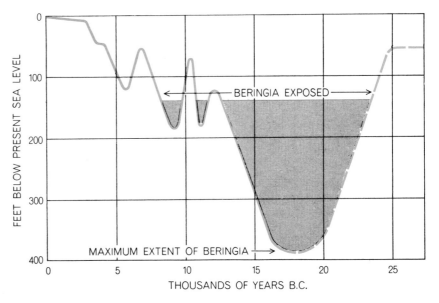

CHANGING SEA LEVEL in late Pleistocene times drowned Beringia 8,000 years ago. The link between Alaska and Siberia had been exposed earlier for two short periods and one long period when it was quite large. The graph is based on one by D. M. Hopkins of the U.S. Geological Survey; dating of sea-level changes before 18,000 B.C. is conjectural.

WORK CREW on the flats below the hill at Onion Portage slowly exposes one of the site's more than 70 levels with traces of human occupation. Silt carried by floodwaters and sand eroded from the hillside had accumulated in the flats to a depth of 20 feet in places.

new light on the relations between various poorly dated or undated Arctic archaeological assemblages. At the start we see Arctic peoples with cultural roots in Siberia adapting themselves to a life of hunting on the treeless tundra of interior Alaska, and later to hunting along the treeless coast. As we can infer from the abundance of microblade edge insets found at Onion Portage, a part of this adaptation involved the efficient use of materials other than wood for weapons, among them antler (and later ivory) spearpoints edged with stone. This indigenous tradition, based on Asian origins, had an uninterrupted development from perhaps as early as 13,000 B.C. until about 6000 B.C.

Sometime before 4000 B.C. we see the arrival at Onion Portage of a forest-adapted tradition that had its origins in the eastern woodlands of the U.S. The advance of the Archaic tradition into Arctic terrain coincided with the postglacial shift in climate that allowed the forests to invade the northern tundra. With the reexpansion of the tundra at the end of the warm period Arctic cultures once again dominated the Kobuk

River region. At the same time they spread rapidly across the entire Arctic area occupied by Eskimos today.

Until Onion Portage was excavated the archaeological record in the Arctic favored the view that early cultural developments there were somehow connected with the Paleo-Indians of the Great Plains. Many scholars suggested that the Arctic and Paleo-Indian cultures shared essentially the same cultural tradition, perhaps originating in the north or perhaps in the Great Plains but in either case occupying northwestern Alaska and Canada sometime between 7000 and 3000 B.C. The suggestion derived its strength primarily from the presence of projectile points almost identical with Paleo-Indian ones at several sites in Alaska and Canada. The projectile points found in the Arctic could not be dated, but it was speculated that they were as much as 7,000 or 8,000 years old. Such antiquity, of course, added strength to the Paleo-Indian hypothesis.

Even before the Onion Portage excavations some contrary evidence had come to light. For example, the Choris complex is rich in projectile points that

are Paleo-Indian in appearance. Yet the Choris complex is firmly dated between 1500 and 1000 B.C.—scarcely half of the minimum age suggested by the Paleo-Indian hypothesis.

The findings at Onion Portage, in my opinion, cast even more doubt on the hypothesis. During the millenniums between 7000 and 3000 B.C.—nearly the entire interval of the postulated contact between (or identity of) the Arctic and the Paleo-Indian cultures—nothing from any occupation level at Onion Portage shows any hint of Paleo-Indian influence. On the contrary, the influence in the earlier part of the interval is Siberian and in the later part Archaic.

We hope that future work at Onion Portage will push the firmly dated record of Arctic prehistory back to even earlier times. We should also like to learn what cultures were developing along the Kobuk River between 6000 and 4000 B.C.— the period for which we have no record at Onion Portage. Meanwhile what we have already learned substantially clarifies the sequence of events at the gateway to the New World.

3

Elephant-Hunting
in North America

by C. Vance Haynes, Jr.
June 1966

*Bones of elephants that vanished from the continent
10,000 years ago are found together with the projectile
points early men used to kill them. Indeed, the hunters
may have caused the elephants' extinction*

Elephant-hunting today is a specialized activity confined to a handful of professionals in parts of Africa and Asia; 11,000 years or so ago it provided a living for one of the earliest groups of humans to inhabit the New World. At that time hunting bands whose craftsmen made a particular kind of stone projectile point by the thousands ranged across North America from the east coast to the west coast, as far north as Alaska and as far south as central Mexico. Two generations ago such a statement would have been hard to support. Since 1932, however, the excavation of no fewer than six stratified ancient sites of mammoth-hunting activity in the western U.S. and the discovery of scores of significant, if less firmly documented, sites elsewhere in North America have proved its validity beyond the possibility of challenge. It is the purpose of this article to present what we know of the lives of these mammoth-hunters and to suggest when they arrived in the New World.

The first evidence that man had been present in the New World much before 2000 B.C. touches only indirectly on the history of the mammoth-hunters. This was a discovery made near Folsom, N.M., by an expedition from the Denver Museum of Natural History in 1926. Careful excavation that year and during the next two seasons uncovered 19 flint projectile points of unusual shape and workmanship lying 10 feet below the surface among the bones of 23 bison. The bison were of a species that paleontologists had thought had been extinct for at least 10,000 years. The Denver Museum excavation at Folsom thus made it plain that as long ago as 8000 B.C. hunters armed with a distinctive type of flint point had inhabited what is now the western U.S. The association of the projectile points with the bison bones made it almost certain that the bison were the hunters' prey; any doubts on this score were settled when Frank H. H. Roberts of the Smithsonian Institution, digging at the Lindenmeyer site in Colorado, found a Folsom point firmly lodged in a bison vertebra.

In 1932 a cloudburst near Dent, Colo., hastened the erosion of a gully near the South Platte River and exposed a large concentration of mammoth bones. Investigators from the Denver Museum went to work at the site; the bones proved to represent 11 immature female mammoths and one adult male. Along with the animal remains they found three flint projectile points and a number of boulders that were evidently not native to the surrounding accumulation of silt. In the 1930's the carbon-14 technique of dating had not yet been invented, but the geologists in the party estimated that the Dent site was at least as old as the Folsom site and perhaps older. Certainly the projectile points found at Dent, although they bore a general resemblance to those found at Folsom, were cruder in work-

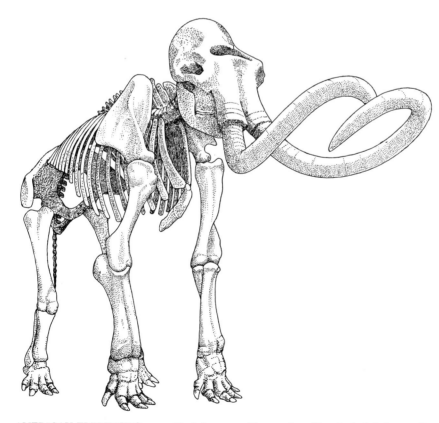

AMERICAN ELEPHANTS were all of the genus *Mammuthus*. They included the woolly mammoth, which also ranged the Old World, and the imperial, confined to North America. This skeleton of one imperial variety, the Columbian, is 12 feet at the shoulder.

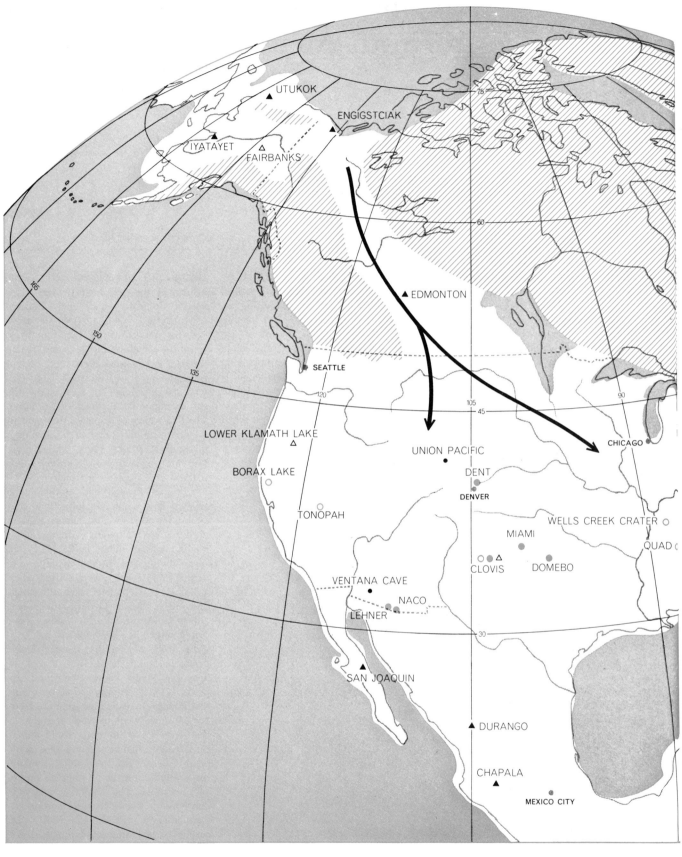

● CLOVIS KILL SITE   ○ CAMP SITE   △ ISOLATED FINDS OF CYLINDRICAL BONE POINTS

ICE-FREE CORRIDOR in western Canada may have opened some 12,000 years ago. The author suggests that the mammoth-hunters who made both the characteristically fluted flint projectile points and the needle-like bone ones left the Bering Strait area earlier than that and reached the unglaciated part of North America some 11,500 years ago. Symbols by the names distinguish among campsites, kill

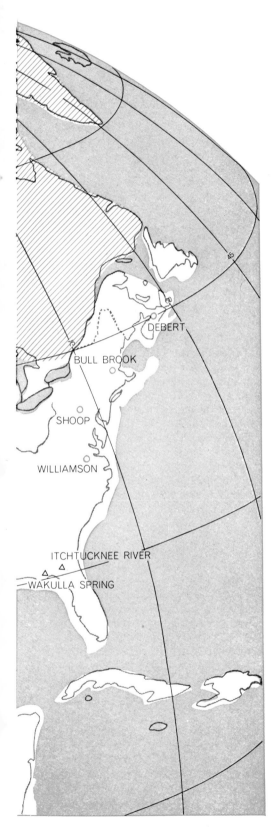

▲ ISOLATED FINDS OF FLUTED FLINT POINTS

sites and significant isolated finds. In the northeast Debert and Bull Brook probably include non-Clovis Paleo-Indian material.

manship. In any case, the excavation at Dent made it evident that early hunters in western North America had preyed not only on extinct bison but also on the mammoth.

Beginning in 1934 John L. Cotter of the Academy of Natural Sciences in Philadelphia excavated a site known as Blackwater Draw near Clovis, N.M., which proved to contain the answer to the relative antiquity of the Folsom and Dent finds. In the Clovis sediments projectile points like those from Folsom were found in the upper strata associated with bison bones. Below these strata, associated with the remains of two mammoths, were four of the cruder, Dent-style projectile points and several flint tools of a kind that could have been used for butchering. Also found at Clovis was an entirely new kind of artifact—a projectile point fashioned out of bone. At the completion of nearly two decades of work at the site by investigators from the Philadelphia Academy and other institutions, students of New World prehistory were generally agreed that two separate groups of hunters had once inhabited western North America. The earlier group, using flint projectile points of the type found in the lower Clovis strata, had been primarily mammoth-hunters; the later group, using Folsom points, had been primarily bison-hunters.

The most obvious characteristic that Clovis and Folsom points have in common is that they are "fluted." After the flint-knapper had roughed out the point's general shape he beveled its base; then, with a deft blow against the beveled base, he detached a long flake, leaving a channel that extended a third or more of the point's length [see illustration page 38]. The fluting, on one or both sides of the point, gave the point a hollow-ground appearance. It has been suggested that the flute channels facilitated the bleeding of the prey, as do the blood-gutters of a modern hunting knife. A more plausible explanation is that the fluting made the point easier to fit into the split end of a wooden shaft. The assumption that the points were hafted in this manner is strengthened by the fact that their edges are generally dulled or ground smooth for a distance from the base about equal to the length of the flute channel. If a sinew lashing was used to mount the point in a split shaft, it would be mandatory to have dull edges where the lashing was wrapped; otherwise the flint would cut through the taut sinew.

To judge from the ease with which

a few self-taught flint-knappers today can turn out a classic Clovis or Folsom point in a matter of minutes by striking raw flint with a "baton" of deer antler or hardwood, it is reasonable to believe that the early hunters also used this technique of baton percussion, at least in roughing out their points. There are even indications that such roughed-out blanks were produced at various flint quarries and then carried back to campsites for the finishing touches. Detaching the channel flake or flakes was obviously the crucial step; once successfully fluted, the point was finished by sharpening the tip, trimming the edges either by rasping or by pressure-flaking, and dulling the lower edges where the lashing would be wrapped around. If the tip of a point broke off, the point might be sharpened again [see top illustration on page 40].

Although the points from any one site exhibit a considerable range in size and appearance, it is usually not difficult to distinguish between Folsom and Clovis points. The fluting of a Folsom point is typically a single channel that extends all the way to the tip of the point or nearly so, and the edges of the point are delicately chipped. A Clovis point is typically larger, with coarsely chipped edges; usually more than one flake has been removed to produce the flute channel and these have "broken out" less than halfway to the tip in what is called a "hinge" fracture. In some cases the hinge fracture broke inward rather than outward, snapping the unfinished point in half. If early man used profane language, such an incident must surely have inspired an epithet or two.

Carbon-14 dating has now established the antiquity of four of the six sites in which mammoth bones are associated with Clovis points. Two of the sites are Clovis itself and Dent; the others are Domebo Canyon in Oklahoma, where a single mammoth was found together with three Clovis points and an assembly of flint butchering tools, and Lehner Ranch Arroyo in New Mexico, where among the bones of nine immature mammoths Emil Haury of the Arizona State Museum uncovered 13 Clovis points and eight butchering tools in 1955 and 1956. It was charcoal from a campfire hearth at the Lehner site that in 1959 yielded the first Clovis carbon-14 dates to be determined; they averaged 11,260 ± 360 years before the present, or a little earlier than 9000 B.C. The carbon-14 dates from Dent, Clovis and Domebo fall in this same time in-

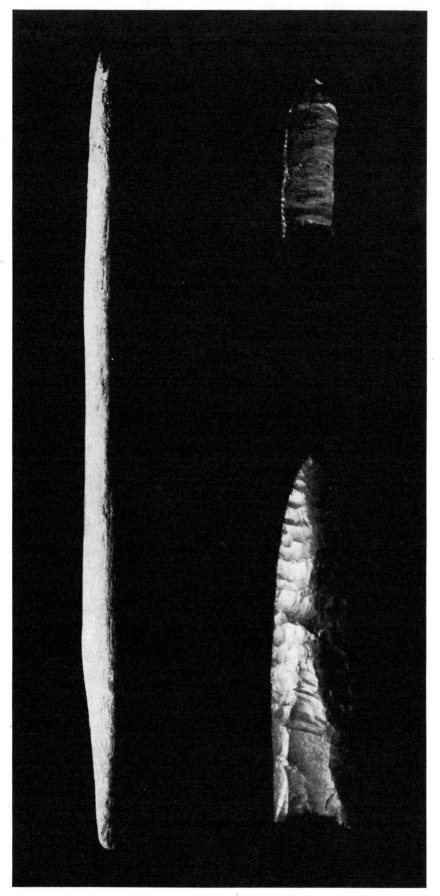

PROJECTILE POINTS used by early hunting groups in North America include one of bone (*left*) and one of flint (*lower right*) found near Clovis, N.M., in the mid-1930's. These artifacts were used to kill mammoths. The smaller flint point (*upper right*) was made by a later group that hunted bison. The first of these were found near Folsom, N.M., in 1926.

terval, as do the dates of two other early sites in the western U.S. that may or may not have Clovis connections. These are Union Pacific, Wyo., where mammoth bones and flint tools are found, and Ventana Cave in Arizona, which has no mammoth remains. The other two stratified Clovis sites that contain mammoth bones—Miami in the Texas Panhandle and Naco, Ariz., where Haury and his associates uncovered the bones of a single mammoth in 1951 with five out of eight Clovis points concentrated in its chest area—have not been dated by the carbon-14 method.

These and other carbon-14 determinations, together with geological analyses, have established a general framework for North American prehistory in the Rocky Mountains, the Great Plains and the Southwest. The earliest period ends about 10,000 B.C.; its fossil fauna include the mammoth and extinct species of camel, horse and bison, but there are no artifacts associated with their remains that positively indicate man's presence. There follows a gap of about 500 years for which information is lacking. In the next period, between 9500 and 9000 B.C., the early fauna is still present and Clovis projectile points are frequently found in association with mammoth remains. In the following period, between 9000 and 8000 B.C., mammoth, camel and horse have all disappeared; only the extinct bison species remains, and the artifacts found among the bison bones include Folsom projectile points rather than Clovis. The next cultural complexes overlap Folsom somewhat and are dated between 8500 and 7000 B.C. Several sites in this span of time are assigned to the Agate Basin complex. Finally, between 7000 and 6000 B.C., the Agate Basin complex is replaced by the Cody complex. These later "Paleo-Indian" cultures do not concern us. What is interesting is that, in spite of their wide geographical distribution, all the dated Clovis sites apparently belong to the same relatively narrow span of time.

Although the Clovis sites mentioned thus far are all in the western U.S., it would be a mistake to think that the mammoth-hunters were confined to that part of North America. Clovis points have been found in every one of the mainland states of the U.S. and there are more Clovis points at any one of three eastern sites than at all the stratified western sites combined. The trouble is that, with a very few exceptions, the eastern Clovis artifacts are found on the surface or only inches below the surface; it is impossible to assign dates to them with any degree of reliability. An example of the complexity of the problem is provided by the Williamson site near Dinwiddie, Va., where Clovis points and Civil War bullets are found side by side in the same plowed field.

In spite of the problem of dating the eastern discoveries, no grasp of the vigor and extent of the mammoth-hunters' culture is possible without consideration of its maximum range. In addition to the sites in the western U.S. already mentioned, Clovis points—flaked from obsidian rather than flint—have been unearthed at Borax Lake, a site north of San Francisco. Here, unfortunately, the stratigraphy is disturbed and artifacts of various ages are mixed

together. Another western Clovis site is near Tonopah, Nev., where fluted points were found on the surface around a dry lake, together with flint scrapers, gravers and perforators. Neither the site nor the artifacts have been described in detail, however, and the Tonopah material is not available for study. (It is in a private collection.)

Projectile points made of bone and ivory, nearly identical with the ones found at Clovis, have also been found elsewhere in the West. Two come from deposits of muck in central Alaska that contain mammoth bones. Unfortunately the Alaskan muck is notorious for its mixed stratigraphy, and the relative ages of artifacts and animal remains in it are not easily determined. The other

bone points have been found at Klamath Lake in California, in deposits as yet undated. These deposits also contain mammoth bones, but the artifacts and animal remains are not in direct association.

In the eastern U.S. large numbers of similar bone points have been found underwater at two locations in Florida: the Itchtucknee River and Wakula Spring. The latter site has also yielded mammoth remains. Something of the difficulty facing investigators who wish to assign dates to such underwater discoveries as the 600 bone points from Wakula Spring can be appreciated when one considers that the same six-foot stretch of sandy bottom may yield a bone point, a mammoth tooth and a

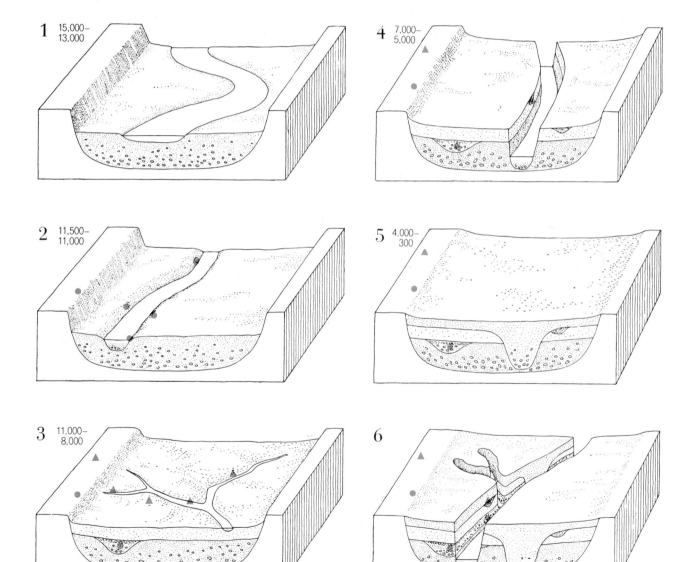

SEQUENCE OF DEPOSITS at a hypothetical valley site shows how a sediment-filled river valley (1) was inhabited by the Clovis mammoth-hunters (2). Dates are given in number of years before the present. Next (3) the Clovis valley sites are covered by fresh sediments on which the later Folsom bison-hunters camped. Both the Clovis and the Folsom campsites on the terrace above the valley escape burial; surface sites of this kind are difficult to date. Later cycles of erosion and deposit (4 and 5) leave the Clovis and Folsom valley sites deeply buried. Finally (6), today's situation is shown; erosion has now bared two superposed kill sites (center).

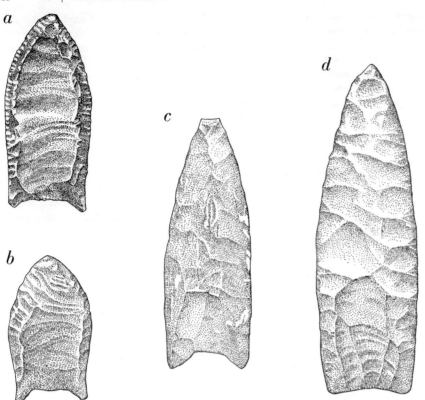

CHARACTERISTIC DIFFERENCES between Folsom ("*a*" and "*b*") and Clovis ("*c*" and "*d*") projectile points include the Folsom point's long neat flute scar, produced by the detachment of a single flake, and the delicate chipping of its cutting edges. Clovis points tend to be coarser and larger; flute scars are short and often show the detachment of more than one flake. The shorter of the Folsom points may have been repointed after its tip broke off.

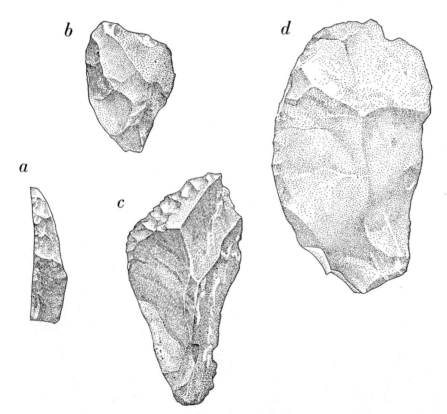

STONE TOOLS found at the Lehner site in New Mexico include keeled scrapers (*a*) and a variety of sidescrapers ("*b*," "*c*" and "*d*"). The latter were made from large flakes of flint knapped on one side. Choppers suitable for butchering were also found at this Clovis site.

soft-drink bottle. The prospect of dating the abundant Clovis finds elsewhere in the East is in most instances not much brighter. Nevertheless, thanks to amateur archaeologists who have taken pains to report the exact location of their surface discoveries, it is now apparent that the greatest concentration of fluted projectile points is centered on Ohio, Kentucky and Tennessee. When the places in which Clovis points have been discovered are plotted on a map, the distribution of the points corresponds closely to that of mammoth fossils and those of the other New World proboscid, the mastodon.

The curious fact remains that, with one possible exception, no Clovis point in the eastern U.S. has ever been found in association with animal bones. The possible exception is a Clovis point found in 1898 at Big Bone Lick in Kentucky, where mammoth bones have also been uncovered. At the time, of course, the point was not recognized for what it was, and there is no evidence that the point was found in association with the mammoth bones.

The major surface discoveries of Clovis artifacts in eastern North America have been made at the Williamson site in Virginia, at the Shoop site near Harrisburg, Pa., at the Quad site in northern Alabama and at Wells Creek Crater in Tennessee [*see illustration on pages 36 and 37*]. To judge from the hundreds of Clovis points and thousands of other flint tools that have been picked up at these locations, each must represent a large campsite.

The same is probably true of Bull Brook near Ipswich, Mass.; hundreds of fluted points from this site have been analyzed by Douglas S. Byers of the R. S. Peabody Foundation in Andover, Mass. Unfortunately the stratigraphy at Bull Brook is disturbed. No campfire hearths or clear-cut levels of human habitation are known; four charcoal samples that may or may not be associated with the flint points yield carbon-14 dates that range from 4990 ± 800 B.C. to 7350 ± 400 B.C. It is evident that the Bull Brook deposits cover a considerable span of time.

The only other significant stratified site in eastern North America that has yielded carbon-14 dates is near Debert in the Canadian province of Nova Scotia. Debert is being studied by investigators from the R. S. Peabody Foundation and the National Museum of Canada. Here fluted projectile points have been found that are neither Clovis nor Folsom in style. The average of carbon-14 dates at Debert is 8633 ± 470 B.C., or roughly 1,000 years later than the Clovis sites in the western U.S.

East or west, buried or exposed, most Clovis discoveries can be classified either as campsites or sites where animals were killed. A campsite is characterized by the presence of a wide variety of flint implements in addition to fluted points. A kill site is characterized by the presence of animal bones together with fluted points and a few flint butchering tools or no other tools at all. Recent excavations at Clovis itself indicate that the area around an extinct lake that attracted game to the site was used by the mammoth-hunters for both killing and camping. Not only butchering tools but also flint scrapers, gravers and knives have been discovered in the lower strata of the Clovis site. Apart from Clovis, however, the only other campsites in the western U.S. appear to be Tonopah, with its mixture of points

and other artifacts, and Borax Lake.

Fortunately the major Clovis sites in the eastern U.S. provide abundant evidence of camp life. Some contain literally thousands of flint implements in addition to the characteristic fluted points; these include choppers, gravers, perforators, scrapers and knives made out of flint flakes. The locations of these sites show the kind of place the mammoth-hunters preferred as a camp. Shoop, Williamson, Quad and Wells Creek Crater are all on high ground, such as a stream-cut terrace or a ridge, overlooking the floodplain of a river or creek.

Analysis of the kill sites, in turn, reveals something about the Clovis people's hunting techniques, although many questions remain unanswered. The number of points found with each kill, for example, is inconsistent. At the Dent site only three Clovis points were

found among the remains of a dozen mammoths. At Naco the skeleton of a single mammoth was associated with eight points. One interpretation of this seeming contradiction is that the Naco mammoth may have been one that got away, escaping its hunters to die alone some time after it was attacked. The 12 mammoths at Dent, according to the same interpretation, were butchered on the spot and the hunters recovered most of their weapons. One piece of negative evidence in support of this interpretation is that no butchering tools were found at Naco. Such tools, however, are also absent from Dent.

The Dent site affords a reasonably clear picture of one hunt. The mammoth bones were concentrated at the mouth of a small gully where an intermittent stream emerges from a sandstone bluff to join the South Platte River. It seems plausible that here the Clovis hunters had stampeded a mam-

STAMPEDED MAMMOTHS were unearthed near Dent, Colo., in 1932 by workers from the Denver Museum of Natural History. Among the bones of 11 immature female elephants and one adult male elephant they found several boulders and three typical Clovis projectile points. Photographed at the site were (*left to right*) Rev. Conrad Bilgery, S.J., an unidentified Regis College student, two Denver Museum trustees (W. C. Mead and C. H. Hanington) and Frederick Howarter of the museum's paleontology department.

moth herd over the edge of the bluff. Some of the animals may have been killed by the fall; others may have escaped. Those that were too badly hurt to fight free of the narrow gully may then have been stunned with boulders—an assumption that helps to explain the presence of these misplaced stones among the mammoth bones—and finally dispatched with spear thrusts. The bag of 11 cows and one bull would have constituted a highly successful day's work, but it may also have been the result of several hunts.

All six mammoths found at Clovis could also have been taken by stampeding a herd, in this case into shallow water where the footing was treacherous. Whether this actually happened, or whether the animals were simply surprised while watering, is impossible to determine. Clovis nonetheless affords a tantalizing glimpse into another of the mammoth-hunters' thought processes. One of the springs that fed the lake contains hundreds of flint flakes and a number of intact flint tools, including three Clovis points. Did the ancient hunters deliberately toss waste chips and usable artifacts into the spring? If not, how did these objects accumulate?

The concept of cutting a herd—separating the young and less dangerous animals from the more formidable adults—may be what is demonstrated by the remains at the Lehner site, where all nine mammoths were immature or even nurslings. At Lehner, as at Domebo (where only a single adult was killed), the animals apparently had been attacked while watering along a spring-fed stream.

Although the way in which the hunters' fluted projectile points were mounted seems clear, the kind of haft on which they were mounted remains unknown. That the points were used as arrowheads seems unlikely; the bow reached the New World or was independently invented there at a much later date. The Clovis points must therefore have been mounted on spears or darts. Whether launched from the hand or propelled by a spear-thrower, neither may have been a weapon of much effectiveness against an infuriated mammoth. It seems possible that, when the prey showed fight, most of the hunters devoted their efforts to keeping the mammoth at bay while a daring individual or two rushed in to drive a spear home to its heart from behind the foreleg.

The analysis of kill sites provides one

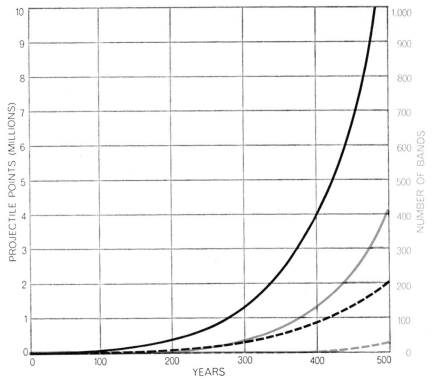

POPULATION INCREASE among the mammoth-hunters in the course of 500 years is calculated on the assumption that an original 30-member hunting band multiplied by a factor of 1.2 or 1.4 each 28-year generation (color). Black curves show the total number of Clovis points produced during 500 years, assuming that one person in four made five each month.

further fact about the Clovis hunters. Although they were evidently specialists in the pursuit of mammoths, they were not unwilling to take other kinds of quarry. At two of the sites—Clovis and Lehner—bison bones are also found.

The fluted projectile point is a highly specialized artifact that must have passed through a considerable period of development, yet no precursors are known in the New World or elsewhere. Obviously the archaeological record is incomplete, and perhaps it will remain so. For the time being, however, this absence of evident precursors suggests that the Clovis people arrived in the New World, already equipped with their specialized tool kit, between 12,000 and 13,000 years ago. Carbon-14 dates obtained during the past 15 years have built up a reasonably consistent picture of the way in which the New World was peopled during the final stages of the Pleistocene ice age. When the most recent glacial period was at its peak, 14,000 to 20,000 years ago, a large portion of the earth's water supply was stored in the Northern Hemisphere's ice sheets. The so-called land bridge between Alaska and Siberia in the area of the Bering Strait, exposed by the low level of the earth's oceans at that time,

was no narrow isthmus but a broad land mass joining Asia and North America in a single continent.

The Bering land mass, however, was not a thoroughfare from the Old World to the whole of the New. The Cordilleran ice cap covered the Canadian Rockies from Vancouver to eastern Alaska, and the Laurentide ice cap covered most of the rest of Canada and much of the northern U.S. These two glacial formations merged at the foot of the Canadian Rockies, leaving central Alaska, the Bering land mass and eastern Siberia unglaciated but cut off from the more southerly Americas by an ice barrier.

A little more than 12,000 years ago there occurred a marked period of glacial retreat known as the Two Creeks interval. Carbon-14 dates indicate that the warm interval came to an end scarcely more than a century or two later, or about 9900 B.C.; another glacial advance began soon thereafter. As we have seen, Clovis points make their first appearance in western North America in 9500 B.C., or roughly half a millennium after the Two Creeks interval. A tenable hypothesis connecting the two events is that the Two Creeks glacial retreat opened a trans-Canadian corridor between the Cordilleran and

CLOVIS BONE POINT, partly cleared of surrounding matrix at lower right, lies in direct association with the bones of a mammoth foreleg. Unearthed at Clovis, this evidence of early man's hunting ability is displayed at the Philadelphia Academy of Natural Sciences.

the Laurentide ice caps. The progenitors of the Clovis people, confined until then to central Alaska but already specialists in big-game hunting, could thus make their way down an ice-free corridor into a world where big game abounded and had scarcely been hunted until that time.

This, of course, is no more than a hypothesis, but it is a useful one on two counts. First, it provides a logical explanation for the abrupt appearance of Clovis points in North America at about 9500 B.C. Second, it is easily tested. All that is needed to destroy the Two Creeks hypothesis, for example, is the discovery of a Clovis site more than 12,000 years old located south of the ice sheet. Thus far no such Clovis site has been found. Meanwhile the Two Creeks hypothesis can also be tested indirectly in demographic terms.

Assuming that the first Clovis people passed through northwestern Canada some 12,000 years ago, they would have had to travel at the rate of four miles a year to reach the most southerly of their western U.S. sites, 2,000 miles away, within 500 years. Is such a rate of human diffusion realistic? Edward S. Deevey, Jr., of Yale University has noted that, under conditions of maximal increase in an environment empty of competitors, mankind's best efforts produce a population increase by a factor of 1.4 in each 28-year generation [see "The

Human Population," by Edward S. Deevey, Jr.; SCIENTIFIC AMERICAN Offprint 608]. James Fitting of the University of Michigan has recently investigated a prehistoric hunting camp in Michigan; he suggests that Paleo-Indian family hunting bands numbered between 30 and 60 indiviuals.

Making conservative use of these findings, I have assumed that the first and only Clovis band to pass down the corridor opened by the Two Creeks interval numbered about 30, say five families averaging six persons each: two grandparents, two parents and two offspring. I have assumed further that one in four knew how to knap flint and produced Clovis points at the rate of five a month. In case Deevey's growth factor of 1.4 is too high, I have also made my calculation with a smaller factor—1.2— on the grounds that a plausible extrapolation probably lies somewhere between the two.

Applying these production rates, I find that in 500 years an original band of 30 mammoth-hunters evolves into a population numbering between 800 and 12,500, comprised of 26 to 425 hunting bands. In the same 500 years the bands' flint-knappers will have made—and left scattered across the land—between two million and 14 million Clovis points. Assuming that the demographic model is a reasonable one, the Clovis hunters could easily have spread across North America from coast to coast in the brief span of time allotted to them. Indeed, if the higher figure is in any way realistic, the rapid increase in the number of mammoth-hunters could easily be one of the main reasons why these animals became extinct in North America sometime around 9000 B.C., leaving the succeeding Folsom hunters with no larger prey than bison.

A Paleo-Indian Bison Kill

4

By Joe Ben Wheat

January 1967

Some 8,500 years ago a group of hunters on the Great Plains stampeded a herd of buffaloes into a gulch and butchered them. The bones of the animals reveal the event in remarkable detail

When one thinks of American Indians hunting buffaloes, one usually visualizes the hunters pursuing a herd of the animals on horseback and killing them with bow and arrow. Did the Indians hunt buffaloes before the introduction of the horse (by the Spanish conquistadors in the 16th century) and the much earlier introduction of the bow? Indeed they did. As early as 10,000 years ago Paleo-Indians hunted species of bison that are now extinct on foot and with spears. My colleagues and I at the University of Colorado Museum have recently excavated the site of one such Paleo-Indian bison kill dating back to about 6500 B.C. The site so remarkably preserves a moment in time that we know with reasonable certainty not only the month of the year the hunt took place but also such details as the way the wind blew on the day of the kill, the direction of the hunters' drive, the highly organized manner in which they butchered their quarry, their choice of cuts to be eaten on the spot and the probable number of hunters involved.

The bison was the most important game animal in North America for millenniums before its near extermination in the 19th century. When Europeans arrived on the continent, they found herds of bison ranging over vast areas, but the animals were first and foremost inhabitants of the Great Plains, the high, semiarid grassland extending eastward from the foothills of the Rocky Mountains and all the way from Canada to Mexico. Both in historic and in late prehistoric times the bison was the principal economic resource of the Indian tribes that occupied the Great Plains. Its meat, fat and bone marrow provided them with food; its hide furnished them with shelter and clothing;

its brain was used to tan the hide; its horns were fashioned into containers. There was scarcely a part of the animal that was not utilized in some way.

This dependence on big-game hunting probably stretches back to the very beginning of human prehistory in the New World. We do not know when man first arrived in the Americas, nor do we know in detail what cultural baggage he brought with him. The evidence for the presence of man in the New World much before 12,000 years ago is scattered and controversial. It is quite

clear, however, that from then on Paleo-Indian hunting groups, using distinctive kinds of stone projectile point, ranged widely throughout the New World. On the Great Plains the principal game animal of this early period was the Columbian mammoth [see the article "Elephant-hunting in North America," by C. Vance Haynes, Jr., beginning on p. 35]. Mammoth remains have been found in association with projectile points that are usually large and leaf-shaped and have short, broad grooves on both sides of the base. These points are typical of the complex of

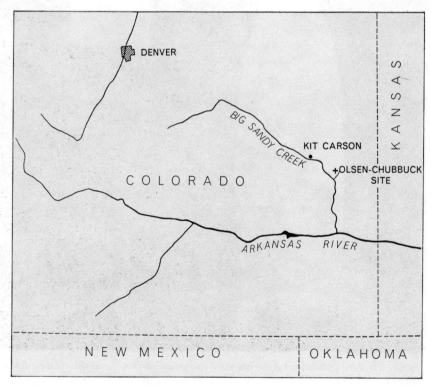

SITE OF THE KILL is 140 miles southeast of Denver. It is named the Olsen-Chubbuck site after its discoverers, the amateur archaeologists Sigurd Olsen and Gerald Chubbuck.

PROJECTILE POINTS found at the site show a surprising divergence of form in view of the fact that all of them were used simultaneously by a single group. In the center is a point of the Scottsbluff type. At top left is another Scottsbluff point that shows some of the characteristics of a point of the Eden type at top right. At bottom left is a third Scottsbluff point; it has characteristics in common with a point of the Milnesand type at bottom right. Regardless of form, all the points are equally excellent in flaking.

cultural traits named the Clovis complex; the tool kit of this complex also included stone scrapers and knives and some artifacts made of ivory and bone.

The elephant may have been hunted out by 8000 B.C. In any case, its place as a game animal was taken by a large, straight-horned bison known as *Bison antiquus*. The first of the bison-hunters used projectile points of the Folsom culture complex; these are similar to Clovis points but are generally smaller and better made. Various stone scrapers and knives, bone needles and engraved bone ornaments have also been found in Folsom sites.

A millennium later, about 7000 B.C., *Bison antiquus* was supplanted on the Great Plains by the somewhat smaller *Bison occidentalis*. The projectile points found in association with this animal's remains are of several kinds. They differ in shape, size and details of flaking, but they have some characteristics in common. Chief among them is the technical excellence of the flaking. The flake scars meet at the center of the blade to form a ridge; sometimes they give the impression that a single flake has been detached across the entire width of the blade [*see the illustration on opposite page*]. Some of the projectile points that belong to this tradition, which take their names from the sites where they were first found, are called Milnesand, Scottsbluff and Eden points. The last two kinds of point form part of what is called the Cody complex, for which there is a fairly reliable carbon-14 date of about 6500 B.C.

Paleo-Indian archaeological sites fall into two categories: habitations and kill sites. Much of our knowledge of the early inhabitants of the Great Plains comes from the kill sites, where are found not only the bones of the animals but also the projectile points used to kill them and the knives, scrapers and other tools used to butcher and otherwise process them. Such sites have yielded much information about the categories of projectile points and how these categories are related in time. Heretofore, however, they have contributed little to our understanding of how the early hunters actually lived. The kill site I shall describe is one of those rare archaeological sites where the evidence is so complete that the people who left it seem almost to come to life.

Sixteen miles southeast of the town of Kit Carson in southeastern Colorado, just below the northern edge of the broad valley of the Arkansas River, lies a small valley near the crest of a low divide. The climate here is semiarid; short bunchgrass is the main vegetation and drought conditions have prevailed since the mid-1950's. In late 1957 wind erosion exposed what appeared to be five separate piles of bones, aligned in an east-west direction. Gerald Chubbuck, a keen amateur archaeologist, came on the bones in December, 1957; among them he found several projectile points of the Scottsbluff type. Chubbuck notified the University of Colorado Museum of his find, and we made plans to visit the site at the first opportunity.

Meanwhile Chubbuck and another amateur archaeologist, Sigurd Olsen, continued to collect at the site and ultimately excavated nearly a third of it. In the late spring of 1958 the museum secured permission from the two discoverers and from Paul Forward, the owner of the land, to complete the excavation. We carried out this work on summer expeditions in 1958 and 1960.

The Olsen-Chubbuck site consists of a continuous bed of bones lying within the confines of a small arroyo, or dry gulch. The arroyo, which had long since been buried, originally rose near the southern end of the valley and followed a gently undulating course eastward through a ridge that forms the valley's eastern edge. The section of the arroyo that we excavated was some 200 feet long. Its narrow western end was only about a foot and a half in depth and the same in width, but it grew progressively deeper and wider to the east. Halfway down the arroyo its width was five feet and its depth six; at the point to the east where our excavation stopped it was some 12 feet wide and seven feet deep. At the bottom of the

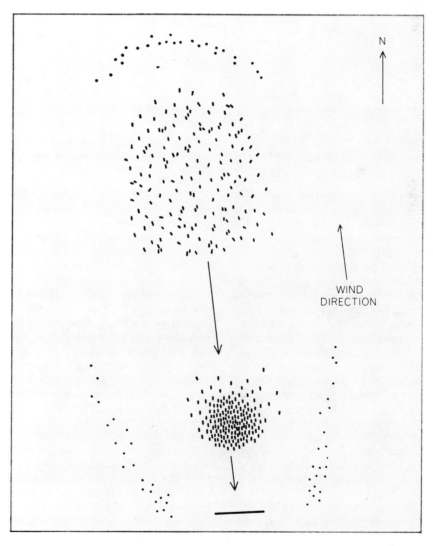

BISON STAMPEDE was probably set off by the Paleo-Indian hunters' close approach to the grazing herd from downwind. Projectile points found among the bones of the animals at the eastern end of the arroyo (*bottom*) suggest that some hunters kept the bison from veering eastward to escape. Other hunters probably did the same at the western end of the arroyo.

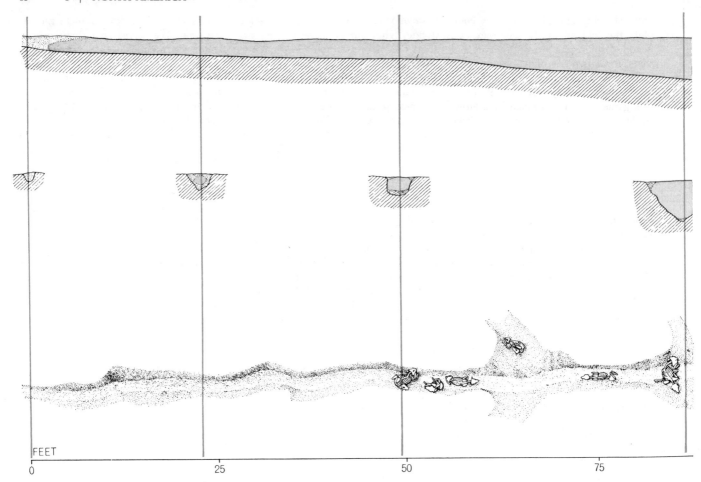

FEET

0   25   50   75

SECTION AND PLAN of the Olsen-Chubbuck site show how the remains of the dead and butchered bison formed a deposit of bones that lined the center of the arroyo for a distance of 170 feet (*color at top*). One part of the site had been excavated by its discoverers

arroyo for its entire length was a channel about a foot wide; above the channel the walls of the arroyo had a V-shaped cross section [*see top illustration on page 50*].

Today the drainage pattern of the site runs from north to south. This was probably the case when the arroyo was formed, and since it runs east and west it seems certain that it was not formed by stream action. Early frontiersmen on the Great Plains observed that many buffalo trails led away from watering places at right angles to the drainage pattern. Where such trails crossed ridges they were frequently quite deep; moreover, when they were abandoned they were often further deepened by erosion. The similarity of the Olsen-Chubbuck arroyo to such historical buffalo trails strongly suggests an identical origin.

The deposit of bison bones that filled the bottom of the arroyo was a little more than 170 feet long. It consisted of the remains of nearly 200 buffaloes of the species *Bison occidentalis*. Chubbuck and Olsen unearthed the bones of an estimated 50 of the animals; the museum's excavations uncovered the bones of 143 more. The bones were found in three distinct layers. The bottom layer contained some 13 complete skeletons; the hunters had not touched these animals. Above this layer were several essentially complete skeletons from which a leg or two, some ribs or the skull were missing; these bison had been only partly butchered. In the top layer were numerous single bones and also nearly 500 articulated segments of buffalo skeleton. The way in which these segments and the single bones were distributed provides a number of clues to the hunters' butchering techniques.

As the contents of the arroyo—particularly the complete skeletons at the bottom—make clear, it had been a trap into which the hunters had stampeded the bison. Bison are gregarious animals. They move in herds in search of forage; the usual grazing herd is between 50 and 300 animals. Bison have a keen sense of smell but relatively poor vision. Hunters can thus get very close to a herd as long as they stay downwind and largely out of sight. When the bison are frightened, the herd has a tendency to close ranks and stampede in a single mass. If the herd encounters an abrupt declivity such as the Olsen-Chubbuck arroyo, the animals in front cannot stop because they are pushed by those behind. They can only plunge into the arroyo, where they are immobilized, disabled or killed by the animals that fall on top of them.

The orientation of the skeletons in the middle and lower layers of the Olsen-Chubbuck site is evidence that the Paleo-Indian hunters had initiated such a stampede. Almost without exception the complete or nearly complete skeletons overlie or are overlain by the skeletons of one, two or even three other whole or nearly whole animals; the bones are massed and the skeletons are contorted. The first animals that fell into the arroyo had no chance to escape; those behind them wedged them tighter into the arroyo with their struggles. Many of the skeletons are sharply twisted around the axis of the spinal column. Three spanned the arroyo, deformed into

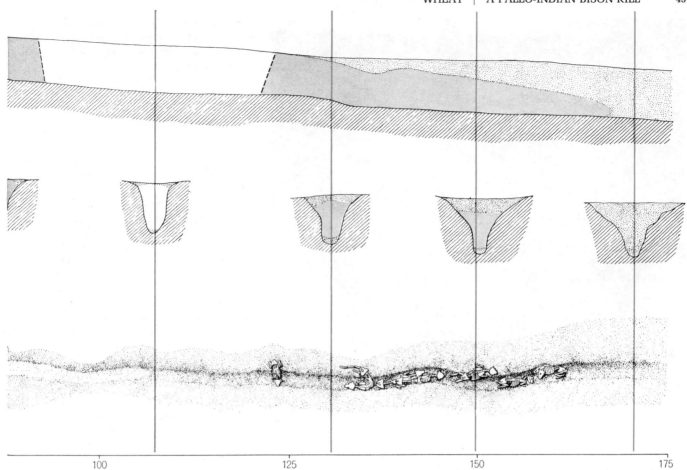

before the author and his associates began work in 1958; this area is represented by the 20-foot gap in the deposit. The shallow inner channel at the bottom of the arroyo can be seen in the plan view (*bottom*); outlines show the locations of 13 intact bison skeletons.

an unnatural U shape. Ten bison were pinned in position with their heads down and their hindquarters up; an equal number had landed with hindquarters down and heads up. At the bottom of the arroyo two skeletons lie on their backs.

The stampeding bison were almost certainly running in a north-south direction, at right angles to the arroyo. Of the 39 whole or nearly whole skeletons, which may be assumed to lie in the positions in which the animals died, not one faces north, northeast or northwest. A few skeletons, confined in the arroyo's narrow inner channel, face due east or west, but all 21 animals whose position at the time of death was not affected in this manner faced southeast, south or southwest. The direction in which the bison stampeded provides a strong clue to the way the wind was blowing on the day of the hunt. The hunters would surely have approached their quarry from downwind; thus the wind must have been from the south.

We have only meager evidence of the extent to which the stampede, once started, was directed and controlled by the hunters. The projectile points found with the bison skeletons in the deepest, most easterly part of the arroyo suggest that a flanking party of hunters was stationed there. It also seems a reasonable inference that, if no hunters had covered the stampede's western flank, the herd could have escaped unscathed around the head of the arroyo. If other hunters pursued the herd from the rear, there is no evidence of it.

Even if the hunters merely started the stampede and did not control it thereafter, it sufficed to kill almost 200 animals in a matter of minutes. The total was 46 adult bulls and 27 immature ones, 63 adult and 38 immature cows and 16 calves. From the fact that the bones include those of calves only a few days old, and from what we know about the breeding season of bison, we can confidently place the date of the kill as being late in May or early in June.

As we excavated the bone deposit we first uncovered the upper layer containing the single bones and articulated segments of skeleton. It was soon apparent that these bones were the end result of a standardized Paleo-Indian butchering procedure. We came to recognize certain "butchering units" such as forelegs, pelvic girdles, hind legs, spinal columns and skulls. Units of the same kind were usually found together in groups numbering from two or three to as many as 27. Similar units also formed distinct vertical sequences. As the hunters had removed the meat from the various units they had discarded the bones in separate piles, each of which contained the remains of a number of individual animals. In all we excavated nine such piles.

Where the order of deposition was clear, the bones at the bottom of each pile were foreleg units. Above these bones were those of pelvic-girdle units. Sometimes one or both hind legs were attached to the pelvic girdle, but by and large the hind-leg units lay separately among or above the pelvic units. The next level was usually composed of spinal-column units. The ribs had been removed from many of the chest vertebrae, but ribs were still attached to some of the other vertebrae. At the top

EXCAVATION at the eastern end of the arroyo reveals its V-shaped cross section and the layers of sand and silt that later filled it. The bone deposit ended at this point; a single bison shoulder blade remains in place at the level where it was unearthed (*lower center*).

BISON SKULL AND STONE POINT lie in close association at one level in the site. The projectile point (*lower left*) is of the Scottsbluff type. The bison skull, labeled 4-F to record its position among the other bones, rests upside down where the hunters threw it.

of nearly every pile were skulls. The jawbones had been removed from most of them, but some still retained a few of the neck vertebrae. In some instances these vertebrae had been pulled forward over the top and down the front of the skull. When the skull still had its jawbone, the hyoid bone of the tongue was missing.

Like the various butchering units, the single bones were found in clusters of the same skeletal part: shoulder blades, upper-foreleg bones, upper-hind-leg bones or jawbones (all broken in two at the front). Nearly all the jawbones were found near the top of the bone deposit. The tongue bones, on the other hand, were distributed throughout the bed. About 75 percent of the single foreleg bones were found in the upper part of the deposit, as were nearly 70 percent of the single vertebrae. Only 60 percent of the shoulder blades and scarcely half of the single ribs were in the upper level.

The hunters' first task had evidently been to get the bison carcasses into a position where they could be cut up. This meant that the animals had to be lifted, pulled, rolled or otherwise moved out of the arroyo to some flat area. It seems to have been impossible to remove the bison that lay at the bottom of the arroyo; perhaps they were too tightly wedged together. Some of them had been left untouched and others had had only a few accessible parts removed. The way in which the butchering units were grouped suggests that several bison were moved into position and cut up simultaneously. Since foreleg units, sometimes in pairs, were found at the bottom of each pile of bones it seems reasonable to assume that the Paleo-Indians followed the same initial steps in butchering that the Plains Indians did in recent times. The first step was to arrange the legs of the animal so that it could be rolled onto its belly. The skin was then cut down the back and pulled down on both sides of the carcass to form a kind of mat on which the meat could be placed. Directly under the skin of the back was a layer of tender meat, the "blanket of flesh"; when this was stripped away, the bison's forelegs and shoulder blades could be cut free, exposing the highly prized "hump" meat, the rib cage and the body cavity.

Having stripped the front legs of meat, the hunters threw the still-articulated bones into the arroyo. If they followed the practice of later Indians, they would next have indulged themselves

BONES OF BISON unearthed at the Olsen-Chubbuck site lie in a long row down the center of the ancient arroyo the Paleo-Indian hunters utilized as a pitfall for the stampeding herd. The bones proved to be the remains of bulls, cows and calves of the extinct species *Bison occidentalis*. Separate piles made up of the same types of bones (for example sets of limb bones, pelvic girdles or skulls) showed that the hunters had butchered several bison at a time and had systematically dumped the bones into the arroyo in the same order in which they were removed from the carcasses. In the foreground is a pile of skulls that was built up in this way.

by cutting into the body cavity, removing some of the internal organs and eating them raw. This, of course, would have left no evidence among the bones. What is certain is that the hunters did remove and eat the tongues of a few bison at this stage of the butchering, presumably in the same way the Plains Indians did: by slitting the throat, pulling the tongue out through the slit and cutting it off. Our evidence for their having eaten the tongues as they went along is that the tongue bones are found throughout the deposit instead of in one layer or another.

The bison's rib cages were attacked as soon as they were exposed by the removal of the overlying meat. Many of the ribs were broken off near the spine. The Plains Indians used as a hammer for this purpose a bison leg bone with the hoof still attached; perhaps the Paleo-Indians did the same. In any case, the next step was to sever the spine at a point behind the rib cage and remove the hindquarters. The meat was cut away from the pelvis (and in some instances simultaneously from the hind legs) and the pelvic girdle was discarded. If the hind legs had been separated from the pelvis, it was now their turn to be stripped of meat and discarded.

After the bison's hindquarters had been butchered, the neck and skull were cut off as a unit—usually at a point just in front of the rib cage—and set aside. Then the spine was discarded, presumably after it had been completely stripped of meat and sinew. Next the hunters turned to the neck and skull and cut the neck meat away. This is evident from the skulls that had vertebrae draped over the front; this would not have been possible if the neck meat had been in place. The Plains Indians found bison neck meat too tough to eat in its original state. They dried it and made the dried strips into pemmican by pounding them to a powder. The fact that the Paleo-Indians cut off the neck meat strongly suggests that they too preserved some of their kill.

If the tongue had not already been removed, the jawbone was now cut away, broken at the front and the tongue cut out. The horns were broken from a few skulls, but there is little evidence that the Paleo-Indians broke open the skull as the Plains Indians did to take out the brain. Perhaps the most striking difference between the butchering practices of these earlier Indians and those of later ones, however, lies in the high degree of organization displayed by the Paleo-Indians. Historical

accounts of butchering by Plains Indians indicate no such efficient system.

In all, 47 artifacts were found in association with the bones at the Olsen-Chubbuck site. Spherical hammerstones and knives give us some idea of what constituted the hunter's tool kit; stone scrapers suggest that the bison's skins were processed at the site. A bone pin and a piece of the brown rock limonite that shows signs of having been rubbed tell something about Paleo-Indian ornamentation.

The bulk of the artifacts at the site are projectile points. There are 27 of them, and they are particularly significant. Most of them are of the Scottsbluff type. When their range of variation is considered, however, they merge gradually at one end of the curve of variation into Eden points and at the other end into Milnesand points. Moreover, among the projectile points found at the site are one Eden point and a number of Milnesand points. The diversity of the points clearly demonstrates the range of variation that was possible among the weapons of a single hunting group. Their occurrence together at the site is conclusive proof that such divergent forms of weapon could exist contemporaneously.

How many Paleo-Indians were pres-

INTACT SKELETON of an immature bison cow, uncovered in the lowest level of the arroyo, is one of 13 animals the Paleo-Indian hunters left untouched. The direction in which many bison faced suggests that the stampede traveled from north to south.

ent at the kill? The answer to this question need not be completely conjectural. We can start with what we know about the consumption of bison meat by Plains Indians. During a feast a man could consume from 10 to 20 pounds of fresh meat a day; women and children obviously ate less. The Plains Indians also preserved bison meat by drying it; 100 pounds of fresh meat would provide 20 pounds of dried meat. A bison bull of today yields about 550 pounds of edible meat; cows average 400 pounds. For an immature bull one can allow 165 pounds of edible meat, for an immature cow 110 pounds and for a calf 50 pounds. About 75 percent of the bison killed at the Olsen-Chubbuck site were completely butchered; on this basis the total weight of bison meat would have been 45,300 pounds. The *Bison occidentalis* killed by the Paleo-Indian hunters, however, was considerably larger than the *Bison bison* of modern times. To compensate for the difference it seems reasonable to add 25 percent to the weight estimate, bringing it to a total of 56,640 pounds. To this total should be added some 4,000 pounds of edible internal organs and 5,400 pounds of fat.

A Plains Indian could completely butcher a bison in about an hour. If we allow one and a half hours for the dissection of the larger species, the butchering at the Olsen-Chubbuck site would have occupied about 210 man-hours. In other words, 100 people could easily have done the job in half a day.

To carry the analysis further additional assumptions are needed. How long does fresh buffalo meat last? The experience of the Plains Indians (depending, of course, on weather conditions) was that it could be eaten for about a month. Let us now assume that half of the total weight of the Olsen-Chubbuck kill was eaten fresh at an average rate of 10 pounds per person per day, and that the other half was preserved. Such a division would provide enough fresh meat and fat to feed 150 people for 23 days. It seems reasonable to assume that the Paleo-Indian band was about this size. One way to test this assumption is to calculate the load each person would have to carry when camp was broken.

The preserved meat and fat, together with the hides, would have weighed about 7,350 pounds, which represents a burden of 49 pounds for each man, woman and child in the group (in addition to the weight of whatever other necessities they carried). Plains Indians are known to have borne loads as great as 100 pounds. Taking into account the likeli-

hood that small children and active hunters would have carried smaller loads, a 49-pound average appears to be just within the range of possibility.

A band of 150 people could, however, have eaten two-thirds of the kill fresh and preserved only one-third. In that case the fresh meat would have fed them for somewhat more than a month. At the end the meat would have been rather gamy, but the load of preserved meat per person would have been reduced to the more reasonable average of 31 pounds.

One possibility I have left out is that the Paleo-Indians had dogs. If there were dogs available to eat their share of fresh meat and to carry loads of preserved meat, the number of people in the group may have been somewhat less. In the absence of dogs, however, it seems improbable that any fewer than 150 people could have made use of the bison killed at the Olsen-Chubbuck site to the degree that has been revealed by our excavations. Whether or not the group had dogs, the remains of its stay at the site are unmistakable evidence that hunting bands of considerable size and impressive social organization were supporting themselves on the Great Plains some 8,500 years ago.

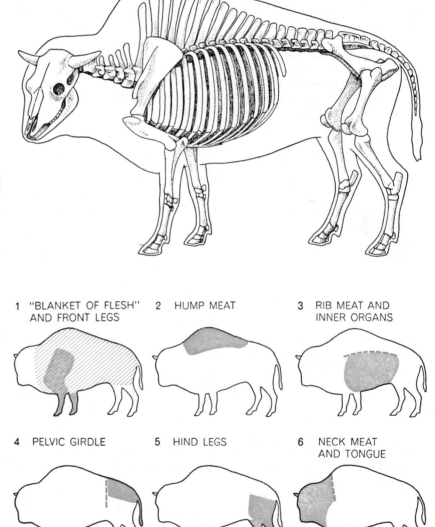

1 "BLANKET OF FLESH" AND FRONT LEGS

2 HUMP MEAT

3 RIB MEAT AND INNER ORGANS

4 PELVIC GIRDLE

5 HIND LEGS

6 NECK MEAT AND TONGUE

BUTCHERING METHODS used by the Paleo-Indians have been reconstructed on the dual basis of bone stratification at the Olsen-Chubbuck site and the practices of the Plains Indians in recent times. Once the carcass of the bison (*skeleton at top*) had been propped up and skinned down the back, a series of "butchering units" probably were removed in the order shown on the numbered outline figures. The hunters ate as they worked.

5

The Hopewell Cult

by Olaf H. Prufer
December 1964

A 1,500-year-old rubbish heap unearthed in southern Ohio holds the answers to some key questions about the ancient Indians who lived there and built huge funeral mounds filled with offerings

As Europeans explored North America, they found that many of the continent's river valleys were dotted with ancient earthworks. Scattered from western New York to North Dakota and south to Louisiana and the Florida Keys were uncounted thousands of burial mounds, temple mounds, hilltop ramparts surrounded by ditches, and earthen walls enclosing scores of acres. Some Colonial scholars were so impressed by these works that they thought they must have been built by an unknown civilized people that had been exterminated by the savage Indians. In due course it became clear that the earthworks had been put up by the Indians' own ancestors, and that they belonged not to one culture but to a series of separate cultural traditions spanning a period of 3,000 years.

Perhaps the most striking assemblage of these works is located in southern Ohio in the valleys of the Muskingum, Scioto and Miami rivers. It consists of clusters of large mounds surrounded by earthworks laid out in elaborate geometric patterns. As early as 1786 one such group of mounds at the confluence of the Muskingum and the Ohio (the present site of Marietta, Ohio) was excavated; it was found to be rich in graves and mortuary offerings. It was not until the 1890's, however, that the contents of the Ohio mounds attracted public attention. At that time many of them were excavated to provide an anthropological exhibit for the Chicago world's fair of 1893. One of the richest sites was on the farm of M. C. Hopewell, and the name Hopewell has been assigned to this particular type of mortuary complex ever since.

More recent excavations have shown that the Hopewell complex extends far beyond southern Ohio. Hopewell remains are found in Michigan and Wisconsin and throughout the Mississippi valley; there are Hopewell sites in Illinois that are probably older than any in Ohio. Typical Hopewell artifacts have been unearthed as far west as Minnesota and as far south as Florida. The mounds of southern Ohio are nonetheless the most numerous and the richest in mortuary offerings.

Thanks to carbon-14 dating it is known that the Hopewell complex first materialized in southern Ohio about 100 B.C. and that the last elaborate valley earthwork was constructed about A.D. 550. Until recently, however, there were other questions to which only conjectural answers could be given. Among them were the following: In what kinds of settlements did the people of southern Ohio live during this period? Where were their habitations located? On what foundation did their economy rest? Answers to these questions can now be given, but first it is necessary to say exactly what the Hopewell complex is.

What is known about the Hopewell complex of Ohio has been learned almost exclusively from the nature and contents of burial mounds. In many places these structures are found in groups enclosed by earthworks linked in a pattern of squares, circles, octagons and parallel lines [*see top illustration on page 56*]. The dimensions of some of the enclosures are immense: the largest known Hopewell earthworks in Ohio—the Newark Works in Licking County—covered four square miles. Many of the burial mounds are also large: the central mounds on the Hopewell farm and at the Seip and Harness sites, all of which are in Ross County, range from 160 to 470 feet in length and from 20 to 32 feet in height. Within the mounds are the remains of numerous human bodies, some of them alone and some in groups. If the bodies were simply interred, they rest on earthen platforms surrounded by log cribs; if they were cremated, the bones are found in shallow basins of baked earth.

The sequence of events in the construction of a major mound seems to have been as follows. Bare ground was first covered with a layer of sand; then a large wooden structure was raised on this prepared floor. Some of the structures were so extensive that it is doubtful that they had roofs; they were probably stockades open to the sky. Individual graves were prepared inside these enclosures; in many cases the burials were covered with low mounds of earth. When the enclosure was filled with graves, the wooden structure was set afire and burned to the ground. Then the entire burial area was covered with layer on layer of earth and stone, forming the final large mound.

The quantity and quality of the grave goods accompanying the burials indicate that the people of the period devoted a great deal of time and effort to making these articles. A marked preference for exotic raw materials is evident. Mica, frequently cut into geometric or animate shapes, was imported from the mountains of Virginia, North Carolina and Alabama [*see illustration on opposite page*]. Conch shells, used as ceremonial cups, came from the Gulf

SILHOUETTED HAND made from a sheet of mica (*opposite page*) is typical of the elaborate grave offerings found at the Hopewell site near Chillicothe, Ohio. Human, animal and geometric figures of mica are characteristic Hopewell funerary goods; they are particularly abundant in southern Ohio.

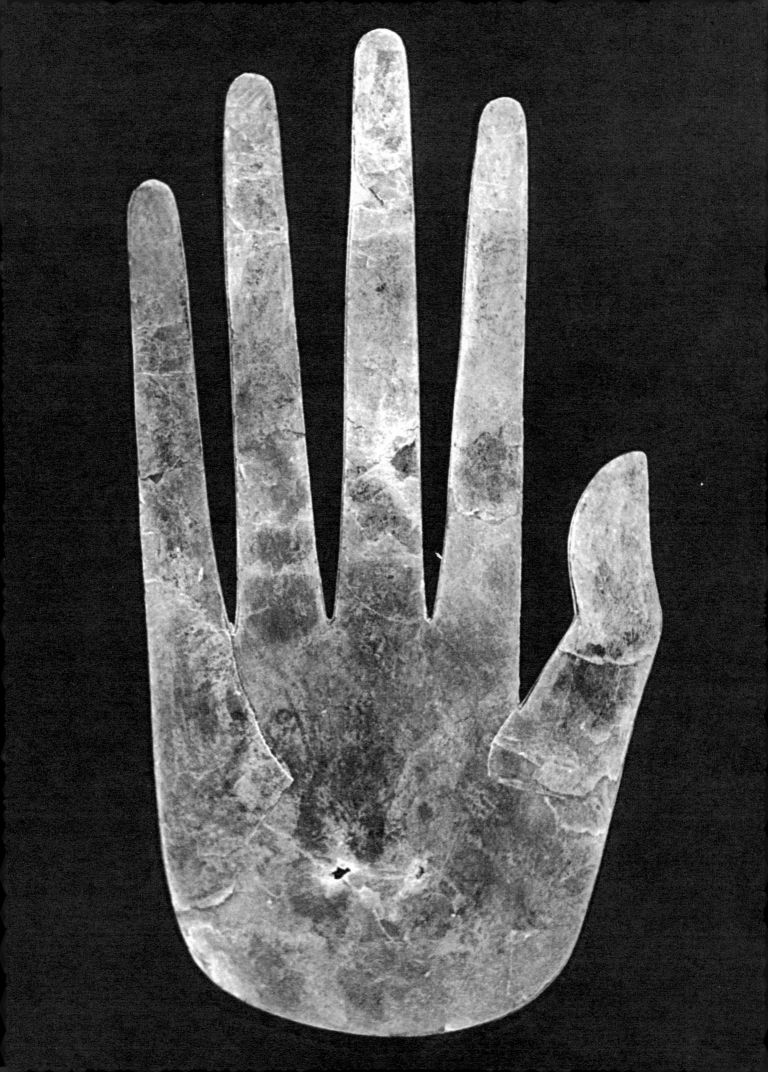

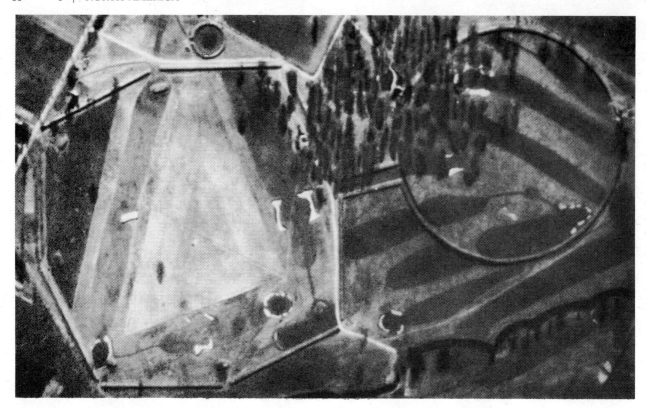

OCTAGON AND CIRCLE in this aerial photograph are a portion of the earthworks marking the most extensive known Hopewell construction: the site at Newark, Ohio. Most of the four-square-mile array (*see original plan below*) has now been obliterated by modern building. Only these figures (now part of a golf course) and another circle (used for years as a fairground) have been preserved.

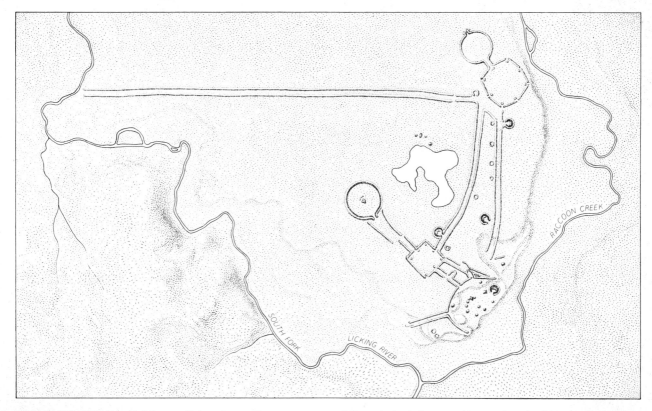

LONG AVENUES bounded by parallel earthen walls constitute the major parts of the Newark site. When first surveyed, the longest parallels (*top*) extended from the paired figures shown in the photograph at top of page to the Licking River, two and a half miles distant. Both circles are quite precise: the fairground circle (*center*) diverges at most 13 feet from a mean diameter of 1,175 feet, and the golf course circle only 4.5 feet from a mean diameter of 1,045 feet. The Newark site has never been systematically excavated.

Coast. Obsidian, exquisitely flaked into large ritual knives, was obtained either from what is now the U.S. Southwest or from the Yellowstone region of the Rocky Mountains. The canine teeth of grizzly bears, frequently inlaid with freshwater pearls, may also have been imported from the Rockies. Copper, artfully hammered into heavy ax blades and into ornaments such as ear spools, breastplates and geometric or animate silhouettes, was obtained from the upper Great Lakes.

Even in their choice of local raw materials the Hopewell craftsmen of Ohio favored the precious and the unusual. Much of their work in stone utilized the colorful varieties of flint available in the Flint Ridge deposits of Licking County. The freshwater pearls came from the shellfish of local rivers, and they were literally heaped into some of the burials. The tombs of the Hopewell site contained an estimated 100,000 pearls; a single deposit at the Turner site in Hamilton County has yielded more than 48,000.

Other typical Hopewell grave furnishings are "platform" pipes [see lower illustration on page 60], elaborately engraved bones of animals and men, clay figurines and highly distinctive kinds of decorated pottery. Projectile points of flint show characteristic forms; the flint-workers also struck delicate parallel-sided blades from prepared "cores."

For the most part these characteristic objects of the Hopewell complex are the same wherever they are found. In spite of this fact the Hopewell complex cannot be classed as a "culture" in the anthropological sense of the word, that is, as a distinct society together with its attendant material and spiritual manifestations. On the contrary, the Hopewell complex was only one segment of the cultural totality in each area where it is encountered. A reconstruction of life in eastern North America from 500 B.C. to A.D. 900 reveals the existence of distinct cultural traditions in separate regions, each rooted in its own past. During the Hopewell phase each of these regional traditions was independently influenced by the new and dynamic religious complex. The new funeral customs did not, however, take the place of the local culture; they were simply grafted onto it. Although the word "cult" has some unfortunate connotations in common usage, it is more appropriate to speak of a Hopewell cult than of a Hopewell culture.

The exact religious concepts that

EARTHWORKS characteristic of the burial cult are found throughout eastern North America. Major Hopewell centers, from the Gulf Coast to the Great Lakes, are named on the map.

SOUTHERN OHIO is the locale of the most abundant and richest Hopewell sites. The majority are found along the Miami, Scioto and Muskingum rivers and range in date from 100 B.C. to A.D. 550. After that no more lowland centers were built; instead hilltops were fortified (*colored dots locate three major examples*). The McGraw site was excavated by the author.

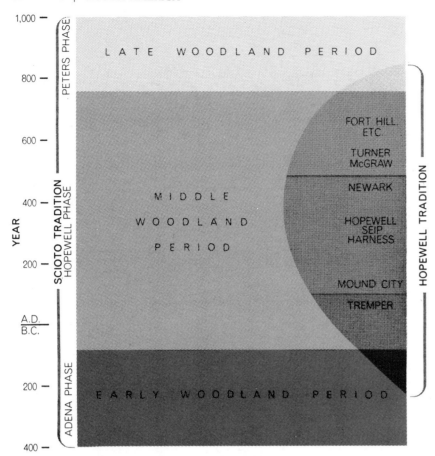

SEQUENCE OF CULTURES in southern Ohio during the rise and decline of the Hopewell funeral complex indicates that a local tradition of Woodland culture, called Scioto, was present in the area before the Hopewell cult appeared and continued both during and after it. The earliest of the Woodland culture periods began about 1200 B.C. in southern Ohio.

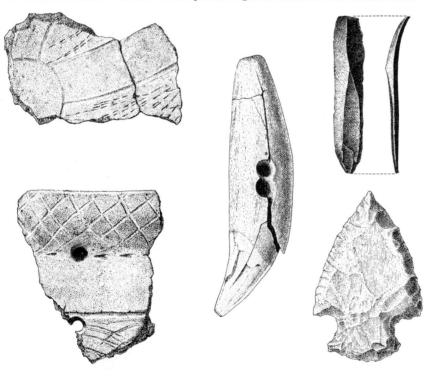

IDENTITY OF FARMSTEAD discovered at the McGraw site as the residence of Indians who participated in the burial cult is proved by the presence of characteristic Hopewell tools and ceremonial objects. The fine, parallel-sided flint blade is typically Hopewell, as is the "Snyders" projectile point. The bear canine and the pottery are standard burial finds.

permitted the successful diffusion of the Hopewell cult necessarily remain unknown. Curiously enough, however, the cult's consumption of exotic materials for grave goods may have provided a mechanism for its diffusion. Procurement of raw materials entailed an exchange system of almost continental proportions; many widely separated areas in North America must have been brought into contact as their natural resources were tapped by practitioners of the Hopewell rites.

Students of the Hopewell remains in southern Ohio have been disturbed for more than a century by the lack of evidence for any habitation sites linked to the great funerary centers. In other Hopewell areas, notably Illinois, large villages are clearly associated with the local ceremonial sites. Years of patient fieldwork in Ohio had failed to produce anything that could legitimately be called a settlement. The extensive enclosures and their associated clusters of burial mounds contain no evidence of habitation to speak of. The little that has been found seems to mark brief squatters' tenancies, probably associated with the construction of the final mounds or with ceremonies that may have been performed from time to time. Clearly the nature of Hopewell society and its settlement patterns in Ohio were markedly different from those in Illinois.

Still another puzzle was the fact that remains of corn have been found at only two Ohio Hopewell sites—Harness and Turner—and in both cases under doubtful circumstances. It was therefore supposed that the Hopewell phase in Ohio was one of simple hunting and collecting and no agriculture. Whether because of this supposition or because earlier investigators were looking for sizable villages, most of the search for Hopewell habitation sites has been confined to regions near the ceremonial centers, leaving the rich bottomlands along the rivers largely unexplored.

While reflecting on all these factors in 1962 I was struck by a possible parallel between the Ohio Hopewell sites and the classic ceremonial sites of certain areas in Middle America, where the religious center remained vacant except on ritual occasions and the population lived in scattered hamlets surrounding the center. To apply such an assumption to the Ohio Hopewell complex meant granting the people agriculture; it meant, furthermore, that the bottomlands were the very zones in which to look for small farming communities. Survey work along the floodplain of the middle and lower Scioto River during the past two years has amply demonstrated the validity of this assumption. Our survey teams from the Case Institute of Technology have turned up 37 small sites—the largest of them little more than 100 feet in diameter—marked by thinly scattered objects on the surface. These objects include sherds of cord-marked pottery, chips of flint, fragments of shell and bone and, most important, the fine, parallel-edged bladelets that are among the characteristic artifacts of the Hopewell complex.

It is certain that many such habitation sites are now lost forever under the accumulated silt of river floodplains and that others have been destroyed by river meandering. A perfect example of flood burial in the making is provided by the McGraw site, which is located on bottomland near an ancient meander of the Scioto River two miles south of Chillicothe. Alva McGraw, the owner of the land, brought the site to our attention in 1962. Surface indications were scanty; over an area 10 feet square we found only a few potsherds, some shell fragments, bits of flint and fire-cracked rocks. The site was on a nearly imperceptible rise of land, the remnant of a knoll that had been almost covered by river silts.

Under ordinary circumstances no archaeologist would have been attracted by such an impoverished find. It happened, however, that this site and similar ones on the McGraw farm were soon to be destroyed by road construction. We therefore decided without much enthusiasm to sound the area with a modest trench. Where the trench cut into the ancient knoll we found no remains at depths lower than the plow zone: eight inches below the surface. But where the trench extended beyond the knoll, proceeding down its slope to the adjacent silt-covered low ground, we struck a dense deposit of residential debris, evidently the refuse heap of an ancient farmstead.

This deposit, a foot thick and 95 by 140 feet in extent, was packed with material. There were more than 10,000 pottery fragments, some 6,000 animal bones, nearly 2,000 identifiable mollusk shells, abundant remains of wild plants and both an ear and individual kernels of corn. In fact, this single rubbish heap contained enough material to answer the questions posed at the beginning of this article.

First, in spite of the pattern of organized village life associated with the Hopewell cult 400 miles to the west in Illinois, the people of southern Ohio lived in small, scattered farm dwellings. This does not mean that the population was sparse; indeed, the size and complexity of the ceremonial earthworks in Ohio imply ample manpower. The significant fact is that the two groups shared a religion but lived quite different secular lives. In seeking parallels for this phenomenon one turns to the early, expansionist days of Christianity or of Islam, when a religion was shared by peoples with sharply contrasting cultures.

Second, the Ohio Hopewell people built their dwellings not near ceremonial centers but on the floodplains of the

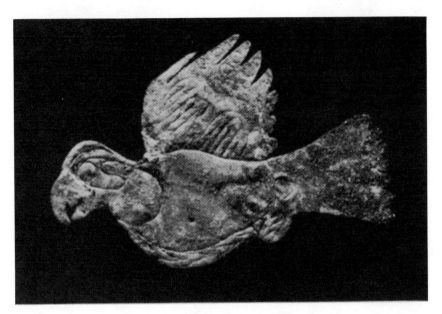

BIRD EFFIGY from Mound City combines cutout and repoussé techniques in copper work. The metal was imported from outcroppings at Isle Royale in Lake Superior. Hopewell funeral offerings of copper include rings, ear spools, breastplates and headdresses, many geometric forms, copper-plated wooden objects and large ax blades, evidently cold-forged.

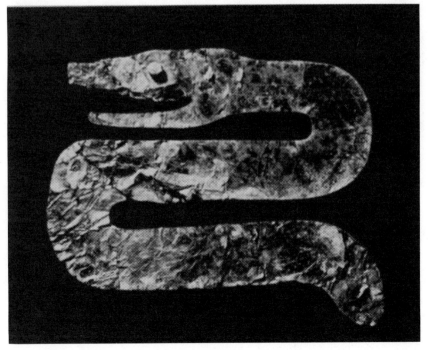

SNAKE EFFIGY from the Turner site is a foot-wide mica silhouette cut from a sheet imported from Virginia or North Carolina. Some Ohio burials were literally blanketed by mica.

HUMAN FIGURES representing a kneeling man and a standing woman are modeled in ter-ra-cotta. Unearthed at the Turner site, they were ritually broken, or "killed," before burial.

PLATFORM PIPE from the Mound City site has a bowl carved to represent a toad. Pipes showing birds, fishes, mammals and human figures were also made for Hopewell burials.

nuts, walnuts and acorns. Other wild plants that have been identified are the hackberry and the wild plum. Apparently corn was the only plant the people cultivated, but the remains make it clear that their knowledge of corn-raising had not been recently acquired. The charred ear of corn from the McGraw site, still bearing a number of kernels, is of a 12-row variety. It appears to be of a type intermediate between the northern flint corn grown in Ohio in late pre-European times and the ancient flint corns and popcorns known from elsewhere in the Western Hemisphere. One of the isolated kernels from the deposit has been identified as belonging to an eight-row or 10-row variety of corn; it possibly represents a full-fledged, although small, member of the northern flint type. These relatively advanced types of corn imply a long period of agricultural activity before the site was first occupied.

The date of the McGraw site's occupation can be estimated both from the style of its artifacts and from carbon-14 determinations; it is roughly A.D. 450. The bulk of the artifacts could have come from any pre-Hopewell site in Ohio; for example, less than 4 percent of the pottery fragments found in the deposit are characteristic of the Hopewell complex. This reinforces the point made earlier: Whenever the influences of the Hopewell cult appear, they are imposed on an already existing culture that for the most part continues in its own ways.

The McGraw site is nevertheless clearly identified as belonging to the Hopewell complex not only by the few Hopewell potsherds but also by other characteristic Hopewell artifacts. Parallel-sided flint bladelets were found in large numbers, and the bulk of the projectile points were of the classic Hopewell type known as "Snyders," after the site of that name in Illinois. The inhabitants of the McGraw farmstead evidently included craftsmen engaged in the production of grave goods for the Hopewell cult: cut and uncut mica was found in abundance. One bear tooth turned up in the midden, with typical countersunk perforations but without any inlay of pearls. There were also two ornaments made of slate that, like the bear-tooth ornament, were unfinished. Perhaps all these objects were discards; this would help to explain their presence in a refuse heap.

The McGraw site therefore casts considerable light on life in southern Ohio

rivers, presumably because the bottom-land was most suitable for agriculture. As for their economy in general, they raised corn, but a substantial part of their food came from hunting, fishing and collecting. Analysis of the animal bones in the McGraw deposit shows that the commonest source of meat was the white-tailed deer. Other game animals that have been identified in the deposit

are the cottontail rabbit and the turkey. River produce was of equal or perhaps greater importance for the larder; we found the bones and shells of a variety of turtles, the bones of nine species of fish and the shells of 25 species of mollusk.

Among the wild-plant foods these people collected were nuts: the deposit contained charred remains of hickory

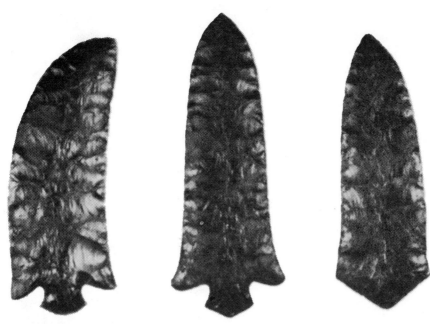

CEREMONIAL BLADES unearthed at the Hopewell site are of obsidian, probably from the Yellowstone area of the Rocky Mountains. The largest (*center*) is 13 inches in length.

In southern Ohio the people of the Early Woodland period were mound builders long before the Hopewell cult arose. They belonged to the Adena culture (which takes its name from a mound site near Chillicothe). The remains of the Adena people show that they were roundheaded rather than longheaded. They lived without contact with the Hopewell cult until about 100 B.C.; at that time, according to carbon-14 determinations, the Tremper mound of Scioto County was raised. This mound contained some 300 crematory burials. Many of the grave offerings are typical of the Adena culture, but some of them show Hopewell influences.

As skulls from later burials indicate, the arrival of the Hopewell cult in Ohio (presumably from Illinois) was accompanied by the arrival of a new population; these people were longheaded rather than roundheaded. How many immigrants arrived is an open question. The total number of individuals found in Ohio Hopewell mounds—an estimated 1,000—can represent only a fraction of the population of this region during the Middle Woodland period. It seems probable that most of the local inhabitants were the roundheaded Adena folk, many of whom may well have continued to live typical Adena lives untroubled by the neighboring Hopewell cultists. The fact that numerous Adena mounds continued to be built during Hopewell times is strong evidence for this.

To judge from their production of Hopewell ceremonial objects, the residents of the McGraw site would not have been undisturbed Adena folk. It is equally unlikely that they were immigrants from Illinois. It seems more probable that the immigrants were a privileged minority who in some way had come to dominate some of Ohio's Adena people, among whom were the farmers of the McGraw site.

during the latter days of the Hopewell phase. Skilled hunters and food-collectors, gifted artisans in a wide range of materials, the people who manufactured the rich grave goods for the ritual burials lived in small scattered farmsteads on the river bottoms.

But were the people who made the grave goods the same as those who were buried in the great Hopewell mounds? Curiously this appears to be unlikely, at least in southern Ohio. To explain why, it is necessary to sketch what is known about the rise and decline of the Hopewell complex against the general background of the various prehistoric cultures in eastern North America.

Of the four successive major culture stages in this part of the New World—Paleo-Indian, Archaic, Woodland and Mississippian—only the third is involved here. In southern Ohio the Woodland stage begins about 1200 B.C. and ends shortly before the arrival of the Europeans. In the entire eastern part of North America, southern Ohio included, the Woodland stage is divided into Early, Middle and Late periods.

Why did the Hopewell complex ultimately disappear? It may be that one part of the answer is plain to see. From their first arrival in southern Ohio until A.D. 550 these cultists evidently not only felt secure in themselves but also appear to have taken no steps to guard from raiders the treasures buried with their dead. After that time, however, no more ceremonial centers were built in open valleys. Instead it seems that every inaccessible hilltop in southern Ohio was suddenly crowned by earthworks that appear to have served a defensive function.

This does not mean that such sites as

MYTHICAL BEAST with four horns and feet with five talons decorates the surface of a narrow stone object 10 inches long. It was found at the Turner site. Its purpose is unknown.

Fort Hill, Fort Ancient and Fort Miami were permanently inhabited strongholds. Quite the contrary; at Fort Hill, for example, a survey of the land surrounding the foot of the hill has revealed several small farmsteads resembling the McGraw site. It is probable that the hilltop earthworks were places of refuge that were occupied only in time of danger. That there were such times is demonstrated by the evidence of fires and massacres at the Fort Hill, Fort Ancient and Fort Miami sites.

What was the nature of the danger? As yet there is no answer, but it is interesting to note that at about this same time the Indian population in more northerly areas first began to protect their villages with stockades. Unrest of some kind appears to have been afoot throughout eastern North America.

This being the case, it is not hard to envision the doom of the Hopewell cult. Whatever its basic religious tenets, the tangible elements of the ceremony were the celebrated grave goods, and the most notable of the goods were produced from imported raw materials. The grave goods were of course cherished for their part in the religious scheme; could the scheme itself be kept alive when the goods were no longer available? I suggest that the Hopewell cult could survive only as long as its trade network remained intact and, further, that the postulated current of unrest in eastern North America during the seventh and eighth centuries A.D. was sufficient to disrupt that network.

Whether or not this caused the collapse of the Hopewell cult, there is no question that it did collapse. By the beginning of the Late Woodland period, about A.D. 750, elaborate burial mounds containing rich funeral offerings were no longer built. For the very reason that Hopewell was only a cult and not an entire culture, however, the distinctive local traditions that had participated in the Hopewell ceremonies now reasserted themselves.

In Ohio this regional tradition is named Scioto [see top illustration on page 58]. Because of the alien nature of the Hopewell ceremonial complex, the phase of the Scioto tradition—called Hopewell—during which the funeral centers were built has a dual status. In terms of chronology the Hopewell phase was only one subdivision of the Scioto tradition. At the same time the Hopewell religious cult must be granted the status of a full-fledged tradition in its own right.

A Pre-Columbian Urban Center on the Mississippi

6

by Melvin L. Fowler
August 1975

About A.D. 1000 there arose in the area north and south of what is now St. Louis the most populous Indian settlements north of Mexico. Foremost among them was Cahokia, which included some 120 mounds

One of the largest earthworks built by ancient man anywhere in the world rises in the U.S. Middle West not far from where the Illinois and Missouri rivers join the Mississippi. Relatively few people other than prehistorians are aware of this colossal monument, and even prehistorians have only recently learned that it marks the center of a 125-square-mile area that contained the most populous pre-Columbian settlements in the New World north of Mexico. Today the area, which includes a floodplain, alluvial terraces and low bluffs along the east bank of the Mississippi north and south of St. Louis, is called American Bottoms. The huge earthwork at its center, a few miles east-northeast of East St. Louis, Ill., is known as Monks Mound. The aggregation of some 120 lesser earthworks that surround it is called Cahokia: the name of an Indian group living in the area at the time of the French colonization early in the 18th century.

Monks Mound, which got its name from a short-lived Trappist settlement, is still an impressive affair [*see illustration on page 71*]. Its base, which rises from a plain lying 417 feet above sea level, measures 1,000 feet from north to south and more than 700 feet from east to west, covering an area of about 15 acres. Its volume is estimated to be 22 million cubic feet; in North America only the Pyramid of the Sun at Teotihuacán and the great pyramid at Cholula are larger. It rises in four steps to a maximum height of 100 feet above the plain. The first terrace, occupying about a fourth of the surface area at that level, is 40 feet high. Three lobelike protrusions in the northwest quadrant of the mound collectively form the second ter-

race, which is some 62 feet high. The third and fourth terraces occupy the northeast quadrant; the fourth terrace, at an elevation of 100 feet, is three feet higher than the third.

For all its impressiveness, Monks Mound is only a part of the even more impressive Cahokia group, and Cahokia in turn is only one, albeit the largest, of 10 large and small population centers and 50-odd farming villages that flourished in American Bottoms about the start of the second millennium (A.D. 1000).

How did these North American population centers arise? The best answer at present is that a complex feedback interaction involving population growth and an advance in agricultural productivity was responsible. Sometime late in the eighth century, it appears, the hoe re-

placed the digging stick in maize agriculture and a variety of maize became available that was better suited to the climate of the Middle West than the southern varieties that had been grown there up to that time.

Archaeologists, both amateur and professional, have worked in American Bottoms for a century, and in recent decades some of the sites that lacked official protection have been partially excavated before local construction destroyed them. Since 1950 at Cahokia alone individual or joint efforts by five universities and at least two museums have resulted in soundings and excavations at a score of localities. Yet only two or three of the 120 Cahokia mounds have been adequately excavated. Meanwhile the mounds that marked prehistoric popula-

CLOSE-UP OF MONKS MOUND, looking to the northwest, gives a sense of its dimensions: 1,000 feet at the base from north to south, more than 700 feet from east to west and 100 feet above the plain at the highest point. The mound is the largest pre-Columbian structure in the New World north of Mexico; it was built in successive stages between A.D. 900 and 1250.

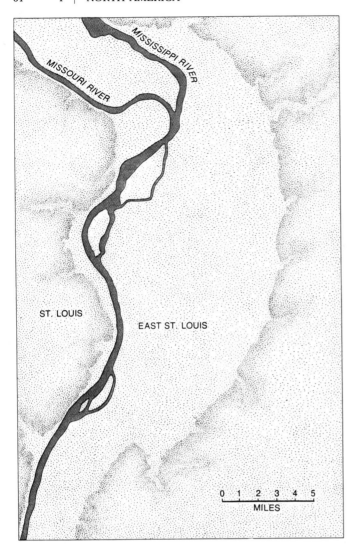

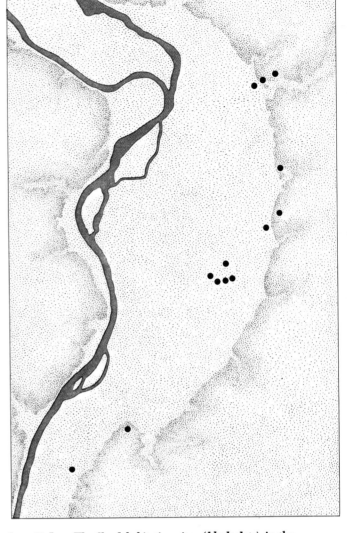

LINE OF BLUFFS (*left*) on both sides of a low floodplain outlines the American Bottoms region at and below the confluence of the Mississippi and Missouri rivers. The river channels shown are the present ones; the numerous lakes, creeks and sloughs occupying much of the bottomland have been omitted. About A.D. 800 (*right*) there were at least 13 Late Woodland habitation sites (*black dots*) in the region. Eight have been recognized on or near the upland bluffs; five, including one where Monks Mound would later rise, have so far been located in the richer bottomland. Farm productivity increased in American Bottoms soon thereafter.

tion centers of equal interest in St. Louis and East St. Louis have been obliterated by urban expansion. Nevertheless, it is possible, thanks to the work of recent years, to trace the evolution of the pre-Columbian settlements in American Bottoms with some degree of confidence.

The sophisticated kind of social and economic organization that is reflected by the construction of earthworks in American Bottoms was not the first to arise in the region. For several hundred years before that people belonging to a widespread culture, known as the Hopewell culture after a site in Ohio, had undertaken the construction of scores of earth enclosures, effigy mounds and other earthworks all through the Middle West. Another feature of the Hopewell culture was a widespread trade in exotic materials from as far away as the Rocky Mountains. Hopewell was a flowering of

what is called the Middle Woodland period in this part of America. After A.D. 500, however, this cultural integration of a large area came to an end. The farming hamlets that thrived in the vicinity of American Bottoms about A.D. 800 were representative of the subsequent Late Woodland period.

The initial phase of the settlement at American Bottoms that led to the rise of Cahokia extended from A.D. 600 to 800. It is called the Patrick phase after A. J. R. Patrick, a physician of Belleville, Ill., who was a pioneer investigator of Cahokia in the latter half of the 19th century. Archaeologists from the University of Illinois at Urbana have excavated Patrick-phase pit deposits at a site at the western extremity of the Cahokia settlement, and our group from the University of Wisconsin at Milwaukee found

Patrick-phase materials in the bottom occupation levels we uncovered below the eastern margin of Monks Mound. Other Patrick-phase remains have been found outside the Cahokia area.

The people of the Patrick phase appear to have been newcomers to American Bottoms, perhaps attracted there from the more typical river-bluff and upland farms by the fertile sandy loams that form the natural terraces and levees of the river valley. The information now available about the Patrick phase and an unnamed century-long phase that followed it is largely obtained from the analysis of pottery fragments gathered by surface collecting and the excavation of refuse heaps. Patrick-phase house sites indicate that residences at this time were rectangular and that the house posts were set in pits. There is little evidence of mound building between 600

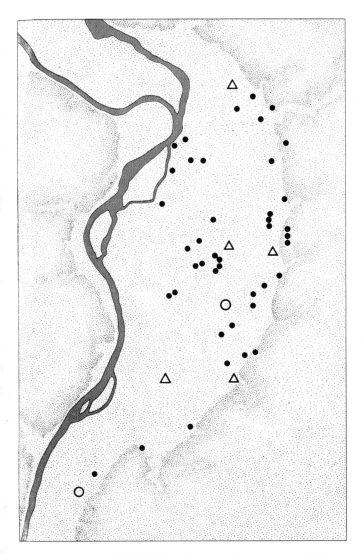

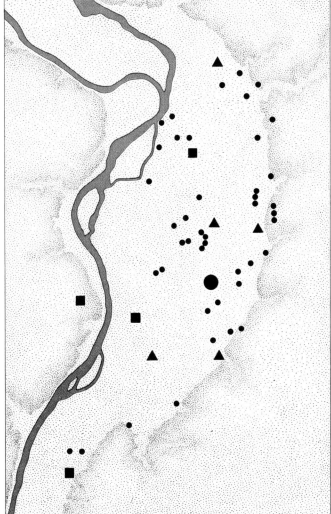

FAIRMOUNT PHASE at Cahokia (*left*), which extended from A.D. 900 to 1050, brought many changes to American Bottoms. Two sites, Cahokia and Lunsford-Pulcher (*open circles*), came to include a number of earth mounds. Farm villages (*dots*) increased in number from 13 to 42. In addition five sites larger than villages arose, four of them near Cahokia (*triangles*); each included at least one platform mound. In the following 200 years (*right*), embracing the Stirling and Moorehead phases at Cahokia, other sites with plazas and platform mounds arose (*squares*). During this time Cahokia (*solid circle*) became the largest community in American Bottoms.

and 900, nor is it clear just how, sometime about 900, people of the Late Woodland period here adopted what American archaeologists call Mississippian culture.

The occupation phase that followed, called Fairmount, continued for 150 years. It was typically Mississippian in culture and includes ample evidence, in the form of mound construction and elaborate burials, that sharp social stratification and a centralized control of resources had arisen among the inhabitants of American Bottoms. Soil cores taken by investigators from Washington University indicate that the first work at Monks Mound probably began at this time. My group's excavation of a small "ridgetop" earthwork, Mound 72 near the middle of the Cahokia group, produced indications that the builders of other mounds in the vicinity followed a plan calling for the overall orientation of the settlement along a north-south axis.

In view of the enormous quantities of fill required for the construction of the Cahokia earthworks, one immediate question is where did the soil come from? The answer is that the builders followed a procedure still used today: they dug "borrow pits." So far nine borrow pits have been located at Cahokia. The largest, about 800 yards southwest of Monks Mound, covered a 17-acre area and was about six feet deep. The second-largest pit covered nearly eight acres and the others ranged from about two acres to less than one acre. A group from the University of Illinois at Urbana has investigated one of the borrow pits that probably supplied the earth fill for an early phase in the construction of Monks Mound. The pit had later served as a trash dump; when it was full, the area was leveled and a large platform mound was built on top of the former excavation.

The builders did some of their digging with tools made from the hard, fine-grained stone known as chert. Quite probably they also worked with wood tools that have long since disintegrated, and they carried the earth fill from the pits to the construction sites in baskets.

Among the earthworks at Cahokia, Monks Mound is unique in shape. Mound 72 is one of six known ridgetop mounds in the group. By far the most common mound shape at Cahokia, however, is the platform mound; 28 square, oblong or oval single-platform mounds and four stepped, or double-platform, mounds have been identified [see *illustration on next two pages*]. In some instances excavation has shown that wood structures were built on the tops of the platform mounds, and so it is generally assumed that all the platform mounds served as building sites. The double-platform mounds presumably were used for structures more important than those on the mounds with only one platform. Just which platforms supported ceremonial buildings and which were residential sites occupied by the Cahokia elite is a question that only additional excavation can answer. A fourth kind of mound was also built; it is conical. There were seven of these mounds at Cahokia, and their shape makes it improbable that they were used as building foundations. They may have been used as burial mounds.

Other mound-building communities arose in American Bottoms during the Fairmount phase. One of them, the Lunsford-Pulcher site some 10 miles south of Cahokia, may even have approached Cahokia in size and importance at the time. Five other sites, four

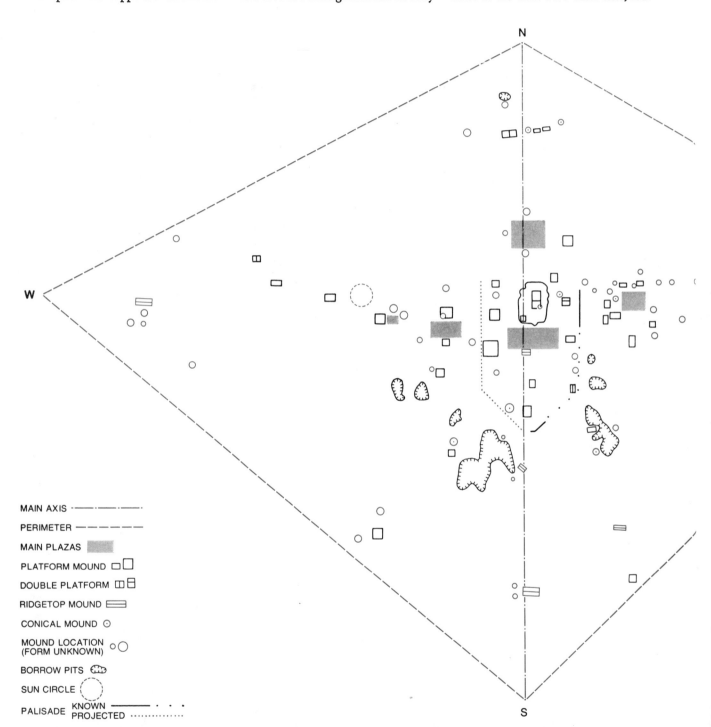

MAIN AXIS ·—·—·—·—·

PERIMETER — — — — —

MAIN PLAZAS ▨

PLATFORM MOUND ▫ ◻

DOUBLE PLATFORM ⊞ ⊟

RIDGETOP MOUND ⊟

CONICAL MOUND ⊙

MOUND LOCATION
(FORM UNKNOWN) ○ ◯

BORROW PITS ⬭

SUN CIRCLE ⦵

PALISADE KNOWN ——— · · ·
          PROJECTED ·············

CAHOKIA MOUNDS once extended three miles from the East Group (*right*) to the Powell Group (*left*), both now destroyed, and 2.25 miles from the Kunneman Group (*top*) to the Rattlesnake Group (*bottom*). When the four cardinal points are bounded (*broken colored line*), the area enclosed is some five square miles. Many of the 120 or so mounds at Cahokia have been obliterated by plowing or construction. Only 92 appear on this plan, and the origi- nal shape of 47 of them can no longer be determined. The remain- ing 45 fall into four classes. There are 28 single platforms and four double platforms; all 32 probably had buildings on them. Seven mounds are conical and six are classified as "ridgetop." Four of the ridgetop mounds may have been intended to mark the two axes of the site. Open colored circles locate the 47 mounds of unknown shape; irregular black areas mark eight of the nine known "borof them quite near Cahokia, are characterized by the construction of at least one platform mound. Elsewhere in the bottomland the number of farming hamlets and villages, all of them without mounds, had increased from a known total of 13 during the Patrick phase to more than three times that number [see illustration on page 65]. Two carbon-14 dates, both based on wood samples excavated at Cahokia, have helped to define the duration of the Fairmount phase. A house site excavated by workers from the University of Illinois at Urbana produced a carbon-14 age reading in the range between A.D. 685 and 985, and wood recovered from a ceremonial posthole underlying Mound 72 produced a reading in the range between A.D. 925 and 1035.

The most intriguing information unearthed so far concerning the intellectual and societal complexity of Mississippian culture about the end of the first millennium is associated with the Fairmount phase. In 1961 archaeologists from the Illinois State Museum undertook salvage archaeology in advance of Federal highway construction at Cahokia. They came on a series of soil stains some 900 yards west of Monks Mound. Tracing the stains, they found that many large upright timbers had once been arrayed in a circle. Within the circular enclosure the inhabitants of Cahokia were probably able, by sighting along certain marker posts, to observe the annual sequence of the solstices and the equinoxes. Solar observations of this kind, of course, can be the basis of a useful agricultural calendar. Several of these woodhenges were built in the same part of Cahokia over the centuries, but the first was built during the Fairmount phase.

Our group from Milwaukee had been struck by the fact that three of the six ridgetop mounds at Cahokia were located respectively at the eastern, southern and western extremities of the settlement. A fourth ridgetop mound, Mound 72, was located at the edge of the largest borrow pit, 800 yards south of Monks Mound. We found the position of Mound 72 suggestive. If one draws a line from Mound 72 to a ridgetop mound in the Rattlesnake group, some 600 yards farther south, a northward extension of the line crosses the southwest corner of the first terrace of Monks Mound. It seemed plausible to us that Mound 72 had served to mark a carefully calculated north-south center line at Cahokia.

To test our hypothesis we excavated a trench at the point in Mound 72 where, according to our prediction, the north-south center line would have crossed the structure. We uncovered a pit that extended well below ground level. At the bottom of the pit we found the impression of the butt of a very large upright timber. The timber itself was gone; perhaps the Fairmount-phase inhabitants had later removed it for use elsewhere. Still present, however, were the remains of logs that had been used to hold the large timber in position. A sample of this wood provided the carbon-14 date mentioned above.

As we continued to excavate Mound 72 it became clear that at the time the marker post was first erected, and continuously thereafter, the locale had served as a burial ground. It was no ordinary cemetery but one evidently reserved for the burial of the elite, perhaps even several generations of the same elite family. It was many years before the mound grew to its final ridgetop shape. We could recognize a succession of building phases; they included no fewer than six separate episodes of burial involving a total of at least 200 individuals.

The first episode, which was probably contemporaneous with the raising of the timber upright, began with the construction of a timber building on level ground. The lack of refuse in association with the building suggests that it was used as a mortuary, or charnel house. Early accounts of European contacts with some Indian groups in the Southeast include descriptions of the storage of the dead in such buildings and of their final burial only at a time that was ceremonially determined. In any event the building was eventually dismantled, and a mound was raised over a group of burials that included the body of one individual who had just died and the bundled bones of several others who had been dead for a long time. This kind of interment is suggestive of a ritual that postpones the burial of lesser kin until a kinsman of high status dies, whereupon all are buried as a group.

The earthwork that was built over this first mass burial was a small platform mound. Nothing was added to the mound for some time, but one pit was dug on the east side and another on the south to accommodate group burials. These pit burials comprised the second episode of burial at the site.

The third episode involved two further excavations and additional construction. One of the excavations was a pit that intruded into the fill covering the pit dug earlier on the south side of the mound. No bodies were buried in the new hole; instead the diggers placed pottery, shell beads and projectile points in the pit and then refilled it. At about the same time a rectangular pit was dug at the southeast corner of the mound and 24 individuals were buried there. Work did not stop with the refilling of the pit but was continued until a mound was raised above it that extended the initial platform mound to the southeast.

Just as the erection of a north-south

E

0   500   1,000
YARDS

row pits" that furnished earth to the builders. A broken colored circle locates the Cahokia woodhenge. Shaded areas outline five possible main plazas. The perimeter palisade surrounding the center of the site has been traced only in part; a dotted line (color) suggests its possible further extension.

marker post suggests sophisticated planning, so the fourth episode of burial at Mound 72 indicates that the social system of Fairmount-phase Cahokia was a distinctly stratified one. First a large pit was excavated about 10 yards southeast of the extension that had been added to the platform mound during the previous episode. Between the pit and the mound extension a small earth mound was raised, and the bodies of four men, with head and hands missing, were placed on top of it. In the pit the bodies of more than 50 young women, all between the ages of 18 and 23, were placed side by side. Finally earth was heaped over both group burials so that the platform mound was extended still farther to the southeast.

Although there is no physical evidence that the young women met a violent death, their closeness in age argues strongly against their having died from disease or from some common disaster. It is difficult to avoid the conclusion that, like the four mutilated men, the women were sacrificed, probably as a part of some kind of funeral ritual.

On whose behalf was the sacrifice made? Not far from the pit, at the place where the timber upright had once stood, we uncovered another group burial. It contained the remains of an individual of obvious importance who had been buried soon after his death. His

TAPERED BEAKER from Cahokia is some nine inches high. Its spiral scroll design is more sophisticated than most of the pottery motifs encountered at the site. The pot is in the collection of the Illinois State Museum.

body had been placed on a platform made up of thousands of shell beads; nearby were a number of bone bundles and the partly disarticulated remains of other individuals.

Not far from this group burial were the remains of three men and three women; buried with them was a wealth of grave goods [*see illustration on page 70*]. A sheet of rolled-up copper, roughly three feet long and two feet wide, had probably come from the Lake Superior region. Several bushels of sheet mica may have been imported from as far to the east as North Carolina. Quantities of arrowheads were present. Some had been freshly flaked from a variety of local materials. Others, including arrowheads made of a black chert found in Arkansas and Oklahoma, had evidently been imported ready-made. None of the arrowheads showed any sign of ever having been used. Finally, there were 15 beautifully polished double-concave stone disks of the kind European visitors later saw used in a sporting event that the Indians of that time called "chunky."

These rich burials were covered by a mound that stood to the southeast of the original (and now twice extended) platform mound. They constitute the fifth episode of burial at Mound 72. It seems reasonable to suppose this episode was contemporaneous with the sacrifice of the young women.

The sixth episode of burial is less spectacular. Ten oblong pits were dug in an area that was then probably near the southwestern edge of the multiple mound. The pits were used for mass burials and in most instances the individuals were buried soon after death. When the last oblong grave was filled, the builders of Mound 72 covered the multiple structure with fresh earth, giving it the ridge-top form that had initially attracted our attention. From the first episode to the last the sequence of burials and mound building seems to have occupied less than 100 years out of the 150-year Fairmount phase.

About A.D. 1050 the Fairmount phase was succeeded by a 100-year phase that has been named Stirling. Cahokia continued to grow during this phase, until the settlement covered between four and five square miles. Excavations of the fourth terrace at Monks Mound by groups from Washington University indicate that about A.D. 1100 the terrace was walled and was the site of one large building and several lesser ones. Work by our group has revealed that other buildings stood on the southwest corner of the lowest terrace at that time.

Elsewhere in American Bottoms other centers marked by mounds, in particular the Lunsford-Pulcher site to the south, began to assume increased stature. The mounds of St. Louis and East St. Louis appear to have been started during the Stirling phase, and another multiple-mound community, the Mitchell site, grew up some eight miles north of Cahokia. All four communities were located close to the major waterways of the region. This suggests that waterborne commerce of the kind indicated by the exotic Fairmount-phase grave goods may by then have become as important to the prosperity of American Bottoms as the high-yield harvests from the bottomland farms.

At some time about A.D. 1150 the Stirling phase at Cahokia was succeeded by the Moorehead phase, named after Warren K. Moorehead of the University of Illinois, who studied the Cahokia mounds almost half a century ago. The Cahokia community attained its highest development during that 100-year phase. At Monks Mound a succession of platform mounds, topped by timber buildings, were built on the lowest terrace. Construction activity is also evident elsewhere. One Moorehead-phase project was the rebuilding of an elaborate timber stockade, probably defensive in nature, that at least partly surrounded both Monks Mound and 16 other mounds in its vicinity.

Traces of this structure were first detected in aerial photographs; they appear as white lines running in a north-south direction to the east of Monks Mound. Our group conducted test excavations of the traces in the latter 1960's and discovered evidence of at least four consecutively constructed stockade systems. The first one, apparently built during the Stirling phase, was a wall made of large logs set on end. At intervals the wall incorporated circular projections, or bastions. The second stockade, probably built early in the Moorehead phase, was similar in design except that the bastions, located at the same points as those of the first stockade, were square rather than circular. A third stockade differed from the second only in minor details, and a fourth phase of construction involved an extensive remodeling of the third stockade.

It proved possible to trace the north-south line of the stockade for about 700 yards in the aerial photographs before it turned toward the southwest. Photo-interpretation suggests that the stockade, after turning, continued to a point some 300 yards due north of Mound 72 and

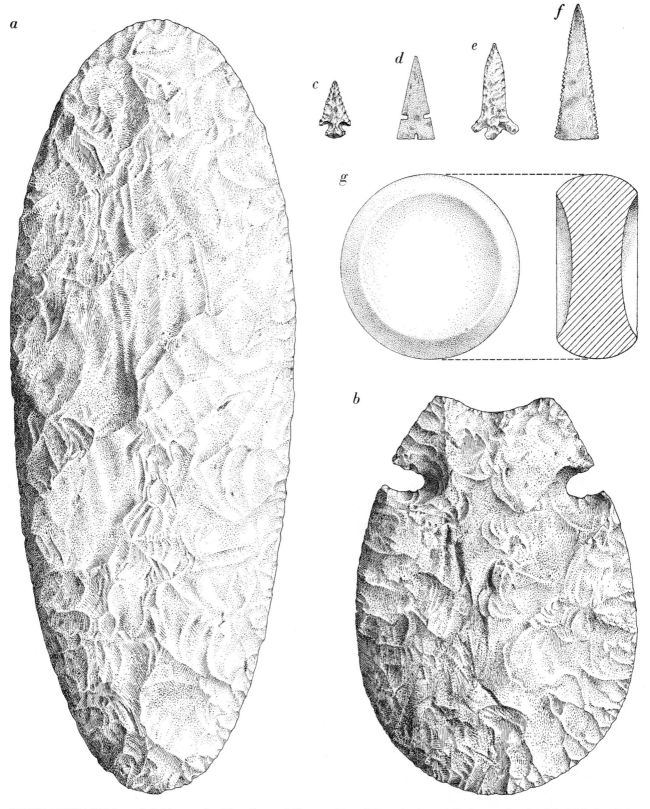

STONE ARTIFACTS from Cahokia, mostly chipped out of flint, range in size from large farm tools to small points. All are shown here at 60 percent actual size. The narrow cutting tool (*a*) is more than a foot long and may have been used like a hoe. The notched oval (*b*) more closely resembles a conventional hoe blade; it is some eight inches long. The smallest point (*c*) is one of several found in Mound 72 that were made from a black chert that is not locally available; the points were probably made in Arkansas or Oklahoma and imported to Cahokia. This example is 1.2 inches long. The triply notched point (*d*), 1.5 inches long, is also from Mound 72, as is the peculiarly tanged point (*e*), 1.7 inches long, that may be an import from Arkansas. The largest point (*f*), 2.5 inches long, is also from Mound 72; it is made from a kind of chert found in southern Illinois. The polished stone that resembles a concave hockey puck (*g*) is identical with those used in historical times by the Indians of the Southeast in the game of "chunky." The specimen, 3.5 inches in diameter, is in the Illinois State Museum. The large tools are in the St. Louis Museum of Science and Natural History. The points, unearthed during the author's excavation of Mound 72, are now at the University of Wisconsin at Milwaukee.

then angled back along a northwest leg, roughly equal to the southwest leg in length, before turning due north again. So far nothing is known about the stockade's northern terminus. If its northern limit was located exactly where the northernmost traces of its east side now seem to end, it would have enclosed some 200 acres in the central part of Cahokia.

The stockade has been called a fortification because it incorporated bastions or perhaps towers. Another interpretation of the structure is possible. Monks Mound and 16 other earthworks, including some of the largest platform mounds at the site, lie within the area more or less enclosed by the stockade. Did the structure perhaps screen off and isolate a central core of the community that had a higher status than the periphery? In the absence of the kinds of data that only further excavation can provide, such questions remain unanswered. In any event evidence other than maintenance of the stockade supports the view that the Moorehead phase saw Mississippian culture reach its peak at American Bottoms. For example, the woodhenge excavations suggest that the last of the

solar observatories was built at this time. Again, to judge by the number of house sites in areas where such sites have been found, the Moorehead-phase population of Cahokia may have approached 40,000.

How was this substantial population distributed? The area outside the stockade, with its many mounds, suggests a pattern. The mounds appear to have been organized in clusters, and each cluster includes platform mounds, plazas and what are probably burial mounds. The clusters suggest the existence of sub-communities located within the larger metropolis.

The distribution of house sites at Cahokia is also suggestive of a pattern of community organization. A ridge runs through the site from east to west; it is along this ridge line, over an area of some 2,000 acres, that the main concentration of housing is found. The houses were spaced at regular intervals, several to an acre. Of pole-and-thatch construction, they were mostly rectangular in floor plan. Evidently once a building site was chosen a succession of structures were built in the same place, suggesting several generations of occu-

pation. The houses show substantial variations in size. Some could have been the residences of persons of high status, while others may have sheltered craftsmen or even farmers.

Finally, evidence of change in the pattern of land utilization, particularly close to the stockade, hints at the social complexity of Cahokia at its height. In one location some 400 yards west of Monks Mound land that was residential at an earlier time was transformed during the Stirling phase into an area of walled enclosures and large public structures. The area was not returned to residential use until after A.D. 1250. The construction of the stockade provides another example. A part of the timber wall appears to have been built through the middle of an active residential area without regard for the residents. All these findings hint at the power of the central authority that directed the destiny of the Cahokia community.

The next phase at American Bottoms, named Sand Prairie, continued from A.D. 1250 until about 1500. The data from Cahokia for this period give the impression of a far lower level of activity. It was now that the area to the west of Monks Mound was reconverted from public uses to private ones and that minor additions were made to the lower part of Monks Mound. At least one mound still supported a public building. This is the Murdock mound, a double-platform structure located at the angle where the east wall of the stockade turns to the southwest. Excavation there by workers from the Illinois State Museum in 1941 uncovered timbers from what was apparently the last stage of construction of a large building. Wood samples gave a carbon-14 age ranging from A.D. 1270 to 1470.

No name has yet been chosen for the final phase at American Bottoms, which extends from A.D. 1500 to 1700, or about the time of contact with Europeans. The pattern, insofar as it has been traced, is one of continuing decline. About all that is certain, as excavations have shown, is that local Indians sometimes visited Monks Mound at the beginning of the 18th century to bury their dead.

Why did the remarkably successful Mississippian culture at American Bottoms fade away? Perhaps the decline was related to the exhaustion of local resources: a lack of timber for public and private buildings, for the stockade and for the sun circle, and the disappearance of the game animals (mainly deer) in the immediate hinterland that had provided a vital part of the inhabi-

RICH CACHE OF GRAVE GOODS was found at Mound 72 together with the bones of six individuals. Above the marker arrow (*lower left*) are a cluster of arrowheads, including many imported from the Ozarks. Above them (*center*) is a group of chunky stones. The cylindrical mass to their right is a rolled sheet of copper from the region of Lake Superior. Parallel with the roll of copper is a row of large and small shell beads; they are from the Gulf coast. The rounded pile just above the chunky stones is a mass of imported sheet mica.

AREA OF CENTRAL PLAZA at Cahokia is seen in this aerial photograph. The view is to the north; the shadows cast by the late afternoon sun accentuate the relief. The conical mound at left is No. 57; the platform mound at right is No. 60. Both were once enclosed by the timber wall that surrounded the plaza and Monks Mound, the 100-foot-high earthwork at upper right that dominated Cahokia.

tants' diet. Even the fertility of the bottomland loam, where the maize was grown, was not inexhaustible. Evidence from elsewhere in North America, for example at Chaco Canyon in New Mexico, indicates that population concentrations and the overuse of local resources go hand in hand.

It is also possible that the decline of the large settlements at American Bottoms, Cahokia in particular, was related to the growing strength of other centers of Mississippian culture. Cahokia had been the largest single Mississippian center and also perhaps the earliest. Its role in the evolution of the Mississippian way of life must have been dominant for centuries. At the same time American Bottoms was a major crossroads, particularly for travel by water. Its northern extremity was marked by the confluence of the Illinois and Mississippi rivers; the Illinois was a highway to the north-northeast and the upper Mississippi was a highway to the north and north-northwest. Just to the south of this confluence the Missouri River, a highway to the west and northwest, also joins the Mississippi. Toward the southern end of American Bottoms a highway into the Ozarks, the Meramec River, enters the Mississippi from the west. And some 150 miles to the south is the confluence of the Mississippi with the second-greatest of North American rivers, the Ohio, a major highway leading to the east and northeast.

The exotic materials found at sites in American Bottoms (for example black chert, probably from the Ozarks; native copper, almost certainly from Lake Superior; sheet mica, possibly from North Carolina; salt from southern Illinois or Missouri; lead from northern Illinois, and marine shells from the Gulf coast) are concrete evidence of the waterborne commerce that presumably kept American Bottoms in contact with other Mississippian or proto-Mississippian areas of North America. In addition many perishable goods, of which no archaeological trace remains, probably moved through Cahokia in the course of this commerce. Meanwhile Mississippian culture expanded to other areas and thrived. When the first Europeans traveled through southeastern North America, even though Cahokia was by then abandoned and unknown, they found many flourishing Mississippian regional centers. The young warriors were playing games with chunky stones, their elders were tending charnel houses and preparing bundles of bones for final burial and (among the Natchez Indians) an elaborate social hierarchy, headed by

BURIAL PLATFORM made of thousands of shell beads, drilled for stringing, supports the skeleton of a man who was buried in the extended position. The burial was found in the part of Mound 72 near where a large post had once stood to mark the north-south axis of Cahokia. The interred man probably held an important social position. All the burials in and under Mound 72 date from the Fairmount phase at Cahokia: A.D. 900 to A.D. 1050.

chiefs called suns, still built mounds and lived on top of them and regularly offered human sacrifices in the ceremonies that attended the burial of people of high status.

It is plausible to suppose that in addition to the handicap of diminishing resources the Mississippians of American Bottoms suffered from a loss of social status and economic power as the other regional centers of Mississippian culture developed their own hinterlands and spheres of influence. This does not alter the fact that the settlements at American Bottoms and at Cahokia in particular offer a nearly unique opportunity to study the rise of a complex society that for centuries controlled the natural resources of an immediate hinterland and also oversaw the distribution of highly valued resources drawn from more distant areas. The processes that led to the rise of such a society, although they are not yet understood in detail, can be suggested in broad outline.

The initial stimulus seems to have been the population expansion and the jump in agricultural productivity. High crop yields and sedentary communities in turn combined to foster further in-

creases in population density; perhaps it was competition for available farmland and the resulting conflict between rival communities that stimulated the evolution of social controls and societal hierarchies.

The fact that one community in American Bottoms, Cahokia, became the dominant community can be understood in these terms. First, Cahokia stands on some of the best agricultural land in the region. Second, a network of sloughs, lakes and creeks gave Cahokia easy access both to the rest of American Bottoms and to the long-distance transport network formed by the big rivers. Cahokia was thus a central place ideally situated both to exploit the resources of the immediate hinterland and to dominate the trade in exotic goods.

So much for the rise of Cahokia, at least in the light of present knowledge. The processes involved in its decline, however, need to be understood quite as much as the processes involved in its rise. Those who plan future studies of American Bottoms should recognize that the question of why Cahokia was abandoned is among the most significant questions that remain unanswered.

The Iroquois Confederacy

by James A. Tuck
February 1971

This alliance of Woodland Indian tribes played a significant role during the European colonization of North America. Excavations in New York now cast new light on their origins and social evolution

Among the Indians in the American Northeast none affected the lives of the European colonists more than the few thousand who lived near Lake Ontario and spoke the Iroquoian language. With firearms acquired in the 17th century, first from the Dutch and then the English, an alliance of five Iroquois tribes forayed east into the maritime provinces of Canada and west as far as the Illinois River. They crushed the nearest of their traditional Algonkian-speaking enemies and even destroyed Iroquois-speaking tribes that did not belong to their confederacy. Since the Algonkians were allies of the French, the Iroquois did much to help the English win control of Canada in the 18th century. Then they fought for both sides during the War of Independence.

The role played by these "Romans of the New World," as the historian Francis Parkman called them, seems out of all proportion to the slim resources at their disposal. How did the Iroquois manage to accomplish so much? The question has made Iroquois prehistory a controversial subject; a leading scholar in the field has remarked that more ink has been spilled over the Iroquois than over any other aboriginal American people. Yet the five tribes of the confederacy never had more than 12,000 members, and probably had considerably fewer. Their fighting men numbered only some 2,200.

Some scholars have maintained that the Iroquois came originally from Georgia and the Carolinas. That area was the home of the "civilized" Cherokees, who spoke an Iroquoian language and whose ready adoption of European ways was considered an indication of their superiority to other Indians. It has also been suggested that the Iroquois came from the north, moving down the valley of the St. Lawrence under pressure from the advancing Algonkians. One source even places the Iroquois homeland in the Pacific Northwest. Not until recently has it been realized that the Iroquois culture might simply have arisen in the area where the European colonists first encountered it.

Today it is clear that the actual origin is the last one. Archaeological evidence collected at more than a score of sites over the past two decades shows that the Onondagas—the key tribe in the confederacy—developed into full-fledged Iroquois from a preceding level of pre-Iroquois culture in the years after A.D. 1000 without ever leaving a 25-by-15-mile area in upper New York State near modern Syracuse. What is true of the Onondagas must surely hold for the other tribes in the confederacy: the Oneidas and Cayugas immediately to the east and the west, the Senecas of the Genesee valley farther to the west and the Mohawks of the Mohawk valley farther to the east.

What is known about the Iroquois in Colonial times is helpful in interpreting their prehistory. Like most of the other aboriginal inhabitants of the region, they were representatives of the Late Woodland period of Northeastern prehistory. Farmers and hunters, they lived in villages in forest clearings, protected from raiders by one or more palisades made of saplings. In the clearing beyond the palisade the women of the village raised corn, beans, squashes and tobacco. The women also collected wild plant foods and the men hunted and fished. Except for dogs, domestic animals were unknown. Inside the palisade stood several "longhouses," which were long indeed: typically they were 25 feet in width and 50 to 100 feet in length. This was the traditional Iroquois form of house, consisting of a framework of saplings covered with sheets of bark. It was divided into apartments that were usually occupied by closely related families. Running down the middle of the house was a corridor where the families living on each side shared fireplaces.

Each of the five tribes of the confederacy occupied two or more such villages, usually only a few miles apart. Village affairs were supervised by a local council. Above the local council was a tribal council, which generally met in the largest village. The tribes were banded together in a "Great League of Peace," the formal name for the confederacy, which was governed by a council of 50 sachems representing all the tribes. Iroquois religious observations marked both the events of the agricultural cycle (with such occasions as a "planting festival" and a "green corn festival") and the progress of the seasons (exemplified by an annual "wild strawberry festival" and similar events).

As a tribe whose leader was prominent in founding the Great League of Peace, the Onondagas were traditionally at the center of confederacy affairs. The tribe was "keeper of the central fire," and the name of their tribal leader, Atotarho, was adopted by an Onondaga when he rose to be sachem. Thus it seems likely that the trends and events of Onondaga prehistory parallel those of the other tribes. All five tribes must have been subjected to much the same environmental and social pressures. Indeed, the career of the Onondagas probably reflects the events taking place among many of the Indians of the American Northeast in the era following the introduction of the cultivation of corn, beans and squashes around 1000 B.C.

The Late Woodland culture of the pre-Iroquois inhabitants of New York is named Owasco after a site at Owasco Lake near the center of the state. The earliest Owasco village that is pertinent to Onondaga prehistory lies some eight

miles north of Skaneateles Lake and is known as the Maxon-Derby site. (This site and others, by the way, take their names from the local landowner or from local topographic features.) The Maxon-Derby site was excavated in 1959 and 1960 by William A. Ritchie of the New York State Museum in Albany. The site covers two acres and includes the floors of seven houses. Two separate carbon-14 analyses show that the village was occupied around A.D. 1100. Apparently it had no palisade of the kind that surrounded the villages of historical times.

The outlines of the seven houses can be traced partially or completely by rows of post molds: dark patches of humus in the subsoil that mark the position of the saplings that once formed the frame. Most of the houses were small, with parallel sides and rounded ends, but two of them appear to be precursors of the Iroquois longhouse: they were 25 feet wide and 60 feet long. The hearths in these larger houses, however, were along one wall rather than in a central corridor. The fact that the houses had several hearths suggests that they sheltered several related families.

The food remains at the Maxon-Derby site included the bones of mammals, birds and fish, the debris of wild plants and charred kernels of corn. Among the artifacts were triangular stone arrow points, bone tools and fired-clay tobacco pipes. All these objects in one way or another foreshadow Iroquois forms. The most abundant artifacts at the site were fragments of pottery; their rims had been decorated with impressions made by the edge of a paddle wrapped with cord.

A second Owasco village, known as the Chamberlin site, is some three miles southeast of the Maxon-Derby site. Early historical records indicate that it was once surrounded by a low ring of earth, which has now disappeared. A field party from Syracuse University excavated the site under my direction in the summer of 1967. Carbon-14 analysis indicates that the village was occupied around A.D. 1290, some two centuries later than the Maxon-Derby village. The pottery showed a corresponding degree of development, although it still clearly represented the late phase of Owasco culture.

The Chamberlin houses in particular show advances along Iroquois lines. Although the hearths are still next to one wall, the houses are more than 80 feet long. I suspect that the obliterated ring of earth once formed the base of a defensive palisade, which may mean that by the end of the 13th century village defense was becoming an important consideration.

Remains at still a third village site only a little east of the Chamberlin site show the transition from the Owasco culture to the nascent culture of the Iroquois. This is the Kelso site, excavated by Ritchie in 1963. The Kelso site actually consists not of one village but of two overlapping villages. Both were heavily fortified; the palisade of one consisted of three concentric rings of saplings. Some of the Kelso houses were small and oval, but the longhouses were nearly 130 feet in length and the hearths are along a central corridor with a door at each end. Although the overlapping outlines of the palisades show there had been two villages, only a single carbon-14 date was obtained. This is A.D. 1390, just a century later than the Chamberlin date. Not only the form of the Kelso longhouses but also the details of decoration on tobacco pipes and pottery allow the site to be assigned to the earliest phase of the full Iroquois culture.

On the basis of the available evidence the connection among the three sites is not entirely clear. It is nonetheless possible that the three villages, considering their closeness in time and space and the similarity of their artifacts, were occupied successively by a single community. Periodic relocations could have been motivated by the need for new supplies of firewood, for new hunting grounds and perhaps for new soil for horticulture.

Four village sites that are comparable in age to the first three and that also reflect the transition from the Owasco culture to the Iroquois are located among the tributaries to Lake Onondaga, some 15 miles farther east. The first of these sites, the Cabin site, was apparently a small, undefended hilltop village. A large trash heap on the steep slope next to the village yielded a wealth of artifacts. These are primarily fragments of pottery but also include triangular arrow points, tobacco pipes of late Owasco

style, bone awls, pins, scrapers and fish-spear points, and a bangle fashioned from the toe bone of a deer [see top illustration on pages 80 and 81]. Another find was a tiny stylized clay effigy of a human face. This may foreshadow the later practice of wearing life-size effigy masks, which became an important feature of Iroquois religious ritual in historical times. No absolute date has been established for the Cabin site, but the inventory of artifacts suggests that it was occupied between A.D. 1250 and 1300.

Four miles to the north are the remains of a two-acre village known as the Furnace Brook site. It is not quite contemporaneous with the Kelso site to the west but, like the Kelso villages, it was completely surrounded by a palisade. Two carbon-14 determinations show that Furnace Brook was occupied between A.D. 1300 and 1370. Some of its houses are small and reminiscent of the ones at the Maxon-Derby site, but Furnace Brook has a longhouse that is of unusual dimensions for the period. It was 22 feet wide and 210 feet long; a door at each end opened on a central corridor where the hearths were located. The artifacts unearthed at Furnace Brook show that, like the Kelso site, it belongs to the earliest phase of the full Iroquois culture.

A third village site less than two miles away is Howlett Hill. It has the well-defined remains of three longhouses. The largest is also of unusual dimensions: it is 334 feet long [see illustration on page 78]. Analysis of charcoal from a post mold of this house yields a carbon-14 date of A.D. 1380, which suggests that the Howlett Hill village may have been a successor to the Furnace Brook one. The increase in longhouse size (the largest at Howlett Hill is a third longer than the largest at Furnace Brook) clearly reflects a similar increase in the number of occupants. In any case, the people of both villages had progressed beyond the Owasco culture to the Iroquois.

The last of the villages in the vicinity of Lake Onondaga is known as the Schoff site. It was partly excavated by our Syracuse University group in 1967, and it proved to have the longest of all the longhouses: it extended almost exactly 400 feet. A limited number of artifacts unearthed at the village include trumpet-shaped tobacco pipes and pottery with incised neck decorations. Both suggest that the villagers had attained the phase of Iroquois cultural development that follows the nascent phase. Analysis of material from the site has provided a carbon-14 date of A.D. 1410.

I have already suggested that the

INDIAN VILLAGE on a hilltop near Syracuse, N.Y., is seen in the photograph on the opposite page during excavation. It is a 14th-century Iroquois site known as Furnace Brook. Stakes mark rotted saplings that formed walls and inner partitions. Dominating the scene is the outline of a structure that was 22 feet wide and 210 feet long: an Iroquois longhouse.

SAVAGE RITUAL at a 15th-century Iroquois village site known as Bloody Hill is evidenced by a bathtub-shaped pit discovered by a Syracuse University team in 1967. A fire burning under the stones transformed the pit into a platform suitable for roasting.

CLOSE-UP OF PIT during its excavation shows pieces of broken and cut human bone. Arrows point to knife marks. Part of a skull was also unearthed. Evidently an adult male had been cooked and eaten. The incident preceded the founding of the Onondaga tribe.

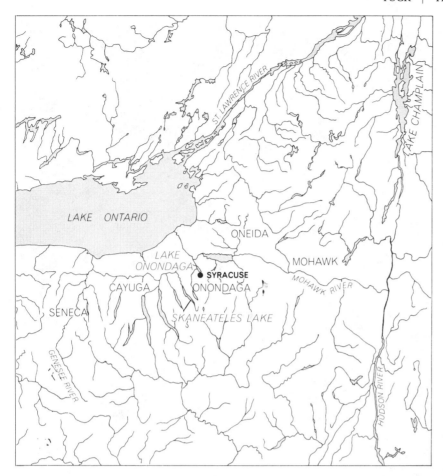

FIVE TRIBES of the Iroquois confederacy were, from west to east, the Senecas, the Cayugas, the Onondagas, the Oneidas and the Mohawks. At the beginning of the 18th century their power extended from Maine to Illinois and from southern Ontario to Tennessee. The Tuscaroras became the sixth after being ousted by white settlers in the Carolinas.

three western sites could have been the successive residences of a single social group. The probability that another single group successively occupied the four central sites is stronger. The four villages are close to one another, and their successive occupation—if I am right—represents a series of moves into fresh territory first from south to north and then south again. Moreover, the three most recent villages are separated in time by no more than a century, and the progressive increase in the size of their longhouses might reflect the natural increase in the group's numbers. Lastly, certain aspects of the assemblage of artifacts at these sites, notably a high percentage of pottery vessels with incised neck decorations compared with the low percentage of this kind of decoration at other sites, suggest a degree of cultural continuity that may be characterized as a "microtradition."

The sequence of sites from Cabin to Schoff therefore appears to reflect the activities of a single group. The group's next move apparently was to abandon the Lake Onondaga watershed altogether. In spite of long and intensive reconnaissance and the excavation of test pits in a zone extending for miles in all directions from the Schoff site, no trace of a successor village has been found. The trail does not, however, grow completely cold.

The largest number of sites in the Onondaga region are found in the area east of Syracuse. The record preserved in these eastern sites extends from nascent Iroquois times through the period of European contact and up to the final decades of the 18th century. Three of the earliest sites in the eastern group are roughly contemporaneous with the Howlett Hill and Schoff sites in the cen-

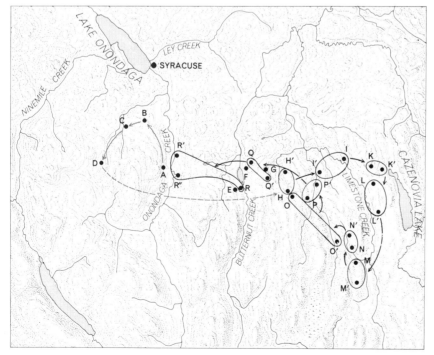

A	CABIN	L'	ATWELL
B	FURNACE BROOK	N	CHASE
		N'	QUIRK
C	HOWLETT HILL	M	SHELDON
D	SCHOFF	M'	DWYER
E	COYE II	O	CARLEY
F	KEOUGH	O'	POMPEY CENTER
G	BLOODY HILL	P	INDIAN HILL
H	BURKE	P'	INDIAN CASTLE
H'	CHRISTOPHER	Q	JAMESVILLE PEN
I	NURSERY	Q'	WESTON
I'	CEMETERY	R	TOYADASSO
K	BARNES	R'	UPPER VALLEY OAKS
K'	MCNAB		
L	TEMPERANCE HOUSE	R''	LOWER VALLEY OAKS

VILLAGE SITES occupied by the Indians who eventually founded the Onondaga tribe are identified by letters on this map. Arrows indicate successive occupations. The period runs from the end of the 13th century through the 18th. Establishment of two adjacent villages (H–H') late in the 15th century marks the foundation of the tribe. Thereafter the tribe usually occupied pairs of villages.

LARGER LONGHOUSE, at the Howlett Hill site, is 334 feet in length. Closely set stakes outline the house wall. Other stakes within the house show where its inner structural supports stood. Numbered placards locate 16 hearths that lined a central corridor.

tral group; the earliest of them is known as Coye II. Like the Kelso site in the west and Howlett Hill in the central group, Coye II is a village that was occupied by people at the nascent phase of Iroquois cultural development. This is evidence that still a third social group in the Onondaga region participated in the transition from the Owasco to the Iroquois culture.

Two sites slightly later than Coye II are Keough and Bloody Hill. Both were small villages. No absolute date is available for Keough but a carbon-14 analysis of material from Bloody Hill places its time of occupation around A.D. 1420. The percentages of similar artifacts of various kinds from both sites are nearly identical, suggesting that the villages were occupied at about the same time.

Bloody Hill has also yielded evidence that ritual torture and cannibalism, which were familiar in historical times, were an established part of the Iroquois culture in the 15th century. In the summer of 1967 our digging exposed a large pit shaped somewhat like a bathtub: it was about eight feet long, four and a half feet wide and two and a half feet

deep. The soil showed signs of having been subjected to intense heat. We found that the pit had been filled with firewood, some of it logs as much as six inches in diameter, which was then ignited. A layer of boulders and cobblestones had been placed on top of the burning logs, and the blaze soon transformed the cobble pavement into a roasting platform. A few scraps of refuse were present on the platform but the principal remains on it were fragments of an adult male's skull and long bones; the bones showed the marks of cutting tools. In the light of later Iroquois practices, it is not difficult to see in these human remains the ordeal and ultimate disposition of a captured enemy. The pit is testimony to the bellicose characteristics of early Iroquois society every bit as eloquent as the village fortifications.

About two miles east of Bloody Hill are two later sites I believe contain evidence of how the village groups of the time reacted to local strife. One of these areas is known as the Christopher site. It appears to cover two acres, and thus it represents a village much larger than either Keough or Bloody Hill. I

suggest that the Christopher site in fact represents a merger of the two earlier communities, probably in the interests of improved security.

The second area, called the Burke site, is another extended village. It was occupied for a considerable time and, as the relocation of its palisade and one of its longhouses indicates, it was rebuilt at least once. The real surprise at the Burke site, however, is the presence of the same pottery-decorating microtradition that was characteristic of the Schoff site and its predecessors in the central area. At Burke we seem to have picked up the trail that had vanished earlier. Not only does the Schoff microtradition reappear at Burke but also one of the Burke longhouses is almost as generous in its proportions as the houses of the central area are. Although it has not yet been fully exposed, it already measures more than 240 feet. Moreover, the forms of the arrow points and tobacco pipes at Burke indicate a gradual evolution from the forms found at Howlett Hill and Schoff. That would be natural. The only available date for the Burke site, based on a carbon-14 study of material prob-

VILLAGE DEFENSE depended primarily on a stout palisade made of timbers brought from the nearby forest and set upright in a ring around the village. The holes indicate where the timbers stood that formed the palisade surrounding the site at Furnace Brook.

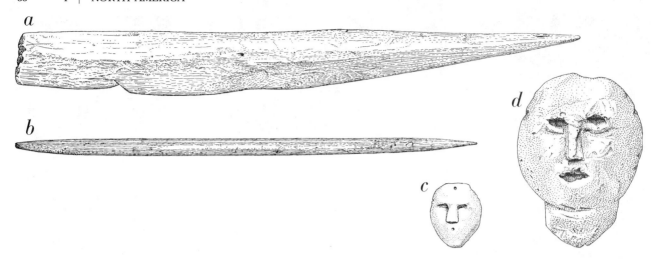

CHARACTERISTIC ARTIFACTS of the Owasco and Iroquois cultures include a bone awl (*a*), a bone point for a fish spear (*b*), an effigy of a human face modeled in clay (*d*) and a bangle fashioned from the toe bone of a deer (*e*). All are from the Cabin site,

ably deposited near the end of the village's occupation, is about A.D. 1480, or almost a century later than the Schoff village.

Why would a group intent on relocation choose to settle only two miles away from a large, well-defended and strange village? The choice has implications that bear on the eventual development of the Iroquois confederacy. It is hard to imagine that two potentially hostile communities could have existed so close together without an understanding, however informal, about mutual defense. At the very least some kind of nonaggression pact would have been needed to prevent clashes that could have been disastrous for one village if not both. I interpret the evidently peaceful coexistence of the inhabitants of the Christopher and Burke sites as an arrangement that marks the founding of the Onondaga tribe. The two groups probably became closely allied between A.D. 1425 and 1450, and it appears that an Iroquois two-village system and a subsequent pattern of intertribal nonaggression alliances may have begun here.

How soon after this time the two allied villages developed a sense of common identity and took a single name is impossible to say, but it should not have been long afterward. ("Onondaga" is an Iroquois word meaning "the people on the hills.") The merger would provide most of the advantages of combining military forces while at the same time avoiding the pressure that too large a concentration of people in a single village would exert on the environment. In this simple balancing of security require-

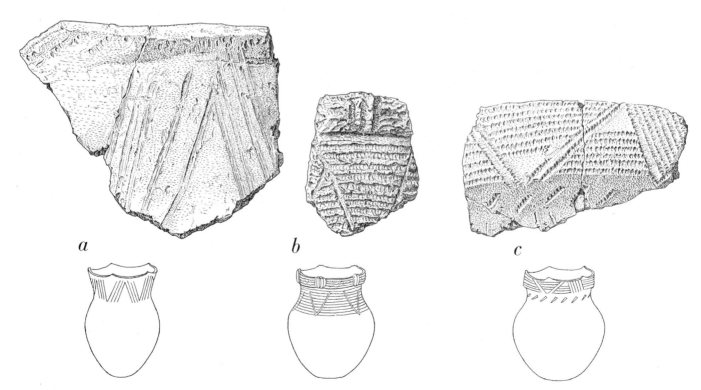

POTTERY DECORATION was applied principally to the neck of cooking vessels by incising lines in the clay or pressing it with a paddle wrapped with cord. The decorated fragments are illustrated two-thirds actual size; the form of the entire vessel is shown schematically below. The first examples are from village sites that may have been occupied successively by the same group: the

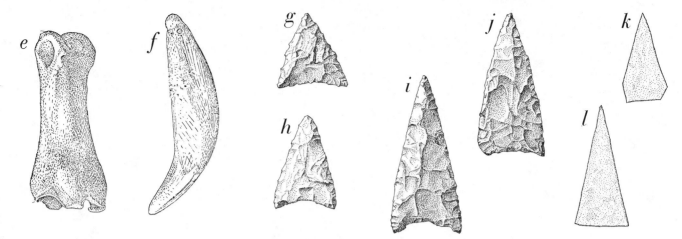

which was occupied around A.D. 1250 or 1300 by a group that was at the Owasco stage of cultural development. The smaller effigy (c), bear tooth (f) and arrow points (g–j) are from later Iroquois sites. Brass arrow points (k, l) mark the arrival of European trade goods.

ments with ecological imperatives, I believe, lies the basis of the later and larger political groupings that gave rise to the Great League of Peace.

For nearly three centuries, beginning with the first removal and resettlement of the twin villages late in the 15th century, the Onondaga tribe shifted its living sites a number of times. Although the removals were surely not simultaneous on each occasion, the general pattern consisted in occupying one smaller and one larger village that were never more than a few miles apart. Before the tribe's final post-Revolution move to the Onondaga reservation, it had occupied nine such pairs of villages. To describe the 18 sites in detail would be unnecessary; a short summary will suffice to complete the record of Onondaga cultural development.

The late prehistoric period of the Iroquois lasted until late in the 16th century. During that time the Onondaga villages were successively relocated in a northeasterly direction. The next, or protohistoric, period was marked by the introduction of European trade goods, although there was no direct contact between the Iroquois and Europeans. During this time the direction of relocation was southward, along the valley of Limestone Creek. Sites with steep approaches were favored, and the villages were usually well fortified. The houses were considerably smaller than the great longhouses of earlier days; the change may be indicative of social evolution that made the traditional house obsolete.

After a few southward removes the Onondagas reached the Allegheny Plateau and began to move northward again

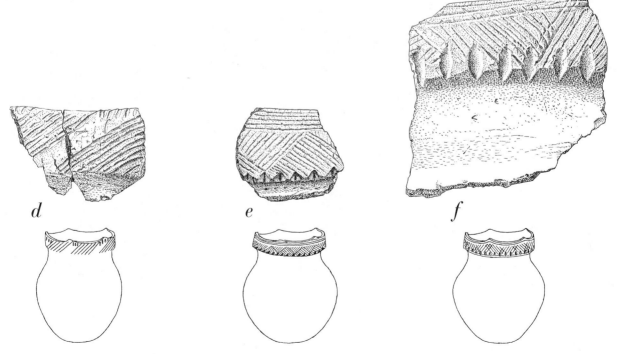

Cabin site (a), inhabited before A.D. 1300, and the Furnace Brook (b), Howlett Hill (c) and Schoff (d) sites, which were inhabited during the 14th century and the early 15th. The next sherd (e), from the Burke site, reveals its Owasco ancestry by its decoration with impressions of the edge of a cord-wrapped paddle. Finally, a fragment from the Cemetery site (f) exemplifies Onondaga ware.

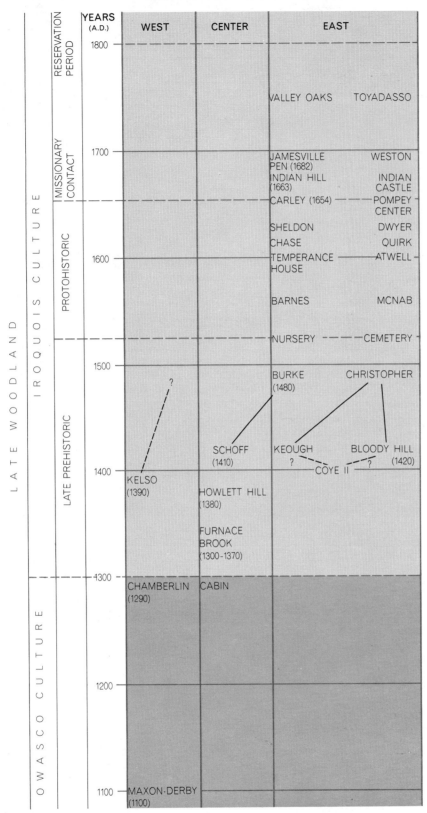

YEARS (A.D.)	WEST	CENTER	EAST	
1800			VALLEY OAKS	TOYADASSO
1700			JAMESVILLE PEN (1682)	WESTON
			INDIAN HILL (1663)	INDIAN CASTLE
			CARLEY (1654)	POMPEY CENTER
			SHELDON	DWYER
			CHASE	QUIRK
1600			TEMPERANCE HOUSE	ATWELL
			BARNES	MCNAB
			NURSERY	CEMETERY
1500			BURKE (1480)	CHRISTOPHER
	?	SCHOFF (1410)	KEOUGH ?	BLOODY HILL ? (1420)
1400	KELSO (1390)	HOWLETT HILL (1380)	COYE II	
		FURNACE BROOK (1300-1370)		
1300	CHAMBERLIN (1290)	CABIN		
1200				
1100	MAXON-DERBY (1100)			

(Left vertical labels: LATE WOODLAND — IROQUOIS CULTURE — RESERVATION PERIOD, MISSIONARY CONTACT, PROTOHISTORIC, LATE PREHISTORIC; OWASCO CULTURE)

CHRONOLOGICAL CHART shows the relative ages of selected Late Woodland Indian sites in the Syracuse area. Three of the oldest lie north of Skaneateles Lake. The artifacts they contain demonstrate a transition from the preceding Owasco culture to nascent Iroquois. The three sites may have been occupied successively by the same group, but no trace of the group is found after A.D. 1390. The four more central sites also show the transition from Owasco culture to Iroquois. Development of a "microtradition" that favors incised decoration of pot necks suggests that they were occupied successively by the same group that subsequently occupied the eastern village represented by the Burke site, where the same microtradition is present. Coalition with a third group of Iroquois villagers is suggested by the proximity of the Burke and Christopher sites. Villages are usually paired thereafter.

along the valley of Butternut Creek. Villages were still located in defensible positions, but they were no longer necessarily protected by steep slopes. A steady decay in native arts and crafts provides a measure of the growing importance of European trade goods. Stone axes, knives and arrow points disappear and metal ones take their place. By the time of the first recorded contact between the Onondagas and Europeans the native manufacture of pottery had become virtually a lost art. We may surmise that many less tangible elements of Iroquois culture had been eroded at the same rate.

On August 5th, 1654, a French missionary, Father Simon LeMoyne, entered the leading Onondaga village. As he writes, he was "singing the ambassador's song and receiving addresses of welcome." The next year two more French priests arrived; they supervised the building of a small bark chapel and started the work of Christianizing the Onondagas. Tradition has it that they came to the village now known as the Indian Hill site. Jesuit records, however, indicate that Indian Hill was not settled until about 1663, so that it is more likely that Father LeMoyne entered an earlier Onondaga village, perhaps the Carley or the Pompey Center site.

A European who came to Indian Hill in 1677 left this eyewitness description: "The Onondagoes have butt one towne, butt it is very large, consisting of about 140 houses, nott fenced; it is situate upon a hill thatt is very large, the banke on each side extending it self att least two miles, all cleared land whereon the corne is planted. They have likewise a small village about two miles beyond thatt, consisting of about 24 houses." (The latter was apparently a village to the south of Indian Hill now called the Indian Castle site.)

The visitor's words attest to the Onondaga two-village settlement pattern and also to the extensive plantings that surrounded the settlements. It further allows us to deduce that the dwellings at Indian Hill were not the traditional Iroquois longhouses; the site is much too small to have accommodated 140 houses of any great size. That the settlement Indian Hill was "nott fenced" is surprising. Evidently by this time the Onondagas no longer built the customary village palisade.

The sites of historical Onondaga villages need further study, but the archaeological work that has been done at Indian Hill so far suggests that by the 1670's European trade goods were predominant. Virtually the only items of native manufacture found there (or at Jamesville Pen, the successor village to Indian Hill) are tobacco pipes.

This was the period of the confederacy's greatest influence. The Iroquois conquered the Huron Indians in 1649, the Tobacco and "Neutral" tribes in 1650, the Eries in 1656 and other groups in succeeding years. By that time the confederacy held sway from the Illinois River in the west to the Kennebec in the east and from the Tennessee River north to the Ottawa. In 1711 the British settlements in North Carolina expelled the Iroquoian-speaking Tuscaroras from their lands. The Tuscaroras moved north and were formally adopted by the Oneidas, increasing the membership of the confederacy from five tribes to six.

The confederacy sided successfully with the British in the many bloody frontier campaigns of the French and Indian Wars, but the War of Independence that followed led to its destruction. Nominally the Great League of Peace remained neutral, but each tribe was left free to choose the side it preferred. Only the Oneidas favored the cause of the Revolution. The Senecas and the Mohawks actively supported the loyalists until Revolutionary punitive campaigns in 1779 defeated them, decimated the Onondagas and brought general destruction to the Iroquois homeland.

The surviving Onondagas took refuge first on a reservation near Buffalo and finally on a parcel of land near Syracuse part of which today constitutes the Onondaga Indian Reservation. Of the other tribes, the Oneidas chose a new home in Wisconsin, and many of the surviving Mohawks and Cayugas remained allied with the loyalists and moved to Canada.

In this summary of some 700 years we first find traces of the early and apparently successive activities of three small Late Woodland Indian groups in the upstate New York area where the Onondaga tribe eventually arose. Around A.D. 1400 we lose track of the westernmost group; its contributions to the Onondaga culture, if any, remain unknown. The villages successively occupied by the other two groups, however, are more easily traced. The movements of one group can be followed for a period of 200 years as it shifts from place to place in an area just west of modern Syracuse. As the group moves, its members acquire Iroquois ways and develop a concern about self-defense that may have arisen because of the increase in population pressure throughout the American Northeast that followed the introduction of agriculture.

Between A.D. 1425 and 1450 the western group leaves its ancestral domain, moves eastward and settles near a community of a similar kind that had inhabited a similar local territory for some generations. Although there is a tradition of warfare and human sacrifice, the strangers' incursion appears to have been peaceful. This strife-free event we take to mark the founding of the Onondaga tribe, the central group in the later Iroquois confederacy. From earlier mergers of small groups and from political unions such as this one, presumably aimed at nonaggression and mutual defense, there seem to have arisen such powerful Iroquois social institutions as the "medicine societies" and perhaps even the system of tribal organization in moieties, or dual groups. Both would have served a socially integrative function in newly formed communities. The medicine society gathers individuals from separate kinship groups into a single unified organization. The moiety system, in turn, ensures a system of complementary rituals and ceremonies, ranging from the exchange of marriage partners between the two halves of the tribe to burial rituals and the elevation of sachems.

The increase in nonhostile contacts between the Iroquois villages and tribes that led to the Great League of Peace can be seen in the archaeological evidence. It appears in the gradual transformation of local microtraditions into patterns that are more broadly homogeneous. This is particularly evident in certain styles of pottery among the Onondagas, the Oneidas and the Mohawks that eventually become almost identical.

The heyday of the confederacy in the 16th century must have been a relatively peaceful time. Although village fortifications testify to a continuing concern about defenses, raids from the outside could not have been nearly as disruptive as the earlier intertribal battles. Over the next two centuries, however, direct and indirect contacts with Europeans, and Iroquois involvement in European quarrels, proved fatal. These contacts brought about the collapse of the Great League of Peace, the steady erosion of the Iroquois way of life and the eventual transformation of the Romans of the New World into wards of a white man's society.

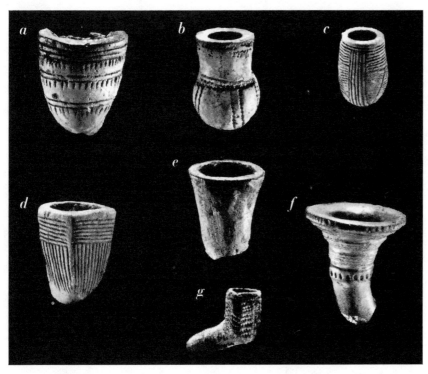

TOBACCO PIPES, a common Woodland Indian artifact, were made in a number of styles. A miniature model (g) shows the form of an intact pipe. The rest have lost their stems and are represented only by their bowls. The conical bowl, decorated with impressions from a cord-wrapped paddle (a), is from the Furnace Brook site and resembles the pipes of the preceding Owasco culture. The pot-shaped (b), barrel-shaped (c) and square bowls (d) are from the same site, an Iroquois village that was occupied between A.D. 1300 and 1370. A somewhat trumpet-shaped bowl (e) from the Bloody Hill site, which was occupied around 1420, presages the form of Iroquois trumpet pipe (f) popular in historical times.

Prehistoric Man in the Grand Canyon

by Douglas W. Schwartz
February 1958

In an oasis at the bottom of the Canyon live the Havasupai Indians, who have now been linked to a vanished people who settled the surrounding plateau in the seventh century A.D.

The Grand Canyon in Arizona was discovered by Spanish explorers in 1540, but so far as is known no white man entered the Canyon itself until two and a half centuries later. In July of 1776 a Franciscan priest, Francisco Thomás Garcés, was traveling on a mission toward the Hopi country, and en route along the Colorado River he heard of an Indian tribe living deep in the Canyon. Since his mission was to convert Indians wherever he found them, Father Garcés asked to be led to the tribe so that he might take them the word of God. With the help of a guide the padre descended by steep trails to a valley almost a mile below the Colorado Plateau, in a small branch of the Colorado River called Cataract Creek. There he found a verdant oasis offering the pleasantest possible contrast to the desert country above. On the canyon bottom, between the bare, brown cliffs, ran a beautiful spring-fed stream,

CATARACT CREEK CANYON is a fork of the Grand Canyon. It is now the home of the Havasupai Indians. On the high ledges of the canyon wall, and atop the sloping rock debris at its base, are the granaries and shelters of an ancient people.

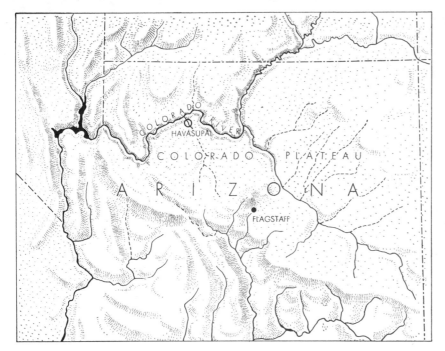

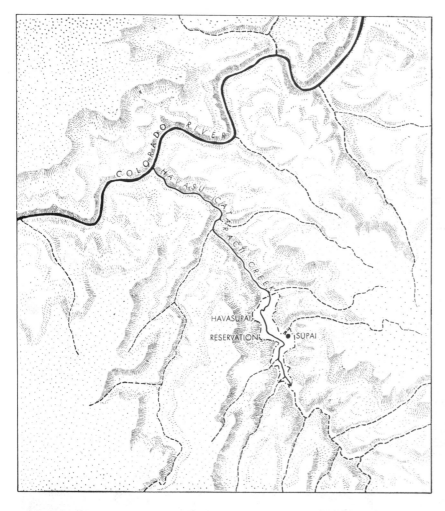

GRAND CANYON of the Colorado River cuts through the Colorado Plateau in northern Arizona. The relation of the Havasupai territory to the Grand Canyon is shown on the map at top. The map at bottom shows the exact location of the Havasupai Reservation in a widening of Cataract Creek Canyon. To the west, on the Coconino Plateau, are the ruins of houses built by the Cohonina people. The author believes they were ancestors of the Havasupai.

creating a green paradise of trees, flowers and luxuriant grass. It was occupied by a village of Indians called the Havasupai—"people of the blue-green water."

Garcés noted that the Havasupai made good use of the life-giving stream. They had developed a system of irrigation ditches to water their hundred or so arable acres, and in their small fields they were growing corn, beans, squash and a few European crop plants—apricots, figs, peaches, alfalfa—which they had obtained from other Indian tribes, who in turn had received them from the Spaniards. Father Garcés also observed a number of other things about the Havasupai's culture during his short stay of several days in the village. At dawn each family went out to work in the fields with digging sticks, hatchets and hoes. But as soon as the sun rose high enough to beat down in the Canyon, generating oven-like heat, everyone retreated from the fields to the huts and shades of the village. The men gossiped at the "sweatlodge," a counterpart of the village drugstore. The women indulged in their favorite sport—gambling with dice made of sticks. The children spent most of their afternoon hours swimming in the fast-flowing stream.

The peripatetic padre moved on, taking away only a momentary picture of these people and knowing little (since he had no interpreter) about their fascinating history and way of life. Not for well over a century was much more heard about the Havasupai. The waves of trappers, prospectors, soldiers, railroad scouting parties and scientific expeditions that overran the Southwest through the 19th century saw little of this shy tribe, which ventured less and less from its canyon retreat. But about 30 years ago Harold S. Colton, director of the Museum of Northern Arizona at Flagstaff, became interested in the history of Indians of the area, for remains going back some 1,200 years had been found on the plateau above the Canyon. He unearthed many old camp sites and houses of a people on the plateau who seemed to have disappeared around 1100 A.D. The mystery of their disappearance, as well as the peculiar isolation of the Havasupai, excited my curiosity when I began to work in the Grand Canyon area eight years ago. I became convinced that the key to the prehistory of the Colorado Plateau and Canyon Indians lay in the Havasupai home at the bottom of the Canyon.

In the winter of 1953-54 I lived with the Havasupai for six months in their canyon village. It was apparent that there was no hope of finding any ancient Havasupai remains in the village area. In early spring and in late summer floods as high as 40 feet often rush down the narrow canyon of Cataract Creek. The Havasupai villages have repeatedly been washed away by these floods. But at such times the Indians have taken refuge, as far back as they can remember, in rock shelters at the base of the cliff walls. We therefore excavated these shelter sites, hoping to find cultural remains of the Indians going back to the beginning of their occupation of the Canyon. The excavations were so successful that, combining information from the diggings in the Canyon and on the Plateau with our knowledge of the present descendants, and injecting a dash of poetic license (if my professional colleagues will not object), it is now possible to reconstruct the general history of the Havasupai for some 13 centuries.

Some time around 600 A.D. a few small family groups of Indians began to settle in the Colorado Plateau area above the Canyon [see map on opposite page]. They came from the west, possibly leaving an overcrowded region. (Colton named them the Cohonina, a Hopi word meaning "those who live to the west.") For a century they lived a frontier life, depending heavily on game and berries for food, searching for water sources, trying out the land for farming and settlement possibilities. After about 100 years they had learned to live off their new land so well that the population began to increase and settlements spread to all parts of the plateau. In the winter months they supplemented their farm crops by hunting near their plateau homes and in the great canyons that bordered them on two sides. It is possible that the Cataract Creek Canyon oasis was discovered during one of these early expeditions and thereafter served as a hunting base.

By 700 or 800 A.D. the plateau settlers had developed an efficient agriculture, were building some stone houses, and were making pottery with designs and decorations borrowed from their Indian neighbors in the Little Colorado and San Juan country to the north and east. In another century or so they had progressed to constructing granaries for their crops and were adopting a new style of house with what looks like a patio at one end. They also built a large, thick-walled structure which may have been a fort or a ceremonial building.

Meanwhile the population had overflowed into Cataract Creek Canyon. The canyon pioneers developed their own way of life, clearing the heavy brush, using the creek to irrigate their patches of land, and developing trails to the plateau a mile above. Possibly the tribe might eventually have split into two groups, one living primarily in the canyon, the other on the plateau. But as Colton observed, around 1100 A.D. the plateau population began to disappear, and within 100 years its settlements were deserted. Our excavations

suggested a likely explanation. It seems that the plateau dwellers, as well as some Indians from other areas, were driven into the canyons by wandering tribes of raiders. The archaeological remains show that the Cataract Creek Canyon population increased greatly at this time. The valley floor became so overcrowded that people took up residence in the rock shelters at the base of the cliffs. Furthermore, they began to build cliff dwellings in the face of the cliffs, no doubt to defend themselves against the raiders. Every avail-

CLIFF SHELTER on a high ledge of the canyon wall is shown according to the author's reconstruction. Now a ruin, it was used as a refuge from floods or enemy raiding parties.

able ledge became a home, and on the large ledges the canyon people erected elaborate structures.

Apparently by the middle of the 13th century the raiding of the area by outside bands had subsided. The Canyon people abandoned their cliff dwellings. By this time they had evolved a new way of life. To find enough food for the large valley population they had had to organize frequent hunting parties to go up on the plateau. Now these

hunting and food-gathering expeditions to the top, particularly in winter, became a fixed feature of Havasupai life. The canyon refugees could not go back to living on the plateau again, even if they had wanted to. Conditions on the old plateau had changed, as the old men may have remarked. The annual rainfall had diminished. The vegetation was no longer as lush; the flowers were not as bright. Farming on the plateau had become impossible.

So the Havasupai developed a double life: summer in the canyon, winter on the plateau. All summer they led a sedentary existence in the valley, watching the crops grow. After the harvest, when the days grew cool, they moved up to the plateau and pitched camp in the cedar thickets. But they could not stay long in any one place: the winter life of hunting and gathering wild fruits and nuts kept them on the move over the great expanses of the plateau. Their rather precarious winter existence gained some security, however, from the crop reserves they were able to bring with them from the canyon. In the spring the Havasupai went back to the canyon village to take up their sedentary farming life again.

For 300 years, until early in the 17th century, the Canyon Indians passed a tranquil existence. They had friendly relations with the Navaho, Hopi, Walapai and other neighboring tribes. Each August the Havasupai invited their neighbors to their annual harvest dance —a five-day feast of eating, dancing, trading and gambling which is still the highlight of Havasupai life today. The Havasupai culture changed little in the three centuries.

But this stability began to break down in the early 1700s. Long before Father Garcés arrived, the coming of the white man was heralded in Cataract Creek Canyon by new goods which filtered to the Havasupai from other tribes. The Spanish settlers themselves did not come near the canyon; the land of the Havasupai was of no use to them. The fact that the little canyon was well hidden from the plundering hands of the conquistadors saved the Havasupai from the fate that overtook many other Southwestern Indian tribes. They retained most of their aboriginal culture: their pottery, clay pipes, stone knives, fire drills, bone tools, bows and arrows, basketry and skin clothing. But through the Hopi they began to receive crockery, metal pans, guns, plants and cloth. When the first white man, Father Garcés, laid eyes on them, they already had horses, cattle and some Old World plants.

Although they have continued to have less contact with white people than almost any other Indian tribe, their culture has gone on adapting itself to the white man's ways. In the middle of the 19th century the unaggressive Havasupai accepted a reservation of only

SHELTERS AND GRANARIES on high ledges illustrate the near-inaccessibility of the sites in which the author excavated early Havasupai remains. A stone house with a window can be seen (upper right) and, below it, a row of granaries on a narrow ledge (bottom).

600 700 800 900 1000 1100 1200 1300 1400 1500 1600 1700 1800 1900

CHANGES OF POPULATION on the Coconino Plateau (*gray line*) and in Cataract Creek Canyon (*black line*) are shown schematically. The plateau population began to decrease in the 12th century, probably because of enemy raids followed by climatic change. The raids filled the canyon with refugees. When the raiders left, canyon population fell.

about 500 acres in the bottom of the Canyon. Secluded in their deep valley, the "people of the blue-green water" have nevertheless, by diffusion from the Hopi and other Indian neighbors and by deliberate education through Federal Government workers, moved rapidly toward immersion in American culture in recent decades. Each year several hundred tourists descend the Canyon to see their blue oasis, with beautiful waterfalls that tumble down the creek bed, and to see the gentle, cheerful Havasupai, now a small group of some 35 families. Their village, Supai, has a post office and a schoolhouse, and on occasion the villagers are treated to Hollywood movies of the "Wild West."

II

MESOAMERICA

II   MESOAMERICA

INTRODUCTION

The ancient ruins of Mesoamerica (that area encompassing much of modern Mexico, Guatemala, Belize, Salvador, and Honduras) have stimulated much archaeological research, and archaeologists now understand the outlines of the "Mesoamerican civilizational system" from its inception around 1200 B.C. until the time of the Spanish Conquest in the early sixteenth century A.D. During this 2,700 year span, ancient Mesoamerican civilization flourished in both the semiarid highlands and tropical rain-forest lowlands of the area. Although the seats of power of Mesoamerican civilization shifted through time, there were strong continuities in material, social, ideological, and other cultural practices.

Complex society first appeared in Mesoamerica in the Gulf Coast lowlands of Mexico among the Olmecs. These people built ceremonial centers, which contained small resident populations. There is much evidence for intensive labor projects in these centers, including large platforms, mounds, and monumental sculptures. The Olmecs were excellent craftsmen. They developed a complex art style and iconography featuring many motifs, including a were-jaguar. The Olmecs obtained a variety of raw materials, such as obsidian and jade, from the neighboring highlands. After a relatively brief florescence lasting about 600 years, the Olmecs declined in power as highland groups in the Valley of Oaxaca and the Basin of Mexico, who had direct access to a variety of raw materials and the potential for intensive agriculture, began to flourish.

In the Basin of Mexico, we now have evidence for the rise of several chiefdoms that competed for economic and political power throughout the first millennium B.C. Eventually, one of the competitors, Teotihuacan, emerged as the most successful. Between about 200 B.C. and A.D. 600, this site grew into a giant urban center that served as the focus for extensive economic, political, and religious interaction throughout much of Mesoamerica. While Teotihuacan was reaching its peak, the lowland Maya were building their Classic civilization in southern Mesoamerica. Although the Maya lowlands witnessed some remarkable achievements in the arts, architecture, astronomy, and sociopolitical organization, the Classic Maya never emerged as a dominant economic or political factor in Mesoamerica in the same way as Teotihuacan or its Central Mexican successors, the Toltecs and the Aztecs.

With the decline of Teotihuacan around A.D. 750, there was an interregnum period of competing centers until about A.D. 900–1000, when the Toltecs, centered at their capital of Tula to the north of the Basin of Mexico, emerged as a dominating force in the region. With the rise of the Teltecs, which marks the beginning of the Postclassic Period in Mesoamerica, militarism and mercantilism became the two main forces in the continuing development of Mesoamerican civilization. Widespread trade linked various parts of Mesoamerica.

For the first time, western Mexico and northern Mexico were drawn into the Mesoamerican orbit. There is also evidence of significant military activities, including the Toltec conquest of the Maya center of Chichen Itza in distant Yucatan.

After the decline of the Toltecs in the thirteenth century A.D., a number of small city-states in Central Mexico began to vie for power. Eventually, one of these groups, a relative latecomer to the competition, emerged as the major power. This was Tenochtitlan, the capital of the Aztecs. In the fifteenth century A.D., the Aztecs consolidated their political and economic control over much of Central Mexico and began to expand their power to other parts of Mesoamerica. Combining the militarism and mercantilism of the Toltecs with the pattern of strong centralized control found at Teotihuacan, the Aztecs started to build the largest, most complex centralized state ancient Mesoamerica had seen. Unfortunately, we will never know how far this development might have progressed, since this civilization was conquered and destroyed by Cortes and his soldiers in A.D. 1521.

Although most archaeological attention has focused on the monumental remains of the great civilizations of Mesoamerica, archaeologists have recently begun to focus their research on periods antedating the rise of complex society. In particular, archaeologists have increasingly addressed questions of the rise of agriculture and settled village life. The most complete published data on the Mesoamerican transition from a nomadic hunting and gathering way of life to a sedentary agricultural life-style come from the Tehuacan Valley, a semiarid upland valley to the south of Mexico City.

The pioneering research of the archaeologist Richard S. MacNeish and his associates in the Tehuacan Valley in the early 1960s has shown that the development of agriculture was not a revolutionary event that took place seemingly overnight and that it did not result immediately in the rise of sedentarism. Through the surveys and excavations of his interdisciplinary team, which focused on ancient flora, fauna, and general environmental conditions, MacNeish was able to establish an archaeological sequence extending from 10,000 B.C. to the Spanish Conquest in the sixteenth century A.D. MacNeish and his scientific collaborators explored the extremely dry caves along the flanks of the Tehuacan Valley, in which were preserved a variety of normally perishable remains, such as corn cobs. From these remains, MacNeish was able to reconstruct the rise of domesticated plants and agriculture. The specifics of this story are discussed in MacNeish's article "The Origins of New World Civilization."

Moreover, MacNeish has been able to present a plausible hypothesis about *how* the increased use of domesticated plants over a 5,000 year period from about 7000 to 2000 B.C. enabled the inhabitants of the Tehuacan Valley to remain in one camp for more than a single season and eventually to live in the same place all year round. *Why* this slow transition took place, however, is still the subject of much archaeological controversy. Although population pressure is often put forward as a principal cause for the transition, the archaeological evidence, at least from the Tehuacan Valley, is equivocal. Nevertheless, the process that MacNeish has documented in the Tehuacan Valley probably occurred, with varying degrees of similarity, in other highland valleys.

With the rise of agriculture and the growth of settled villages in Mesoamerica, the stage was set for the growth of more complex societies. One of the most impressive developments took place in the highland valley of Teotihuacan, just northeast of the Basin of Mexico where modern Mexico City is located. Between approximately 1000 and 200 B.C., the relatively small valley of Teotihuacan competed with a number of its neighbors in and around the Basin of Mexico for power and wealth. Toward the end of the first millennium B.C., two principal sites emerged from this competition, Teotihuacan and Cuicuilco (in the southwestern part of the Basin). This competition was cut short when a volcano near Cuicuilco erupted and covered the agricultural fields with lava, leaving Teotihuacan as the sole major power.

The recent research of Rene Millon and his colleagues has given us, for the first time, an idea of just how rapidly and how large Teotihuacan grew. As Millon discusses in his article "Teotihuacan," within a few hundred years after the fall of Cuicuilco, Teotihuacan had developed into a city of great size and complexity. Millon's intensive mapping and survey of the urban zone have shown that, by A.D. 400, the city of Teotihuacan covered 20 square kilometers and may have had over 150,000 to 200,000 people. Not only has Millon's project revealed the heretofore unappreciated size of the city, it has shown how complex was its internal economic, political, and social organization. For example, there were over 500 specialized production centers in the city. These centers manufactured the obsidian tools, pottery, and other items that provided the economic base for Teotihuacan's development.

The question of how and why Teotihuacan was able to grow to such monumental proportions is obviously of keen interest to archaeologists. Clearly, the rich obsidian resource in the Teotihuacan Valley, the potential for intensive agriculture through irrigation, and the natural access for trade to the east and south were three of the principal factors in Teotihuacan's rise to prominence. The agricultural potential of the valley could have provided the resources to feed a rapidly growing population, which could have profitably mined the obsidian, manufactured obsidian tools, and traded them.

Recent archaeological surveys by William T. Sanders and his associates have indicated the great importance of agricultural land for site location and site development in the Basin of Mexico and surrounding valleys. Moreover, Sanders has shown that irrigation was an important aspect of agricultural development well before the rise of Teotihuacan. The administrative and labor requirements of large-scale irrigation systems must also have been crucial factors in the growth of complex political entities such as Teotihuacan.

Michael D. Coe, in his article "The Chinampas of Mexico," shows how an even more intensive form of agriculture, the *chinampa* system, also contributed to cultural developments in the Basin of Mexico. Although many archaeologists might disagree with Coe's contention that *chinampas* were an important aspect of the greater Teotihuacan agricultural system in the first millennium A.D., they certainly played a critical role in the growth of ancient Mexico's last great state prior to the arrival of the Spanish—the Aztec state.

Within a relatively few years from the founding of the Aztec capital of Tenochtitlan (at modern Mexico City) in A.D. 1325, the Aztecs transformed this swampy island into one of the most highly developed urban centers in Pre-Columbian America. Through a program of land reclamation, the Aztecs literally built up their city from the swamps. A large dike was constructed across a constricted part of Lake Texcoco in order to keep this saline lake from polluting the freshwater lakes to the south. These lakes were the location of the *chinampas*, or artificially constructed plots of agricultural land. The *chinampas* were fertilized by rich mud, which was collected in boats from the swamps, and human waste and garbage recycled from Tenochtitlan. These plots yielded some of the great quantities of food needed to support the huge urban center at Tenochtitlan. In addition, the Aztecs built extensive systems of drains and aqueducts to bring fresh water from the mainland. As Coe succinctly points out, "The entire chinampa zone . . . represented a gigantic hydraulic scheme based on land drainage and the manipulation of water resources."

While the highlands of Mexico saw the rise of agriculture, settled villages, and urbanism, the tropical rain-forest lowlands of Mesoamerica also witnessed some important developments in Pre-Columbian civilization. As noted previously, the first complex society in Mesoamerica, the Olmec, rose to prominence in the Gulf Coast lowlands of Tabasco and Veracruz. The ancient Maya developed their fascinating civilization in southern Mesoamerica, cen-

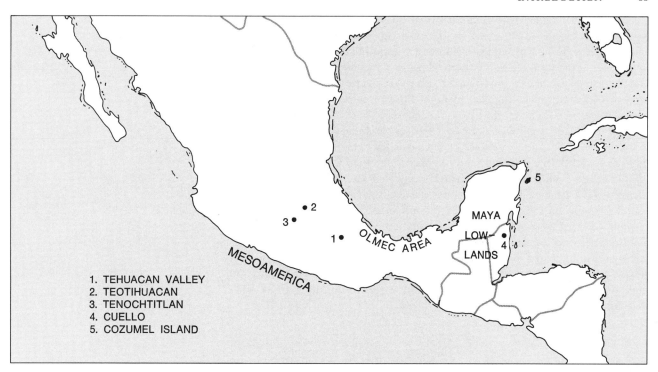

1. TEHUACAN VALLEY
2. TEOTIHUACAN
3. TENOCHTITLAN
4. CUELLO
5. COZUMEL ISLAND

A map showing the general boundaries of Mesoamerica and the locations of the archaeological sites and regions discussed in the articles in this section.

tering on the Yucatan peninsula and including parts of modern Mexico, Guatemala, Belize, Honduras, and Salvador. The well-known Maya Classic Period, which was characterized by a complex social and political organization as well as achievements in architecture, astronomy, and other intellectual areas, dates from A.D. 300–800. However, the Maya lowlands were first occupied centuries earlier.

Recent excavations by Norman Hammond at the site of Cuello in northern Belize have uncovered the earliest known remains of human occupation in the Maya lowlands. As Hammond discusses in his article "The Earliest Maya," his research has revealed a house platform that may date as early as 2500 B.C. This platform was associated with a distinctive class of pottery and evidence that the inhabitants practiced agriculture. Hammond's discoveries provide one of the earliest dates for the use of pottery in Mesoamerica, and they raise a number of questions about the invention and dispersion of pottery in the New World and the rise of sedentary agricultural villages in Mesoamerica. If Hammond's initial discoveries are confirmed, and there is every reason to believe that they will be, his research will have a great impact on Maya studies in particular and Mesoamerican studies in general.

The Cuello data have shown that the Maya lowlands were occupied more than 1,000 years earlier than previously thought. They further indicate that the growth of complex society in Maya lowlands was a much longer and slower process than archaeologists have indicated in most recent discussions of the rise of Classic Maya civilization. Older views had postulated that the jungle lowlands had first been occupied by simple village agriculturalists by about 900 B.C. Slow population growth and cultural development marked most of the first millennium B.C., with the first clear indications of the emergence of more complex social and political forms appearing by 300 B.C. The next 500 years were a time of rapid growth and increased contacts with neighboring groups. Classic Maya civilization, with its characteristic social, political, and intellectual forms, clearly had emerged by A.D. 300.

Most archaeological investigation of the Maya area has focused on the well-known Classic civilization, with its great monumental and artistic achievements. From the sudden collapse of Classic Maya civilization and the relative depopulation of the southern Maya lowlands around A.D. 800, many Maya archaeologists have inferred that Maya civilization began to decline at that time. In particular, the final phase of Pre-Columbian Maya civilization, after the fall of Chichen Itza in the thirteenth century A.D., has often been viewed as decadent. However, recent research on ancient Maya trading systems that flourished after the collapse of Classic Maya civilization, as reported in Sabloff and Rathje's "The Rise of the Maya Merchant Class," has indicated that the Late Postclassic or Decadent Period (from A.D. 1250 to 1519), rather than being a time of cultural degeneration, witnessed growing mercantile developments, mass production of goods, and an increased standard of living. Sabloff and Rathje argue that a reexamination of traditional views of the Decadent Period are necessary if we are to understand the cultural development of this neglected but fascinating period of Pre-Columbian Maya history. They further argue that careful consideration of ancient Maya merchants and their long-distance trading activities should be an important part of such reexamination.

The Origins of
New World Civilization

by Richard S. MacNeish
November 1964

*In the Mexican valley of Tehuacán bands of hunters
became urban craftsmen in the course of 12,000 years.
Their achievement raises some new questions about the
evolution of high cultures in general*

Perhaps the most significant single occurrence in human history was the development of agriculture and animal husbandry. It has been assumed that this transition from food-gathering to food production took place between 10,000 and 16,000 years ago at a number of places in the highlands of the Middle East. In point of fact the archaeological evidence for the transition, particularly the evidence for domesticated plants, is extremely meager. It is nonetheless widely accepted that the transition represented a "Neolithic Revolution," in which abundant food, a sedentary way of life and an expanding population provided the foundations on which today's high civilizations are built.

The shift from food-gathering to food production did not, however, happen only once. Until comparatively recent times the Old World was for the most part isolated from the New World. Significant contact was confined to a largely one-way migration of culturally primitive Asiatic hunting bands across the Bering Strait. In spite of this almost total absence of traffic between the hemispheres the European adventurers who reached the New World in the 16th century encountered a series of cultures almost as advanced (except in metallurgy and pyrotechnics) and quite as barbarous as their own. Indeed, some of the civilizations from Mexico to Peru possessed a larger variety of domesticated plants than did their European

conquerors and had made agricultural advances far beyond those of the Old World.

At some time, then, the transition from food-gathering to food production occurred in the New World as it had in the Old. In recent years one of the major problems for New World prehistorians has been to test the hypothesis of a Neolithic Revolution against native archaeological evidence and at the same time to document the American stage of man's initial domestication of plants (which remains almost unknown in both hemispheres).

The differences between the ways in which Old World and New World men achieved independence from the nomadic life of the hunter and gatherer are more striking than the similarities. The principal difference lies in the fact that the peoples of the Old World domesticated many animals and comparatively few plants, whereas in the New World the opposite was the case. The abundant and various herds that gave the peoples of Europe, Africa and Asia meat, milk, wool and beasts of burden were matched in the pre-Columbian New World only by a half-domesticated group of Andean cameloids: the llama, the alpaca and the vicuña. The Andean guinea pig can be considered an inferior equivalent of the Old World's domesticated rabbits and hares; elsewhere in the Americas the turkey was an equally inferior counterpart of the Eastern Hemisphere's many

varieties of barnyard fowl. In both the Old World and the New, dogs presumably predated all other domestic animals; in both beekeepers harvested honey and wax. Beyond this the New World list of domestic animals dwindles to nothing. All the cultures of the Americas, high and low alike, depended on their hunters' skill for most of their animal produce: meat and hides, furs and feathers, teeth and claws.

In contrast, the American Indian domesticated a remarkable number of plants. Except for cotton, the "water bottle" gourd, the yam and possibly the coconut (which may have been domesticated independently in each hemisphere), the kinds of crops grown in the Old World and the New were quite different. Both the white and the sweet potato, cultivated in a number of varieties, were unique to the New World. For seasoning, in place of the pepper and mustard of the Old World, the peoples of the New World raised vanilla and at least two kinds of chili. For edible seeds they grew amaranth, chive, panic grass, sunflower, quinoa, apazote, chocolate, the peanut, the common bean and four other kinds of beans: lima, summer, tepary and jack.

In addition to potatoes the Indians cultivated other root crops, including manioc, oca and more than a dozen other South American plants. In place of the Old World melons, the related plants brought to domestication in the New World were the pumpkin, the

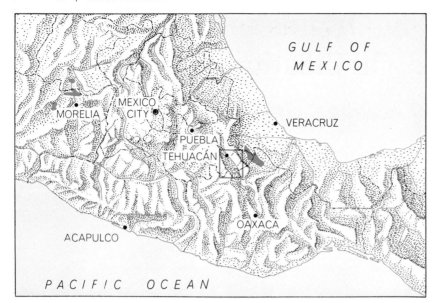

TEHUACÁN VALLEY is a narrow desert zone in the mountains on the boundary between the states of Puebla and Oaxaca. It is one of the three areas in southern Mexico selected during the search for early corn on the grounds of dryness (which helps to preserve ancient plant materials) and highland location (corn originally having been a wild highland grass).

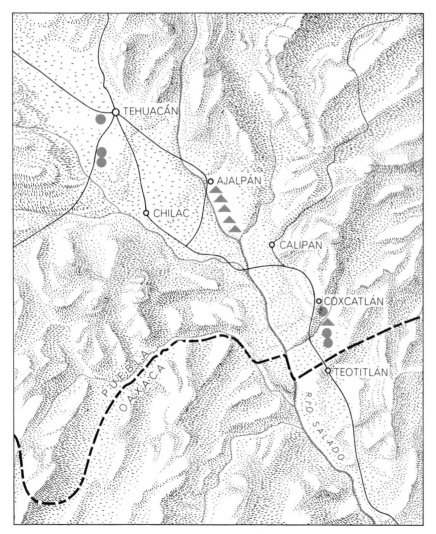

SIX CAVES (*dots*) and six open-air sites (*triangles*) have been investigated in detail by the author and his colleagues. Coxcatlán cave (*top dot at right*), where early corn was found in 1960, has the longest habitation record: from well before 7000 B.C. until A.D. 1500.

gourd, the chayote and three or four distinct species of what we call squash. Fruits brought under cultivation in the Americas included the tomato, avocado, pineapple, guava, elderberry and papaya. The pioneering use of tobacco—smoked in pipes, in the form of cigars and even in the form of cane cigarettes, some of which had one end stuffed with fibers to serve as a filter—must also be credited to the Indians.

Above all of these stood Indian corn, *Zea mays*, the only important wild grass in the New World to be transformed into a food grain as the peoples of the Old World had transformed their native grasses into wheat, barley, rye, oats and millet. From Chile to the valley of the St. Lawrence in Canada, one or another of 150 varieties of Indian corn was the staple diet of the pre-Columbian peoples. As a food grain or as fodder, corn remains the most important single crop in the Americas today (and the third largest in the world). Because of its dominant position in New World agriculture, prehistorians have long been confident that if they could find out when and where corn was first domesticated, they might also uncover the origins of New World civilization.

Until little more than a generation ago investigators of this question were beset by twin difficulties. First, research in both Central America and South America had failed to show that any New World high culture significantly predated the Christian era. Second, botanical studies of the varieties of corn and its wild relatives had led more to conflict than to clarity in regard to the domesticated plant's most probable wild predecessor [see "The Mystery of Corn," by Paul C. Mangelsdorf; SCIENTIFIC AMERICAN Offprint 26]. Today, thanks to close cooperation between botanists and archaeologists, both difficulties have almost vanished. At least one starting point for New World agricultural activity has been securely established as being between 5,000 and 9,000 years ago. At the same time botanical analysis of fossil corn ears, grains and pollen, together with plain dirt archaeology, have solved a number of the mysteries concerning the wild origin and domestic evolution of corn. What follows is a review of the recent developments that have done so much to increase our understanding of this key period in New World prehistory.

The interest of botanists in the history of corn is largely practical: they study the genetics of corn in order to produce improved hybrids. After the wild ancestors of corn had been sought for nearly a century the search had narrowed to two tassel-bearing New World grasses—teosinte and *Tripsacum*—that had features resembling the domesticated plant. On the basis of crossbreeding experiments and other genetic studies, however, Paul C. Mangelsdorf of Harvard University and other investigators concluded in the 1940's that neither of these plants could be the original ancestor of corn. Instead teosinte appeared to be the product of the accidental crossbreeding of true corn and *Tripsacum*. Mangelsdorf advanced the hypothesis that the wild progenitor of corn was none other than corn itself—probably a popcorn with its kernels encased in pods.

Between 1948 and 1960 a number of discoveries proved Mangelsdorf's contention to be correct. I shall present these discoveries not in their strict chronological order but rather in their order of importance. First in importance, then, were analyses of pollen found in "cores" obtained in 1953 by drilling into the lake beds on which Mexico City is built. At levels that were estimated to be about 80,000 years old—perhaps 50,000 years older than the earliest known human remains in the New World—were found grains of corn pollen. There could be no doubt that the pollen was from wild corn, and thus two aspects of the ancestry of corn were clarified. First, a form of wild corn has been in existence for 80,000 years, so that corn can indeed be descended from itself. Second, wild corn had flourished in the highlands of Mexico. As related archaeological discoveries will make plain, this geographical fact helped to narrow the potential range—from the southwestern U.S. to Peru—within which corn was probably first domesticated.

The rest of the key discoveries, involving the close cooperation of archaeologist and botanist, all belong to the realm of paleobotany. In the summer of 1948, for example, Herbert Dick, a graduate student in anthropology who had been working with Mangelsdorf, explored a dry rock-shelter in New Mexico called Bat Cave. Digging down through six feet of accumulated deposits, he and his colleagues found numerous remains of ancient corn, culminating in some tiny corncobs at the lowest level. Carbon-14 dating indicated that these cobs were between 4,000 and 5,000 years old. A few months later, exploring the La Perra cave in the state of Tamaulipas far to the north of Mexico City, I found similar corncobs that proved to be about 4,500 years old. The oldest cobs at both sites came close to fitting the description Mangelsdorf had given of a hypothetical ancestor of the pod-popcorn type. The cobs, however, were clearly those of domesticated corn.

These two finds provided the basis for intensified archaeological efforts to find sites where the first evidences of corn would be even older. The logic was simple: A site old enough should have a level of wild corn remains older than the most ancient domesticated cobs. I continued my explorations near the La Perra cave and excavated a number of other sites in northeastern Mexico. In them I found more samples of ancient corn, but they were no older than those that had already been discovered. Robert Lister, another of Mangelsdorf's co-workers, also found primitive corn in a cave called Swallow's Nest in the Mexican state of Chihuahua, northwest of where I was working, but his finds were no older than mine.

If nothing older than domesticated corn of about 3000 B.C. could be found to the north of Mexico City, it seemed logical to try to the south. In 1958 I went off to look for dry caves and early corn in Guatemala and Honduras. The 1958 diggings produced nothing useful, so in 1959 I moved northward into Chiapas, Mexico's southernmost state. There were no corncobs to be found,

EXCAVATION of Coxcatlán cave required the removal of one-meter squares of cave floor over an area 25 meters long by six meters wide until bedrock was reached at a depth of almost five meters. In this way 28 occupation levels, attributable to seven distinctive culture phases, were discovered. Inhabitants of the three lowest levels lived by hunting and by collecting wild-plant foods.

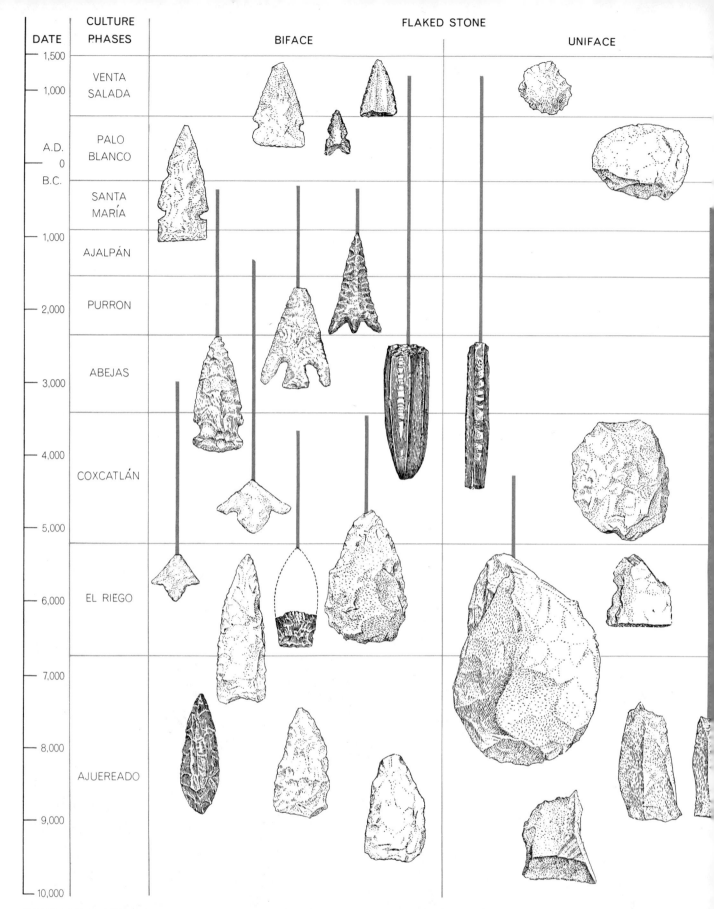

STONE ARTIFACTS from various Tehuacán sites are arrayed in two major categories: those shaped by chipping and flaking (*left*) and those shaped by grinding and pecking (*right*). Implements that have been chipped on one face only are separated from those that show bifacial workmanship; both groups are reproduced at half their natural size. The ground stone objects are not drawn to a common scale. The horizontal lines define the nine culture phases thus far distinguished in the valley. Vertical lines (*color*) indicate the extent to which the related artifact is known in cultures other than the one in which it is placed. At Tehuacán the evolution of civilization failed to follow the classic pattern established by the Neolithic Revolution in the Old World. For instance, the mortars,

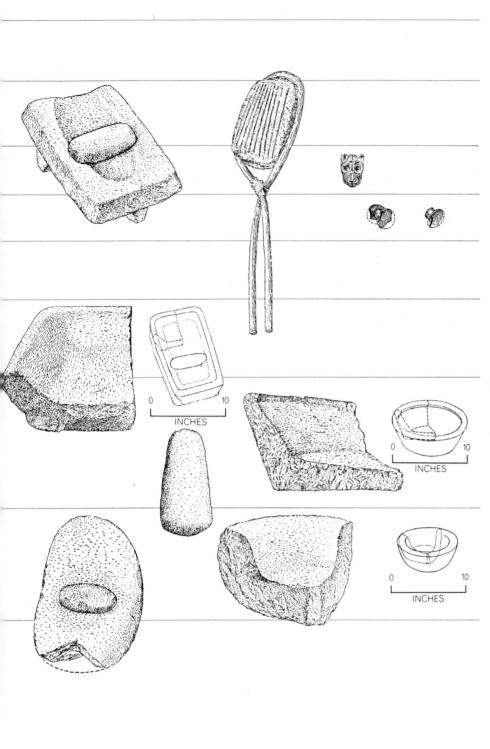

pestles and other ground stone implements that first appear in the El Riego culture phase antedate the first domestication of corn by 1,500 years or more. Not until the Abejas phase, nearly 2,000 years later (marked by sizable obsidian cores and blades and by grinding implements that closely resemble the modern mano and metate), do the earliest village sites appear. More than 1,000 years later, in the Ajalpán phase, earplugs for personal adornment occur. The grooved, withe-bound stone near the top is a pounder for making bark cloth.

but one cave yielded corn pollen that also dated only to about 3000 B.C. The clues provided by paleobotany now appeared plain. Both to the north of Mexico City and in Mexico City itself (as indicated by the pollen of domesticated corn in the upper levels of the drill cores) the oldest evidence of domesticated corn was no more ancient than about 3000 B.C. Well to the south of Mexico City the oldest date was the same. The area that called for further search should therefore lie south of Mexico City but north of Chiapas.

Two additional considerations enabled me to narrow the area of search even more. First, experience had shown that dry locations offered the best chance of finding preserved specimens of corn. Second, the genetic studies of Mangelsdorf and other investigators indicated that wild corn was originally a highland grass, very possibly able to survive the rigorous climate of highland desert areas. Poring over the map of southern Mexico, I singled out three large highland desert areas: one in the southern part of the state of Oaxaca, one in Guerrero and one in southern Puebla.

Oaxaca yielded nothing of interest, so I moved on to Puebla to explore a dry highland valley known as Tehuacán. My local guides and I scrambled in and out of 38 caves and finally struck pay dirt in the 39th. This was a small rock-shelter near the village of Coxcatlán in the southern part of the valley of Tehuacán. On February 21, 1960, we dug up six corncobs, three of which looked more primitive and older than any I had seen before. Analysis in the carbon-14 laboratory at the University of Michigan confirmed my guess by dating these cobs as 5,600 years old—a good 500 years older than any yet found in the New World.

With this find the time seemed ripe for a large-scale, systematic search. If we had indeed arrived at a place where corn had been domesticated and New World civilization had first stirred, the closing stages of the search would require the special knowledge of many experts. Our primary need was to obtain the sponsorship of an institution interested and experienced in such research, and we were fortunate enough to enlist exactly the right sponsor: the Robert S. Peabody Foundation for Archaeology of Andover, Mass. Funds for the project were supplied by the National Science Foundation and by the agricultural branch of the Rockefeller

EVOLUTION OF CORN at Tehuacán starts (*far left*) with a fragmentary cob of wild corn of 5000 B.C. date. Next (*left to right*) are an early domesticated cob of 4000 B.C., an early hybrid variety of 3000 B.C. and an early variety of modern corn of 1000 B.C. Last (*far right*) is an entirely modern cob of the time of Christ. All are shown four-fifths of natural size.

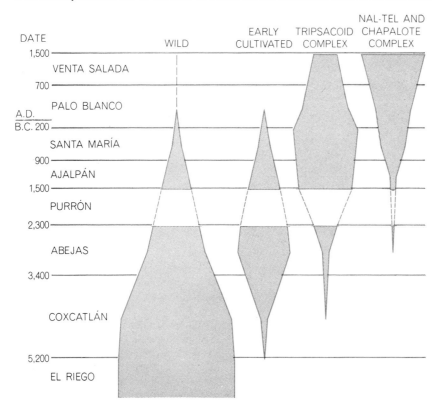

MAIN VARIETIES OF CORN changed in their relative abundance at Tehuacán between the time of initial cultivation during the Coxcatlán culture phase and the arrival of the conquistadors. Abundant at first, wild corn had become virtually extinct by the start of the Christian era, as had the early cultivated (but not hybridized) varieties. Thereafter the hybrids of the tripsacoid complex (produced by interbreeding wild corn with introduced varieties of corn-*Tripsacum* or corn-teosinte hybrids) were steadily replaced by two still extant types of corn, Nal-Tel and Chapalote. Minor varieties of late corn are not shown.

Foundation in Mexico, which is particularly interested in the origins of corn. The project eventually engaged nearly 50 experts in many specialties, not only archaeology and botany (including experts on many plants other than corn) but also zoology, geography, geology, ecology, genetics, ethnology and other disciplines.

The Coxcatlán cave, where the intensive new hunt had begun, turned out to be our richest dig. Working downward, we found that the cave had 28 separate occupation levels, the earliest of which may date to about 10,000 B.C. This remarkably long sequence has one major interruption: the period between 2300 B.C. and 900 B.C. The time from 900 B.C. to A.D. 1500, however, is represented by seven occupation levels. In combination with our findings in the Purrón cave, which contains 25 floors that date from about 7000 B.C. to 500 B.C., we have an almost continuous record (the longest interruption is less than 500 years) of nearly 12,000 years of prehistory. This is by far the longest record for any New World area.

All together we undertook major excavations at 12 sites in the valley of Tehuacán [*see bottom illustration on page* 98]. Of these only five caves—Coxcatlán, Purrón, San Marcos, Tecorral and El Riego East—contained remains of ancient corn. But these and the other stratified sites gave us a wealth of additional information about the people who inhabited the valley over a span of 12,000 years. In four seasons of digging, from 1961 through 1964, we reaped a vast archaeological harvest. This includes nearly a million individual remains of human activity, more than 1,000 animal bones (including those of extinct antelopes and horses), 80,000 individual wild-plant remains and some 25,000 specimens of corn. The artifacts arrange themselves into significant sequences of stone tools, textiles and pottery. They provide an almost continuous picture of the rise of civilization in the valley of Tehuacán. From the valley's geology, from the shells of its land snails, from the pollen and other remains of its plants and from a variety of other relics our group of specialists has traced the changes in climate, physical environment and plant and animal life that took place during the 12,000 years. They have even been able to tell (from the kinds of plant remains in various occupation levels) at what seasons of the year many of the floors in the caves were occupied.

Outstanding among our many finds was a collection of minuscule corncobs that we tenderly extracted from the lowest of five occupation levels at the San Marcos cave. They were only about 20 millimeters long, no bigger than the filter tip of a cigarette [*see top illustration on opposite page*], but under a magnifying lens one could see that they were indeed miniature ears of corn, with sockets that had once contained kernels enclosed in pods. These cobs proved to be some 7,000 years old. Mangelsdorf is convinced that this must be wild corn—the original parent from which modern corn is descended.

Cultivated corn, of course, cannot survive without man's intervention; the dozens of seeds on each cob are enveloped by a tough, thick husk that prevents them from scattering. Mangelsdorf has concluded that corn's wild progenitor probably consisted of a single seed spike on the stalk, with a few pod-covered ovules arrayed on the spike and a pollen-bearing tassel attached to the spike's end [*see bottom illustration at right*]. The most primitive cobs we unearthed in the valley of Tehuacán fulfilled these specifications. Each had the stump of a tassel at the end, each had borne kernels of the pod-popcorn type and each had been covered with only a light husk consisting of two leaves. These characteristics would have allowed the plant to disperse its seeds at maturity; the pods would then have protected the seeds until conditions were appropriate for germination.

The people of the valley of Tehuacán lived for thousands of years as collectors of wild vegetable and animal foods before they made their first timid efforts as agriculturists. It would therefore be foolhardy to suggest that the inhabitants of this arid highland pocket of Mexico were the first or the only people in the Western Hemisphere to bring wild corn under cultivation. On the contrary, the New World's invention of agriculture will probably prove to be geographically fragmented. What can be said for the people of Tehuacán is that they are the first whose evolution from primitive food collectors to civilized agriculturists has been traced in detail. As yet we have no such complete story either for the Old World or for other parts of the New World. This story is as follows.

From a hazy beginning some 12,000 years ago until about 7000 B.C. the people of Tehuacán were few in number. They wandered the valley from season to season in search of jackrabbits, rats, birds, turtles and other small animals, as well as such plant foods as be-

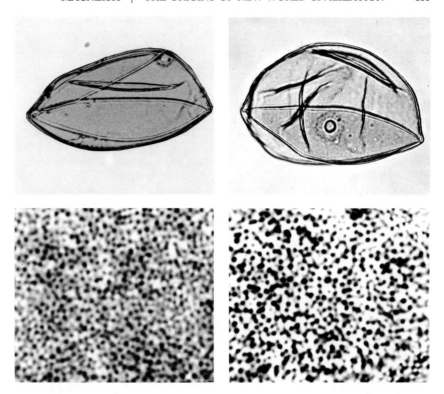

ANTIQUITY OF CORN in the New World was conclusively demonstrated when grains of pollen were found in drilling cores taken from Mexico City lake-bottom strata estimated to be 80,000 years old. Top two photographs (*magnification 435 diameters*) compare the ancient corn pollen (*left*) with modern pollen (*right*). Lower photographs (*magnification 4,500 diameters*) reveal similar ancient (*left*) and modern (*right*) pollen surface markings. The analysis and photographs are the work of Elso S. Barghoorn of Harvard University.

THREE NEW WORLD GRASSES are involved in the history of domesticated corn. Wild corn (*reconstruction at left*) was a pod-pop variety in which the male efflorescence grew from the end of the cob. Teosinte (*center*) and *Tripsacum* (*right*) are corn relatives that readily hybridized with wild and cultivated corn. Modern corn came from such crosses.

came available at different times of the year. Only occasionally did they manage to kill one of the now extinct species of horses and antelopes whose bones mark the lowest cave strata. These people used only a few simple implements of flaked stone: leaf-shaped projectile points, scrapers and engraving tools. We have named this earliest culture period the Ajuereado phase [*see illustration on pages 100 and 101*].

Around 6700 B.C. this simple pattern changed and a new phase—which we have named the El Riego culture from the cave where its first evidences appear—came into being. From then until about 5000 B.C. the people shifted from being predominantly trappers and hunters to being predominantly collectors of plant foods. Most of the plants they collected were wild, but they had domesticated squashes (starting with the species *Cucurbita mixta*) and avocados, and they also ate wild varieties of beans, amaranth and chili peppers. Among the flaked-stone implements, choppers appear. Entirely new kinds of stone tools—grinders, mortars, pestles and pounders of polished stone—are found in large numbers. During the growing season some families evidently gathered in temporary settlements, but these groups broke up into one-family bands during the leaner periods of the year. A number of burials dating from this culture phase hint at the possibility of part-time priests or witch doctors who directed the ceremonies involving the dead. The El Riego culture, however, had no corn.

By about 5000 B.C. a new phase, which we call the Coxcatlán culture,

had evolved. In this period only 10 percent of the valley's foodstuffs came from domestication rather than from collecting, hunting or trapping, but the list of domesticated plants is long. It includes corn, the water-bottle gourd, two species of squash, the amaranth, black and white zapotes, the tepary bean (*Phaseolus acutifolius*), the jack bean (*Canavalia ensiformis*), probably the common bean (*Phaseolus vulgaris*) and chili peppers.

Coxcatlán projectile points tend to be smaller than their predecessors; scrapers and choppers, however, remain much the same. The polished stone implements include forerunners of the classic New World roller-and-stone device for grinding grain: the mano and metate. There was evidently enough surplus energy among the people to allow the laborious hollowing out of stone water jugs and bowls.

It was in the phase following the Coxcatlán that the people of Tehuacán made the fundamental shift. By about 3400 B.C. the food provided by agriculture rose to about 30 percent of the total, domesticated animals (starting with the dog) made their appearance, and the people formed their first fixed settlements—small pit-house villages. By this stage (which we call the Abejas culture) they lived at a subsistence level that can be regarded as a foundation for the beginning of civilization. In about 2300 B.C. this gave way to the Purrón culture, marked by the cultivation of more hybridized types of corn and the manufacture of pottery.

Thereafter the pace of civilization in

the valley speeded up greatly. The descendants of the Purrón people developed a culture (called Ajalpán) that from about 1500 B.C. on involved a more complex village life, refinements of pottery and more elaborate ceremonialism, including the development of a figurine cult, perhaps representing family gods. This culture led in turn to an even more sophisticated one (which we call Santa María) that started about 850 B.C. Taking advantage of the valley's streams, the Santa María peoples of Tehuacán began to grow their hybrid corn in irrigated fields. Our surveys indicate a sharp rise in population. Temple mounds were built, and artifacts show signs of numerous contacts with cultures outside the valley. The Tehuacán culture in this period seems to have been strongly influenced by that of the Olmec people who lived to the southeast along the coast of Veracruz.

By about 200 B.C. the outside influence on Tehuacán affairs shifted from that of the Olmec of the east coast to that of Monte Alban to the south and west. The valley now had large irrigation projects and substantial hilltop ceremonial centers surrounded by villages. In this Palo Blanco phase some of the population proceeded to full-time specialization in various occupations, including the development of a salt industry. New domesticated food products appeared—the turkey, the tomato, the peanut and the guava. In the next period—Venta Salada, starting about A.D. 700—Monte Alban influences gave way to the influence of the Mixtecs. This period saw the rise of true

COXCATLÁN CAVE BURIAL, dating to about A.D. 100, contained the extended body of an adolescent American Indian, wrapped in a pair of cotton blankets with brightly colored stripes. This bundle in turn rested on sticks and the whole was wrapped in bark cloth.

cities in the valley, of an agricultural system that provided some 85 percent of the total food supply, of trade and commerce, a standing army, large-scale irrigation projects and a complex religion. Finally, just before the Spanish Conquest, the Aztecs took over from the Mixtecs.

Our archaeological study of the valley of Tehuacán, carried forward in collaboration with workers in so many other disciplines, has been gratifyingly productive. Not only have we documented one example of the origin of domesticated corn but also comparative studies of other domesticated plants have indicated that there were multiple centers of plant domestication in the Americas. At least for the moment we have at Tehuacán not only evidence of the earliest village life in the New World but also the first (and worst) pottery in Mexico and a fairly large sample of skeletons of some of the earliest Indians yet known.

Even more important is the fact that we at last have one New World example of the development of a culture from savagery to civilization. Preliminary analysis of the Tehuacán materials indicate that the traditional hypothesis about the evolution of high cultures may have to be reexamined and modified. In southern Mexico many of the characteristic elements of the Old World's Neolithic Revolution fail to appear suddenly in the form of a new culture complex or a revolutionized way of life. For example, tools of ground (rather than chipped) stone first occur at Tehuacán about 6700 B.C., and plant domestication begins at least by 5000 B.C. The other classic elements of the Old World Neolithic, however, are slow to appear. Villages are not found until around 3000 B.C., nor pottery until around 2300 B.C., and a sudden increase in population is delayed until 500 B.C. Reviewing this record, I think more in terms of Neolithic "evolution" than "revolution."

Our preliminary researches at Tehuacán suggest rich fields for further exploration. There is need not only for detailed investigations of the domestication and development of other New World food plants but also for attempts to obtain similar data for the Old World. Then—perhaps most challenging of all —there is the need for comparative studies of the similarities and differences between evolving cultures in the Old World and the New to determine the hows and whys of the rise of civilization itself.

SOPHISTICATED FIGURINE of painted pottery is one example of the artistic capacity of Tehuacán village craftsmen. This specimen, 2,900 years old, shows Olmec influences.

Teotihuacán

by René Millon
June 1967

The first and largest city of the pre-Columbian New World arose in the Valley of Mexico during the first millenium A.D. At its height the metropolis covered a larger area than imperial Rome

When the Spaniards conquered Mexico, they described Montezuma's capital Tenochtitlán in such vivid terms that for centuries it seemed that the Aztec stronghold must have been the greatest city of pre-Columbian America. Yet only 25 miles to the north of Tenochtitlán was the site of a city that had once been even more impressive. Known as Teotihuacán, it had risen, flourished and fallen hundreds of years before the conquistadors entered Mexico. At the height of its power, around A.D. 500, Teotihuacán was larger than imperial Rome. For more than half a millennium it was to Middle America what Rome, Benares or Mecca have been to the Old World: at once a religious and cultural capital and a major economic and political center.

Unlike many of the Maya settlements to the south, in both Mexico and Guatemala, Teotihuacán was never a "lost" city. The Aztecs were still worshiping at its sacred monuments at the time of the Spanish Conquest, and scholarly studies of its ruins have been made since the middle of the 19th century. Over the past five years, however, a concerted program of investigation has yielded much new information about this early American urban center.

In the Old World the first civilizations were associated with the first cities, but both in Middle America and in Peru the rise of civilization does not seem to have occurred in an urban setting. As far as we can tell today, the foundation for the earliest civilization in Middle America was laid in the first millennium B.C. by a people we know as the Olmecs. None of the major Olmec centers discovered so far is a city. Instead these centers—the most important of which are located in the forested lowlands along the Gulf of Mexico on the narrow Isthmus of Tehuantepec—were of a ceremonial character, with small permanent populations probably consisting of priests and their attendants.

The Olmecs and those who followed them left to many other peoples of Middle America, among them the builders of Teotihuacán, a heritage of religious beliefs, artistic symbolism and other cultural traditions. Only the Teotihuacanos, however, created an urban civilization of such vigor that it significantly influenced the subsequent development of most other Middle American civilizations—urban and nonurban—down to the time of the Aztecs. It is hard to say exactly why this happened, but at least some of the contributing factors are evident. The archaeological record suggests the following sequence of events.

A settlement of moderate size existed at Teotihuacán fairly early in the first century B.C. At about the same time a number of neighboring religious centers were flourishing. One was Cuicuilco, to the southwest of Teotihuacán in the Valley of Mexico; another was Cholula, to the east in the Valley of Puebla. The most important influences shaping the "Teotihuacán way" probably stemmed from centers such as these. Around the time of Christ, Teotihuacán began to grow rapidly, and between A.D. 100 and 200 its largest religious monument was raised on the site of an earlier shrine. Known today as the Pyramid of the Sun, it was as large at the base as the great pyramid of Cheops in Egypt [see *bottom illustration on page 114*].

The powerful attraction of a famous holy place is not enough, of course, to explain Teotihuacán's early growth or later importance. The city's strategic location was one of a number of material factors that contributed to its rise. Teotihuacán lies astride the narrow waist of a valley that is the best route between the Valley of Mexico and the Valley of Puebla. The Valley of Puebla, in turn, is the gateway to the lowlands along the Gulf of Mexico.

The lower part of Teotihuacán's valley is a rich alluvial plain, watered by permanent springs and thus independent of the uncertainties of highland rainfall. The inhabitants of the valley seem early to have dug channels to create an irrigation system and to provide their growing city with water. Even today a formerly swampy section at the edge of the ancient city is carved by channels into "chinampas": small artificial islands that are intensively farmed. Indeed, it is possible that this form of agriculture, which is much better known as it was practiced in Aztec times near Tenochtitlán, was invented centuries earlier by the people of Teotihuacán.

The valley had major deposits of obsidian, the volcanic glass used all over ancient Middle America to make cutting and scraping tools and projectile points. Obsidian mining in the valley was apparently most intensive during the city's early years. Later the Teotihuacanos appear to have gained control of deposits of obsidian north of the Valley of Mexico that were better suited than the local material to the mass production of blade implements. Trade in raw obsidian and obsidian implements became increasingly important to the economy of Teotihuacán, reaching a peak toward the middle of the first millennium A.D.

The recent investigation of Teotihuacán has been carried forward by specialists working on three independent but related projects. One project was a monumental program of excavation and reconstruction undertaken by Mexico's National Institute of Anthropology, headed by Eusebio Dávalos. From 1962 to 1964 archaeologists under the direction of Ignacio Bernal, director of the

National Museum of Anthropology, unearthed and rebuilt a number of the structures that lie along the city's principal avenue ("the Street of the Dead"); they have also restored Teotihuacán's second main pyramid ("the Pyramid of the Moon"), which lies at the avenue's northern end. Two of the city's four largest structures, the Pyramid of the Sun and the Citadel, within which stands the Temple of Quetzalcoatl, had been cleared and restored in the 1900's and the 1920's respectively. Among other notable achievements, the National Institute's work brought to light some of the city's finest mural paintings.

As the Mexican archaeologists were at work a group under the direction of William T. Sanders of Pennsylvania State University conducted an intensive study of the ecology and the rural-settlement patterns of the valley. Another group, from the University of Rochester, initiated a mapping project under my direction. This last effort, which is still under way, involves preparing a detailed topographic map on which all the city's several thousand structures will be located. The necessary information is being secured by the examination of surface remains, supplemented by small-scale excavations. One result of our work has been to demonstrate how radically different Teotihuacán was from all other settlements of its time in Middle America. It was here that the New World's urban revolution exploded into being.

It had long been clear that the center of Teotihuacán was planned, but it soon became apparent to us that the extent and magnitude of the planning went far beyond the center. Our mapping revealed that the city's streets and the large majority of its buildings had been laid out along the lines of a precise grid aligned with the city center. The grid was established in Teotihuacán's formative days, but it may have been more intensively exploited later, perhaps in relation to "urban renewal" projects undertaken when the city had become rich and powerful.

The prime direction of the grid is slightly east of north (15.5 degrees). The basic modular unit of the plan is close to 57 meters. A number of residential structures are squares of this size. The plan of many of the streets seems to repeat various multiples of the 57-meter unit. The city's major avenues, which run parallel to the north-south axis, are spaced at regular intervals. Even the river running through the center of the city was canalized to conform to the grid. Miles from the city center the remains of buildings are oriented to the grid, even when they were built on slopes that ran counter to it. A small design composed of concentric circles divided into quadrants may have served as a standard surveyor's mark; it is sometimes pecked into the floors of buildings and sometimes into bare bedrock. One such pair of marks two miles apart forms a line

exactly perpendicular to the city's north-south axis. The achievement of this kind of order obviously calls for an initial vision that is both audacious and self-confident.

A city planner's description of Teotihuacán would begin not with the monumental Pyramid of the Sun but with the two complexes of structures that form the city center. These are the Citadel and the Great Compound, lying respectively to the east and west of the city's main north-south avenue, the Street of the Dead. The names given the various structures and features of Teotihuacán are not, incidentally, the names by which the Teotihuacanos knew them. Some come from Spanish translations of Aztec names; others were bestowed by earlier archaeologists or by our mappers and are often the place names used by the local people.

The Street of the Dead forms the main axis of the city. At its northern end it stops at the Pyramid of the Moon, and

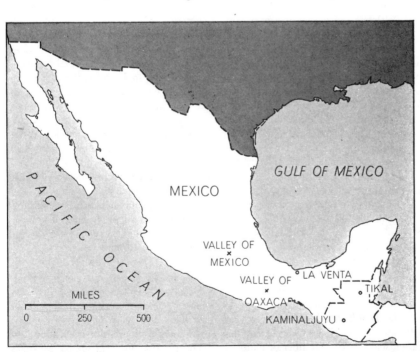

EARLY CIVILIZATION in Middle America appeared first in the lowlands along the Gulf of Mexico at such major centers of Olmec culture as La Venta. Soon thereafter a number of ceremonial centers appeared in the highlands, particularly in the valleys of Oaxaca, Puebla and Mexico. Kaminaljuyu and Tikal, Maya centers respectively in highlands and lowlands of what is now Guatemala, came under Teotihuacán's influence at the height of its power.

CEREMONIAL HEART of Teotihuacán is seen in an aerial photograph looking southeast toward Cerro Patlachique, one of a pair of mountains that flank the narrow valley dominated by the city. The large pyramid in

we have found that to the south it extends for two miles beyond the Citadel-Compound complex. The existence of a subordinate axis running east and west had not been suspected until our mappers discovered one broad avenue running more than two miles to the east of the Citadel and a matching avenue extending the same distance westward from the Compound.

To make it easier to locate buildings over so large an area we imposed our own 500-meter grid on the city, orienting it to the Street of the Dead and using the center of the city as the zero point of the system [see bottom illustration, p. 113]. The heavy line defining the limits of the city was determined by walking around the perimeter of the city and examining evidence on the surface to establish where its outermost remains end. The line traces a zone free of such remains that is at least 300 meters wide and that sharply separates the city from the countryside. The Street of the Dead,

East Avenue and West Avenue divide Teotihuacán into quadrants centered on the Citadel-Compound complex. We do not know if these were formally recognized as administrative quarters of the city, as they were in Tenochtitlán. It is nonetheless possible that they may have been, since there are a number of other similarities between the two cities.

Indeed, during the past 25 years Mexican scholars have argued for a high degree of continuity in customs and beliefs from the Aztecs back to the Teotihuacanos, based partly on an assumed continuity in language. This hypothetical continuity, which extends through the intervening Toltec times, provides valuable clues in interpreting archaeological evidence. For example, the unity of religion and politics that archaeologists postulate at Teotihuacán is reinforced by what is known of Aztec society.

The public entrance of the Citadel is a monumental staircase on the Street of the Dead. Inside the Citadel a plaza

opens onto the Temple of Quetzalcoatl, the principal sacred building in this area. The temple's façade represents the most successful integration of architecture and sculpture so far discovered at Teotihuacán [see bottom illustration on page 116].

The Great Compound, across the street from the Citadel, had gone unrecognized as a major structure until our survey. We found that it differs from all other known structures at Teotihuacán and that in area it is the city's largest. Its main components are two great raised platforms. These form a north and a south wing and are separated by broad entrances at the level of the street on the east and west. The two wings thus flank a plaza somewhat larger than the one within the Citadel. Few of the structures on the platforms seem to have been temples or other religious buildings. Most of them face away from the Street of the Dead, whereas almost all the other known structures along the avenue face toward it.

the foreground is the Pyramid of the Moon. The larger one beyond it is the Pyramid of the Sun. Many of the more than 100 smaller religious structures that line the city's central avenue, the Street of the Dead, are visible in the photograph. South of the Pyramid of the Sun and east of the central avenue is the large enclosure known as the Citadel. It and the Great Compound, a matching structure not visible in the photograph, formed the city's center. More than 4,000 additional buildings, most no longer visible, spread for miles beyond the center. At the peak of Teotihuacán's power, around A.D. 500, the population of the city was more than 50,000.

One therefore has the impression that the Compound was not devoted to religious affairs. In the Citadel there are clusters of rooms to the north and south of the Temple of Quetzalcoatl, but the overall effect conveyed by the temples and the other buildings that surround the Citadel's plaza is one of a political center in a sacred setting. Perhaps some of its rooms housed the high priests of Teotihuacán.

The plaza of the Compound is a strategically located open space that could have been the city's largest marketplace. The buildings that overlook this plaza could have been at least partly devoted to the administration of the economic affairs of the city. Whatever their functions were, the Citadel and the Compound are the heart of the city. Together they form a majestic spatial unit,

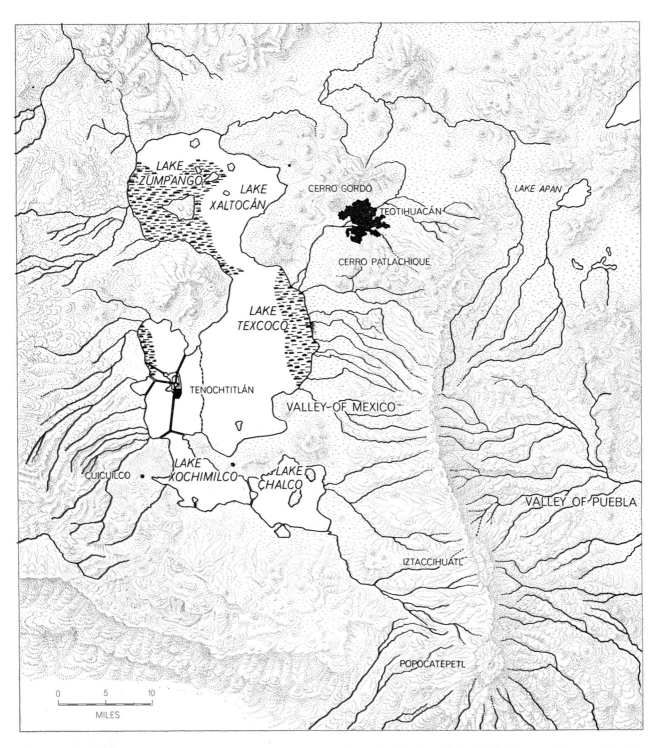

VALLEY OF MEXICO was dominated by shallow lakes in late pre-Hispanic times; in the rainy season they coalesced into a single body of water. Teotihuacán was strategically located; it commanded a narrow valley a few miles northeast of the lakes that provided the best route between the Valley of Mexico and the Valley of Puebla, which leads to the lowlands along the Gulf of Mexico (*see map at bottom of page 108*]. It was an important center of trade and worship from 100 B.C. until about A.D. 750. Centuries after its fall the Aztec capital of Tenochtitlán grew up in the western shallows of Lake Texcoco, 25 miles from the earlier metropolis.

a central island surrounded by more open ground than is found in any other part of Teotihuacán.

The total area of the city was eight square miles. Not counting ritual structures, more than 4,000 buildings, most of them apartment houses, were built to shelter the population. At the height of Teotihuacán's power, in the middle of the first millennium A.D., the population certainly exceeded 50,000 and was probably closer to 100,000. This is not a particularly high figure compared with Old World religious-political centers; today the population of Mecca is some 130,000 and that of Benares more than 250,000 (to which is added an annual influx of a million pilgrims). One reason Teotihuacán did not have a larger population was that its gleaming lime-plastered residential structures were only

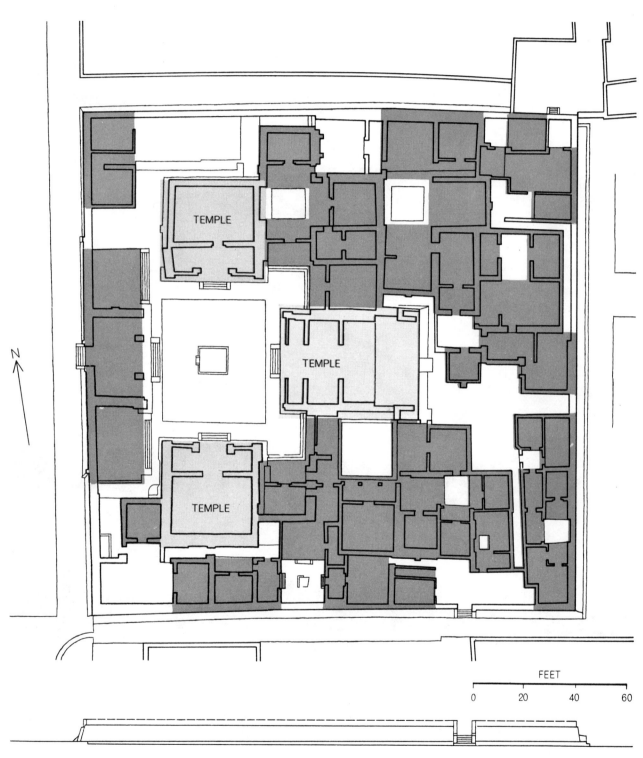

SOUTH ELEVATION

APARTMENT HOUSE typical of the city's many multiroomed dwellings was excavated in 1961 by Laurette Séjourné. The outer walls of the compound conform with the 57-meter module favored by the city's planners. Within its forbidding exterior (*see south façade at bottom of illustration*) individual apartments comprised several rooms grouped around unroofed patios (*smaller white areas*).

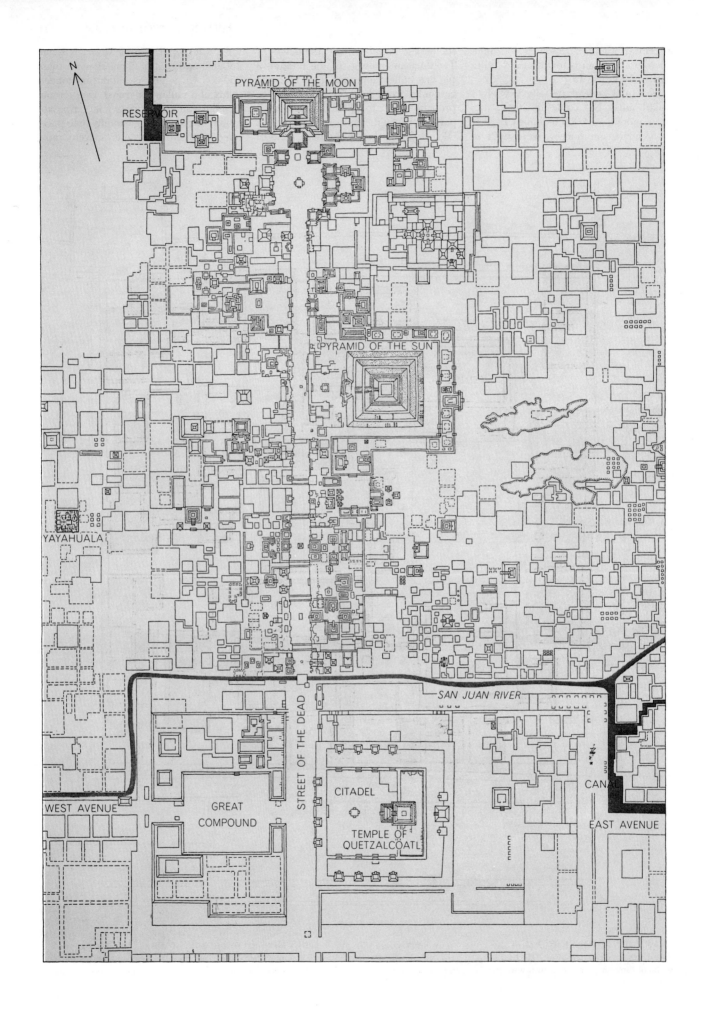

one story high. Although most of the inhabitants lived in apartments, the buildings were "ranch-style" rather than "high-rise."

The architects of Teotihuacán designed apartments to offer a maximum of privacy within the crowded city, using a concept similar to the Old World's classical atrium house [*see illustration on page 111*]. The rooms of each apartment surrounded a central patio; each building consisted of a series of rooms, patios, porticoes and passageways, all secluded from the street. This pattern was also characteristic of the city's palaces. The residential areas of Teotihuacán must have presented a somewhat forbidding aspect from the outside: high windowless walls facing on narrow streets. Within the buildings, however, the occupants were assured of privacy. Each patio had its own drainage system; each admitted light and air to the surrounding apartments; each made it possible for the inhabitants to be out of doors yet alone. It may be that this architectural style contributed to Teotihuacán's permanence as a focus of urban life for more than 500 years.

The basic building materials of Teotihuacán were of local origin. Outcrops of porous volcanic rock in the valley were quarried and the stone was crushed and mixed with lime and earth to provide a kind of moisture-resistant concrete that was used as the foundation for floors and walls. The same material was used for roofing; wooden posts spaced at intervals bore much of the weight of the roof. Walls were made of stone and mortar or of sunbaked adobe brick. Floors and wall surfaces were then usually finished with highly polished plaster.

What kinds of people lived in Teotihuacán? Religious potentates, priestly bureaucrats and military leaders presumably occupied the top strata of the city's society, but their number could not have been large. Many of the inhabitants tilled lands outside the city

and many others must have been artisans: potters, workers in obsidian and stone and craftsmen dealing with more perishable materials such as cloth, leather, feathers and wood (traces of which are occasionally preserved). Well-defined concentrations of surface remains suggest that craft groups such as potters and workers in stone and obsidian tended to live together in their own neighborhoods. This lends weight to the hypothesis that each apartment building was solely occupied by a "corporate" group, its families related on the basis of occupation, kinship or both. An arrangement of this kind, linking the apartment dwellers to one another by webs of joint interest and activity, would have promoted social stability.

If groups with joint interests lived not only in the same apartment building but also in the same general neighborhood, the problem of governing the city would have been substantially simplified. Such organization of neighborhood groups could have provided an intermediate level between the individual and the state. Ties of cooperation, competition or even conflict between people in different neighborhoods could have

created the kind of social network that is favorable to cohesion.

The marketplace would similarly have made an important contribution to the integration of Teotihuacán society. If the greater part of the exchange of goods and services in the city took place in one or more major markets (such as the one that may have occupied the plaza of the Great Compound), then not only the Teotihuacanos but also the outsiders who used the markets would have felt a vested interest in maintaining "the peace of the market." Moreover, the religion of Teotihuacán would have imbued the city's economic institutions with a sacred quality.

The various social groups in the city left some evidence of their identity. For example, we located a walled area, associated with the west side of the Pyramid of the Moon, where large quantities of waste obsidian suggest that obsidian workers may have formed part of a larger temple community. We also found what looks like a foreign neighborhood. Occupied by people who apparently came to Teotihuacán from the Valley of Oaxaca, the area lies in the western part of the city. It is currently under study by

CITY CENTER is composed of two sets of structures, the Great Compound and the Citadel (*bottom of illustration on opposite page*). They stand on either side of the Street of the Dead, the main north-south axis of the city. A pair of avenues approaching the center of the city from east and west form the secondary axis. The city's largest religious monuments were the Pyramid of the Sun, the Pyramid of the Moon and the Temple of Quetzalcoatl, which lies inside the Citadel. Yayahuala (*left of center*) was one of many residential compounds. Its architecture is shown in detail on page 111.

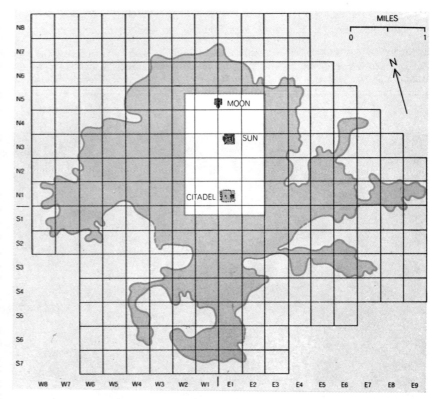

IRREGULAR BOUNDARY of Teotihuacán is shown as a solid line that approaches the edges of a grid, composed of 500-meter squares, surveyed by the author's team. The grid parallels the north-south direction of the Street of the Dead, the city's main avenue. One extension of the city in its early period, which is only partly known, has been omitted. A map of Teotihuacán's north-central zone (*light color*) is reproduced on page 112.

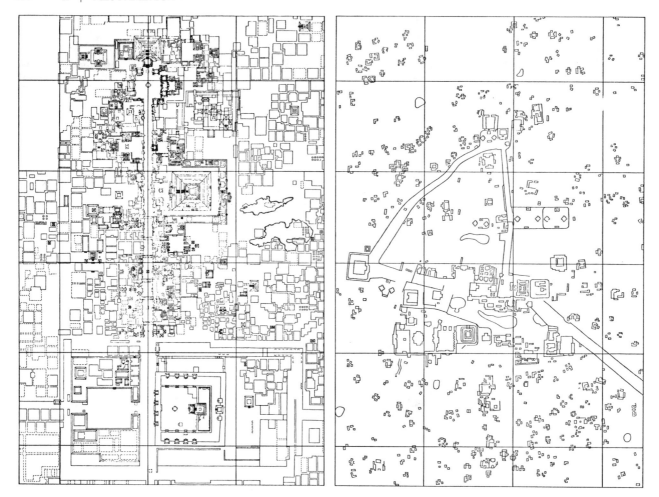

DENSITY OF SETTLEMENT at Teotihuacán is compared with that at Tikal, largest of the lowland Maya ceremonial centers in Middle America. The maps show the central area of each settlement at the same scale. The data for Teotihuacán (*left*) are from surveys by the author and the Mexican government. Those for Tikal (*right*) are from a survey by the University of Pennsylvania. Even though its center included many public structures, Teotihuacán's concentrated residential pattern shows its urban character.

PYRAMID OF THE SUN is as broad at the base as the great pyramid of Cheops in Egypt, although it is only half as high. It was built over the site of an earlier shrine during Teotihuacán's first major period of growth, in the early centuries of the Christian era.

John Paddock of the University of the Americas, a specialist in the prehistory of Oaxaca. Near the eastern edge of the city quantities of potsherds have been found that are characteristic of Maya areas and the Veracruz region along the Gulf of Mexico. These fragments suggest that the neighborhood was inhabited either by people from those areas or by local merchants who specialized in such wares.

We have found evidence that as the centuries passed two of the city's important crafts—the making of pottery and obsidian tools—became increasingly specialized. From the third century A.D. on some obsidian workshops contain a high proportion of tools made by striking blades from a "core" of obsidian; others have a high proportion of tools made by chipping a piece of obsidian until the desired shape was obtained. Similar evidence of specialization among potters is found in the southwestern part of the city. There during Teotihuacán's period of greatest expansion one group of potters concentrated on the mass production of the most common type of cooking ware.

The crafts of Teotihuacán must have helped to enrich the city. So also, no doubt, did the pilgrim traffic. In addition to the three major religious structures more than 100 other temples and shrines line the Street of the Dead. Those who visited the city's sacred buildings must have included not only peasants and townspeople from the entire Valley of Mexico but also pilgrims from as far away as Guatemala. When one adds to these worshipers the visiting merchants, traders and peddlers attracted by the markets of Teotihuacán, it seems likely that many people would have been occupied catering to the needs of those who were merely visiting the city.

Radical social transformations took place during the growth of the city. As Teotihuacán increased in size there was first a relative and then an absolute decline in the surrounding rural population. This is indicated by both our data from the city and Sanders' from the countryside. Apparently many rural populations left their villages and were concentrated in the city. The process seems to have accelerated around A.D. 500, when the population of the city approached its peak. Yet the marked increase in density within the city was accompanied by a reduction in the city's size. It was at this time, during the sixth century, that urban renewal programs may have been undertaken in areas

HUMAN FIGURE, wearing a feather headdress, face paint and sandals, decorates the side of a vase dating from the sixth century A.D. Similar figures often appear in the city's murals.

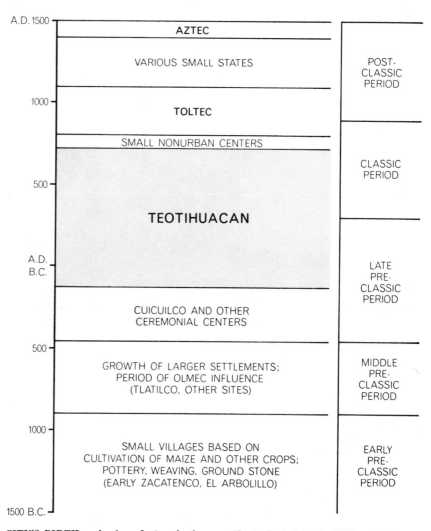

CITY'S BIRTH took place during the late pre-Classic Period in the Valley of Mexico, about a century before the beginning of the Christian era. Other highland ceremonial centers such as Cuicuilco in the Valley of Mexico and Cholula in the Valley of Puebla were influential at that time. Although Teotihuacán fell in about A.D. 750, near the end of the Classic Period, its religious monuments were deemed sacred by the Aztecs until Hispanic times.

PYRAMID OF THE MOON, excavated in the early 1960's by a Mexican government group under the direction of Ignacio Bernal, stands at the northern end of the Street of the Dead. The façade presented to the avenue (*above*) consists of several interlocking, truncated pyramids thrusting toward the sky. The structure, 150 feet high and 490 feet wide at the base, is smaller than the Pyramid of the Sun but is architecturally more sophisticated.

TEMPLE OF QUETZALCOATL is the major religious structure within the Citadel, the eastern half of Teotihuacán's city center. The building is believed to represent the most successful integration of sculpture and architecture to be achieved throughout the city's long history. A covering layer of later construction protected the ornate façade from damage.

where density was on the rise.

Such movements of rural and urban populations must have conflicted with local interests. That they were carried out successfully demonstrates the prestige and power of the hierarchy in Teotihuacán. Traditional loyalties to the religion of Teotihuacán were doubtless invoked. Nevertheless, one wonders if the power of the military would not have been increasingly involved. There is evidence both in Teotihuacán and beyond its borders that its soldiers became more and more important from the fifth century on. It may well be that at the peak of its power and influence Teotihuacán itself was becoming an increasingly oppressive place in which to live.

The best evidence of the power and influence that the leaders of Teotihuacán exercised elsewhere in Middle America comes from Maya areas. One ancient religious center in the Maya highlands—Kaminaljuyu, the site of modern Guatemala City—appears to have been occupied at one time by priests and soldiers from Teotihuacán. Highland Guatemala received a massive infusion of Teotihuacán cultural influences, with Teotihuacán temple architecture replacing older styles. This has been recognized for some time, but only recently has it become clear that Teotihuacán also influenced the Maya lowlands. The people of Tikal in Guatemala, largest of the lowland Maya centers, are now known to have been under strong influence from Teotihuacán. The people of Tikal adopted some of Teotihuacán's artistic traditions and erected a massive stone monument to Teotihuacán's rain god. William R. Coe of the University of Pennsylvania and his colleagues, who are working at Tikal, are in the midst of evaluating the nature and significance of this influence.

Tikal provides an instructive measure of the difference in the density of construction in Maya population centers and those in central Mexico. It was estimated recently that Tikal supported a population of about 10,000. As the illustration at the top of page 114 shows, the density of Teotihuacán's central area is strikingly different from that of Tikal's. Not only was Teotihuacán's population at least five times larger than Tikal's but also it was far less dispersed. In such a crowded urban center problems of integration, cohesion and social control must have been of a totally different order of magnitude than those of a less populous and less compact ceremonial center such as Tikal.

What were the circumstances of Teotihuacán's decline and fall? Almost certainly both environmental and social factors were involved. The climate of the region is semiarid today, and there is evidence that a long-term decline in annual rainfall brought the city to a similar condition in the latter half of the first millennium A.D. Even before then deforestation of the surrounding hills may have begun a process of erosion that caused a decrease in the soil moisture available for crops. Although persistent drought would have presented increasingly serious problems for those who fed the city, this might have been the lesser of its consequences. More ominous would have been the effect of increasing aridity on the cultivators of marginal lands and the semisedentary tribesmen in the highlands north of the Valley of Mexico. As worsening conditions forced these peoples to move, the Teotihuacanos might have found themselves not only short of food but also under military pressure along their northern frontier.

Whether or not climatic change was a factor, some signs of decline—such as the lowering of standards of construction and pottery-making—are evident during the last century of Teotihuacán's existence. Both a reduction in population and a tendency toward dispersion suggest that the fabric of society was suffering from strains and weaknesses. Once such a process of deterioration passed a critical point the city would have become vulnerable to attack.

No evidence has been found that Teotihuacán as a whole had formal defenses. Nonetheless, the valley's drainage pattern provides some natural barriers, large parts of the city were surrounded by walls or massive platforms and its buildings were formidable ready-made fortresses. Perhaps the metropolis was comparatively unprotected because it had for so long had an unchallenged supremacy.

In any case, archaeological evidence indicates that around A.D. 750 much of central Teotihuacán was looted and burned, possibly with the help of the city's own people. The repercussions of Teotihuacán's fall seem to have been felt throughout civilized Middle America. The subsequent fall of Monte Alban, the capital of the Oaxaca region, and of many Maya ceremonial centers in Guatemala and the surrounding area may reasonably be associated with dislocations set in motion by the fall of Teotihuacán. Indeed, the appropriate epitaph for the New World's first major metropolis may be that it was as influential in its collapse as in its long and brilliant flowering.

FEATHERED SERPENT, from one of the earlier murals found at Teotihuacán, has a free, flowing appearance. The animal below the serpent is a jaguar; the entire mural, which is not shown, was probably painted around A.D. 400. It may portray a cyclical myth of creation and destruction. The city's principal gods were often represented in the form of animals.

LATER SERPENT GOD, with a rattlesnake tail, is from a mural probably painted less than a century before the fall of Teotihuacán. The figure is rendered in a highly formal manner. A trend toward formalism is apparent in the paintings produced during the city's final years.

The Chinampas of Mexico

by Michael D. Coe
July 1964

*They are highly productive farm plots surrounded on
at least three sides by canals. Created in an ancient
drainage project, they were the economic foundation
of the Aztec empire*

When the Spanish conquistadores entered Mexico in 1519,
they found most of the peoples
in the region unwillingly paying tribute
to the emperor of the Aztecs, who ruled
from a shimmering island capital in a
lake on the site of modern Mexico City.
Less than 200 years earlier the Aztecs
had been a small, poor, semibarbaric
tribe that had just settled in the area
after centuries of wandering in search
of a home. Shortly after their arrival
they fought with their neighbors and
were obliged to retreat to two small
islands in the lake. There they adopted
a unique form of land reclamation and
agriculture known as the chinampa system. This system, which had long been
practiced on the margins of the lake,
was one of the most intensive and
productive methods of farming that
has ever been devised. It provided
the Aztecs with land to live on and
with the first surplus of food they had
ever known. Their new wealth enabled
them to create a standing army that
soon subjugated nearby peoples. Driv-
en by the demands of their sun-god for
sacrificial captives, and supported by
chinampa agriculture (which was also
practiced by some of their vassals), the
Aztecs quickly expanded their empire
throughout Mexico.

The Spaniards toppled the Aztecs
within two years and razed their magnificent pyramid temples, but the chinampa system has persisted to the present. Now, after enduring for perhaps
2,000 years, it too appears to be facing
extinction.

Chinampas are long, narrow strips of
land surrounded on at least three sides
by water. Properly maintained, they
can produce several crops a year and
will remain fertile for centuries without
having to lie fallow. The important role

they have played in the long history of
Mexico is probably unknown to the *chinamperos* who tend them and to the
many tourists who visit the most famous chinampa center: the town of
Xochimilco south of Mexico City.

In Xochimilco the guides relate the
charming story that chinampas are, or
once were, "floating gardens." This is a
tall tale that goes back at least to 1590,
when a Father Acosta included it in his
*Natural and Moral History of the In-
dies:* "Those who have not seen the
seed gardens that are constructed on
the lake of Mexico, in the midst of the
waters, will take what is described here
as a fabulous story, or at best will believe it to be an enchantment of the
devil, to whom these people paid worship. But in reality the matter is entirely feasible. Gardens that move on
the water have been built by piling
earth on sedges and reeds in such a
manner that the water does not destroy
them, and on these gardens they plant
and cultivate, and plants grow and
ripen, and they tow these gardens from
one place to another."

Acosta may have been deceived by
the rafts of water vegetation that even
today are towed to the chinampas and
dragged onto them as compost. The
real interest of a chinampa town such
as Xochimilco lies not in its fables and
its tourist attractions—flower-garlanded
boats plying canals, waterborne maria-
chi bands and floating soft-drink pur-
veyors—but in the problem of the nature
and origin of the chinampas and the relation of this form of agriculture to the
rise of the pre-Columbian civilizations
of central Mexico.

The chinampa zone is located in the
Valley of Mexico, a landlocked basin
entirely surrounded by mountains of

volcanic origin. The valley, which is a
mile and a half above sea level, has an
extent of some 3,000 square miles. In
pre-Spanish times a sheet of water,
called by the Aztecs the Lake of the
Moon, covered a fourth of the valley
during the rainy summer season. In the
dry winter season evaporation reduced
this shallow body of water to five separate lakes: Zumpango on the north,
Xaltocán and Texcoco in the center and
Xochimilco and Chalco on the south
[*see illustration on following page*]. The
last two were really a single lake divided by an artificial causeway. Villages
were established in the valley sometime late in the second millennium
B.C.; since then the valley has supported
dense populations of farmers. During
the first or second century A.D. the
populous city of Teotihuacán, which
covered at least eight square miles at
the northeastern edge of the valley,
came to dominate the region. Although
Teotihuacán was overthrown as long
ago as A.D. 600, its enormous pyramid
temples still stand. The last, most powerful and best known of the civilized
states of the valley before the arrival
of the Spanish was the empire of the
Aztecs, centered on the island of Tenochtitlán-Tlatelolco in the western part of
Lake Texcoco.

Since the Spanish conquest in 1521
man has drastically changed the valley.
In the colonial era the water was partly
drained in the course of reclaiming land
for agriculture. Far more, however, was
removed by a great tunnel bored
through the mountains to the north in
1900, during the rule of Porfirio Díaz.
The valley has been further dried out
by the tapping of springs and digging
of wells to provide water for the rapid
growth of Mexico City. Of the estimated
six billion cubic meters of water avail-

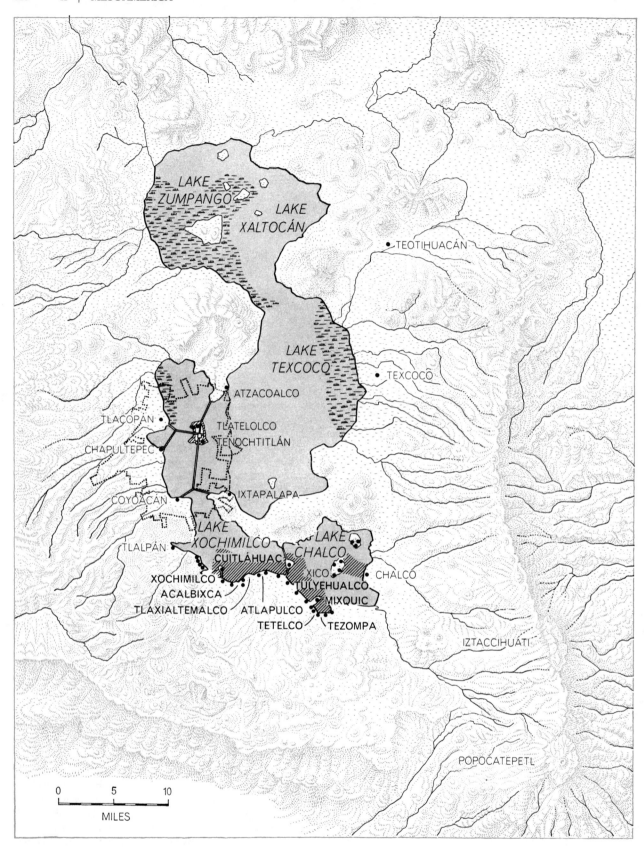

CHINAMPA AREAS (*hatched*) and the Valley of Mexico are shown as they appeared in summer at the time of the Spanish conquest in 1521. In the rainy summer season the five lakes coalesced into one large lake: the Lake of the Moon. Tenochtitlán-Tlatelolco was the Aztec capital. The dotted line marks the limits of modern Mexico City. The broken line between Atzacoalco and Ixtapalapa shows the location of the great Aztec dike that sealed off and protected the chinampas from the salty water of Lake Texcoco. Causeways and aqueducts leading to the Aztec capital are also shown. The names of the nine chinampa towns that remain today are given in heavy type. The large black dots without names are the sites of the freshwater springs that fed the chinampa zones.

able in the valley each year, 744 million cubic meters is consumed by the urban population. Most of the rest evaporates. As a result only isolated puddles of the Lake of the Moon remain, including parts of Lake Texcoco and Lake Xochimilco. Dehydration has so weakened the underlying sediments that the larger buildings of Mexico City are sinking at the rate of about a foot a year.

The removal of the water has also had a disastrous effect on the chinampas. From ancient times down to the past century or so many chinampa towns—small urban centers surrounded by the lovely canals and cultivated strips—existed on the western and southern margins of the old Lake of the Moon. Today only nine remain, and eight of them are probably doomed. Xochimilco alone may endure because of its importance as a tourist center.

In a masterly study of Xochimilco published in 1939 the German geographer Elizabeth Schilling established to the satisfaction of most interested scholars that the chinampa zone is an example of large-scale land reclamation through drainage. Recently detailed aerial photographs have confirmed her judgment. These show Xochimilco to be a network of canals of various widths laid out generally at right angles to one another to form a close approximation of a grid. This could not have been achieved by a random anchoring of "floating gardens." Departures from the pattern have probably come about through destruction and rebuilding of the chinampas, which are easily ruined by flooding and neglect.

To the trained observer the photographs reveal carefully planned canals that drained the swampy southern shore

CHINAMPA GARDENS and canals that surround each of them on at least three sides form a grid pattern in this vertical air view. The grid "tilts" about 16 degrees east of north. Many of the canals that appear to be silted up are simply covered with waterweeds. Part of the town of Xochimilco, south of Mexico City, is at lower left. First canals were dug 2,000 years ago to drain swampy areas.

ANCIENT AZTEC MAP of a portion of Tenochtitlán-Tlatelolco shows that it was a chinampa city. Six to eight plots are associated with each house. Profile of the householder and his name in hieroglyphs and in Spanish script appear above each house. Footprints indicate a path between plots or beside a canal. This is a copy of a small part of the damaged map, which is in the National Museum of Anthropology in Mexico City.

of Lake Xochimilco, where water flowing in from numerous springs had been held in the spongy soil. Here the water table was higher than the surface of the open lake to the north. The canals permitted the spring water to flow freely into Lake Xochimilco and thence into Lake Texcoco, which was deeper. The peaty sediments then released much of the trapped water. Mud dug out in making the canals was piled between them, adding height to the narrow islands and peninsulas that constitute the chinampas. The sides of the garden plots were held in place by posts and by vines and branches woven between them. Later living willow trees replaced many of these wattle walls. Until a few decades ago the water flowed out of Lake Xochimilco into Lake Texcoco through the willow-bordered Canal de la Viga, which carried native women to the market of Mexico City in canoes laden with the rich produce of Xochimilco. Now abandoned, the canal is largely silted up.

In many ways this remarkable drainage project resembled land-reclamation schemes elsewhere, such as those in the fens of eastern England or the polders of the Netherlands. It was unique, however, in the kind of farm plots that resulted, in the technique of their cultivation and in their enormous productivity. Each chinampa is about 300 feet long and between 15 and 30 feet wide. The surrounding canals serve as thoroughfares for the flat-bottomed canoes of the farmers. Ideally the surface of the garden plot is no more than a few feet above the water. Before each planting the *chinamperos*, using a canvas bag on the end of a long pole, scoop rich mud from the bottom and load it into their canoes. The mud is then spread on the surface of the chinampas. In the wet season (June through October) water held in the chinampa provides enough moisture for the crops; toward the end of the dry season, when the canals are lower, the plots must be watered. After a number of years the surface of a chinampa is raised too high by the repeated application of mud and must be lowered by excavation. The surplus soil is often removed to a new or rebuilt chinampa.

New chinampas are made, naturally enough, by cutting new canals, which today is accomplished with power dredges. Older plots that have fallen into disrepair are often reconditioned. In both operations rafts of water vegetation are cut from the surface of the canals, towed to the plot and dragged

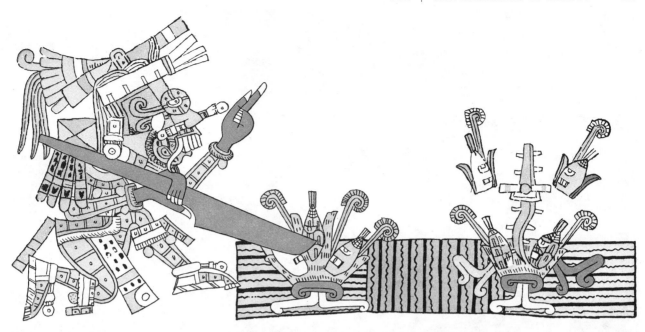

DIGGING WITH A "COA," the cultivating stick of the ancient Mexicans, the rain-god tills magic maize. The drawing is copied from a late preconquest Mexican religious work. The *coa* is considerably broader near the digging end than it is toward the handle.

into place one on top of another until they reach the desired height. After that they are covered with the usual mud. Thus each plot has its own built-in compost heap.

An essential element in chinampa farming is the technique of the seed nursery, which has been thoroughly investigated by the anthropologist Pedro Armillas of Southern Illinois University and the geographer Robert West of Louisiana State University. The nursery, at one end of the chinampa near a canal, is made by spreading a thick layer of mud over a bed of waterweeds. After several days, when the mud is hard enough, it is cut into little rectangular blocks called *chapínes*. The *chinampero* makes a hole in each *chapín* with a finger, a stick or a small ball of rag, drops in the seed and covers it with manure, which now comes from cattle but in Aztec days came from humans. For protection against the occasional winter frosts the seedbed is covered with reeds or old newspapers. During dry weather the sprouting plants are watered by hand. Finally each seedling is transplanted in its own *chapín* to a place on the chinampa, which has been cultivated and leveled with a spade or hoe (the Aztecs employed a

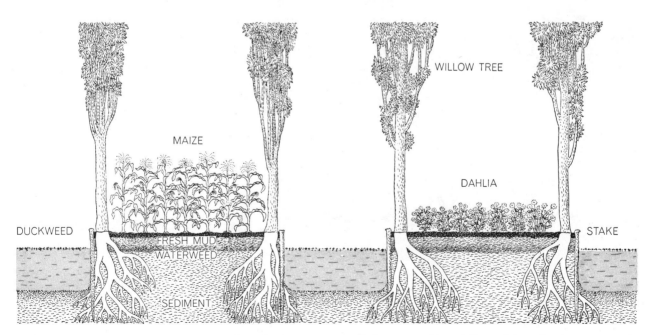

CROSS-SECTION DIAGRAM of chinampas and canals gives an idea of their construction. Fresh mud from bottom of canals and weeds for compost beneath the mud keep the chinampas fertile. Trees and stakes hold the sides of the chinampas firmly in place.

SEED NURSERY, made from small squares of rich mud, is an essential element of chinampa farming. Each square, or *chapín*, holds one seed and manure for it. When seedlings sprout, they will be transplanted in the *chapines* to places on the chinampa.

SCOOPING UP MUD from the bottom of the canal, the *chinamperos* load it into their canoe. They will spread the mud on the chinampa plot before setting out the new crop.

digging stick called a *coa*) and then covered with canal mud. The only crop for which the seedbed stage is not necessary is maize, which is planted directly in the chinampa.

The *chinamperos* report that they usually harvest seven different kinds of crop a year from each plot, of which two are maize. Crops raised today at Xochimilco include five varieties of maize, beans, chili peppers, tomatoes and two kinds of grain amaranth—all of which were cultivated before the Spanish arrived. Also grown are vegetables introduced from Europe, such as carrots, lettuce, cabbages, radishes, beets and onions. Xochimilco means "place of the flower gardens" in the Nahuatl language spoken by the Aztecs and still used today by the older people of the chinampa towns. The growing of flowers for sale goes back to the preconquest era, when flowers were offered on the altars of the pagan gods. Native species have imaginative Nahuatl names: *cempoaxóchitl* ("twenty flower," a marigold), *oceloxóchitl* ("jaguar flower"), *cacaloxóchitl* ("crow flower"). The gardens produce dozens of varieties of dahlia, the national flower of Mexico. European flowers include carnations, roses and lilies.

Carp and other fishes abound in the canals and are netted or speared by the *chinamperos*. Another inhabitant of the canals is the axolotl, a large salamander valued by zoologists as a laboratory animal and prized by the people of Xochimilco for its tender meat and lack of hard bones. Water birds were once caught in nets but are now scarce due to the indiscriminate use of firearms.

A basic question for the archaeologist and the historian is: How old are the chinampas? The traditional histories of the peoples of central Mexico list the Xochimilcas as one of eight tribes (the Aztecs were another) that came into the valley after a migration from a legendary home in the west. They were settled at Xochimilco by A.D. 1300 and were ruled by a succession of 17 lords. In 1352 and again in 1375 they were defeated by the Aztecs; finally, in the 15th century, they were incorporated into the Aztec state, which had absorbed the rest of the chinampa zone as well.

Some recent archaeological evidence makes it appear certain that Xochimilco, and by extension the other chinampa towns, existed long before the Xochimilcas arrived. A local newspaperman and booster of Xochimilco, José Farias

Galindo, has been collecting fragments of ancient pottery and clay figurines found by the *chinamperos* in the mud of the canals and in the garden plots. It is evident that such signs of human residence must postdate the initial digging of the canal system; until that had been done no one could have lived in the tangled marshes. Aztec bowls, dishes and figurines of gods and goddesses abound in Farias Galindo's collection, as might be expected from the many references to Xochimilco in Aztec documents. Of particular interest is the much older material that has been found. This includes a bowl of Coyotlatelco ware made between A.D. 600 and 900, heads broken from figurines of the Teotihuacán III culture, which flourished between A.D. 200 and 600, and Teotihuacán II figurine heads, which are as old as the beginnings of the great city of Teotihuacán in the first and second centuries A.D. Therefore it is likely that the chinampas of Xochimilco were planned and built almost 2,000 years ago.

Who was responsible? The only power in central Mexico at that time capable of such an undertaking was the growing Teotihuacán state, so that whoever built Teotihuacán also created the chinampas. Another piece of information points to the same conclusion. The grid of the Xochimilco canals is not oriented to the cardinal directions but to a point 15 to 17 degrees east of true north. So are the streets of the ruined city of Teotihuacán, and so are the grids of most of the other chinampa towns. We do not know why this is, but there were probably astrological reasons. It has been said that an urban civilization as advanced and as large as Teotihuacán must have been based on irrigation agriculture, but field archaeologists can find no trace of large-scale irrigation works. It seems far more likely that the growth of Teotihuacán was directly related to the establishment and perfection of the chinampas on the southern shore of the lake. Successive peoples and powers entered the valley and took advantage of the same system.

On the eve of the Spanish conquest Xochimilco was a flourishing island town under Aztec control, with at least 25,000 inhabitants—craftsmen as well as farmers. Cortes wrote of its "many towers of their idols, built of stone and mortar." The town, which was and still is on higher and drier ground than the chinampas, was approached from the south by a causeway crossing many canals. Its numerous wooden bridges could be raised to delay the approach

of enemies. At the mainland end of the causeway was a large market; this is now the center of town. Xochimilco was divided into 18 *calpullis*, each with its own name. The Aztec institution of the *calpulli* is not well understood, but it seems to have been a local ward based on kinship. Their names survive today, and every *chinampero* knows to which ward he belongs. The *calpullis* were grouped into three larger units; the town as a whole was ruled by a native lord closely related to the Aztec emperor.

Wills, petitions and other documents filed early in the colonial period show that in Xochimilco land tenure, as well as the social system, was basically the same as that in the Aztec capital of Tenochtitlán-Tlatelolco. There were three categories of chinampa lands: (1) chinampas belonging to the *calpullis*, which could be used by a *calpulli* member to support himself and his family as long as he did not leave the land uncultivated for two years in succes-

sion; (2) office land, which belonged to the position filled by a noble official but not to him personally; (3) private land, which could be disposed of as the individual saw fit.

The island capital of the Aztecs was also surrounded by chinampas. The National Museum of Anthropology in Mexico City possesses a remarkable Aztec map on a large sheet of native paper made from the inner bark of a fig tree. This document, studied in recent years by Donald Robertson of Tulane University, shows a portion of the Aztec capital generally covering the section that is now buried under the railroad yards of Mexico City. In all likelihood it was drawn up as a tax record by Aztec scribes and used by bureaucrats into the period of Spanish domination. The similarity of the plan to that of modern Xochimilco is obvious. It shows a network of canals laid out in a grid, with the larger canals crossing the pattern diagonally. Roads

POTTERY FIGURINES of the types found in the chinampas and canals of Xochimilco were made in Aztec times, A.D. 1367 to 1521 (*top three*), during the Teotihuacán III period, A.D. 200 to 600 (*middle four*), and in the Teotihuacán II era, A.D. 1 to 200 (*bottom*). This ancient evidence of human occupation indicates that the chinampas are 2,000 years old.

and footpaths parallel the major canals, which the Spaniards said were crossed by wooden bridges.

The plan depicts some 400 houses, each with the owner's head in profile and his name in hieroglyphs. The Spanish later added Spanish transliterations of the names and also drawings of churches and other colonial structures. The property surrounding each house consists of six to eight chinampas. It was the cutting of canals and the construction of chinampas by the poor and hungry Aztecs who first came here in the 14th century A.D. that filled in the swampy land between the low rocky islands on which they had camped. The work eventually resulted in the coalescence and enlargement of the islands into the marvelous capital city that so impressed the conquistadores.

The more substantial houses of stone and mortar occupied the central sections of the capital, where the land was higher and firmer. In the very center were such large public buildings as the pyramid temples and the palaces of the emperor and his chief nobles. The bulk of the population was nonagricultural, consisting of priests, politicians, craftsmen, traders and soldiers. Nevertheless, Tenochtitlán-Tlatelolco was a chinampa city; the Spanish described it as another Venice. Thousands of canoes laden with people and produce daily plied the hundreds of canals, which were bright green with water vegetation. An Aztec poet has described the beauty of his native home:

The city is spread out in circles of
*   jade,*
Radiating flashes of light like quetzal
*   plumes.*
Beside it the lords are borne in boats:
Over them spreads a flowery mist.

The real basis of the native economy in the Valley of Mexico was the chinampa zone, which extended all the way from Tenochtitlán-Tlatelolco south to the shore of Lake Xochimilco and then east into Lake Chalco. The rest of the land in the valley, although it produced crops, was far less favorable to farming because of the arid climate. The chinampas, however, presented two difficult problems apart from those involved in their cultivation and day-to-day maintenance. One problem was to keep the water level high, the other was the prevention of floods.

The valley had no external outlet. Year after year over the millenniums nitrous salts had been swept down into

RUINS OF TEOTIHUACÁN, the large city that dominated much of Mexico from about A.D. 100 to 600, are still among the most impressive in Mexico. The rise of this great urban center may have been made possible by the development of the chinampas to the south.

the Lake of the Moon by the summer rains and had been concentrated by evaporation in the eastern part of Lake Texcoco. It was essential to keep the deadly salts away from the chinampas. For this reason the chinampas could only function properly if they were fed constantly by freshwater springs, which maintained the water level and held back the salt water. Such springs are found today in greatest abundance south of Lake Xochimilco, where chinampa towns still exist. Long ago there were adequate springs on the island of Tenochtitlán-Tlatelolco, but the rapid growth of the Aztec capital and its associated chinampas made the springs inadequate. The problem was solved by the construction of aqueducts to bring fresh water from mainland springs. It has sometimes been assumed that the sole purpose of the aqueducts was to carry drinking water to the inhabitants of the capital, but, as the ethnohistorian Angel Palerm of the Pan American Union has noted, their thirst must have been incredible.

These covered masonry watercourses were no mean structures. The first was completed in the reign of Montezuma I (1440–1468); it brought water over a causeway from the west into the city from a large spring at the foot of Chapultepec hill. Cortes wrote that the flow was "as thick as a man's body." A second aqueduct was built by the emperor Ahuítzotl (1486–1502). For this aqueduct a spring at Coyoacán, on a point of land separating Lakes Texcoco and Xochimilco, was enlarged; the aqueduct ran along the causeway that led north to Tenochtitlán-Tlatelolco. Ahuítzotl's effort was initially crowned with disaster: the volume of water was so great that violent floods resulted. The flow of the spring diminished, it was recorded by pious Aztec chroniclers, only when the emperor sacrificed some high officials and had their hearts thrown into it, along with various valuable objects.

The second major problem of the chinampas—periodic flooding by salty water—was also finally solved by construction works. The nitrous salts, which had already made the waters of the eastern part of Lake Texcoco unsuitable for chinampas, rose and moved into the chinampa zone during the summer rains, in spite of the flow from the springs. The problem apparently became acute only in the Aztec period, when, according to the pollen chronology worked out by Paul B. Sears of Yale University, the climate of the region seems to have been wetter than at any time since the end of the last ice age. The floods nearly destroyed the entire economy of the Valley of Mexico. In the 15th century Nezahualcóyotl, the poet-king of Texcoco, supervised for his relative Montezuma I the construction of an enormous dike of stones and earth enclosed by stockades interlaced with branches. The dike, on which 20,000 men from most of the towns of the valley labored, extended 10 miles across the Lake of the Moon from Atzacoalco on the north to Ixtapalapa on the south. It sealed off the Aztec capital and the other chinampa towns from the rest of Lake Texcoco, leaving them in a freshwater lagoon. The three stone causeways connecting the capital with the mainland were pierced in several places and floodgates were installed to provide partial control of the water level in the lagoon.

The entire chinampa zone, then, represented a gigantic hydraulic scheme based on land drainage and the manipulation of water resources. The Aztecs refined and exploited it to establish a vast empire for the glory of their gods and the profit of their rulers. Defeated peoples were quickly organized as tributaries under the watchful eye of a local Aztec garrison and military governor. Twice a year they had to render a huge tribute to Tenochtitlán-Tlatelolco. The Aztec tribute list records that every year the capital received 7,000 tons of maize, 4,000 tons of beans and other foods in like quantity, as well as two million cotton cloaks and large amounts of more precious materials such as gold, amber and quetzal feathers. In fact, in supporting the dense population of the capital, variously estimated at 100,000 to 700,000 (the latter figure is highly unlikely), tribute greatly outstripped local production in importance.

It would probably be no exaggeration to say that the chinampas gave the ancient peoples of the Valley of Mexico intermittent sway over most of the country for 1,500 years before the arrival of the Spaniards. For this reason a detailed study of all aspects of this unique system as it now operates should be made before the chinampas disappear altogether in the name of progress.

12

The Earliest Maya

by Norman Hammond
March 1977

Archaeological excavations in Belize in Central America have pushed back the origins of the Maya to 2500 B.C. The buildings and pottery uncovered clearly foreshadow the splendor of the Classic Maya period

The collapse of Maya civilization, culturally the most advanced of any in the pre-Columbian New World, has inspired almost as many explanations as there are students of American prehistory. An unanswered question of equal importance is how Maya civilization first arose. Until recently that question has received relatively little attention, but its cogency is now greatly increased. Work over the past two seasons on the eastern margin of the Maya area in Belize (formerly British Honduras), often regarded as a backwater, has pushed the beginnings of the Maya Formative (or Preclassic) period back by more than 1,500 years, from about 900 B.C. to perhaps as long ago as 2600 B.C. The new findings place this Early Formative Maya culture among the oldest settled societies in Mesoamerica or, for that matter, in the entire New World.

The term Mesoamerica is often mistakenly thought to be synonymous with Central America: the region extending from southern Mexico to Panama. The term is actually much narrower. Prehistorians define it as the culturally unified area that in pre-Columbian times embraced southern Mexico (including Yucatán), Guatemala, Belize and the western parts of Honduras and El Salvador. The last and politically the most developed of the Mesoamerican civilizations was the Aztec, which the Spanish conquistadors overthrew in 1521. The Aztec capital, Tenochtitlán, was situated where Mexico City stands today, and Aztec political power was centered on the high plateau of Mexico.

Not all Mesoamerican civilizations had this highland focus. The Olmec, one of the earliest of the complex societies in the region, built major ceremonial centers on the low-lying coastal plain of the Gulf of Mexico; examples are San Lorenzo and La Venta. At the same time the Olmec zone of cultural influence and Olmec trade extended into much of the high plateau.

To the east of both the Aztec and the Olmec area in Mexico lies the peninsula of Yucatán and, south of the peninsula, the northern lowlands of Guatemala (the Petén) and Belize. In this southern area during the first millennium of the Christian Era what are regarded as the outstanding characteristics of Maya civilization emerged. This was the start of the Maya Classic period. Extending from about A.D. 250 to 900, the Classic period witnessed the development of mathematics, nontelescopic astronomy and calendrical calculations more advanced than any in other parts of the New World. The data were expressed in a hieroglyphic script utilizing more than 800 characters, many of which still defy decipherment. Paralleling these purely intellectual achievements the Classic Maya civilization gave employment to a school of vase painters as talented as those of Classical Greece and to architects whose great temple pyramids and sacred precincts still amaze the visitor of today.

In common with a number of other students of Mesoamerican prehistory I have been concerned in recent years with the factors underlying the rise of Maya civilization. My own work has taken the form of a series of field studies examining the demographic and economic aspects of the Maya Formative period. The geographical focus of our project, established jointly by the British Museum and the Centre of Latin American Studies at the University of Cam-

MAYA ARCHITECTURE OF THE EARLY FORMATIVE PERIOD is shown in reconstructions based on the partial excavation at Cuello, a site in northern Belize, of two plaster-covered earth platforms that were the foundations for timbered superstructures. The two small superstructures, one circular and one oblong, are alternative conceptions of the timber-and-thatch building that occupied the older of the two platforms, which was probably circular in plan and some six meters in diameter. The platform was built directly on an old soil surface that included burned wood suitable for carbon-14 analysis; the date of construction appears to fall

bridge in 1973, was inspired by the late Sir Eric Thompson, who pointed out the archaeological importance of northern Belize. Physiographically the region is a continuation of the lowlands. To the south and west the Petén, the Classic Maya heartland in northern Guatemala, forms a rain-forest zone with numerous rivers and lakes. To the north the Yucatán peninsula forms an arid zone: a karst landscape of sinkholes, caverns and underground streams. Northern Belize lies within the rain-forest zone but borders on the arid zone. Two of its major valleys are those of the Rio Hondo and the New River. Following the two rivers upstream, one moves south and west toward the Petén heartland [see illustration on page 131].

A second reason for selecting the area is that decades of intermittent exploration (mainly by Thomas Gann, a physician and amateur archaelogist, between 1896 and 1936) have uncovered a number of major and minor archaeological sites that evidently were occupied in Late Formative times, a period extending from about 300 B.C. to A.D. 250. Finally, the people of Belize are greatly interested in their country's past, and the government encourages archaeological research. As a result we have enjoyed the friendliest cooperation not only with the government, through the Archaeological Commissioner, Joseph O. Palacio, but also with such representatives of the private sector as Belize Sugar Industries, Maya Airways and G. A. Roe Insurance Services, all of which are generous sponsors of our work.

A line drawn along the 18th parallel defines the southern boundary of our research area in northern Belize; the eastern boundary is the Caribbean, and the western and northern boundaries are the Mexican border along the Rio Hondo and across Chetumal Bay. The entire research area covers some 3,500 square kilometers. During our first field season, in 1973, we concentrated on locating as many archaeological sites as possible. These we classified in terms of size and complexity: scattered, informal residential clusters; formal clusters grouped around a central plaza, and ceremonial precincts, minor or major, surrounded by residential areas of varying extent. We also established a rough regional chronology based on the pottery uncovered in test excavations at several sites. The pottery chronology was achieved by comparing styles and style changes with those already established for pottery from elsewhere in the Maya region, either discovered in association with dated inscriptions (which first appear in about A.D. 250) or dated by means of carbon-14 analysis.

All together we plotted some 60 sites, most of them last occupied during the Classic period and most located in the higher and drier western part of the region: areas of raised ground between the Rio Hondo and the New River and between the New River and Freshwater Creek. Three sites included ceremonial precincts ranging in size from medium to large, and one of them, Nohmul, was surrounded by more than 20 square kilometers of residential settlements. Each of the three ceremonial precincts included a large elevated acropolis, building foundations surrounding large plazas, several tall temple pyramids and at least one parallel-sided court where the sacred ball game had been played.

All three of the major sites, Nohmul, Aventura and El Pozito, are located along the same stretch of high ground, the ridge between the Rio Hondo and the New River. It is easy to visualize the three as the capitals of separate Classic Maya principalities. The lesser sites that surround them are comparable to the towns and villages around the cathedral cities of medieval Europe. One of these lesser sites, located almost exactly midway between Nohmul and El Pozito, stands on land owned by the Cuello family, who hospitably gave us permission to investigate it.

We named the site after its owners. Examination in 1974 of a partially destroyed mound at the site revealed pottery of an unfamiliar type that we had also encountered in the lowest levels of our test excavations at Nohmul and elsewhere. At those sites the unfamiliar pottery was associated with recognizable wares of the Maya Middle Formative period (from 900 to 300 B.C.). The Cuello sherds, however, had no such associations. Was the unfamiliar ware perhaps even older and indigenous? Or had

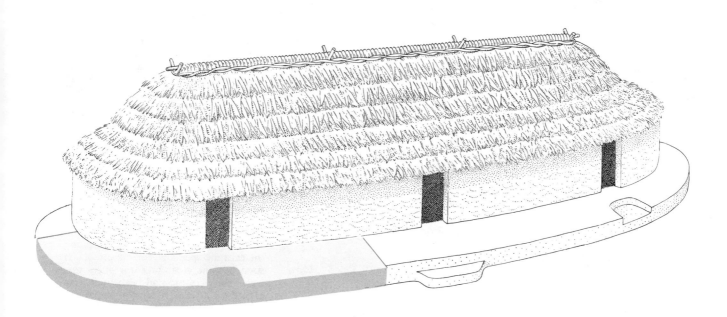

between 2500 and 2400 B.C., making the platform the oldest architectural endeavor known in Mesoamerica. That a superstructure of some kind once stood on the platform is evident from numerous postholes (see illustration on page 138). The larger and more recent platform (above) was apparently oblong, some five meters wide and more than 10 meters long, with rounded ends. At the point where one end begins to curve a niche was built into the side of the platform; evidence that the plaster lining of the niche had been renewed suggests that it served as a step for mounting the platform from the patio in front. The platform was probably built between 1700 and 1500 B.C. Considerations of symmetry suggest the second niche shown here, and the small size of both niches suggests the centrally located additional step. The restoration, however, is conjectural; indeed, only those parts of both platforms shown in color have been excavated.

AGES OF EARLY POTTERY IN THE NEW WORLD vary from site to site over a range of 1,200 years. In Mesoamerica (*colored rectangle*) pottery from the Tehuacán valley is estimated to be 4,800 years old and pottery from Puerto Marquez 5,200 years old. Pottery superior in quality to both, recently found in Belize, includes some that is 4,600 years old. One site in the U.S., Stallings Island, has yielded pottery nearly that old, but the most ancient New World pottery now known is from sites in South America: the pottery from Real Alto averages 5,000 years in age, and that from Valdivia and Puerto Hormiga respectively averages 5,600 and 5,800 years.

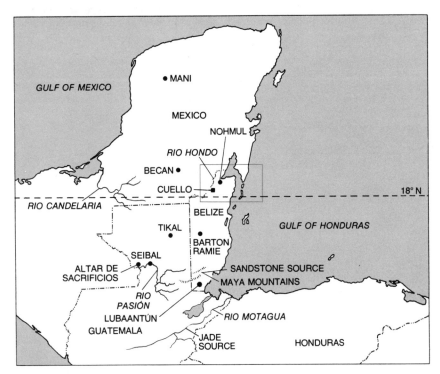

MAYA LOWLANDS consist of three parts of Mesoamerica: the Yucatán peninsula of Mexico, the Petén region of Guatemala and Belize. Classic Maya civilization reached its apogee in about A.D. 700 in the tropical forest of the Petén; Tikal was a major Classic ceremonial center. Until recently the earliest lowland pottery known was from sites on the Rio Pasión. Ascribed to the Maya Middle Formative period, the wares are dated at about 900 B.C. The earliest lowland pottery now known is that of the Swasey ceramic complex, unearthed at Cuello. Carbon-14 dates for Swasey wares extend from 1250 to 2600 B.C. Swasey pottery, unearthed at four other sites in northern Belize, has also been found at two sites in Yucatán: Becan and Mani.

it been made elsewhere in the first millennium B.C. and reached the sites in northern Belize as an import?

The question could be answered only by excavation. Moreover, the location of Cuello midway between two major ceremonial sites suggested other possible benefits that might accrue from further investigation. What was the nature of the contacts between Nohmul and El Pozito in the Classic period? If the major centers were indeed the capitals of principalities, where was the frontier between them? With questions of this kind in mind we decided to carry out a small-scale excavation at Cuello during our next field season, in 1975.

Cuello lies five kilometers west of Orange Walk Town, capital of the district of Orange Walk. The most obvious part of the uncleared site is a small ceremonial precinct of the Classic period consisting of two linked plazas, each with a small temple pyramid. No stone superstructures survive anywhere at the site, and it is probable that not only the temples but also the many residences and other structures were built of perishable materials: timber frames with palm-thatch roofs.

To the south of the ceremonial precinct we located a series of large platforms. One of them, about four meters high and 80 meters long, particularly attracted our attention because on it was a small temple pyramid, about eight meters high. The pyramid was simply too small for such a large platform. This architectural discontinuity suggested that the temple was a late addition, perhaps built after the platform had been abandoned for some time. On the eroded sides of the temple pyramid we found potsherds of the Classic period. Perhaps, like the unfamiliar pottery we had found in 1973, the platform belonged to the earlier Formative period. Certainly its four meters of material should contain traces of a long period of growth; such had proved to be the case with the large platform at the North Acropolis in Tikal, the great Maya ceremonial center in the Petén.

Work began early in 1975 on the selected structure, designated Platform 34 on the Cuello site map, under the supervision of Duncan Pring, then a graduate student at the University of London and the ceramic specialist for the project. It soon became clear that our guess was right; the pyramid had been built long after the platform. A layer of debris had accumulated on the plaster surface of the platform, evidence that the structure had been out of service for some time, before the pyramid was built directly on top of the debris.

We cut down into the platform, exposing a succession of well-preserved plaster floors. Between the successive layers of plaster we found thin deposits

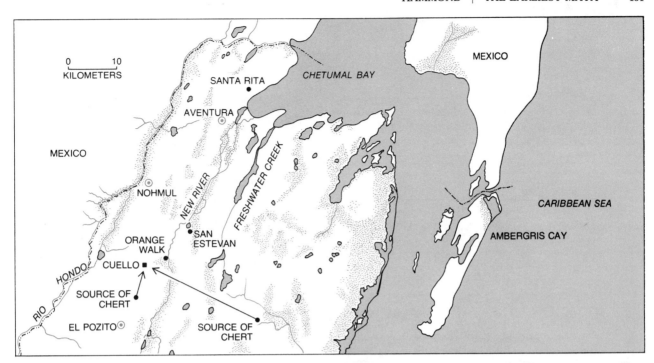

MAYA SITES IN NORTHERN BELIZE include three large enough to rank as regional ceremonial centers (*color*): Aventura, El Pozito and Nohmul. All are situated on the higher ground between two streams, the Rio Hondo and the New River, that empty into Chetumal Bay. The Cuello site is midway between El Pozito and Nohmul, about five kilometers west of Orange Walk Town. The inhabitants of the site early in the Maya Formative period brought the colored chert they preferred as a raw material for edged tools from two nearby sources, seven and 27 kilometers away. To collect the marine shells they made into ornaments required a minimum round trip of 100 kilometers.

of debris and an occasional thicker layer containing potsherds, animal bones, snail shells and small quantities of burned wood. Two meters down the potsherds included some of the unfamiliar type, this time in association with the remains of pottery identifiable as products of the Middle Formative period. Some 70 centimeters below this the potsherds were all of the unfamiliar type; this was the case thereafter until the excavation reached bedrock at a depth of about four meters.

The finding settled one of our hypothetical questions. The examples of the unfamiliar ware that we had encountered in the early levels of Belize sites elsewhere were not imports. The presence of the ware signified that each site had an even longer history than had been supposed. Until the time of our probes the earliest-known kinds of pottery in the Maya lowlands had been products of the Middle Formative period unearthed at two sites in the Petén: Seibal and Altar de Sacrificios on the Rio Pasión. There Gordon R. Willey of Harvard University had turned up pottery of an early phase of the Middle Formative associated with material that yielded carbon-14 dates equivalent to slightly later than 900 B.C. Nowhere in the lowlands had any pottery been unearthed that unquestionably belonged to the Early Formative period (then estimated to run from 1500 to 900 B.C.).

All the ceramic complexes of northern Belize are named after local rivers or lagoons, and so we designated our unknown pottery the Swasey ceramic complex after a nearby tributary of the New River. Obviously the sherds from the lower levels in the Cuello platform were older than the pottery from Seibal and Altar de Sacrificios. The question was, how much older? In the traditional view of early influences in Mesoamerica the Olmec civilization, centered on the Gulf Coast of Mexico west of the Maya area, is considered a probable source of the stimuli affecting the earliest aspects of Maya culture. The period of Olmec influence began around 1300 B.C. Was the Swasey complex early enough to have predated possible Olmec contacts and thus to have inaugurated a cultural tradition independent of Olmec influences?

This remained the question foremost in our minds during the summer and fall of 1975 as two laboratories, one at the University of Cambridge and the other at the University of California at Los Angeles, undertook to make carbon-14 determinations on samples of burned wood from the platform excavation at Cuello. Here two points should be made about carbon-14 dates. First, the dates I am citing are "calibrated." That is, the variations in the regularity of carbon-14 readings, revealed by the analysis of samples of known age from the long-lived bristlecone pine, have been eliminated. Hence the dates represent true calendar years, A.D. or B.C.,

rather than carbon-14 laboratory years.

Second, there is a degree of statistical uncertainty in carbon-14 dating, as is apparent in the laboratory notation. Take as an example the notation 1000 B.C. ±100. The 1000 B.C. date, usually a mean figure that combines the results of two or more tests of the sample material, is known as the "central" figure; the ±100 indicates odds of roughly two to one in favor of the specimen's age falling somewhere between 1100 and 900 B.C. Statistically this range on each side of the central figure constitutes one standard deviation. If one extends the range to two standard deviations, which in this example would be from 1200 to 800 B.C., the likelihood that the age of the specimen will fall somewhere between these extremes is increased from 68 percent to 97 percent. Extensions of this kind appear in the illustration on page 121. When two such extensions overlap, the two carbon-14 dates are said to be statistically inseparable.

The first carbon-14 date to come through was from Roy Switsur and Alan Ward at Cambridge. It was for a specimen of wood found in a midden deposit representing the transition between the earlier, or Swasey, phase at Cuello and its successor Middle Formative phase, Lopez Mamom. The date of this level proved to be about 1250 B.C., or more than three centuries earlier than the pottery from Willey's Middle Formative sites in the Petén.

The date suggested not only that the

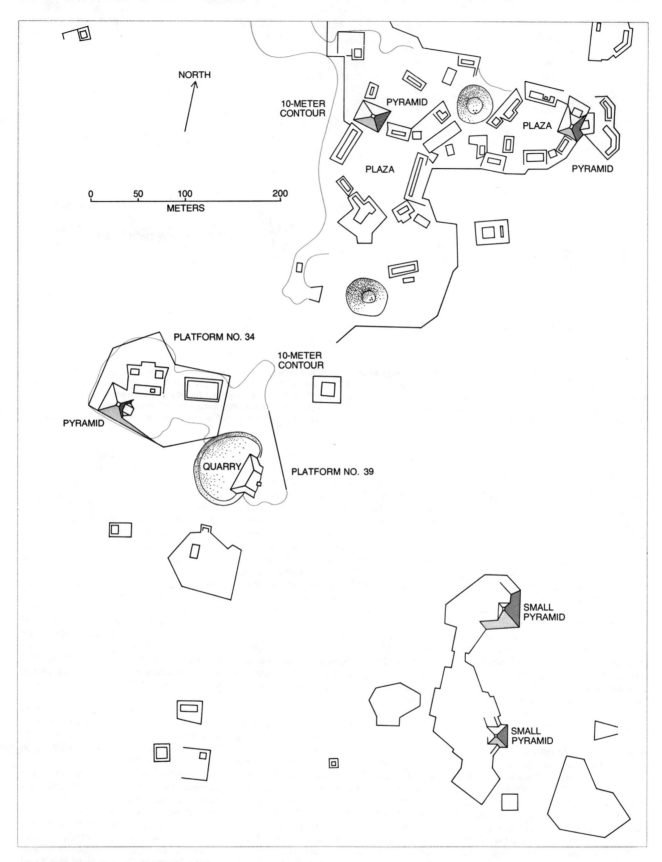

NORTHERN BELIZE SITE, Cuello, is outlined in part; the plan is taken from a survey still in progress. In Classic Maya times Cuello was a minor ceremonial center, its principal focus being two adjacent plazas flanked by pyramids (*top*). Earlier, during the Formative period, the focus was to the south and west and included a massive platform identified by the mappers of the site as Platform No. 34. It was built in the Late Formative period, as was a second, partially destroyed platform, No. 39, situated some 180 meters to the east of No. 34. The area excavated in 1976 (*color*), overlapping a test trench dug during the previous season, bordered on a small pyramid on Platform No. 34 that was not added to the structure until Classic times. Age of the platforms and pyramids at lower right is not yet known.

Middle Formative period began earlier than had been supposed but also that the Swasey complex could well represent a hitherto unknown lowland Maya Early Formative period. Moreover, the Swasey upper levels were at least contemporaneous with the Olmec. Two additional dates from Cambridge, one for a Middle Formative layer of the platform and one for a Late Formative layer, reinforced our confidence in the antiquity of the transition deposit.

In November we received the carbon-14 determinations from Rainer Berger at U.C.L.A. A sample from a level immediately below the transition deposit yielded an almost identical reading; a sample from a somewhat lower level indicated a date perhaps two centuries earlier. The agreement between the findings of the two laboratories gave us confidence in the most surprising determination of all. Wood from the lowest midden uncovered in the probe of the Cuello platform, located just above bedrock, was assigned a carbon-14 date by the U.C.L.A. laboratory that ranged from 2450 to 2750 B.C. and thus had a central value equivalent to 2600 B.C. In effect one season of work at Cuello had pushed back the antiquity of the Maya by a full millennium and the prehistory of the lowlands by more than 1,600 years. Moreover, the establishment of such an early date for the possible inception of the Maya Formative period had effectively removed the Olmec civilization from further consideration as the initial stimulus of Maya culture and even suggested the possibility that Maya culture acted as an influence on the emergent Olmec society.

The great antiquity of the Swasey pottery complex had even wider implications. Up to the time of our discovery the earliest-known examples of a ceramic tradition in Mesoamerica had been pottery from two areas in Mexico west of the Maya zone: the Purrón ware of the Tehuacán valley and the Pox pottery of Puerto Marquez on the Pacific coast. Broadly speaking, the Tehuacán pottery (about 2800 B.C.) appears to be coeval with Swasey ware, and the Puerto Marquez pottery, although a good deal earlier (about 3200 B.C.), is statistically inseparable from Swasey because the dates overlap when they are extended by two standard deviations.

Stylistically, however, the Swasey ware is much more sophisticated than either the Purrón or the Pox. In contrast to their limited repertory the Swasey ware has a wide range of forms, finishes and decorations. Could these lowland products of the Early Formative period in the Maya area represent the starting point of a pottery tradition that later expanded over much of Mesoamerica?

Our single very early carbon-14 date from Cuello was clearly in urgent need of confirmation. Furthermore, the nar-

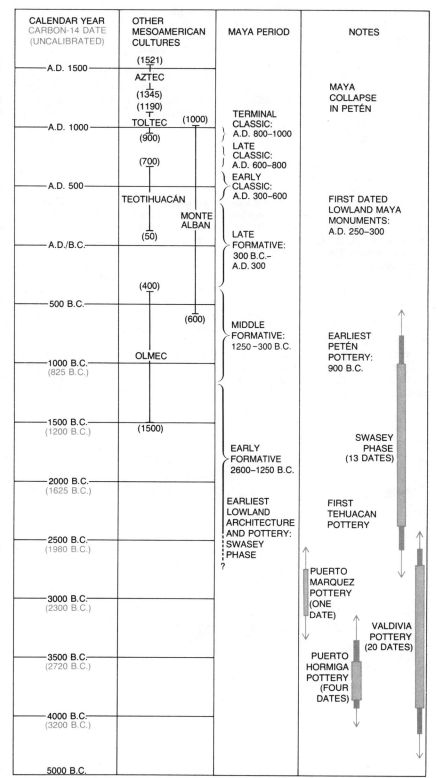

MAYA CHRONOLOGY over a span of 3,500 years is seen against the perspective of other contemporary and later Mesoamerican civilizations' rise and decline. Dates in black (*left*) show calendar years; dates in color are the equivalent carbon-14 years; these have not been calibrated to eliminate their inconsistency, which increases with samples of increasing age. The range of sample age determinations is indicated in four instances by arrows of varying thickness (*color*): for the Swasey ceramic complex at Cuello, for the Mexican Pacific site Puerto Marquez, where pottery slightly earlier than Swasey has been found, and for two South American sites with even earlier pottery. Heads of arrows show maximum ranges of dates, extended from the central carbon-14 reading by ±20 percent (two standard deviations). Wider line measures a one-deviation extension. Where several dates are known the widest line (*light color*) shows the dates' central range. The lowland Formative period was formerly thought to begin in about 900 B.C.

row shaft cut into Platform 34 had provided virtually no information about the economy or the cultural repertory of the Swasey-phase inhabitants of the site, a population that seemed to have a good claim to being the earliest Maya. We therefore decided to put in a short season of further excavations at Cuello in March and April of last year.

That excavation season was supervised by Sara Donaghey of the York Archaeological Trust, which also supplied our group with a drafter, Sheena Howarth, and a conservator, Jim Spriggs. A prime necessity was an accurate map of the site, and work on it had been undertaken in the 1975 season by Michael Walton, an English architect, and Basilio Ah, a Mopan Maya from southern Belize. The two had previously mapped the Maya ceremonial center of Lubaantún [see "The Planning of a Maya Ceremonial Center," by Norman Hammond; SCIENTIFIC AMERICAN, May, 1972]. Ah continued the mapping in 1976, working with another architect, Frederick Johnson of Honolulu. In its present state the map shows the ceremonial precinct at Cuello, surrounded by a scatter of residential compounds [see illustration on page 132.] Three massive

platforms, spaced several hundred meters apart, lie south of the later center of Cuello along a line running a little south of east. The westernmost of the three is Platform 34, which reached its present dimensions in Late Formative times. The final construction work on the central structure, Platform 39, also took place in the Late Formative period; the age of the easternmost platform has not yet been determined.

The 1976 excavation was confined to a 10-by-10-meter square on Platform 34, its four sides facing the four cardinal directions. Two quadrants of the square were excavated: a five-meter square at the northeast corner and another at the southwest corner. The western side of the southwest quadrant incorporated the 1975 shaft, so that we knew roughly what old floors and midden layers to expect at what depths in the new parts of the excavation. By digging diagonally opposed quadrants we also had the benefit of exposing continuous 10-meter vertical sections through the platform, one running from north to south and the other from east to west.

The 1975 shaft provided excellent guidance during the first two weeks of

the season, a time devoted to peeling away successive plaster floor surfaces and screening accumulations of debris. As we passed a floor at a depth of about a meter, however, we encountered two features unlike any we had unearthed in 1975. The first was a layer of rubble, burned plaster and earth, evidence that some structure or structures even older than the platform had been deliberately destroyed. The second, to the south and east of the first, was the surface of a massive rubble dump. Its rough lumps of limestone and chert filled these two sides of the excavation.

Further digging revealed that the layer of rubble, burned plaster and earth covered the remains of two structures that had stood just beyond the rubble dump. We then turned to the task of removing the one-meter layer of rubble. It soon became clear that the rubble had been used to fill up a sunken patio and that the two structures had once stood on individual platforms on the north and west sides of the patio. (We reached the limits of our grid before the south and east sides of the patio were exposed.) The plaster floor of the patio was found to be in a good state of preservation under the rubble.

EXAMPLES OF SWASEY WARES include two of the most abundant variety, Consejo Red (*a, b*). The pots have a cream underslip and a red surface slip. The second shallow dish (*c*), incised with a series of chevrons, is also representative of the Consejo group; its rim and interior are decorated with a red slip. The last two vessels are assigned to other groups of the eight within the Swasey complex. Pot *d* carries a "reserved" design, produced by applying a red slip over an orange underslip. The third dish (*e*), covered inside and out with a buff slip, has been further decorated with fine incisions that form a repeated *X* pattern and frame a false suspension lug. The Swasey-complex groups include 25 ceramic varieties; most of the ones seen here were reconstructed by Louise Christianson from sherd studies.

The 1975 shaft had missed both the west edge of the patio and the rubble fill by about a meter; what we had taken to be earlier floors of the great platform were in fact the interior floors of successive buildings that had stood on the west side of the patio. Further excavation made it plain that in this part of the site the construction of Platform 34 had been preceded by the deliberate razing of the buildings bordering the patio and the filling of the sunken area with rubble.

We were able to place the time of the remodeling toward the end of the Middle Formative period, about 400 B.C. The work had involved a considerable communal effort. Two facts make this clear. First, the limestone available locally at Cuello differs in texture from the limestone used to fill in the sunken patio. Second, there is no chert at all available at Cuello. The nearest source of both fill materials is at least two kilometers from the site.

Platform 34, like the other two great platforms, is obviously a ceremonial structure rather than a residential one. The communal aspect of its construction would thus also seem to involve ceremonial behavior. But what about the structures that had been burned and buried earlier? Were they temples or perhaps residences for a social elite? Or had they been some ordinary cluster of dwellings, razed to make way for the great platform? The evidently ritual nature of the demolition and covering up suggests that the razed structures had been ceremonial ones.

The more impressive of the two buildings had stood on the north side of the patio. A stairway led from the patio up to an open terrace at the front. The front wall of the building, which has been so far only partly excavated, was constructed of small, rounded limestone boulders, laid in courses and covered with a facing of plaster. The doorframe was made out of stiff, perhaps pounded, earth with a core of rubble to give it added strength. The terrace, of similar earth-and-rubble construction, was covered with plaster. Except in the staircase area the plaster finish ran down the face of the terrace and blended into the plaster floor of the patio.

As we dug down, exposing the floor of the building, we found a human burial sealed under the threshold. Such graves are not uncommonly associated with Maya structures and have come to be known as foundation burials. The skeleton was that of a young male, lying on its right side with its head pointing west. In the grave was a small, plain pottery jar and a string of beads made out of mollusk shells and jade.

The second building, on the west side of the patio, had been razed level with the patio floor. Only the outline of its entrance stairway and front wall could

be seen, and the plaster patio floor near it showed signs of intense fire. As we extended our excavation of the area we found that the west edge of the patio at the time of the razing (about 400 B.C.) had in preceding periods been shifted somewhat to the east. Preserved under the Middle Formative buildings and the patio floor were the remains of structures representing three successive periods of construction during the Swasey phase; they constitute the earliest Maya architecture known.

The most recent of the three Swasey buildings is represented by a structure with a poorly preserved floor. Its plaster surface had covered an earlier hole that had once supported the butt of a large timber upright. Remnants of the upright timber, still present in the hole, yielded a carbon-14 reading some three centuries earlier than the readings for samples from this construction period located elsewhere. This suggests that the upright had been a quite mature tree when it was cut down and set in place. On balance the carbon-14 determinations suggest a date of from 1700 to 1500 B.C. for this final Swasey construction period.

The structure was evidently a low platform; its straight east façade had been at least 10 meters long and perhaps substantially longer. At its south end it swept around to the west in a curve, and

to judge from what we can see of this feature the platform had been at least five meters wide. Where the curve begins a niche was set into the edge of the platform near the top. Indications that the plaster lining of the niche had been renewed suggest that it was used as a step by those climbing from the sunken patio to the top of the platform. A similar niche may exist at the unexcavated north end of the platform. The small size of the niche we uncovered seems also to argue for the existence of a central stair. The top of the platform supported a timber superstructure, as was evident from a series of postholes, but no certain plan for the timber structure could be determined.

The structure that represents the next Swasey architectural phase was buried under the last one. It fronts on the same line, but its façade was curved rather than straight. A modest earth-filled platform, it was a mere 30 centimeters high. From what we can see we estimate that it was some seven meters long and four to five meters wide. It had a plaster top and a plaster facing, reinforced along its upper edge with a line of rough stones probably intended to minimize erosion. Like the platform that succeeded it, it had supported timber-framed superstructures; the evidence of the postholes indicates that two such structures had occupied the platform in succession. Both had rounded sides rather than

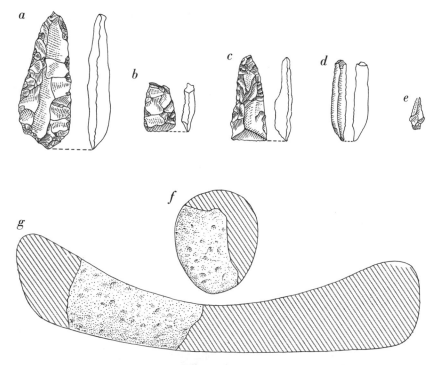

STONE IMPLEMENTS UNEARTHED AT CUELLO were made chiefly by flaking chert (*top*) or by grinding sandstone (*bottom*). The large tool (*a*) is 15 centimeters long; it is typical of the general-utility choppers of the Formative period. Next (*b, c*) are small axe-adzes that may have served for finer work. The long parallel-sided blade (*d*) is much like later Maya work in obsidian. The small point (*e*) probably was used as a drill or punch rather than as a projectile. Fragments of pinkish sandstone (*f, g*) imported from the Maya Mountains 150 kilometers away are shown in restoration here: a mano and metate, the Mesoamerican corn mill.

straight ones, and the earlier of the two was the larger one. Carbon-14 determinations from numerous samples, some contemporaneous with the platform and some from a succeeding layer, suggest a date for the platform between 2300 and 2000 B.C. Both platforms fronted a plaster-floored patio that covered essentially the same area as the Middle Formative patio had.

The oldest of the three Swasey structures came to light at the juncture of our two five-by-five-meter quadrants and had evidently been built at a time before the Early Formative pattern of constructing platforms around a patio perimeter had become established. So far we have uncovered what appears to be part of a circular platform with a three-meter radius. If our preliminary interpretation is correct, the surface area of the platform would have exceeded 28 square meters.

Like the later Swasey structures the platform was built of earth and had a plaster surface; it supported a timber superstructure and rested directly on a substrate of long-buried soil. The soil is mixed with quantities of trash and other debris of occupation apparently derived from dwelling sites that stood outside our area of excavation. Burned wood from this buried soil has yielded a carbon-14 date that falls between 2500 and 2400 B.C. This would place the date of construction of the earliest platform at Cuello substantially more than 4,000 years ago, making it the earliest example of architecture known in Mesoamerica and one of the earliest in the New World.

The three successive examples of Early Formative architecture unearthed at Cuello may be said, if we take the liberty of rounding the dates, to be roughly 4,400, 4,100 and 3,600 years old. The existence of architectural traditions typical of Classic Maya dwellings, such as plastered floors and platforms with timber-framed superstructures, in the lowlands that long ago is indicative of a developmental period for Maya culture of far greater duration than has been supposed.

Our excavations last year provided significant data on the economy of the lowland Maya during the Early Formative period. For example, we found five more human burials, all associated with the Swasey structures. One was a child four or five years old, three were adult males and the fifth was a young adult female. The biological anthropologist for the project, Frank P. Saul of the Medical College of Ohio, concludes that all four adults show abnormally advanced tooth wear, suggesting the presence of an abrasive substance in their daily diet.

The abrasive could have been either of two abrasives that are found in the diet of the Maya today. One is lime, which is in the diet because the Maya steep the kernels of maize in slaked lime before boiling them; the process softens the hard coating of the kernel and also releases certain amino acids in the maize that would otherwise be unassimilable. The other abrasive is grit derived from the stone roller (mano) and milling table (metate) that are still used today to crush the maize kernels into corn meal. Fragments of these grinding stones, which can also be used to grind seeds other than maize, have been unearthed in the earliest of the kitchen middens at Cuello. They were made out of two distinctive kinds of sandstone that were not of local origin.

For the present it is only an assumption that maize was cultivated at Cuello in the Early Formative period. We recovered a large sample of carbonized plant remains at the site, but they are still being analyzed by Barbara Pickersgill of the University of Reading and their identity is not yet known. It is possible that the lowland economy at this period included such root crops as manioc and sweet potato, but proof is unlikely to be forthcoming because identifiable remains of these plants seldom survive prolonged burial in a tropical lowland soil.

Hunting amplified the diet of the early Maya at Cuello. The bones of both the white-tailed deer (*Odocoileus virginianus*) and the agouti (*Dasyprocta* sp.), unearthed from Swasey-phase middens, have been identified by Elizabeth S. Wing of the Florida State Museum. Snails are also represented; the shells of five edible species, the swamp-dwelling *Pomacea flagellata* in particular, have been identified by Lawrence Feldman of the University of Missouri at Columbia. Between 40 and 60 percent of the snail shells were found in deposits of kitchen refuse.

Among the snails are a number of species, seldom if ever eaten, that are common to forest, freshwater and marine environments. Entirely unrepresented in the Swasey material, however, is one snail subspecies (*Neocyclotus dysoni cookei*) that is characteristic of areas that have been burned over and are rich in leaf humus. This suggests that if the Swasey-phase Maya of Cuello did cultivate maize, they did not practice milpa agriculture: planting corn in a field that is prepared by felling and burning the natural brush. Quite the opposite evidence is found in the Middle Formative phase that followed: shells of the swamp snail *Pomacea* decrease in number until they account for only 16 percent of the total, whereas the proportion of the milpa-dwelling *Neocyclotus* rises from zero to 55 percent.

Feldman interprets this change in the snail sample as evidence that the Maya of the succeeding phase were draining swampy land, thereby diminishing the area suitable for *Pomacea* and bringing the drained land under cultivation. Support for his view comes from the findings of a survey group under the direction of Alfred Siemens of the University of British Columbia and Dennis E. Puleston of the University of Minnesota. This group, working just west of us along the Rio Hondo, on the boundary between Mexico and Belize, has mapped a series of raised-field complexes. The fields were formed in riverside swamps by digging drainage canals and using the spoil from the canals to construct platforms that stand above water level. A wood post retrieved from the bank of one of the Rio Hondo canals has yielded a carbon-14 date that falls at about the end of the Swasey phase at Cuello, or about the time of the decline of the swamp snails.

What was grown on these platforms? Perhaps corn, perhaps root crops, perhaps even a "cash" crop such as cacao. Certainly the construction and maintenance of the raised-field complexes would have required some degree of communal cooperation not inconsistent with a structured society and an elite class. As for the need for a cash crop, the presence of imported materials at Cuello suggests that the early Maya there had reason to produce something with which to barter. (In later centuries the cacao bean was a widely accepted form of currency throughout Mesoamerica.)

The foundation burial on the north side of the patio under Platform 34 and two of the five earlier graves included beads of jade and shell among the burial offerings. In addition one of the Swasey graves contained a lump of hematite, the hard iron-ore pigment used in powdered form for pottery decoration and body painting. The shells and the hematite could have been obtained within the Maya lowlands and perhaps even in northern Belize, but the jade could not. The nearest known source of the distinctive green gemstone is some 350 kilometers away, in the Motagua valley on the margin of the Guatemala highlands. The presence of jade beads in these early graves is proof of the existence of an extensive exchange network in this part of Mesoamerica more than 3,500 years ago.

Other materials utilized by the Swasey-phase inhabitants of Cuello may also have been obtained through exchange, but the sources were closer. The Maya Mountains of Belize, some 150 kilometers south of Cuello, were evidently the source of the pink-hued kinds of sandstone used to make manos and metates. Richard Wilk of the University of Arizona traced the brightly colored chert the inhabitants favored as a raw material for edged tools to two nearby sources; one, a notable chert workshop at Colha, is 27 kilometers from Cuello and the other, at Richmond Hill, is seven kilometers away. The shells of marine mollusks found at the site must have been transported over a minimum distance of 50 kilometers.

The high quality of the early pottery at Cuello calls for a brief description of the Swasey ceramic inventory. All in all, the variety of vessel forms and surface finishes is considerable, and the workmanship is consistently expert. In type

the pots range from rough, unslipped pieces—"earthenware" in modern terminology—to thinner-walled pieces with smooth and glossy surfaces, probably comparable in prestige value and in function to today's porcelains. As the ceramics specialist with the project, Pring has surveyed the Cuello findings from the Early Formative period through the Late Formative, and he sees in them a record of a single, continuous process of development.

The earliest entity in the sequence, the Swasey ceramic complex, can be subdivided into some 25 varieties on the basis of combinations of vessel shape and surface appearance [see illustration on page 134]. The commonest are plain, smooth-slipped red bowls: Ramgoat Red and Consejo Red. Ramgoat Red bowls, the earlier of the two varieties, have only a single layer of red slip on their surface. The Consejo Red bowls, which gradually replace the Ramgoat

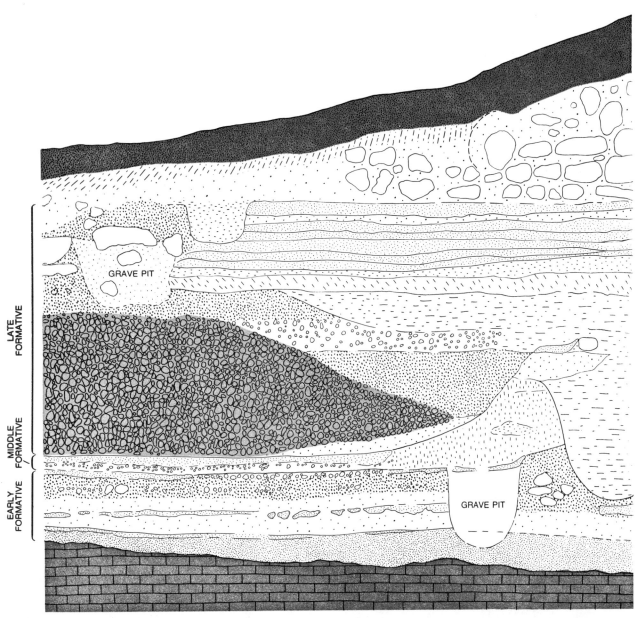

CROSS SECTION of the southwestern five-meter square excavated at Cuello shows the southern exposure of successive strata, from a layer of soil (color, top) that accumulated after the site was deserted in about A.D. 900 to bedrock (color, bottom) some five meters below the surface. Rock-filled area at right, just below the soil, is the stair platform of the Classic-period pyramid that was built on top of a platform of the Late Formative period in about A.D. 600; the stippled layers under the Classic pyramid represent the successive renewals of the plaster floors that formed the surface of the Late Formative platform. A wood sample from the third of these floors yielded a carbon-14 date equivalent to 200 B.C. The massive rubble fill (light color, left), which was not exposed by a 1975 test trench, rests on the plaster floor of a patio built in Middle Formative times. This floor and the one under it end abruptly at the right, evidence that structures facing the patio were razed in about 425 B.C. to clear the way for the Late Formative construction. Samples of wood from the stratum between the two floors date to about 800 B.C. The lowest plaster floor of all, covering an ancient soil that rests on bedrock, is 4,500 years old.

Red as the commonest ceramics, have a cream-colored underslip under the red surface, which gives them a glossier, lighter and more consistent tone.

Other notable Swasey-complex varieties include vessels with two-tone surfaces—red on cream, black on red and red on orange—and vessels with surface colors other than red: cream, black, orange, brown and buff. Still others have incised surface decorations: bold chevrons or multiple incisions forming an X pattern. A few have animal heads modeled in the round on the rim or on the wall; so far Pring has recognized a frog or toad, a monkey and a turtle.

One particularly striking type of vessel is a long-necked bottle with burnished decorations on an unslipped gray surface. None of the bottles found at Cuello are intact, but the overall character of the material is quite similar to that of ceramics found at Mani in northern Yucatán in 1942 by the late George Brainerd. That was in the days before carbon-14 dating, but Brainerd nonetheless assigned the pottery to the period of about 1500 B.C. His accuracy must be accounted an inspired guess.

The overall impression conveyed by the Swasey ceramic complex is one of liveliness and variety in both color and decoration. The vessels are indisputably the product of a mature technology rather than an emerging one. Yet these are the earliest ceramics from the Maya lowlands and among the earliest in all Mesoamerica. Where did this technology evolve?

The earliest Swasey-phase remains known are some 4,500 years old. Any answer to the pottery puzzle must therefore be sought in areas where ceramics were known before that time. One possible answer is that the precursor or precursors of the Swasey ceramic complex are to be found in the Maya lowlands, perhaps at Cuello itself or perhaps at other equally early sites. In addition to being uncovered at Mani, well to the north, Swasey-complex pottery has been found at four adjacent sites in Belize: Nohmul, El Pozito, Santa Rita and San Estevan. A few sherds have also come from Becan, a site located almost in the center of the Yucatán peninsula. At none of these other sites has the age of the Swasey-complex pottery been established by carbon-14 dating. A recent carbon-14 date, however, is available from the central Belize site of Barton Ramie, more than 100 kilometers south of Cuello. The date is about 1500 B.C., which falls within the range of the Swasey carbon-14 dates at Cuello. If one also accepts the probability that the earliest Maya occupation of Mani, some 270 kilometers northeast of Cuello, was contemporary with the earliest-known Swasey phase, then a swath of the lowlands some 400 kilometers in length from north to south (from Mani to Barton Ramie), would seem to have been settled by the Maya of the Formative period, no matter how sparsely, at least 600 years earlier than was formerly believed.

What are the prospects that further work at Cuello will uncover still earlier horizons of occupation? Three carbon-14 determinations made at U.C.L.A. late last year provide an ambiguous hint. Samples of burned wood, from layers at the site that have already yielded a sequence of carbon-14 dates firmly linked to the Cuello stratigraphic succession, give considerably earlier readings. The ages of the samples range from early in the fourth millennium B.C. to the middle of the millennium, or from about 6,000 to 5,500 years ago. It is clear from the archaeological context that the much older wood was trash, swept up for construction fill more than a millennium after it had been burned. The fire that burned the wood could have been either a forest fire due to natural causes or the result of human activity in the Cuello area. We calculate the chance that the site was occupied more than 4,750 years ago at about 50–50.

There are alternatives to the possibility of an early evolution of Mesoamerican ceramics centered in the Maya lowlands. One is that ceramics are known to have been made in central and Pacific-coast Mexico and even in the southeastern U.S. some 4,500 years ago. None of the ceramics from these areas, however, have either the variety or the sheer panache of the Swasey ceramic complex.

Pottery 4,500 years old is also known from Monagrillo in Panama, and in northwestern South America pottery has been unearthed that is at least 6,000 years old. The principal South American sites are Puerto Hormiga on the coast of Colombia and Valdivia in southern Ecuador, but it seems likely that during the millennium before the oldest examples of the Swasey ceramic complex first appeared pottery was being made in South America all the way from the Gulf of Guayaquil to the Gulf of Venezuela, both along the coast and in the highlands of the Andes. As for possible relations between this early New World ceramic focus and Mesoamerica, Donald Lathrap of the University of Illinois maintains that there are close resemblances between 4,500-year-old pottery from Real Alto, a site in southern Ecuador that he excavated recently, and the Swasey-complex pottery from Cuello.

For the moment it seems prudent to leave the question open. The origins of Maya pottery may have been local or they may have been exotic. If it was the latter, then a South American stimulus seems more likely than any other now in evidence. What can be said unequivocally is that in the Swasey phase at Cuello we see not only in the pottery but also in the architecture and in the use of stone artifacts the beginning of the cultural tradition that is known as Classic Maya nearly 3,000 years later. Where its creators came from, and when, are questions we hope one day to answer.

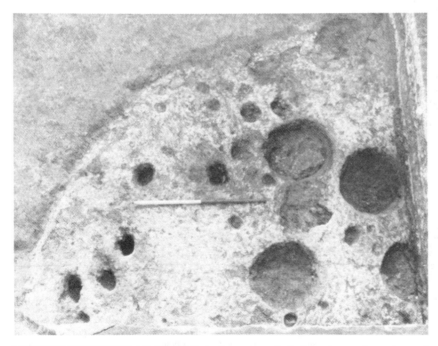

EARLIEST STRUCTURE AT CUELLO, a plaster-covered platform, is seen from above after partial excavation. It was constructed some 4,500 years ago. Its curved edge suggests that the platform was circular in overall shape; two possible reconstructions of the timber structure that stood on it are shown on page 128. The postholes in the plaster surface offer little guidance on the shape of the structure. Large holes are ovens dug into the platform at a slightly later date.

The Rise of a Maya Merchant Class

by Jeremy A. Sabloff and William L. Rathje
October 1975

The centuries just before the Spanish conquest are usually viewed as a time of Maya decline and decadence. A review of the evidence suggests instead that new leaders were pursuing new objectives

The eighth century was a turbulent period in world history. In the Old World the victory of Charles Martel at Tours had halted the Moslem advance in Europe, but the Moslems, having besieged Constantinople for a second time, were still strong enough to keep the Mediterranean as their private sea and at the same time to crush the Maitraka dynasty in India and drive the T'ang dynasty's frontier guards out of Chinese Turkestan. In the New World, although no one in the Old World was aware of it, a period of economic prosperity and cultural flowering in what are now Mexico and Guatemala was ending in disaster. In the highlands of Mexico the great urban center at Teotihuacán was sacked and burned around A.D. 700; in the southern part of the Yucatán lowlands the Classic civilization of the Maya collapsed, its magnificent ceremonial centers ceased to function and the region was depopulated. The aftermath of this New World debacle is our concern here.

Many students of Maya prehistory characterize the period between the collapse in the southern lowlands and the arrival of the Spanish conquistadors as an era of slow decline for all the Maya, in both the southern and the northern lowlands. Few New World writings predating the 16th-century arrival of the Spanish have survived, and what has survived is intelligible only in part. Those who undertake to reconstruct pre-Columbian events therefore must depend largely on archaeological evidence.

Such evidence can be interpreted in more than one way. For example, two decades ago Tatiana Proskouriakoff presented a brief account of several seasons' work conducted at Mayapán in northern Yucatán by the Carnegie Institution of Washington [see "The Death of a Civilization," by Tatiana Proskouriakoff; SCIENTIFIC AMERICAN, May, 1955]. A large walled city, Mayapán flourished from the middle of the 13th century to the middle of the 15th. The most neutral of scholars' terms for this period in Middle America is Late Postclassic; many simply call it "the decadent period." The Carnegie workers found that most of the high standards of civilization maintained by the Maya during the Early and Late Classic periods (A.D. 300–800) were virtually nonexistent at Mayapán. The imposing structures carefully built of masonry, the monumental stone sculpture adorned with inscriptions, even such a comparatively modest skill as the production of fine polychrome-painted pottery—all were conspicuous by their absence. That is why Proskouriakoff titled her account "The Death of a Civilization."

Recent archaeological investigations on the island of Cozumel, off the east coast of Yucatán, lead us to a contrary interpretation of that period in Maya history. Instead of decline and cultural stagnation we see a cultural reorientation: a transfer of authority to new hands and a consequent pursuit of new objectives. Before presenting the evidence from Cozumel and offering a reinterpretation of the older evidence it will be useful to describe the general scene.

The first major city-state in North America arose in the highland Valley of Mexico around the time of the beginning of the Christian Era. The site of its ruins is today called Teotihuacán. Between A.D. 250 and 600 the city's numerous neighborhoods—some religious, some bureaucratic and many industrial-mercantile—reached their point of highest development. A house count conducted by René Millon of the University of Rochester in the 1960's suggests that at the city's apogee no fewer than 75,000 people lived in it; the number may have been as high as 125,000. Among the city's workers were craftsmen who produced such valued export goods as pottery, obsidian artifacts and various ornaments made of semiprecious stones. The craftsmen formed a key element in an economy that carried wares overland from Teotihuacán to parts of Mexico and Guatemala hundreds of kilometers away. If the demands of trade were the same then as they were later, the trade apparatus brought back to the city an abundance of commodities, some exotic (such as feathers, aromatic resin and cacao beans) and some ordinary (such as salt and cotton cloth).

During the period when Teotihuacán enjoyed the benefits of long-range overland trade a parallel development was taking place in the lowlands of Guatemala and southeastern Mexico [see *illustration on page 145*]. The people involved in this southern florescence were the Maya. Their history goes back to at least the middle of the first millennium B.C., but it was not until the Early Classic period (A.D. 300–600) that the record of their remarkable achievements literally began to be hewn in stone. At Tikal, the greatest of the Classic Maya cities in the southern lowlands, is a stone monument bearing a date equivalent to A.D. 292.

The Maya custom of erecting dated monuments has been a great convenience to scholars. It has made possible the reconstruction of a fairly exact chronological record of Maya activities. For example, dates on monuments in the southern lowlands indicate that the Maya were active there during much the same time that the Maya in the northern lowlands were building such great centers as Dzibilchaltún. The monument

ECONOMIC ARENA was dominated from the beginning of the Christian Era until the Spanish conquest in the 16th century, first by traders from Teotihuacán and then by traders from nearby Tollan. Both cities were in the Mexican highlands, and the trade routes were overland. When Teotihuacán fell, a group of Maya, the Putun, began trading by sea instead of overland. The principal Putun sea route, around Yucatán, is shown on the opposite page.

dates also provide evidence that the seventh century, the traditional time of transition from the Early Classic period to the Late Classic, was a turning point that reflected more than local Maya events.

Unrest was rife in Mexico proper during much of the seventh century. It was at the end of the century that Teotihuacán was burned. The effect of the event was widely felt. As the influence of Teotihuacán over Middle America faded, Maya civilization during the Late Classic period (A.D. 600–800) was able to reach new heights. Older ceremonial centers expanded significantly in size and new ones were founded; such hallmarks of Classic civilization as ball courts, palaces and great temples were erected. A new mastery of technique and style was achieved both in monumental sculpture and in polychrome pottery design. The population at the great Maya centers expanded rapidly. For example, it is estimated that at the beginning of the period the population of Tikal was between 30,000 and 50,000.

These trends brought Maya civilization to its highest point but they also laid the foundations for its sudden collapse. In little more than a century, between A.D. 770 and 890, the ceremonial centers were abandoned; not one monument in the southern lowlands bears a date later than A.D. 900. The factors responsible for the collapse of Classic civilization in the southern lowlands and the depopulation of the area are complex and do not concern us here. They

appear to include an overtaxing of the lowland environment and external pressures of an economic and military kind.

At about the time of the Classic Maya collapse, however, another city-state in the highlands of Mexico began to fill the vacuum left by the destruction of Teotihuacán. Mexican scholars identify the city as Tollan (modern Tula), the capital of the Toltecs, and tradition dates its founding at about A.D. 900. Smaller and economically less important than Teotihuacán, Tollan nevertheless made itself felt as a military power.

The Tollan import-export trade extended to the west, north and south of the Valley of Mexico. Concerning the trade to the south, archaeological analyses of imported pottery unearthed at Tollan indicate that overland trade routes extended to Costa Rica and Nicaragua. As far as their nearer neighbors, the Maya, were concerned the most spectacular evidence of Toltec influence is found at Chichén Itzá.

Originally built by the Maya of the Late Classic period, Chichén Itzá was enlarged and rebuilt in Toltec style during the 10th century. The great center probably represents the height of Toltec influence on Maya architecture. The influence of the militant emigrants from Tollan was not limited to architecture, however. By A.D. 1000 the Toltec had assumed political sway over much of the northern lowlands. The traditional interpretation of the Maya archaeological record accepts that date as the start of the period of decline known as the Early Postclassic.

Some 200 years later Tollan was burned just as Teotihuacán had been half a millennium earlier. By A.D. 1224 Chichén Itzá stood abandoned, and Toltec power was extinguished in Yucatán. In the traditional interpretation the Maya decline of the Early Postclassic period deepened at about this time into the Maya decay of the Late Postclassic.

The scene is now set. The actors who enter are Maya from the gulf coast lowlands that are today the states of Tabasco and Campeche. Analyses of postconquest documents by such scholars as Ralph L. Roys, France V. Scholes and J. Eric S. Thompson identify these people as a group known as the Putun. They spoke a dialect unlike the Yucatec Maya dialect heard generally throughout Yucatán; it was Chontal Maya, one of the dialects of the Cholan Maya group. The niche in society that the Putun occupied was a new one: the seafaring merchant.

The importance of trade among the peoples of Middle America is difficult to overemphasize. The economic influence of Teotihuacán had led to a growing secularization of life and the development of a market economy not only in highland Mexico but also elsewhere. At the same time an initial emphasis on trade in luxury goods had gradually been transformed into a demand for the ordinary commodities that were obtainable from distant sources. The trade itself, however, had been almost exclusively overland. In an economy that lacked both wheeled vehicles and pack animals this meant that transport capacity was limited to what a trader and his porters, hired or slave, could carry on their back.

With the collapse of Teotihuacán's political and economic empire at the start of the eighth century the seafaring Putun found themselves in a unique position. No central organization remained to handle the procurement and export of the many kinds of raw materials and other goods produced in the greater Maya region. For example, salt was an important Maya export. It was collected from natural salt pans along the gulf coast of the Yucatán Peninsula and in the northern coastal lagoons. Cacao beans are another example. The beverage made from them was the Mexicans' gift to the Old World; the English word "chocolate" is a corruption of the Nahuatl word for the drink. The beans served another purpose: they were used as currency- throughout Middle America. Early Spanish explorers found that the cost of a strong slave was 100

GULF OF MEXICO

DZIBILCHALTÚN

NORTHERN LOWLANDS

MAYAPÁN

CHICHÉN ITZÁ

COZUMEL

PUUC HILLS

YUCATÁN

TULUM

QUINTANA ROO

CHAMPOTÓN

CAMPECHE

M E X I C O

CANDELARIA

HONDO

TABASCO

BELIZE

PALENQUE

P E T É N

TIKAL

B E L I Z E

USUMACINTA

SOUTHERN LOWLANDS

MAYA MOUNTAINS

CHIAPAS

GULF OF HONDURAS

BAY ISLANDS

DULCE

MOTAGUA

CHAMELECÓN

GUATEMALA

COPÁN

H O N D U R A S

- - - - - PUTUN SEA ROUTE

A SALT   D OBSIDIAN
B CACAO   E COPPER
C JADE   F QUETZAL PLUMES

PUTUN SEA ROUTE connected the gulf coast of Yucatán, close to overland trade routes from highland Mexico, with ports in the Gulf of Honduras on the opposite side of the peninsula. Cozumel, an island just off the east coast, was an important midway point for the maritime merchants who traded in salt, cloth, cacao, jadeite, feathers, obsidian and copper.

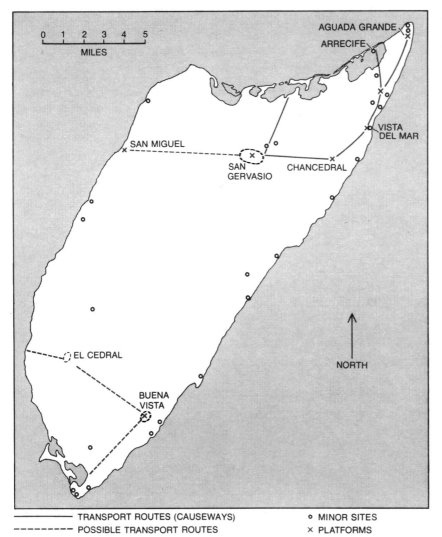

0 1 2 3 4 5
MILES

AGUADA GRANDE
ARRECIFE

VISTA
DEL MAR

SAN MIGUEL

SAN
GERVASIO   CHANCEDRAL

NORTH

EL CEDRAL

BUENA
VISTA

—————— TRANSPORT ROUTES (CAUSEWAYS)   ○ MINOR SITES
- - - - - - - POSSIBLE TRANSPORT ROUTES   × PLATFORMS

ISLAND OF COZUMEL, more than 175 square miles in extent, has 34 pre-Columbian sites. Sites on the coast probably gave residents of the island early warning of approaching vessels. Storage platforms high enough to stay dry during seasonal floods were connected to coastal shipping points by a system of all-weather causeways. The shrine of the goddess Ix Chel, which drew many Maya pilgrims to Cozumel, may have been located at San Gervasio.

cacao beans. Tabasco, on the border of the southern lowlands, was a major cacao-producing area. A third article of trade was cotton cloth; Maya weavers excelled in the production of cotton textiles. A fourth was honey, a major Maya export.

Not only were the Putun in the right place at the right time to take over the interrupted trade in these products and others but also, being seafarers, they were able to transport the merchandise more effectively than any overland trader. It was not simply a matter of a better means of transportation; the Putun planned for convenience and efficiency. For example, the Putun potters were pioneers in the mass production of simple shapes. They specialized in a hard, thin-walled ware that archaeologists call Fine Orange. And the pottery

was not merely mass-produced; it was often shaped so that the finished products could be nested for ease of shipment [see top illustration on page 148].

The long-distance coastwise trade route of the Putun eventually extended from Tabasco to the Gulf of Honduras, with the island of Cozumel acting as an entrepôt. Little is known of the Putun boats, which are described by early European visitors as being log dugouts of various sizes. Spanish accounts refer to canoes carrying as many as 50 men. Pictures of Maya canoes executed by Maya artists always show smaller craft. That may be because the artists drew canoes only big enough to accommodate the occupants; the largest number of passengers shown is seven. In any event, by the time of the first Spanish contacts the Putun dialect had become the lingua

franca of trade throughout the Maya area. The merchants' reputation as voyagers was such that Thompson calls them the "Phoenicians of the New World."

The literature of European exploration tells of an encounter between a Spanish ship and the oceangoing canoe of what may well have been a Putun trader. The contact occurred during the fourth voyage of Columbus, who was looking over one of the Bay Islands off the coast of Honduras. Late in July, 1502, his ship came alongside a large dugout, eight feet wide and "as long as a galley." It was being propelled by some 20 paddlers. The captain, probably the trader-owner, is described as an old man. Apparently he had taken his family along on the voyage: a palm-leaf shelter amidships was occupied by women and children. Unlike the naked Indians of the Caribbean with whom Columbus was familiar, the women wore cotton garments and hid their faces from Spanish stares with brightly colored shawls. The canoe's cargo included a number of these shawls and other cotton clothing, such as dyed sleeveless shirts. There were also long wood "swords" edged with obsidian or flint, cast copper bells, copper hatchets and crucibles for melting copper. What the Maya voyagers valued most, judging by the way they searched the canoe bottom for any that were spilled, were cacao beans. The Spanish took samples of all the Maya merchandise and gave the canoeists some trinkets in exchange. The two vessels then parted, but not before Columbus had seized the old captain to serve as an interpreter.

The Putun expansion had begun toward the end of the eighth century. It was not exclusively economic; the traders also made their military power felt. Their early contacts with highland Mexico must have given them an initial strategic advantage over their neighbors. Among their arms were various Mexican weapons unfamiliar to other Maya at the time, notably darts and dart throwers. It appears certain that the Putun expansion in one direction, along the borders of the southern lowlands, was a factor in the collapse of Classic Maya civilization there. At the same time the expansion in the other direction, into and across the northern lowlands, contributed to a late flowering in that Maya area.

By the end of the 12th century, as Proskouriakoff has shown, many artistic aspects of Classic Maya civilization had long been in a state of decay. In the traditional interpretation such decay reflects a generalized social decline. In reality, however, the economic life of Maya civilization during those centuries was becoming increasingly complex and vigorous. The assembly and distribution of both raw materials and manufactured goods were expanding rapidly. For example, in the manufacture of pottery mass-production methods had replaced the traditional piecework. At the same time the standard of living among the non-elite was on the rise; the intricate system of long-distance trade gave the farm population access to the wide variety of new materials the traders brought back to Yucatán from other areas. Perhaps most important of all, as religious authority became decentralized the developing market economy provided something to take its place: a mercantile authority.

In the course of the Putun's trade-oriented political expansion in the northern lowlands of the Yucatán Peninsula they seem to have been governed by a cultural ethic that was new among the Maya. What might be called mercantile pragmatism, it reflected the ascendancy of a merchant class at the expense of the old theocracy. In characterizing the so-called decadent period of Maya civilization most archaeologists have neglected to take into account either the rise of the new class or the significance of their new cultural ethic. Archaeological findings on the island of Cozumel provide a corrective to this neglect.

Cozumel has an area of more than 175 square miles. Over the years the Mexican National Institute of Anthropology and History has registered more than a score of archaeological sites on Cozumel, most of them along the coast [see illustration on opposite page]. Investigations by such scholars as A. Escalona Ramos and William T. Sanders indicate that the first Maya inhabitants arrived on the island at a time around the beginning of the Christian Era.

Cozumel remained a quiet backwater until the beginning of the Terminal Classic period, around A.D. 800. Thereafter the importance of the island grew; among other reasons was the fact that it was the site of a shrine that was visited by pilgrims from all parts of Yucatán. Cozumel reached its peak between A.D. 1300 and 1500, the period of supposed Maya decadence. This record of insular rise and preeminence is so closely synchronous with the rise of the Putun that when early in the 1970's an opportunity arose for us to reconnoiter Cozumel, we were eager to take advantage of it. Our respective institutions (the Peabody Museum of Archaeology and Ethnology at Harvard University and the Department of Anthropology at the University of Arizona) agreed to undertake an expedition, and the National Geographic Society contributed financial support. We worked on the island with the authorization and cooperation of the Mexican National Institute in 1972 and 1973 as directors of a joint Cozumel project. Our objective was to learn how the island had been useful to the Putun traders and whether or not the archaeological record at Cozumel reflected the traders' mercantile culture.

The largest pre-Columbian structures on Cozumel are of a kind that would be of little interest to students of aesthetics. They nonetheless represent a major investment in labor and materials by the Putun. The primary importance of Cozumel to the traders was its strategic location as a stopover and as a storage depot. The island is low, however, and is subject to flooding during seasonal rains or hurricanes. The Putun therefore built huge stone platforms, high enough to be safely out of the reach of floodwaters, at more than half a dozen sites. The platforms were constructed of limestone rubble. The largest is at Buena Vista; it consists of a group of connected platforms, averaging five meters in height,

which cover an area of more than seven hectares (17 acres).

All the platforms on Cozumel appear to have been built during the three-century span of the "decadent" Late Postclassic period. Although the main motive for building them must have been to provide a safe storage place during floods, it is not the only motive that can be imagined. For example, certain Putun goods, such as salt, came to market seasonally. If such goods are stored by the ultimate consumer, there may be a seasonal oversupply and a price drop. If they are stored by the merchant, using large spaces such as the Cozumel platforms, the price will remain stable. The investment of time and effort in building the platforms would thus have been sensible from more than one mercantile point of view.

Another major construction program on Cozumel was the building of raised stone causeways; these seem to have provided all-weather links between freight-transfer points at the water's edge and the storage platforms inland. Like the platforms, the causeways were built of limestone rubble. They are not easy to trace today, except in a few places where they still provide dry footing across permanently swampy areas.

One large causeway passes through a free-standing arch that is now in ruins. Both causeway and arch seem to have served a purpose other than a mercantile one. The arch evidently marked the main entrance to a group of ruins now known as the San Gervasio zone. This may be where the famous pilgrims' shrine stood: the temple sacred to the goddess Ix Chel. The causeway may therefore have been a pilgrims' road to Ix Chel's shrine or to some other important religious precinct. In the Maya pantheon Ix Chel was the consort of Itzamna; she played a rather superior Juno to his Jupiter, being not only the goddess of the moon but also the patroness of weaving, medicine and

SEVEN-PASSENGER CANOE, the largest represented in Maya art, was among several subjects delicately incised on animal bone and buried with other grave goods in a tomb located under Temple I at Tikal. The paddlers and their grotesque passengers are all members of the Maya pantheon; the fine drawing, incompletely preserved in some parts, is an example of Early Classic craftsmanship. The only descriptions of larger Maya canoes are by European observers; the largest log dugouts are said to have carried 50 men.

childbirth. Visits to her shrine were frequent, perhaps because the only speaking oracle in the Maya world was located there.

Even if the San Gervasio causeway did not serve commerce directly, the Putun might have considered it a good investment. Those who came to worship on Cozumel could well have remained to trade. For that matter, the pilgrim traffic alone would have been an important source of income for the islanders.

An unexpected discovery of the Cozumel project was an islandwide system of walled fields [see illustration below]. The walls were evidently built during the same three centuries of the so-called decadent period. Like the platforms and the causeways, they consist of limestone rubble. They vary in height from half a meter to a meter and a half. The walls almost certainly marked the boundaries of fields that the island's farmers fertilized by burning and then

planted to maize, beans, squash or other crops. Although the fields are somewhat irregular in shape, the average area enclosed is 4,000 square meters, or about one acre.

It is possible that the prosperity of Cozumel at the height of Putun power was accompanied by an increase in population sufficient to place island land at a premium. If this was the case, the walls may have marked property lines as well as field boundaries. The effort invested in constructing such an enclosure system invites the speculation that the walls represent a shift by the Putun from the traditional Maya pattern of farmland held in common to one of farmland held as private property.

The construction of a system of coastal defense points was another Putun activity on Cozumel that called for a considerable investment of time and labor. Fourteen of those structures still stand along the leeward and windward shores of the island. Spanish accounts of early

contacts with the Maya describe fires being lighted on top of the structures as beacons to warn the island's inhabitants when raiders were approaching.

The structures of this early-warning network vary in size and in architectural style. In addition to their defensive function some may have served as shrines or fulfilled other purposes. All, however, seem to have been built during the same 300-year period, and there is evidence that at one time the network included at least 20 coastal structures.

Settlements on the Yucatán mainland opposite Cozumel during this period were fortified. Tulum is a good example: the cliff on which it stands provided protection on the seaward side and wall systems guarded the landward approaches. Cozumel, however, had no natural defenses. Moreover, the island's many field walls were not high enough to be used defensively. The Putun seem to have relied mostly on building storage areas, residences and administrative and

BOUNDARY WALLS of the agricultural field system at Cozumel appear as faint white traces in this aerial photograph of a newly cleared part of the San Gervasio zone in the northern part of the island. The islandwide system of field walls suggests the possibility that the Putun rulers of Cozumel may have abandoned the tradition of communal farmland in favor of private land ownership.

religious structures some distance inland from the defenseless coast. The interior areas were nonetheless linked to certain coastal points by the causeway system. If an enemy approached, the coast watchers could alert the population so that inland forces could use the causeways to concentrate at the threatened point on the coast.

Two other archaeological findings at Cozumel help to fill out the picture of a pragmatic mercantile people. First, the houses built by the traders had imposing façades: under the thatch that shaded the portico in front of the house rose a stone wall, smoothly plastered and often decorated with bright paintings. The wall was broken by doors that led into the dim interior [see *illustration on next page*]. This wall, however, was the only masonry construction in the house. The inviting doorways led directly into a thatch-roofed interior of about the same area as the thatched portico, enclosed by three walls made only of poles. These masonry false fronts, somewhat resembling the set of a Hollywood "Western," were built not only on Cozumel but also elsewhere in Putun-dominated Yucatán.

The other finding was the discovery of several caches of ax blades made from the green jadeite the Maya preferred for ceremonial objects. When one uncovers such a cache at a site of the Classic period, the workmanship of the jade is to be marveled at. In the Late Postclassic caches at Cozumel, however, quality is minimal. Almost all the ax blades are broken or otherwise damaged. One has the impression of bargain merchandise: seconds and irregulars.

What conclusions can be drawn from this picture of a pragmatic mercantile class? We have constructed a model based on our interpretation of the Cozumel fieldwork and on a reinterpretation of findings made elsewhere in Yucatán by other investigators. In broad outline the model would probably hold true for a rising merchant class in many different societies, but in its details it is peculiarly Maya. Its principal suggestion is that the developments of the three so-called decadent centuries, traditionally taken as indications of social decline, appear quite logical and progressive when they are regarded from a non-elite viewpoint. In other words, one has a very different view of Maya civilization looking at it from the bottom rather than from the top. Consider some of the Cozumel findings from that viewpoint.

The Putun dominance of Yucatán is

TIME INTERVAL	MEXICO PROPER	MAYA AREA	PERIOD AT COZUMEL
900 B.C. TO 300 B.C.	(1250 B.C.) OLMEC (600 B.C.) (400 B.C.)	MIDDLE PRECLASSIC (FIRST OCCUPATION OF MAYA LOWLANDS)	(ISLAND UNOCCUPIED)
300 B.C. TO A.D. 300	(A.D. 50)	LATE PRECLASSIC (GROWTH OF CEREMONIAL CENTERS)	LATE FORMATIVE (ISLAND FIRST OCCUPIED)
A.D. 300 TO A.D. 600	TEOTIHUACAN MONTE ALBAN	EARLY CLASSIC (RISE OF MAYA CLASSIC CIVILIZATION)	EARLY PERIOD I (OCCUPATION CONTINUES)
A.D. 600 TO A.D. 800	(A.D. 700)	LATE CLASSIC (PREEMINENCE OF CITIES SUCH AS TIKAL)	EARLY PERIOD II (OCCUPATION CONTINUES)
A.D. 800 TO A.D. 1000	(A.D. 900) (A.D. 1000)	TERMINAL CLASSIC (COLLAPSE IN SOUTHERN LOWLANDS)	PURE FLORESCENT (PERIOD OF PROMINENCE BEGINS)
A.D. 1000 TO A.D. 1250	TOLTEC (A.D. 1190)	EARLY POSTCLASSIC (PREEMINENCE OF CHICHÉN ITZÁ)	MODIFIED FLORESCENT (INCREASING PROMINENCE)
A.D. 1250 TO A.D. 1520	(A.D. 1345) AZTEC (A.D. 1521)	LATE POSTCLASSIC (PREEMINENCE OF MAYAPÁN UNTIL CA. A.D. 1450)	DECADENT (COZUMEL APOGEE CA. A.D. 1400)
A.D. 1520 TO A.D. 1600	SPANISH CONQUEST AND COLONIAL PERIOD		(DRASTIC POPULATION DECLINE)

MAYA CHRONOLOGY, from the first occupation of the lowlands until arrival of the Spanish, is compared with successive periods at Cozumel (right) and in Mexico proper (left).

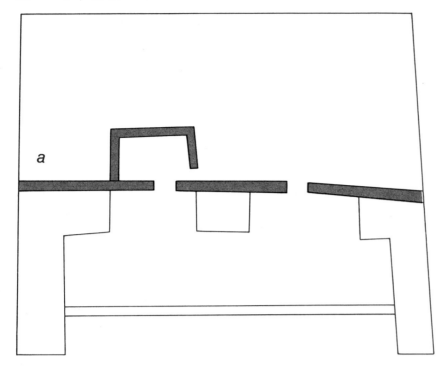

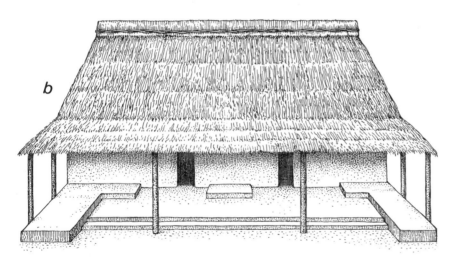

FALSE-FRONT HOUSE, its investment in masonry construction confined to one wall (*a*, *color*), is an example of applied Putun pragmatism. All a visitor to the house could see was a shady thatched portico (*b*), backed by a smoothly plastered and brightly painted wall. Only prying eyes would discover that the rest of the house was simple pole-and-thatch (*c*). House plan seen here was unearthed at San Gervasio; Mayapán contains similar structures.

evidence that the earlier theocratic elite had yielded power to a mercantile class. Just as other merchants have tried to do throughout history, the Putun wanted to keep their capital liquid. To spend the profits of commerce on high-quality grave goods was of no possible use to them; less than perfect jade serves the dead just as well. By the same token the raising of great monuments did little to benefit trade; a dry warehouse is more useful than a lofty temple. Nevertheless, appearances are always important. An inexpensive false front, heavily plastered to conceal shoddy masonry, made a logical investment. Such a house wall might not endure generation after generation, but the Putun were not building for posterity.

Some further examples emphasize the pragmatism of Cozumel's merchant rulers, men whose survival depended on quick reactions to changing economic and political circumstances. One such change came with the collapse of Toltec power in the 13th century. When Chichén Itzá, the paramount Toltec city in Yucatán, was suddenly abandoned, the entire Yucatecan trading network lost its prime central place. To reestablish the lost link a new center was founded within a few years: Mayapán. A fact strongly supporting the view that the new city was built to take the place of the old is that the earliest buildings at Mayapán almost literally reproduce the central core of Chichén Itzá on a smaller scale.

Some indications in the archaeological literature imply that the founders of Mayapán came from Cozumel, with the full support of the island's rulers. Such an action would have been logical; it was certainly in the interests of the Putun on Cozumel to stabilize the disrupted Yucatán trade network as soon as possible.

An even more drastic change accompanied the first probing Spanish voyages from Cuba to Yucatán: Córdoba's three ships in 1517, Grijalva's four in 1518 and Cortes' 11-ship fleet in 1519. The mainland Maya ambushed Córdoba's men when they landed on the north coast of Yucatán and killed many of them when they landed on the west coast. Grijalva landed twice on Cozumel without incident; the islanders simply retreated into the interior when the Spanish approached. Even when Grijalva sent a bilingual Jamaican who lived on Cozumel to summon the Maya chiefs to a meeting, they refused to respond. This passive behavior contrasts sharply with the hostile reaction of the mainland Maya to Grijalva's landings.

Cortes and his fleet met with quite a

SCOUTING CANOE, with a single paddler and two armed warriors aboard, is lying just off the coast in this copy of a wall painting from the Temple of the Warriors at Chichén Itzá. The warriors are carrying Mexican weapons: dart throwers in hand and quivers of darts next to their round shields. They may represent the vanguard of the Toltecs who rebuilt Chichén Itzá during the 10th century.

different response on Cozumel, if one is to believe the eyewitness account of Bernal Díaz. By chance one ship (Díaz was aboard) arrived at the island ahead of the rest of the flotilla. As when Grijalva landed at Cozumel, the inhabitants fled into the interior. In one deserted settlement the Spanish landing party appropriated 40 "fowl" (presumably turkeys) and the contents of a shrine, including some gold pendants heavily alloyed with copper. They also seized three Putun stragglers.

Cortes arrived soon afterward and ordered the release of the prisoners. Returning to them all the articles taken from the shrine (the fowl had been eaten) and adding some Spanish trade goods as gifts, Cortes asked them to seek out their leaders and arrange a meeting. The next day the chief official of the settlement appeared, followed by the men, women and children who had fled. "They went about among us," Díaz reported, "as if they had been friendly with us all their lives."

Cortes knew that when Córdoba had landed on the west coast of Yucatán in 1517, the Maya, on seeing the Spaniards, had called out "Castilan." To a good subject of Castile and León this seemed too much of a coincidence to be put aside, and Cortes asked the Cozumel chiefs if they knew of any other Spaniards in the area. The chiefs replied that indeed two Spaniards were living on the mainland nearby, and that "some traders had spoken to them two days before."

Cortes now asked the traders to take letters to his unknown countrymen, together with trade goods in the event that they had to be ransomed from the Maya who held them. He then sent the traders to the mainland in one of his smaller vessels. The result was the rescue from slavery of Geronimo de Aguilar, who had been cast away on the Yucatán coast in 1511 during a voyage from Panama to Santo Domingo. Aguilar, whose Maya was by now fluent, promptly joined Cortes as an interpreter. (The other Spaniard, a shipmate of Aguilar's, elected to remain in Yucatán with his Maya wife and their children.)

Soon thereafter Cortes desecrated what appears to have been Ix Chel's shrine. The Spaniards had no knowledge of the deity's identity, but Díaz states that the temple was one that was visited by many pilgrims from the mainland. Moreover, he actually heard what may have been the speaking oracle ("an old Indian in a long cloak") deliver what Díaz called a "black sermon." Cortes also heard the oracle, and after loftily telling the island chiefs that no good

would come of idolatry, he had his men destroy the temple images and ordered Maya masons to build a new altar. When it was finished, Cortes placed an image of the Virgin Mary on it and added a timber cross. His actions did not make the people of Cozumel take up arms or

flee. They seemed unperturbed and even burned incense before the new holy image.

How is one to interpret the difference between the hostile Maya of the mainland and the neutral Maya on Cozu-

EASE OF TRANSPORTATION dictated the uniformity in diameter and wall slope of these shallow Maya basins; their shape let them be stacked for shipment. The basins were found on Cozumel. They are probably Putun traders' merchandise brought from northern Yucatán.

MAYA GODDESS, Ix Chel, is portrayed carrying two images of the rain god, Chac, in this wall painting from a temple at Tulum, a Late Postclassic site on the mainland opposite Cozumel. Ix Chel's shrine on Cozumel had the only oracle known in the ancient Maya world.

mel? For one thing, as long-range traders the Putun were accustomed to encountering foreigners. If they believed the strangers' intentions were hostile, which may have been how they viewed Grijalva and the men of Cortes' first ship, they did what they could to avoid contact. Word would have long since reached them through trade channels about the slaughter the Spaniards could accomplish with their strange and fearful weapons.

Perhaps too the Putun already sensed the Spaniards' political and economic potential. It is clear that they chose to overlook the actions of Cortes at Ix Chel's temple. Again, their acknowledgment that Spaniards were to be found on the mainland and their delivery of Cortes' messages were acts of gratuitous goodwill. There is evidence, in their farewell to Cortes, that the pragmatic Putun

may by then have seen in the Spaniards the wave of the future. Before Cortes embarked the Putun asked for and received a "letter of recommendation" that they could show to other Spanish voyagers calling at Cozumel in order to ensure their future good treatment at Spanish hands.

As a final example of Putun pragmatism, consider the shrine of Ix Chel and its oracle. Can it be mere coincidence that the only oracular shrine in the Maya world was located on Cozumel? Oracles are in a far better position to be flexible in the endorsement of social and cultural change than the conservative priests who follow ritual in other kinds of shrine. There is even an example of this type of flexibility from modern Maya history. During the long and bloody "War of the Castes" that disrupted Yucatán periodically from 1847 to 1901 the rebellious

Maya regularly turned for guidance to Chan Santa Cruz, a shrine in the fastness of Quintana Roo. There the priests spoke for the gods through the medium of three "talking crosses," dictating the war policy of the rebels.

It is time for a final question. Can a period of history that witnesses the rise of a merchant class, the development of a new ethic and a substantial increase in economic complexity (including such events as the introduction of mass manufacture and an improvement in the general standard of living) be fairly considered the decadent last gasp of a dying civilization? Looking from the top down, from the viewpoint of an elite, the answer is perhaps yes. Looking from the bottom up, we think, the answer is clearly no. In examining the past one should not be limited to any one social point of view.

III

SOUTH AMERICA

III   SOUTH AMERICA

INTRODUCTION

The most spectacular archaeology in South America involving monumental architecture has occurred in Peru and adjacent portions of highland Bolivia. Indeed, this Peru-Bolivian culture area is often compared to Mesoamerica, with the two areas representing the high peaks of Pre-Columbian cultural development. It was in Mexico that Cortes encountered the Aztec civilization in all its glory and power, and it was in Peru that the other great Spanish conquistador, Pizarro, confronted the impressive domain of the Incas. Both areas had native historical traditions that interested sixteenth-century Spanish scholars and eventually made possible a degree of intellectual understanding of the native past with a richness of detail that was not afforded anywhere else in the New World. With the general advancement of archaeological research, other parallels between the two areas have emerged. In both, there is a long history of plant domestication and settled village life. Similarly, each saw the early rise of complex societies, the subsequent development of urban life, and the formation of state and empire. No other areas of the Americas were so heavily populated and densely settled as Mesoamerica and Peru-Bolivia.

In a Peru-Bolivia, as in Mesoamerica and other parts of the New World, early hunting-collecting cultures date back to remote times. Of course, the very earliest evidences of human presence are rather sketchily documented by scattered finds of lithic tools, and little can be said regarding the life-style of these most ancient populations. But, as in North and Central America, more specialized lithic implements and weapons appear after about 10,000 B.C., and these are standardized enough and are found in a sufficient number of sites to define specialized modes of hunting and other subsistence practices. Such hunters and collectors inhabited both the highlands and the coast, and there is accumulating evidence that these people practiced seasonal migration between highland and coastal areas. After about 4000 B.C., coastal settlers appear to have become more firmly anchored to the littoral and to marine foods from the rich fishing waters of the Pacific. In the opinion of some investigators, such as M. E. Moseley, this marine food dependence led to year-round village sedentism and eventually to the beginnings of complex societies in the coastal valleys.

The centuries of this transition from seminomadism to sedentism and from simple to complex social orders (from about 2500 B.C. to 1800 B.C.) were obviously crucial, and the archaeological record for this period is complicated, so that controversies have inevitably arisen. To understand these issues in a broader setting, it is necessary to shift the narrative back to the highlands. After 4000 B.C., both plant and animal domestication grew steadily in importance in the highland valleys. Many food plants were probably first domesticated here;

others were early imports from either the South American tropical forests or, via the Andean chain, from distant Mesoamerica. Maize, which occurs in Peruvian highland sequences by 2500 B.C., is most probably such a Mesoamerican import. It is found in coastal middens by 2000 B.C., if not earlier, and other cultigens, such as the lima bean, appear appreciably earlier on the coast. The question is thus posed as to how important agriculture may have been in Peruvian societies from 2500 B.C. to 1800 B.C. Was it merely a supplement to hunting and fishing? When did it achieve the dominant economic role? The picture is further complicated, for the highlands especially, by llama and alpaca domestication and herding and its economic potential.

In any event, by at least 1800 B.C., Peruvian coastal populations were primarily dependent upon farming, and the highland populations on farming and herding. This radiocardon date is a mean estimate taken to mark the beginning of the Initial Period of Peru-Bolivian archaeological chronology. This date is given particular archaeological significance by the fact that it is also the approximate date for the introduction of pottery to the area. This Initial Period was a time of rapid population growth and sociopolitical development, as indicated by the construction of huge public buildings and temples. Irrigation agriculture, which was to play such an important part in Peruvian civilization, was instituted in the coastal valleys at this time; and, quite possibly although less certainly, highland irrigation and terracing had comparably early beginnings. The Initial Period closes with the first appearances of Chavin art, the defining horizon style of the Early Horizon. This is dated to about 1200 B.C. The style takes its name from the great temple and residential complex of Chavin de Huantar in the north highlands of Peru. This highly sophisticated Chavin art incorporates a number of life forms that are recognizable, in spite of their stylization and grotesqueness, as caymans, jaguars, serpents, eagles, and humans. The presence of the cayman and jaguar motifs, both tropical lowland animals, suggests religious and ideological elements from that source; but the stylistic synthesis of these motifs was, insofar as we now know, a highland achievement. Like the Olmec style of Mesoamerica, Chavin art is pervasive and is expressed in various media and at various scales, from monumental stone sculptures to pottery ornamentations. It spread widely in Peru. The forces behind this dissemination are matters of speculation, but religious or cult diffusion seems most likely. As with the Olmec of Mesoamerica, the Chavin synthesis, whatever its social, political, or religious nature, gave a coherence to the cultures of the Peru-Bolivian area that was to find expression again in later periods. Thus, after the regional cultures of the Early Intermediate Period (200 B.C.–A.D. 600), the Huari-Tiahuanaco style of the Middle Horizon (A.D. 600–1000) embodies elements suggestive of the myths and ideologies of Chavin. Middle Horizon unification was, however, much more definitely defined, and it was prompted by military force, most likely a conquest empire. The Late Intermediate Period (A.D. 1000–1460) of the Peru-Bolivian chronology was again characterized by regional styles and states; and, as is well known from history, the Inca Empire unification of the Late Horizon (A.D. 1460–1532) absorbed these regional entities in the greatest of all native American conquest states. It seems a safe speculation that the Huari-Tiahuanaco Middle Horizon prepared the way for the Inca Empire, as earlier the Chavin Early Horizon prepared for the Middle Horizon.

No other South American culture area displays the same kind of internal coherence as the Peru-Bolivian area. All other areas are either more diverse or their shared traits are much less complex and specific than those of the Peru-Bolivian cultural tradition. The area of the northern Andes and southern Central America—sometimes referred to as the Intermediate Area because of its geographical position between Mesoamerica and Peru—is characterized by striking regional diversity. There are no horizon styles binding together Ecuador, Colombia, and the Isthmian regions.

A map showing the locations of archaeological sites and regions discussed in the articles in this section.

Archaeological research has progressed rapidly in the Intermediate Area in recent years. It is now known, for example, that agricultural villages and ceramics appear even earlier there than in Mesoamerica or Peru. The area is also known for its sophisticated developments in metallurgy and ceramics in later Pre-Columbian periods; but monumental architecture was never developed in the Intermediate Area to the extent that it was in the areas to the north and south, perhaps because it is a corollary of state power.

Long archaeological sequences are known from the Carribbean area, including the West Indes. The problem of the first peopling of these islands is the theme of Cruxent and Rouse's article "Early Man in the West Indies." Pottery-making and root crop farming also made an early appearance in the Amazon Basin. We have mentioned that tropical-forest domesticated plants found their way into the Peru-Bolivian area at an early time, and the whole complex question of the interrelationships of Andean and Amazonian cultures remains a major one for archaeological research. The nature of lowland plant cultivation in prehistoric times is treated in Parsons and Denevan's article "Pre-Columbian Ridged Fields."

Other culture areas, or culture-historical spheres, on the South American continent can only be mentioned in this brief summary. The South Andes of Argentina and Chile is one such area. It, too, has a long agricultural history, but one that would appear to have been derivative from Peru-Bolivia, as the South Andean cultures are marginal in other ways to events and developments in the area to the north. Eastern Brazil, the Chaco, and Pampean southern South America are other areas with distinct culture histories. Pre-Columbian peoples occupied the continent all the way to its southernmost extremities. Indeed, one of archaeology's most important findings is that there were early hunters in the vicinity of the Strait of Magellan as early as 9000 B.C.

This finding is part of the larger question of the dating of human presence in South America addressed by MacNeish in his article "Early Man in the Andes." MacNeish aligns himself with those who favor a very early presence of man in the Americas (*ca.* 40,000 years ago or earlier.). He advances this view with proper cautions, but he bases his bold argument on some recent findings of his own in the Peruvian Andes, on radiocarbon dates on these and on other early finds in various parts of the Americas from Alaska to Cape Horn, and on the styles of the lithic remains or industries under consideration and a comparison of these with possible Old World prototypes. He calls the earliest American industry the Core Tool tradition, defined by crude chopping and scraping tools made by the shaping of boulders or cores. Such implements characterize his lowest Peruvian cave levels, for which he has a radiocarbon date of 22,000 B.C. This date is well short of 40,000 years, but his argument is that the migration of early populations from north to south through the Americas, after crossing into Alaska from Asia, was slow and that the Peruvian Paccaicasa stone tools had been made by peoples who still retained very ancient, Lower Paleolithic modes of flint chipping. This same "delayed" effect continued up through the Peruvian cave sequences, with older forms of tools still being used in South America at a time when newer forms were already in use in North America. A Flake and Bone Tool tradition of his Ayacucho complex, dating from 13,000 B.C. to 10,000 B.C., reflects a technological ancestry of a greater age in North America and, more remotely, in Asia. Finally, in upper levels in his cave stratigraphy in the Ayacucho Valley, MacNeish found tools belonging to the "Specialized Bifacial Point Tradition," which are related to the classic "Paleo-Indian" lithic industries that date after 10,000 B.C. in North America and a bit later than this in South America.

MacNeish's thesis is daring and provacative. To offer a more cautious interpretation, MacNeish's cave excavations offer a strong argument for human presence in mid-Andean South America by some 20,000 years ago, a finding generally consistent with the developing consensus that the Americas had been inhabited since at least 20,000 to 30,000 years ago. The extension back to 40,000 years or more is a hypothesis extrapolated beyond present facts for the purpose of stimulating the search for new data.

Although there are evidences for human occupation on the Venezuelan mainland back to 10,000 B.C. and earlier, no evidence has been found for such an early occupation of the islands of the West Indies. It is possible, although not yet proven, that early migrants made their way into the Greater Antilles as early as 5000 B.C. Radiocarbon dates from lithic sites on the island of Hispaniola go back to *ca.* 2500 B.C., and earlier dates may be extrapolated through further archaeological interpretation. This hypothesis is detailed in Cruxent and Rouse's article "Early Man in the West Indies." The authors employ, although in not quite so sweeping a manner as MacNeish, the concept of the technological evolution of flint chipping industries that takes its original model from Old World sequences. Thus, they describe the earliest lithic tools on Hispaniola, those of the Casimiroid tradition, as "Early Paleo-Indian" because the complex lacked projectile points, which they identify as markers of "Late Paleo-Indian" traditions. Of course, all the West Indian absolute dates are much later than dates for any kind of Paleo-Indian remains from the continental mainlands. This is an example of archaeologists' sometimes confusing use of both stage sequences and strictly chronological sequences. Perhaps the most interesting aspect of the Cruxent and Rouse article, however, is their hypothesis that attempts to explain the diverse nature of the artifacts and industries of early West Indian cultures found from island to island. They argue that such lack of cultural uniformity can best be explained by several different sources or points of origin for the earliest migrants to the islands and that the apparent geographical randomness of archaeological distributions on the islands resulted from raft travel and the vagaries of sea currents from mainland to archipelago.

The next two South American articles move away from the subject of early man to the subject of later Peruvian civilizations. The article by Schaedel on "The Lost Cities of Peru" has an ironic title, in that modern inhabitants of the region live over the ancient adobe cities of the North Coast of Peru, but the Pre-Columbian structures are often so enormous and extensive that they have been taken for granted as mere eroded clay hills of the landscape. Aerial photography has helped to delineate patterns and site layouts. Considerable archaeological research has taken place since Schaedel originally wrote this article, and we know now that the Moche, or Mochica, civilization of the Early Intermediate Period did indeed build cities. The capital center of Moche is one such city, with extensive, but now buried, residential areas surrounding the huge pyramid and palace complex for which the site is famous. Middle Horizon (Huari-Tiahuanaco) and Chimu Kingdom urban layouts are more readily visible, as Schaedel indicates. The article, with its pictures and plans, gives a good idea of the immensity of ancient Peruvian settlements and constructions.

Isbell's article on "The Prehistoric Ground Drawings of Peru" addresses the more esoteric problem of the strange markings on the desert floor in the vicinity of Nazca on the South Coast. Obviously, great expenditures of time and effort went into the making of these long lines or "roads," various geometrical designs, and stylized life-form figures. For the most part, they are executed on such a scale that they can only be appreciated by present-day observers from the air. What was their purpose? Archaeologists are not sure of an answer and may never be. Because of their forms and designs, which closely resemble the figures on Nazca (Early Intermediate Period) pottery, they can be related to this culture and time; but hypotheses explaining them as astronomical or star lines or perhaps actual roadways are not well supported by the diversity and complexity of the evidence. Isbell offers the interesting theory that the markings, like other types of community ceremonial effort on a large scale, are the remains of labor-intensive activities that "drained off" economic surpluses and held population levels stable. The pyramid-building and temple-building projects of other parts of Peru and the Americas would have had the same effects. Later in Peru, such surpluses and public labor were directed toward warehousing and military constructions. The idea has the quality of a "general field theory" of human social behavior, and many archaeologists and social historians would not agree; but Isbell's employment of it here is a good example of attempting to place archaeological findings in a larger theoretical setting.

"Pre-Columbian Ridged Fields" by Parsons and Denevan calls attention to several relatively recent discoveries that undoubtedly have a bearing on the growth of native American cultures in many parts of South America. Like Pre-Columbian urban patterns and the ground drawings of Nazca, these discoveries were made through aerial surveys. In some cases, as with the "lost cities" or the drawings, they had been noted in a limited way in on-the-ground field explorations, but their scope and significance were understood from the aerial overviews. The authors discuss and describe artificially raised fields in the riverine lowlands of northern Colombia, in the Guayas Basin of Ecuador, in the Amazonian drainage Mojos region of lowland Bolivia, and along the Surinam coast. The magnitude of the remains is proof that such constructions must have been an economically significant factor in ancient agriculture. Tropical-forest farming was not, obviously, all of the shifting-field swidden system. In various places and times, it was more stable, more labor-intensive, and undoubtedly more productive than the swidden method. Parsons and Denevan call attention to other places in South America where the ridged fields may also have been used. Such ridges are found extensively in lowland swampy country of the Maya civilization in Mesoamerica, too.

These five South American articles sample some of the diversity of archaeological interests on that continent and its nearby islands. They also indicate different possible orientations for archaeology—the necessary alliances with geology and oceanography in the early man studies, the ties with Inca and Spanish conquest history and socioeconomic theory in the Peruvian articles, and the links to agriculture and agronomy in Parsons and Denevan's article. Archaeology cannot afford to ignore these or numerous other aids from related disciplines as it goes about building up a body of culture-historical data and seeking ways to explain the past.

Early Man in the Andes

14

by Richard S. MacNeish
April 1971

*Stone tools in highland Peru indicate that men lived
there 22,000 years ago, almost twice the old estimate.
They also imply that the first cultural traditions of the
New World had their roots in Asia*

Recent archaeological discoveries in the highlands of Peru have extended the prehistory of the New World in two significant respects. First, the finds themselves indicate that we must push back the date of man's earliest known appearance in South America from the currently accepted estimate of around 12,000 B.C. to perhaps as much as 20,000 B.C. Second and even more important is the implication, in the nature of the very early Andean hunting cultures now brought to light, that these cultures reflect Old World origins of even greater antiquity. If this is so, man may have first arrived in the Western Hemisphere between 40,000 and 100,000 years ago. The discoveries and the conclusions they suggest seem important enough to warrant this preliminary report in spite of the hazard that it may prove to be premature.

The new findings were made in 1969 and 1970 near Ayacucho, a town in the Peruvian province of the same name. All the sites lie within a mountain-ringed valley, most of it 6,500 feet above sea level, located some 200 miles southeast of Lima [*see top illustration on page 161*]. The valley is rich in prehistoric remains (we noted some 500 sites during our preliminary survey) and archaeological investigations have been conducted there since the 1930's. For me and my associates in the Ayacucho Archaeological-Botanical Project, however, the valley was interesting for other reasons as well.

A number of us had already been involved in a joint archaeological-botanical investigation at Tehuacán in the highlands of Mexico under the sponsorship of the Robert S. Peabody Foundation for Archaeology. Our prime target was early botanical evidence of the origin and development of agriculture in the area. This we sought by archaeological methods, while simultaneously recording the relation between agricultural advances and the material evidence of developing village life (and ultimately urban life) in Mexico before the Spanish conquest. By the time our fieldwork at Tehuacán had been completed in the mid-1960's we had gained some understanding of the changes that had come about in highland Mesoamerica between its initial occupation by preagricultural hunters and gatherers around 10,000 B.C. and the rise of pre-Columbian civilization [see the article "The Origins of New World Civilization," by Richard S. MacNeish, beginning on page 97].

There was, however, at least one other major New World center that had been the site of a similar development from hunting bands to farmers and city folk. This is western South America. Its inhabitants had cultivated some plants that were unknown to the farmers of Mesoamerica, and they had domesticated animals that were similarly unique to the region. Mesoamerica certainly interacted with South America, but the earliest stages of this second regional development apparently took place in isolation. It seemed logical that the record of these isolated advances might provide the foundation for functional comparisons with the Tehuacán results and perhaps lead us to some generalizations about the rise of civilization in the New World.

This was the objective that brought several veterans of the Tehuacán investigation, myself included, to Peru. The work was again sponsored by the Peabody Foundation, where I now serve as director. Reconnaissance of a number of highland areas led us to select the Ayacucho valley as the scene of our investigations. Our decision was based primarily on ecological grounds: within a radius of 15 miles the varied highland environment includes areas of subtropical desert, thorn-forest grassland, dry thorn forest, humid scrub forest and subarctic tundra [*see bottom illustration on page 161*]. It is the consensus among botanists who have studied the question that many of the plants first domesticated in western South America were indigenous to the highlands and that their domestication had probably taken place in Peru. The Peruvian ecologist J. A. Tosi had concluded that the most probable locale for the event would be a highland valley that included a wide range of environments. An additional consideration was that the area where we worked should contain caves that could have served as shelters in the past and thus might prove to be the repositories of animal and plant remains. The Ayacucho valley met both requirements.

Two caves in the valley have in fact turned out to be particularly rich repositories. One of them, located about eight miles north of the town of Ayacucho, is known locally as Pikimachay, or Flea Cave. It lies some 9,000 feet above sea level on the eastern slope of a hill composed of volcanic rock; the mouth of the cave is 40 feet high in places and 175 feet wide, and the distance from the front of the cave to the deepest point inside it is 80 feet. Rocks that have fallen from the roof occupy the northern third of the interior of the cave and form a pile that reaches a height of 20 feet. In 1969 Flea Cave yielded the single most dramatic discovery of the season. During our last week of excavation a test trench, dug to a depth of six feet near the south end of the cave, revealed stone tools in association with bones of an extinct ground sloth of the same family as the fossil North American sloth *Megatherium*. One of the bones, a humerus, has

been shown by carbon-14 analysis to be 14,150 (±180) years old.

The other notable cave site, some 11 miles east of the town of Ayacucho, is known locally as Jayamachay, or Pepper Cave. Although Pepper Cave is as high and nearly as wide as Flea Cave, it is only 15 feet deep. Excavations were made at Pepper Cave with rewarding results in both the 1969 and the 1970 seasons. Because the significance of the findings at this site arises largely from a comparison of the material from both caves, I shall first describe the strata at Flea Cave.

What has been revealed in general by our work at all the cave and open-air sites in the Ayacucho valley (a total of 12 excavations) is a series of remains representative of successive cultures in an unbroken sequence that spans the millenniums from 20,000 B.C. to A.D. 1500. The archaeological sequence documents man's progression from an early hunter to an incipient agriculturist to a village farmer and finally to the role of a subject of imperial rule. The material of the most significance to the present discussion, however, is contained in the strata representing the earliest phases of this long prehistoric record. These strata have yielded a succession of stone-tool types that began some 20,000 years ago and continued until about 10,500 years ago. The earliest part of the record is found in the lowest levels at Flea Cave.

The oldest stratified deposit in the cave lies in a basin-like hollow in the lava flow that forms the cave floor. The stratum lies just above the bedrock of the basin. Labeled Zone k, the stratum consists of soils, transported into the cave by natural means, that are mixed with disintegrated volcanic tuffs from the rocks of the cave itself. Zone k is eight inches deep. Just before the deposition of the stratum ended, some animal vertebrae and a rib bone (possibly from an extinct ground sloth) were deposited in it. So were four crude tools fashioned from volcanic tuff and a few flakes that had been struck from tools. One of the flakes is of a green stone that could only have come from outside the cave.

DEEP CUT through part of an open-air archaeological site at Puente in highland Peru is seen in the photograph on the opposite page. The record preserved in the successive strata at Puente extends from the first appearance of pottery in the 16th century B.C. to about 7000 B.C., when the Andes were inhabited by hunters specializing in the pursuit of big game.

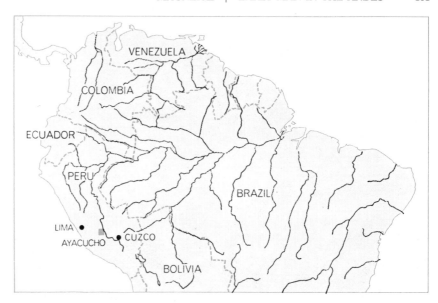

AYACUCHO VALLEY, between Lima and Cuzco, is undergoing joint botanical and archaeological investigation that will allow comparisons with a study of Tehuácan, in Mexico. The Robert S. Peabody Foundation for Archaeology is the sponsor of both studies.

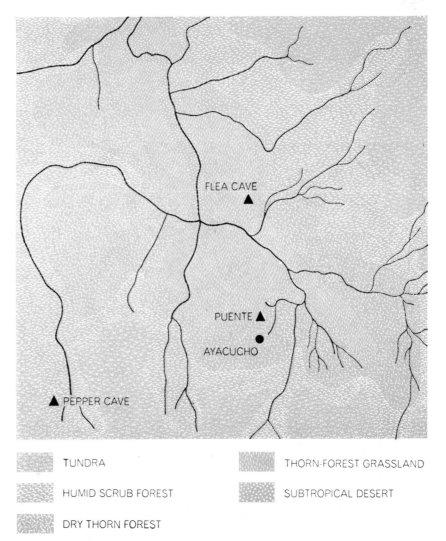

TUNDRA

HUMID SCRUB FOREST

DRY THORN FOREST

THORN-FOREST GRASSLAND

SUBTROPICAL DESERT

MAJOR SITES in the Ayacucho valley include Puente, near the town of Ayacucho, Flea Cave, a few miles north of Puente, and Pepper Cave, a few miles southwest. The existence of five distinct zones of vegetation in the valley (key) was a factor in its selection for study.

FLEA CAVE, the site that contains the oldest evidence of man's presence thus far unearthed in South America, lies at an altitude of 9,000 feet in an area of intermingled thorn forest and grassland. The mouth of the cave (*center*) is 175 feet wide and 40 feet high.

PEPPER CAVE, the other major cave site in the Ayacucho area, lies at an altitude of 11,000 feet on a hill where humid scrub forest gives way to upland tundra vegetation. The lowest strata excavated at Pepper Cave are evidently the product of local glacial outwashes.

The soils in Zone k are neutral in terms of acidity, which suggests that the vegetation outside the cave when the soils were formed was of the grassland variety, in contrast to the dry thorn-forest vegetation found today. The period of deposition that formed Zone k may have begun more than 23,000 years ago. It remains to be seen whether the climate at that time, as indicated by the neutral acidity of the soil, can be exactly correlated with any of the several known glacial fluctuations in the neighboring Andes.

Three later strata, all containing the bones of extinct animals and additional stone implements, overlie Zone k. They are labeled, in ascending order, zones j, i1 and i. Zone j is a brown soil deposit 12 inches thick. In various parts of this stratum we unearthed three vertebrae and two rib fragments of an extinct ground sloth and the leg bone of a smaller mammal, perhaps an ancestral species of horse or camel. Zone j yielded 14 stone tools; like those in Zone k, they are crudely made from volcanic tuff. There are in addition some 40 stone flakes, evidently the waste from toolmaking. Carbon-14 analysis of one of the ground-sloth vertebrae shows it to be 19,600 (±3,000) years old.

Zone i1, above Zone j, is a deposit of a more orange-colored soil; it is 15 inches thick, and it contains tools and both fossilized and burned animal bone. Carbon-14 analysis of one of the bones, a fragment of sloth scapula, indicates that it is 16,050 (±1,200) years old. The soils of zones j and i1 are both quite acid, suggesting that they were formed when the climate was less arid and the vegetation outside Flea Cave included forest cover.

The uppermost of the four strata, Zone i, consists of 18 inches of a slightly browner soil. The soil approaches that of Zone k in neutral acidity, suggesting a return to drier climatic conditions. Distributed through the deposit are crude stone artifacts, waste flakes and the bones of sloth and horse. Carbon-14 analysis of one of the bones shows it to be 14,700 (±1,400) years old.

The stone tools from all four of the lowest Flea Cave strata are much alike. There are 50 of them in all, uniformly large and crude in workmanship. The tool types include sidescrapers, choppers, cleavers, "spokeshaves" and denticulate (sawtoothed) forms. Most of them were made from volcanic tuff, which does not flake well, and it takes a skilled eye to distinguish many of them from unworked tuff detached from the

YEARS BEFORE PRESENT (ESTIMATED)	ASSOCIATED C-14 DATES (YEARS BEFORE PRESENT)		TOOL COMPLEX	CLIMATE AND VEGETATION	POSSIBLE GLACIATION STAGE
	FLEA CAVE	PEPPER CAVE			
8,000	f1	C 8,250 (±125)	JAYWA	MODERN CLIMATE AND VEGETATION	ICE IN HIGH ANDES ONLY
		D 8,360 (±135)			
	8,860 (±125)	E			
	f2	F	PUENTE		
		G			
		H 8,980 (±140)			
		I			
	ROCKFALL	J			
		J1 9,460 (±145)	HUANTA	COOL	FINAL ICE RETREAT
		J2			
		J3			
		K			
		L			
		M			
12,000	g	N		COLD	FINAL ICE ADVANCE
		GRAVEL	BLADE, BURIN, LEAF-POINT?		
	h			WARM FOREST	INTERSTADIAL
	h 14,150 (±180)		AYA-CUCHO		
	h1			COLD GRASSLAND	ICE ADVANCE
16,000	i 14,700 (±1,400)				
	i1 16,050 (±1,200)		PACCAI-CASA	WARM FOREST	INTERSTADIAL?
	j 19,600 (±3,000)				
20,000	k	ROCK FLOOR		COLD GRASSLAND	EARLY ICE ADVANCE?

SEQUENCE OF STRATA at the major Ayacucho cave sites is correlated in this chart with the five earliest tool complexes that have been identified thus far. Carbon-14 determinations of the age of certain strata are shown in relation to estimates of the overall temporal sequence. The climate and vegetation are linked to probable stages of glaciation.

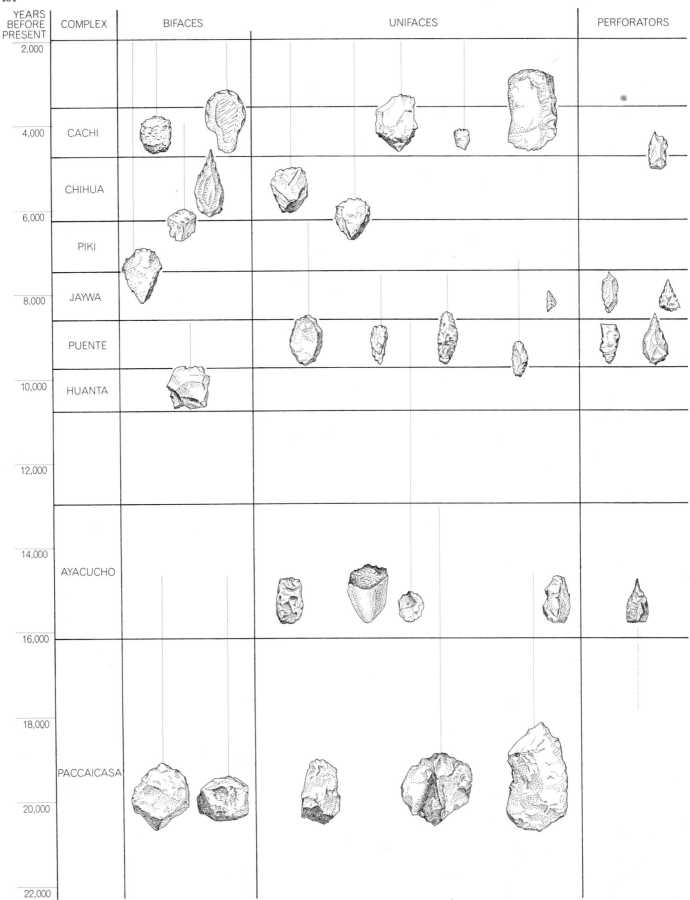

YEARS BEFORE PRESENT	COMPLEX	BIFACES	UNIFACES	PERFORATORS
2,000				
4,000	CACHI			
	CHIHUA			
6,000	PIKI			
8,000	JAYWA			
	PUENTE			
10,000	HUANTA			
12,000				
14,000	AYACUCHO			
16,000				
18,000				
20,000	PACCAICASA			
22,000				

KINDS OF TOOLS discovered at 12 excavations in the Ayacucho valley appear in this chart in association with the complex (*names at left*) that first includes them. No complex more recent than the Puente, some 9,000 years old, is relevant to man's earliest arrival

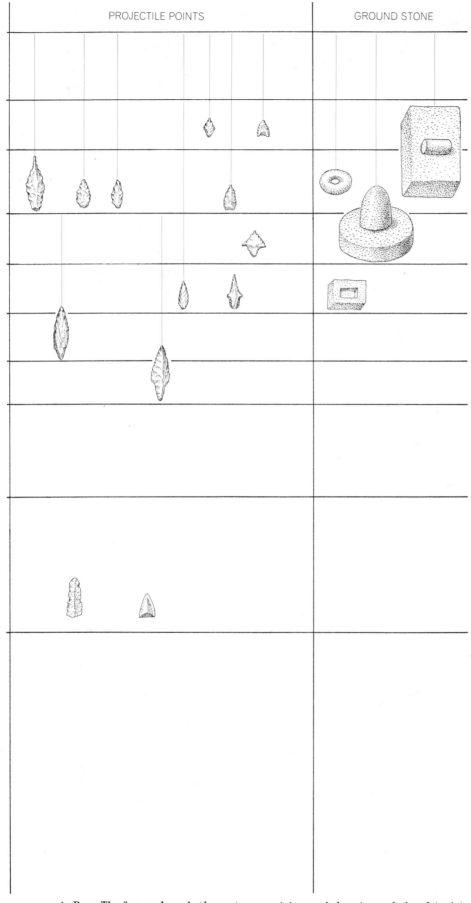

PROJECTILE POINTS	GROUND STONE

in Peru. The first crude tools (*bottom*) are reminiscent of chopping tools found in Asia. In the next complex projectile points first appear; some were made out of bone (*far right*).

cave walls by natural processes. A few of the tools, however, were made from other materials, such as rounded pebbles and pieces of basalt, that were collected outside the cave and carried back to be fashioned into implements. The tools in these four levels represent the earliest assemblage of tools, or tool complex, unearthed so far at a stratified site anywhere in South America. We call it the Paccaicasa complex, after a nearby village. The men who fashioned its distinctive tools occupied the Ayacucho valley from as much as 22,000 years ago to about 13,000 years ago.

The strata at Flea Cave that contain the Paccaicasa complex were excavated during the 1970 season. The previous year we thought we had already reached bedrock when we reached the top of the stratum just above Zone i: it was a very hard, yellowish layer of soil that included numerous small flakes of volcanic tuff. With the season nearly at an end we proceeded no farther. The yellow layer, now known as Zone h1, actually turned out to lie just above bedrock over an area of some 150 square yards of cave floor except for the natural basin near the south end of the cave. Digging into this stratum with some difficulty at the start of the 1970 season, we found that its 20-inch depth contained not only the bones of sloth, horse and possibly saber-toothed tiger but also numerous flakes of waste stone and some 70 tools, most of them quite different from the crude tuff artifacts of the strata below. A few tools of the older kind were present in Zone h1, but the majority are made from such materials as basalt, chalcedony, chert and pebbles of quartzite.

The use of new tool materials is also characteristic of Zone h, a 12-inch stratum of softer, light orange soil that overlies Zone h1. Here, however, the animal remains include many not found in the older strata. A kind of ancestral camel appears to be represented in addition to the sloth and the horse. There are also the remains of the puma, the hog-nosed skunk, an extinct species of deer and several unidentified species, possibly including the mastodon. This larger faunal assemblage suggests a return of the countryside around Flea Cave to forest cover. Indeed, the soil of Zone h is strongly acid, unlike the neutral soils of Zone i and Zone h1.

The tools in Zone h are abundant; in addition to more than 1,000 fragments of waste stone there are some 250 finished artifacts. Some of these artifacts are in the "core" tradition of tool manufacture: they were made by removing

LIMB BONE of an extinct ground sloth (*center*) was found at Flea Cave in a stratum that also contained stone and bone tools representative of the Ayacucho complex. Carbon-14 analysis of the bone shows that the stratum was deposited at least 14,000 years ago.

flakes from a stone to produce the desired shape. Among them are both the choppers and spokeshaves typical of the lower strata and new varieties of tool such as split-pebble scrapers and fluted wedges. The core tools are outnumbered, however, by tools consisting of flakes: burins, gravers, sidescrapers, flake spokeshaves, denticulate flakes and unifacial projectile points (points flaked only on one side). The unifacial points are the oldest projectile points found at Ayacucho.

At this stage the inhabitants of Flea Cave were also fashioning tools out of bone: triangular projectile points, polishers, punches made out of antler and "fleshers" formed out of rib bones. There is even one polished animal toe bone that may have been an ornament.

Zone h is the rich stratum that yielded the 14,000-year-old sloth humerus in 1969. The change in tool materials apparent in Zone h1 and the proliferation of new tool types in Zone h suggest that at Flea Cave a second tool complex had taken the place of the earlier Paccaicasa complex. We have named the distinctive assemblage from these two strata the Ayacucho complex.

The stratum immediately overlying Zone h is found in only a few parts of the excavation. It consists of a fine, powdery yellow soil that is neutral in acidity. This sparse formation, labeled Zone h,

has so far yielded only three stone artifacts: a blade, a sidescraper and a large denticulate scraper. The lack of soil acidity suggests that the interval represented by Zone *h* was characterized by dry grassland vegetation. Further investigation may yield enough artifacts to indicate whether or not the stratum contains a distinctive tool complex suited to the changed environment. For the time being we know too little about Zone *h* to come to any conclusions.

For the purposes of this discussion the Flea Cave story ends here. Above Zone *h* at the time our work began was a three-foot layer of fallen rock, including some individual stones that weighed more than three tons. This rock was apparently associated with the much heavier fall in the northern half of the cave. A small stratum above the rock debris, labeled Zone f1, contained charcoal, the bones of modern deer and llamas, and a few well-made bifacial tools (stone tools flaked on both sides). These tools closely resemble tools of known age at Puente, an open-air site near Ayacucho where only the remains of modern animals have been found. On this basis one can conclude that the time of the rockfall at Flea Cave was no later than 10,000 years ago. It is worth mentioning that before any of the strata below the rock layer could be excavated, the rocks had to be

broken up by pickax and carried out of the cave. The three-foot rock stratum was labeled Zone g.

The strata that tell the rest of our story are in a deep deposit in the southeast corner of Pepper Cave. Situated at an altitude of nearly 11,000 feet, this cave is surrounded today by humid scrub forest. It is adjacent to a tributary of the Cachi River, whose bed lies 150 feet below the level of the cave. The bottom stratum of the deep deposit at Pepper Cave consists of stratified sands and gravels close to the top of a high waterbuilt terrace. This fluvial deposit is labeled Zone N. It is overlain by a threefoot layer of rocks that have fallen from the roof of the cave, mixed with stratified sands that indicate a continuation of fluvial terrace building. The mixed stratum comprises zones M and L. Preliminary geological studies suggest that the terrace was formed by outwash from the final advance of the Andean glaciers. There is no evidence of human activity in the three lowest strata at Pepper Cave.

Overlying these sterile layers is a 28-inch stratum of windblown sand and disintegrated volcanic tuff that has been labeled Zone K. Artifacts were found in the upper four inches of the deposit, and a few were also unearthed in one reddish area near the bottom of it. The artifacts represent a new complex of tools that was also found in the next three strata:

floors of human habitation that are labeled in ascending order zones J3, J2 and J1. No animal remains have been recovered from Zone K, but the three J zones contain the bones of horses, of extinct species of deer and possibly of llamas.

The characteristic artifacts of the new tool complex, which we have named Huanta after another town in the valley, include bifacially flaked projectile points with a "fishtail" base, gravers, burins, blades, half-moon-shaped sidescrapers and teardrop-shaped end scrapers. A carbon-14 analysis of one of the animal bones from the uppermost stratum, Zone J1, indicates that the Huanta complex flourished until about 9,500 years ago.

The five strata overlying the Huanta complex at Pepper Cave, like the single layer above the rockfall at Flea Cave, hold remains typical of the Puente complex. These strata have been designated zones J through F. One stratum near the middle, Zone H, is shown by a carbon-14 analysis of charcoal to have been laid down about 9,000 years ago. This date is in good agreement with the known age of material excavated at the Puente site. The contents of the strata above the Puente complex zones at Pepper Cave (zones E through A), like the contents of zones f1 through a at Flea Cave, will not concern us here.

Having reviewed the facts revealed at Ayacucho, let us consider their broader implications. What follows is not only interpretive but also somewhat speculative; it goes well beyond the direct evidence now at our disposal. Stating the implications straightforwardly, however, may serve two useful purposes. First, in doing so we are in effect putting forward hypotheses to be proved or disproved by future findings. Second, in being explicit we help to define the problems that remain to be solved.

Let us first consider the implications of our evidence concerning changes in vegetation and climate. Remains of the Puente complex overlie the sequences of earlier strata at both caves: they are on top of the material of uncertain character at Flea Cave and on top of the Huanta complex at Pepper Cave. To judge from carbon-14 measurements, the earliest appearance of the Puente complex, with its advanced tools and remains of modern animal species, may have been around 9,700 years ago. At about that time, then, the association of early man and extinct animals in this highland area evidently came to an end.

We have not yet completed the soil studies and the analyses of pollens in the soil that will add many details to the record of climate and vegetation. For the time being, however, I tentatively propose that the last of the pre-Puente strata at Flea Cave (Zone h) and the sterile zones N through L at Pepper Cave coincide with the last Andean glacial advance. Zone h at Flea Cave, with its acid soil and remains of forest animals, appears to represent an earlier "interstadial" period in the glacial record—a breathing spell rather than a full-scale retreat. Zones h1 and i, below Zone h, are characterized by the remains of different animals and by soil of neutral acidity, suggesting a colder climate and a glacial advance. Evidence from the still earlier zones i1 and j suggests a second interstadial period of relative warmth. Zone k, the lowest in the Flea Cave excavation, apparently represents another period of advancing ice. If the Ayacucho evidence holds true for Andean glacial activity in general, the South American glacial advances and retreats do not coincide with those of the Wisconsin glaciation in North America [see illustration on this page]. This apparent lack of correlation presents interesting problems. If glaciation is caused by worldwide climatic change, why are the South American oscillations so unlike the North American ones? If, on the other hand, widespread climatic change is not the cause of glaciation, what is? The precise sequence of Andean glacial advances and retreats obviously calls for further study.

What are the implications of the Aya-cucho findings with respect to early man, not only in South America but also elsewhere in the New World? The results of local studies of the earliest phases of prehistory in South America are all too seldom published, so that the comments that follow are particularly speculative. Having warned the reader, let me suggest that the Paccaicasa complex in the Peruvian central highlands may well represent the earliest stage of man's appearance in South America.

To generalize from Ayacucho material, this earliest stage seems to be characterized by a tool assemblage consisting of large corelike choppers, large sidescrapers and spokeshaves and heavy denticulate implements. This I shall call the Core Tool Tradition; it is certainly represented by the Paccaicasa assemblage in South America and may just possibly be represented in North America by the controversial finds at the Calico site in the Mojave Desert north of Barstow, Calif. In South America the Core Tool Tradition appears to have flourished from about 25,000 years ago to 15,000 years ago.

Man's next stage in South America I call the Flake and Bone Tool Tradition. The only adequate definition of this tradition so far is found in the Ayacucho tool complex. That complex is characterized by a reduction in the proportion of core tools and a sudden abundance of tools made out of flakes: projectile points, knives, sidescrapers, gravers, burins, spokeshaves and denticulate tools.

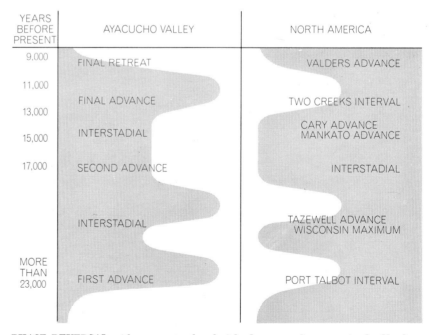

YEARS BEFORE PRESENT	AYACUCHO VALLEY	NORTH AMERICA
9,000	FINAL RETREAT	VALDERS ADVANCE
11,000	FINAL ADVANCE	TWO CREEKS INTERVAL
13,000		
15,000	INTERSTADIAL	CARY ADVANCE / MANKATO ADVANCE
17,000	SECOND ADVANCE	INTERSTADIAL
	INTERSTADIAL	TAZEWELL ADVANCE / WISCONSIN MAXIMUM
MORE THAN 23,000	FIRST ADVANCE	PORT TALBOT INTERVAL

PHASE REVERSAL with respect to the glacial advances and retreats in the Northern Hemisphere during the final period of Pleistocene glaciation appears to characterize the record of fluctuations preserved at Ayacucho. The graph compares estimated Andean advances, retreats and interstadial phases with the phases of the Wisconsin glaciation.

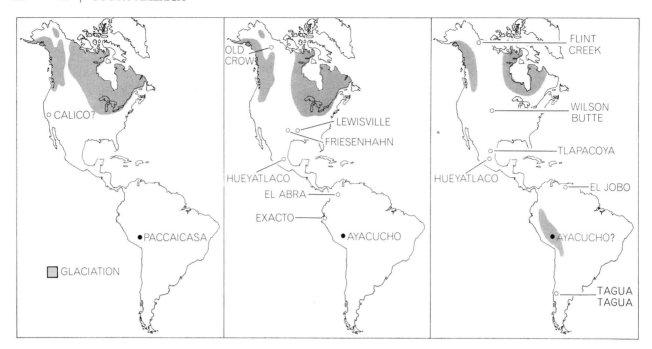

THREE TRADITIONS in New World prehistory are the Core Tool Tradition (*left*), the Flake and Bone Tool Tradition (*center*) and the Blade, Burin and Leaf-Point Tradition (*right*). The age of each tradition in North America, in cases where the age of a representative site is known, is substantially greater than it is in South America, suggesting that they stem from earlier Old World roots.

An important element in the tradition is the presence of bone implements, including projectile points, awls and scrapers. The Flake and Bone Tool Tradition apparently flourished from about 15,000 years ago to 13,000 or 12,000 years ago. Elsewhere in South America, although the evidence is scanty, the tradition may be reflected in surface finds attributed to the Exacto complex of coastal Ecuador and in flake tools from the El Abra cave site in highland Colombia; the El Abra material is estimated to be 12,500 years old. Some of the rare worked flakes from the Chivateros "red zone" of coastal central Peru may also represent this tradition [see "Early Man in South America," by Edward P. Lanning and Thomas C. Patterson; SCIENTIFIC AMERICAN, November 1967]. Not all the North American sites that may be representative of the tradition are adequately dated. Where dates are available, however, they are from 10,000 to more than 20,000 years earlier than their South American counterparts.

The third South American stage I call the Blade, Burin and Leaf-Point Tradition. At present it is very poorly represented at our highland sites, consisting only of the three artifacts from Zone *h* at Flea Cave. The tradition is far better defined, however, in the El Jobo phase of Venezuela, where double-ended points, blades, burins and corelike scrapers have been unearthed in association with the bones of extinct animals. The

El Jobo phase is not adequately dated, but estimates suggest that its tool industry flourished roughly between 10,000 and 14,000 years ago. A small amount of material found at Laguna de Tagua Tagua in central Chile may also belong to this third tradition; carbon-14 analysis indicates that the Chilean material is about 11,300 years old. The precise duration of the Blade, Burin and Leaf-Point Tradition is not yet known. My guess is that it flourished from 13,000 or 12,000 years ago until 11,000 or 10,000 years ago. Like the preceding tradition, it is represented at sites in North America that, where age estimates exist, appear to be somewhat older.

Seen from the perspective of the Ayacucho valley, early man's final stage in South America, which I call the Specialized Bifacial Point Tradition, appears to have flourished from 11,000 or 10,000 years ago to 9,000 or 8,000 years ago. At Ayacucho the tradition is defined in the Huanta complex at Pepper Cave and in the later Puente complex there and elsewhere in the valley. It is characterized by bifacially flaked projectile points that evidently represent a specialization for big-game hunting. The tradition's other characteristic implements include specialized end scrapers and knives suited to skinning and butchering. Elsewhere in South America the tradition is represented at Fell's Cave in southern Chile, where a number of carbon-14 determinations suggest ages clustering

around 11,000 years ago. Other artifacts probably in this tradition are those from a stratum overlying the red zone at Chivateros (which are evidently some 10,000 years old), from Toquepala Cave in southernmost Peru (which are about 9,500 years old) and from a number of other South American sites. Sites representative of the Specialized Bifacial Point Tradition in North America are almost too numerous to mention.

What might these four postulated traditions signify concerning man's arrival in the New World from Asia? Considering first the latest tradition—the Specialized Bifacial Point Tradition—we find a bewildering variety of complexes throughout North America at about the time when the late Paleo-Indian stage ends and the Archaic Indian stage begins. Nearly all the complexes have something in common, however: a specialization in bifacially flaked projectile points of extraordinary workmanship. I suggest that these specialized point industries all belong to a single tradition, that for the most part they represent local New World developments and that there is little use in trying to trace them to some ancestral assemblage on the far side of the Bering Strait. Carbon-14 analysis of charcoal from Fort Rock Cave in Oregon indicates that the earliest known specialized projectile points in the New World are some 13,200 years old. On the basis of this finding I propose that the Specialized Bifacial Point Tradition originated in the New World, beginning about 14,000 years ago in North America, and reached South America 3,000 to 4,000 years later.

North American artifacts related to the preceding tradition—the Blade, Burin and Leaf-Point Tradition—in South America include material from Tlapacoya and Hueyatlaco in Mexico, respectively some 23,000 and 22,000 years old, and material at least 15,000 years old from the lower levels of Wilson Butte Cave in Idaho. Some artifacts of the Cordilleran tradition in Canada and Alaska may also be related to the South American tradition. Again there apparently is a lag in cultural transmission from north to south that at its longest approaches 10,000 years. If there was a similar lag in transmission from Asia to North America, it is possible that the Blade, Burin and Leaf-Point Tradition originated with the Malt'a and Buret tool industries of the Lake Baikal region in eastern Siberia, which are between 15,000 and 30,000 years old.

As for the still older Flake and Bone Tool Tradition, adequately dated North American parallels are more difficult to find. Artifacts from Friesenhahn Cave in central Texas and some of the oldest material at Hueyatlaco show similarities to tools in the Ayacucho complex, but in spite of hints that these North American sites are very old the finds cannot be exactly dated. There are bone tools from a site near Old Crow in the Canadian Yukon that carbon-14 analysis shows to be from 23,000 to 28,000 years old. It is my guess that the Yukon artifacts belong to the Flake and Bone Tool Tradition, but many more arctic finds of the same kind are needed to change this guess into a strong presumption. A few flake tools from the site at Lewisville, Tex., may also be representative of the Ayacucho complex. Their estimated age of 38,000 years is appropriate. Figuring backward from the time the tradition appears to have arrived in South America, it would have flourished in North America between 25,000 and 40,000 years ago. Is it not possible that the Flake and Bone Tool Tradition is also an import from Asia? Perhaps it came from some Old World source such as the Shuitungkuo complex of northern China, reportedly between 40,000 and 60,000 years old.

We now come to the most difficult question, which concerns the oldest of the four traditions: the Core Tool Tradition. I wonder if any of my more conservative colleagues would care to venture the flat statement that no Core Tool

Tradition parallel to the one in the Paccaicasa strata at Flea Cave will ever be unearthed in North America? If it is found, is it not likely that it will be from 40,000 to as much as 100,000 years old? To me it seems entirely possible that such a core-tool tradition in the New World, although one can only guess at it today, could be derived from the chopper and chopping-tool tradition of Asia, which is well over 50,000 years old. (An example of such a tradition is the Fenho industry of China.) I find there is much reason to believe that three of the four oldest cultural traditions in the New World can be derived from specific Old World predecessors. That seems to be the most significant implication of our findings at Ayacucho. However much this conclusion may be modified by future work, one thing is certain: our knowledge of early man in the New World is in its infancy. An almost untouched province of archaeology awaits exploration.

YEARS BEFORE PRESENT	SOUTH AMERICA	MEXICO CENTRAL AMERICA	U.S. AND CANADA	EASTERN ASIA	
9,000	PUENTE HUANTA	IZTAPAN LERMA			SPECIALIZED POINT TRADITION
10,000	FELL'S CAVE (11,000)	AJUREADO			
11,000	EL JOBO		PLAINVIEW FOLSOM CLOVIS		
12,000	TAGUA TAGUA (11,300)		FORT ROCK CAVE (13,200)		
13,000	AYACUCHO				
14,000	EL ABRA (12,500)		WILSON, BUTTE (15,000)		
15,000	AYACUCHO (14,150)				
16,000					
20,000	PACCAICASA (19,600)	HUEYATLACO (21,850) TLAPACOYA (23,150)			BLADE, BURIN, LEAF-POINT TRADITION
25,000		HUEYATLACO	MALT'A-BURET U.S.S.R.		
30,000			FRIESENHAHN CAVE OLD CROW (23,000-28,000)		
40,000			LEWISVILLE (38,000)		FLAKE BONE TOOL TRADITION
50,000			CALICO (?)	SHUITUNG-KUO, CHINA	
60,000				FENHO, CHINA	CORE TOOL TRADITION
75,000					

OLD WORLD SOURCES of the three earliest prehistoric traditions in the New World are suggested in this chart. A fourth and more recent tradition, marked by the presence of finely made projectile points for big-game hunting, seems to have been indigenous rather than an Old World import. Although much work will be required to establish the validity of all three proposed relationships, the foremost weakness in the hypothesis at present is a lack in the Northern Hemisphere of well-dated examples of the core-tool tradition.

Early Man
in the West Indies

by José M. Cruxent and Irving Rouse
November 1969

*Until recently it seemed that the islands of the
Caribbean were uninhabited up to about the
time of Christ. Now it appears that men may have
arrived 5,000 years earlier. How did they get there?*

When and by whom the islands of the West Indies were first settled is a matter of debate among archaeologists. The debate may soon be intensified: evidence recently discovered suggests that people of the Paleo-Indian age, the earliest period in New World prehistory, reached one of the main islands 7,000 years ago. If this is so, it means that New World hunters managed to cross the Caribbean when their level of culture was no more advanced than that of the Paleolithic age in the Old World.

It is our intention in this article to present the new evidence and to relate it to older knowledge and conjecture about the aboriginal settling of the West Indies. Let us first briefly review the geography of the area, with special reference to the various island chains that provide natural migration routes outward from the mainland.

The West Indies consist of two major island chains and three minor ones. The southernmost major chain, the Lesser Antilles, consists of many small islands forming an arc along the eastern side of the Caribbean and separating it from the Atlantic. Starting near the mouth of the Orinoco River in Venezuela, the chain extends northward and then curves around to the northwest, so that its last members (the Virgin Islands) almost touch the first of the Greater Antilles.

The island next to the Virgin Islands is Puerto Rico. Starting there, the Greater Antilles extend westward along the north side of the Caribbean. The next islands in the chain are Hispaniola (politically divided between Haiti and the Dominican Republic) and Jamaica, which lies somewhat to the south. The chain ends with Cuba, whose western tip nearly fills the gap between the peninsulas of Yucatán and Florida at the mouth of the

Gulf of Mexico. The Greater Antilles are much larger and better endowed with natural resources than the other islands of the West Indies, and today they are also much more populous.

Of the three lesser chains the southernmost stretches along the coast of Venezuela from the mouth of the Orinoco on the east to Lake Maracaibo on the west. Its main islands are Trinidad, which is the easternmost, and two smaller clusters: the Venezuelan islands of Margarita, Coche and Cubagua in the middle and the Dutch islands of Bonaire, Curaçao and Aruba in the west. The chain does not have a generally accepted name. In Spanish it is called the Leeward Islands, but the same name is used in English for a group of former British possessions in the Lesser Antilles. Here we shall call the chain the South Caribbean islands.

The next of the lesser chains crosses the Caribbean from Central America almost to Jamaica, following a submerged mountain ridge. Today this chain consists mainly of banks, reefs and cays, but two of its islands (Providencia and San Andrés, which are part of Colombia) are of fair size. When the sea level was lower a few thousand years ago, the chain formed a nearly continuous series of stepping-stones leading to the Greater Antilles. This group also lacks a generally accepted name; here we shall call them the Mid-Caribbean islands.

The last of the lesser chains consists of the Bahamas, which lie to the north and east of Hispaniola and Cuba and extend northward for some distance along the east coast of Florida. A series of small coral islets, they provide the best stepping-stone route between the mainland to the north and eastern Cuba and Hispaniola to the south.

Prevailing winds and currents in the Caribbean strongly favor some directions of travel over others. The trade winds blow from the northeast, making voyages in a westerly direction easy in both the Greater Antilles and the South Caribbean chain. The currents favor movement to the west and also movement from South America north to the major island chains. The South Equatorial Current flows across the Atlantic to the coast of Guiana and is deflected northwestward through the South Caribbean chain and the southernmost Lesser Antilles. The North Equatorial Current follows a similar course through the northern Lesser Antilles to the Greater Antilles. Still farther north, the Canaries Current skirts the north coast of Hispaniola and flows through the Bahamas. The effect of the currents is reinforced by the flow of the two major rivers of northern South America: the Orinoco and the Magdalena. Both discharge into the sea with such force that debris is carried offshore for miles to be picked up by the South Equatorial Current and, in the case of the Orinoco, carried some distance into the Lesser Antilles.

Given these conditions, one would expect that the West Indies were populated from South America. This was true at the time of the first European voyages to America. When the Spaniards reached the area, they found that both the Lesser and the Greater Antilles were inhabited by Indians who spoke Cariban and Arawakan, languages that are widespread in eastern South America. The inhabitants' material culture belonged to the final pre-Columbian age, or period of development, in the Caribbean area; that age is known as the Neo-Indian. This means that the Caribs and Arawaks made pottery. Coincidentally they also knew the art of farming and were skilled mariners, so that it is easy to understand their successful expansion through most of the West Indies.

The Neo-Indians, however, were relative newcomers to the islands. We now know that they migrated from South America at about the time of Christ, entered the Greater Antilles about A.D. 250 and did not populate their most norther-

ly territory, the Bahamas, until A.D. 1000. As they moved along they overran an earlier West Indian population. When the Spaniards arrived, the earlier people existed only as remnants in western Cuba, in a few small Cuban offshore islands and in southwestern Hispaniola.

The earlier inhabitants' material culture belonged to the preceding Meso-Indian age. They knew nothing of pot-

tery; they made their distinctive artifacts by grinding stone and by chipping flakes of flint. They did not know farming and fed themselves instead by fishing and gathering shellfish and wild vegetable foods. After a few decades under Spanish administration the remnant Meso-Indians, together with nearly all the Neo-Indians, had become extinct.

Perhaps because the Meso-Indians

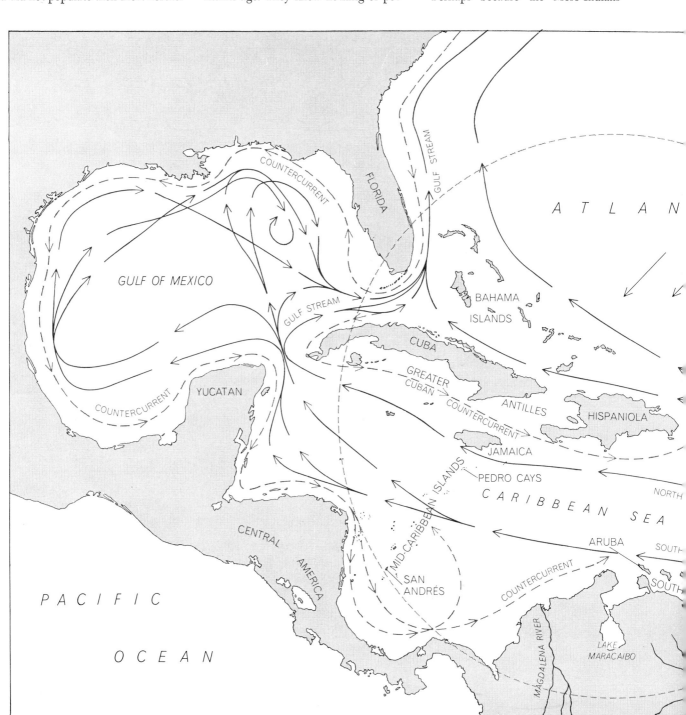

ISLAND CHAINS of the West Indies include the Greater Antilles (consisting of Cuba, Jamaica, Hispaniola and Puerto Rico), the Lesser Antilles (beginning with the Virgin Islands and ending with Grenada), the South Caribbean islands (from Trinidad, the most easterly, to Aruba, the most westerly), the Mid-Caribbean islands (extending from San Andrés to Pedro Cays) and the Bahama Islands (extending from Hispaniola to Florida). Hispaniola is geographically central (*broken circle*). The route to it from Vene-

were fishermen and presumably at home on the water the question of how and when they reached their island homes remained of limited interest to scholars until evidence of an even earlier West Indian population was discovered in recent years. These discoveries, both in the islands and on the adjacent mainland, now make it clear that, no matter how early the Meso-Indian occupation of the

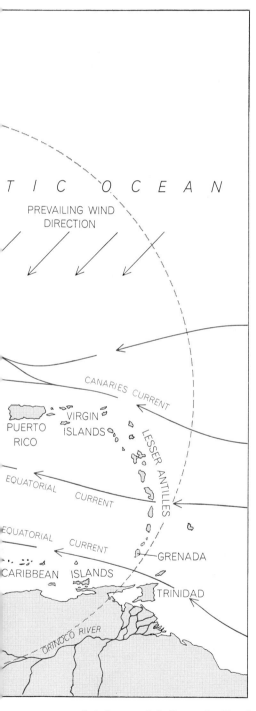

West Indies may have been, even earlier Paleo-Indian occupations preceded it. The sites—in Florida, Cuba and Hispaniola—were identified as Paleo-Indian by the absence of ground-stone artifacts; the only stone implements were made of flaked flint. How and when these primitive hunting peoples reached the islands are questions that have also stimulated increased interest in Meso-Indian origins.

Meso-Indian sites are found in both the Greater Antilles and the islands of the South Caribbean chain. They are not known anywhere in the Lesser Antilles, with the exception of a site on St. Thomas, the member of the Virgin Islands group that is closest to Puerto Rico. How, then, did the Meso-Indians reach the Greater Antilles? The Meso-Indians who settled in the South Caribbean chain must have come from the Venezuelan mainland. There is no convincing evidence, however, that the Meso-Indians who settled in the Greater Antilles had moved to their final destination through the Lesser Antilles, as the Caribs and Arawaks had. Nor is there any conclusive evidence that the Meso-Indians followed either of the alternative routes: from Florida by way of the Bahamas or from Central America by way of the Mid-Caribbean chain.

There is still another alternative. The Meso-Indians in the Greater Antilles may simply have been descendants of the Paleo-Indians, and their more advanced material culture may have evolved on the spot. If that is the case, there are two further possibilities. The ancestral Paleo-Indians may have reached the islands during their initial period of development: the Early Paleo-Indian age, when their artifacts consisted of simple, unhafted flint flakes and crude flint pounders and choppers. Or they may have arrived during the subsequent period: the Late Paleo-Indian age, when some artifacts (particularly projectile points, which were unknown in the Early Paleo-Indian age) were made in shapes suitable for hafting.

Hispaniola lies near the geographic center of the West Indies; it is nearly equidistant from the other three islands in its chain. It is also roughly equidistant from Venezuela and Colombia to the south, Central America and Yucatán to the west and Florida to the north. This pivotal position made Hispaniola preeminent in West Indian cultural development during the Neo-Indian age. Was it also preeminent in the preceding ages? As we shall see, the answer appears to be yes.

The first evidence that Hispaniola harbored any archaeological remains earlier than Neo-Indian ones was unearthed a century ago, but it was not until 1933 that an unquestioned Meso-Indian site was excavated. The digging was done for the Museum of the American Indian by Godfrey J. Olsen at Île à Vache, an island near the southwest tip of Haiti. The site was a large mound of discarded shells from which Olsen excavated single-bitted and double-bitted ground-stone axes, ground-stone mortars and pestles and a number of other objects. Some of the stones, evidently ceremonial, were engraved with elaborate designs. The designs are reminiscent of motifs seen on Hispaniolan pottery of the Neo-Indian age. It is quite possible, in fact, that the Île à Vache culture complex was contemporaneous with the Neo-Indian occupation of Hispaniola. The site is in a part of the island where Meso-Indians managed to survive until historical times.

Two years after Olsen's work five pre-pottery sites were excavated near Fort Liberté in northeastern Haiti by Froelich G. Rainey, then at Yale University's Peabody Museum, and one of us (Rouse). All five sites represented a single Meso-Indian complex that was given the name Couri. The Couri complex is clearly earlier than the Île à Vache one. Its ground-stone artifacts include vessels, milling stones, balls, pegs and double-bitted axes, but the decoration is unsophisticated [*see illustration on page 177*]. Only one stone vessel and a pendant made of shell bore simple rectilinear designs. The Couri people also made some tools out of flint, including large knives, scrapers and projectile points that have central stems for hafting. There are even some "backed blades," with one edge blunted by chipping, as in the Upper Paleolithic age of the Old World.

The Yale excavations stimulated Haitian archaeologists in their own search for pre-pottery sites. In 1940 Edward Mangonès of the Haitian Bureau of Ethnology found two deposits of flint tools in an area north of Port-au-Prince. Other investigators subsequently located six more sites in the same general area. All of them can apparently be grouped in the same complex, named Cabaret after the best-known of the eight localities. The absence of ground-stone artifacts means that the Cabaret complex belongs to one of the Paleo-Indian ages. Included among its flint artifacts are projectile points, showing that the Cabaret people were of the Late Paleo-Indian age; the points have stems for hafting. Among

zuela is by way of the Lesser Antilles, from Florida by way of the Bahamas, from Yucatán by way of Cuba and from Central America via the islands of the Mid-Caribbean chain.

174

FOUR SUCCESSIVE AGES of prehistory on Hispaniola, a major island of the West Indies, are represented by these artifacts. They are (a, b) two fragments of Arawak pottery, typical of the most recent, Neo-Indian age; (c) an engraved stone bowl from Île à Vache and (d) a stone "pin" from a Couri culture site, both shaped by grinding and representative of the Meso-Indian age, whose people preceded and later coexisted with the Neo-Indians; (e) a flint projectile point from a Cabaret culture site, typical of the preceding Late Paleo-Indian age, and finally (f) a flint chopper of the more ancient Early Paleo-Indian age discovered at Rancho Casimira.

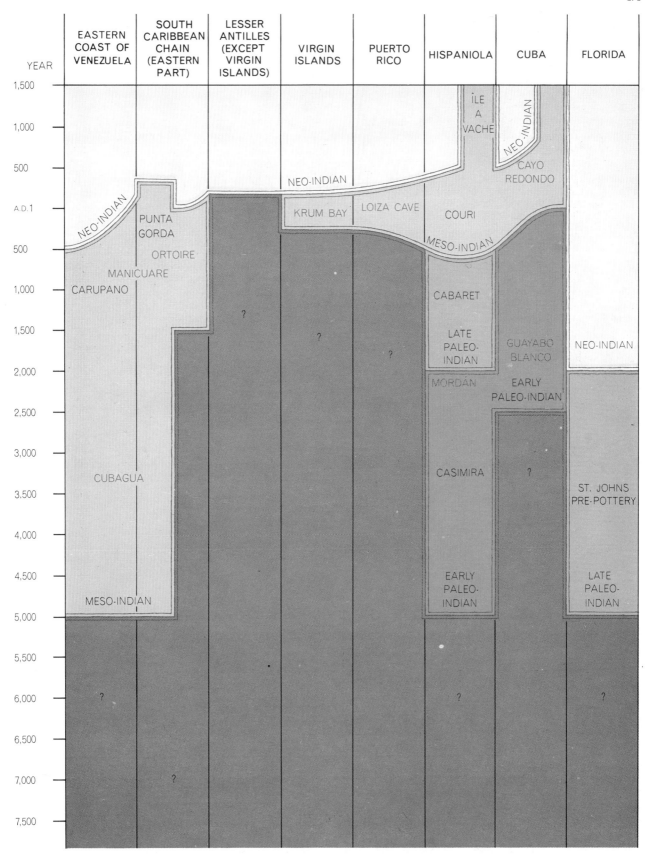

PREHISTORIC AGES were entered at different times in different parts of the West Indies. The Neo-Indian age, characterized by a knowledge of pottery, began in Florida, for example, about 2000 B.C. and in Venezuela late in the first millennium B.C. It had not yet begun in parts of Cuba and Hispaniola, however, at the time of the first European contact. On Hispaniola the Early Paleo-Indian age may have been introduced by migrants as long ago as 5000 B.C. By that time the inhabitants of Florida were representative of the Late Paleo-Indian age and the inhabitants of Venezuela had entered the subsequent prehistoric period, the Meso-Indian age. Many West Indian complexes are of uncertain age, but the dates indicated for the names shown in color are based on carbon-14 findings.

the other artifacts are long, narrow flakes of flint with ends that have been retouched [*see illustration on page 178*]. In their retouching the Cabaret workers took pains to reduce or eliminate the "bulbs of percussion" or the "striking platforms" that are present on the long flakes because of the way they are made. This presumably facilitated setting the flakes in hafts for use as scrapers or as knives.

The most recently discovered pre-pottery sites on Hispaniola also appear to be the island's oldest. They are located some 50 miles west of Santo Domingo on the island's south coast and were excavated in 1963 by the Dominican archaeologist Luis Chanlatte and one of us (Cruxent). In the 1920's the Danish archaeologist Gudmund Hatt had collected flint artifacts there, near the village of Barreras, and had reported that the region was rich in flint. At Mordán, a village near Barreras, Chanlatte and Cruxent excavated the first of their sites, a thick deposit of prehistoric refuse, primarily marine shells that had been brought from the seashore less than a mile away.

A trench two meters wide and four meters long was dug in the Mordán refuse deposit to a depth of one meter.

In the top 25 centimeters of the trench fragments of pottery were common, but they became scarcer in the next 25 centimeters and were absent in the two lowest 25-centimeter sections. The lowest sections contained a number of flint artifacts; no projectile points were among them. All four sections contained small fragments of animal bone; none of the bones could be identified by species, but some were fishbones. In the bottom section a hearth yielded charcoal samples for carbon-14 analysis.

For a distance of at least three miles in all directions from Mordán the ground is littered with flint boulders and angular flint fragments embedded in the soil and half-exposed by erosion. These provided the raw material from which the Mordán workers fashioned their tools. The long flakes were apparently struck from cores with prismatic cross sections; we say "apparently" because no cores were recovered. The flakes, however, show the bulbs of percussion and prepared striking platforms characteristic of flints struck from such cores.

The Mordán workers did not follow the Cabaret practice of retouching their flakes to facilitate hafting. The absence of hafting and of projectile points shows that the complex belongs to the Early Paleo-Indian age. A few of the flakes

show crude retouching on the edges, but most of them were apparently used just as they came from the core. The only secondary flaking visible on them is due to wear. They seem to have served as knives and scrapers, possibly for the manufacture of baskets.

Two other sites were found a short distance inland from Mordán. Both contained flint artifacts but no shell refuse or pottery. At one of them, Rancho Casimira, a two-by-two-meter trench was dug to a depth of 50 centimeters. No charcoal or hearths were found; the contents consisted exclusively of crudely made artifacts and waste flint of poorer quality than the Mordán flint. The upper 25-centimeter section at Casimira bore flint of a quality slightly superior to that in the lower section, as if the Casimira workers had used any flint at hand in the beginning but had later succeeded in finding a source of better material. Nonetheless, only a few of the flakes seem to be from prismatic cores, all the artifacts are strikingly larger and heavier than their Mordán counterparts and the flakes have thick, unretouched ends that would certainly have precluded hafting. None of the implements show evidence of retouching. Signs of wear indicate that the blades were used as scrapers and some of the heavier pieces served as pounders and choppers [*see illustration on pages 179 and 180*].

With the exception of Mordán and Casimira, all the Hispaniola sites described here were excavated before carbon-14 dating had been developed. In recent years work at a number of sites in the West Indies and on the mainland has produced a substantial list of carbon-14 dates. In the case of the Meso-Indian complexes of the Greater Antilles these dates have tended to cluster around the beginning of the Christian era. We had assumed that the same was probably true of the Cabaret complex in Hispaniola. The absence of projectile points and hafting preparations from the Mordán and Casimira complexes placed them in the Early Paleo-Indian age, however, and we eagerly awaited the carbon-14 analysis of the Mordán charcoal.

The samples yielded three dates: 2190 (±130) B.C., 2450 (±170) B.C. and 2610 (±80) B.C. This meant that we had been at least 2,000 years off in our estimate of when man first reached Hispaniola. Indeed, in view of the virtual certainty that the Casimira complex substantially predates the Mordán, the Casimira complex could date back as far as 5000 B.C. In any case the unexpected antiquity of

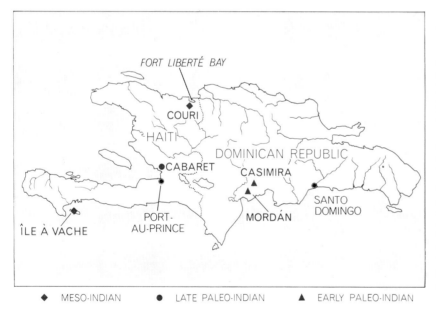

◆ MESO-INDIAN   ● LATE PALEO-INDIAN   ▲ EARLY PALEO-INDIAN

HISPANIOLA, politically divided between Haiti and the Dominican Republic, has a number of archaeological sites representative of the Meso-Indian and Paleo-Indian ages of New World prehistory. The artifacts unearthed at Île à Vache and Couri in Haiti are made out of stone that was shaped by grinding; they are therefore representative of the Meso-Indian age. At sites near Cabaret, also in Haiti, the artifacts are made from chipped flint. They include projectile points and thus belong to the preceding Late Paleo-Indian age. The sites at Mordán and Rancho Casimira in the Dominican Republic yielded Early Paleo-Indian artifacts. Carbon-14 dates show that the Mordán site is at least 4,000 years old. The Casimira site is apparently even older; it may have been first occupied as long as 7,000 years ago.

the Mordán complex has made us revise our views concerning the chronology of the Paleo- and Meso-Indian complexes throughout the West Indies [see illustration on page 175].

Where do these new findings lead us? Let us put forward the hypothesis that the Casimira complex did appear on Hispaniola about 5000 B.C. What are the implications of this early date? One implication stems from the improbability that lower material cultures are derived from higher ones. For this reason the Casimira people are not likely to have been emigrants from either the northern or the southern mainland; they could scarcely have come from Florida because Florida's inhabitants were then in the Late Paleo-Indian age, and they could scarcely have come from Venezuela because by that time Venezuela's inhabitants were Meso-Indians.

If, on the other hand, Casimira is only slightly older than Mordán, there would seem to be no obstacle to attributing the complex to migrants from Cuba, where the Early Paleo-Indian age did not end until the time of Christ. The assumption of a later date for the Casimira complex would therefore appear to be fatal to our hypothesis, and the reader may view with suspicion our selection of the date that appears to serve the hypothesis best. Nonetheless, we can offer considerable evidence in support of this choice.

Let us first dispose of the weakest alternative: a migration from the south. One would have to assign Casimira a date hundreds and perhaps thousands of years earlier than 5000 B.C. before one could find a well-substantiated Early Paleo-Indian population available to emigrate from either Venezuela or the South Caribbean islands. The carbon-14 dates for the Meso-Indian culture sequence in that region run from 750 B.C. back to 3800 B.C., and it appears that a safe initial date for the Meso-Indian age there would be about 5000 B.C. We have no secure carbon-14 dates for the two Paleo-Indian ages in Venezuela, but we have reason to believe the transition from the Early to the Late Paleo-Indian age in that region took place about 12,000 years ago.

What about the possible migration from Florida? We know that the Neo-Indian age began in Florida about 2000 B.C. Near the headwaters of the St. Johns River a number of sites of an earlier age have been excavated. One of the principal artifacts, unearthed in large numbers, is a kind of gouge made by breaking a triangular section from the outer whorl of a conch shell and grinding one edge of it. These gouges are found in association with pins made of bone and with flint projectile points that are flaked on both sides. There are no carbon-14 dates for the sites, but the absence of ground-stone artifacts and the presence of projectile points suggest that St. Johns is a complex of the Late Paleo-Indian age. This complex is dated between 5000 and 2000 B.C. If Casimira is somewhat more recent than 5000 B.C., one could envision a migration from Florida as its source, except for two facts: neither the shell gouge, the characteristic St. Johns artifact, nor the St. Johns type of projectile point has ever been found on Hispaniola.

There remains the possibility of migration from Cuba. If the date of Casimira is closer to 2500 B.C. than to 5000 B.C., some of the Early Paleo-Indians of a complex known as Guayabo Blanco might have migrated to Casimira. Carbon-14 analysis indicates that the Guayabo Blanco complex was in existence as early as 2050 B.C., and it is our opinion that the complex or something quite like it existed in Cuba at least a few hundred years earlier. Could this complex be the source of Casimira? We think not: the artifacts of the Guayabo Blanco complex are made chiefly of shell and not of flint. They include shell vessels and, as in the St. Johns complex, the principal tool is the shell gouge. Objects made of flint are rare, which suggests that they may have been trade items. Unlike the flint artifacts of the St. Johns complex, none are projectile points.

The nearly contemporary age of the Mordán and Guayabo Blanco complexes and the absence of projectile points at both sites point to the closeness of the Hispaniolan and Cuban complexes of the Early Paleo-Indian age. Still, two facts—the paucity of flint tools at the Cuban site and the total absence of shell gouges on Hispaniola—seem to rule out intimate cultural ties between the two complexes. It seems more likely that Cuba's Early Paleo-Indian complex was

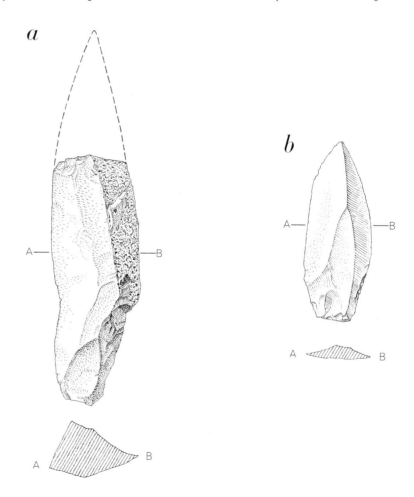

FLINT TOOLS of Paleo-Indian workmanship are from sites of the Cabaret complex in Haiti. The projectile point (a) has been given a lateral stem to allow hafting. Its tip is missing; the broken line suggests its original appearance. The flake (b) has also been reworked at one end for hafting; it was probably a scraper. Both belong to the Late Paleo-Indian age.

derived from Florida, although we know too little about the pre-pottery cultures of Florida to state this as a certainty.

With Venezuela, Florida and Cuba evidently ruled out as sources of the Casimira complex, only one mainland area remains: Central America. It is a further part of our hypothesis that the Casimira people pushed out from Central America into the Caribbean, traveling by way of the Mid-Caribbean island chain first to Jamaica and then to Hispaniola. This part of our hypothesis has weaknesses, at least for the present. For example, although a flint-working tradition like that at Casimira and Mordán is known in Central America, the mainland version is considerably more developed and its artifacts have been found only in a Neo-Indian context. We suggest

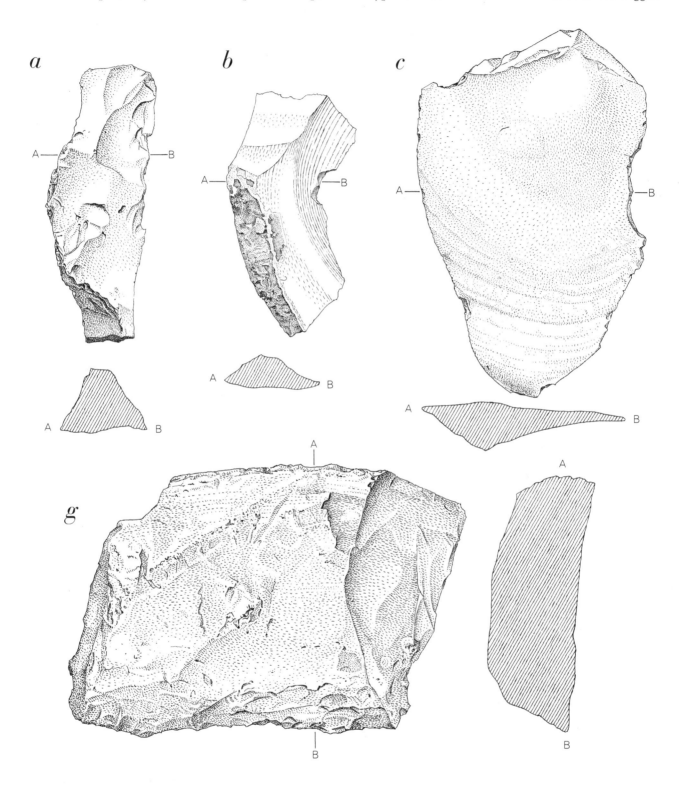

OLDEST-KNOWN TOOLS on Hispaniola, made from an inferior grade of flint, were excavated at Rancho Casimira in the Dominican Republic. Among them are narrow scrapers that are often quite long (a, b, d, e), broad scrapers, both large (c) and small (h),

that the Central American tradition has Paleo- and Meso-Indian antecedents that remain to be discovered. Another weakness is that no prehistoric habitation sites of any kind have been reported on the Mid-Caribbean islands and no Paleo- and Meso-Indian ones have been found on Jamaica. No one has systematically looked for such sites, however, and the absence of reports does not necessarily mean an absence of sites.

Two further questions remain to be answered with respect to our hypothesis: Why did the Casimira people leave the mainland and how? We believe the answer to both questions is implicit in the nature of the flint implements at Casimira. The scrapers, pounders and choppers are typical of the tools made by the big-game hunters of the Late Paleo-Indian age on the mainland, who used

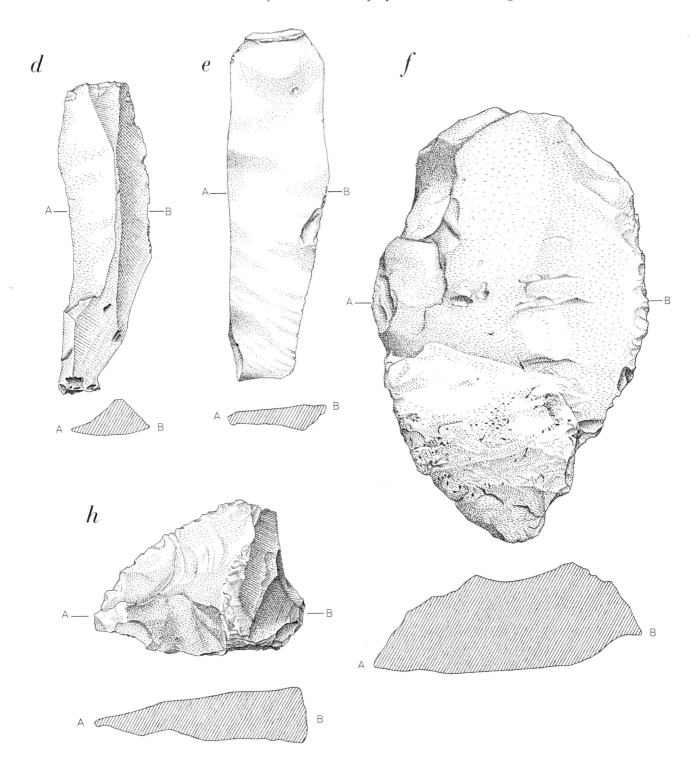

and massive chopping tools (*f*, *g*). Lacking projectile points, the Casimira people lived in the Early Paleo-Indian age. Their tools are nevertheless typical of mainland big-game hunters; they may have hunted large sea mammals such as the seal and the manatee.

180

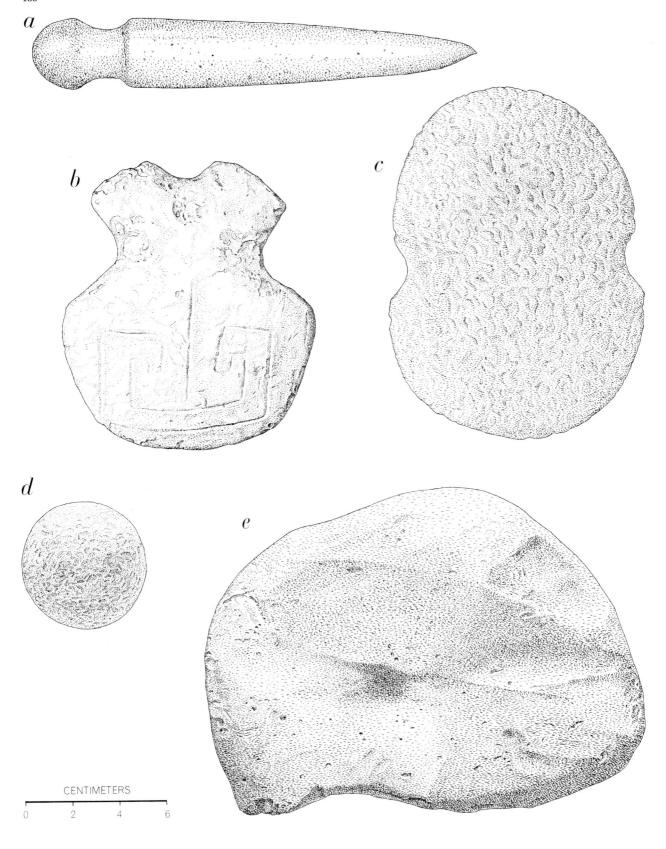

CENTIMETERS

0   2   4   6

MESO-INDIAN ARTIFACTS from two sites in Haiti were made by grinding the desired shapes out of stone. The uses of the stone pin (*a*) and the engraved stone (*b*) from Île à Vache are not known; the Meso-Indians who made them may have been contemporaneous with the pottery-making Neo-Indians who reached Hispaniola about A.D. 500. The other artifacts are from sites of the Couri com-plex. They are a double-bitted axe (*c*), a stone sphere of unknown function (*d*) and a large stone with a shallow depression (*e*), pos-sibly used as a kind of mortar for preparing wild vegetables. All but the large stone are shown two-thirds actual size. The Couri sites also belong to the Meso-Indian age but are clearly earlier in date than the more sophisticated complex unearthed at Île à Vache.

them to butcher and process their quarry. The implication that the Casimira people were hunters of big game does not mean that they did not also kill smaller animals and collect various vegetable foods, but large mammals would have been their main prey. Furthermore, we must assume that the Casimira people were at home on the water; wherever they came from, they did, after all, reach Hispaniola. Therefore their principal prey could easily have been large sea mammals. If we may judge by early Spanish accounts, manatees and seals once ranged among the islands in large numbers. Finally, we can logically expect that the Casimira people used rafts in pursuit of their quarry. So much for the "why"; we would assume that a mainland people followed sea mammals out to Hispaniola.

The "how" is far more conjectural. Rafts are largely at the mercy of winds and currents. Even assuming that the Casimira people could have equipped their rafts with mat sails, they would still have only been able to travel before the wind, and the prevailing winds are from the northeast. One can always conjure up a chance storm to drive a hunting party far out to sea, thus making at least the first migration accidental. The assembly of a viable breeding population on a remote island through pure chance, however, seems quite unlikely. We prefer to think of the Casimira people's moving purposefully out along the Mid-Caribbean chain (which, because of the lower sea level at the time, must have consisted of many more islands). Presumably they took advantage of winds and currents that would be in their favor at certain times of the year.

Arriving on Hispaniola, the hunters

SCREEN SIFTER, suspended by ropes, was used to separate the seashell debris at the Mordán site from the animal bones, flint tools and other artifacts that the deposit contained.

would have found a supply of the flint from which they were accustomed to making their tools. There would have been sea mammals along the shore and quantities of vegetable food and fresh water, which were probably scarce on many of the Mid-Caribbean islets. All in all, it is easy to see why the Casimira people would have settled down once they reached Hispaniola.

Our hypothesis runs counter to an assumption common among New World prehistorians that Paleo-Indians could only travel overland. We suggest that this assumption be reexamined. It seems entirely possible to us that various Paleo-Indians were using rafts both for river crossings and for coastwise travel in very early times. The first Americans need not have been restricted to overland routes for their movements, as many have supposed.

16

The Lost Cities of Peru

by Richard P. Schaedel
August 1951

*How aerial photography and the jeep combined to give
an overall view of the many cultures that flourished on
the north Peruvian coast before the Inca conquest*

TWO technological conveniences developed in recent years have become highly useful tools in archaeology. They are the jeep and aerial photography. The jeep, a "mechanical burro" that can go almost anywhere, gives the archaeologist a relatively rapid means of reaching and reconnoitering archaeological sites in out-of-the-way places. Aerial photography adds a new dimension to exploration. Not only does it bring to light ruins in unexplored areas that might never have been discovered otherwise, but it allows the archaeologist a bird's-eye view in addition to the worm's-eye view with which he has had to be content in the past. Exploring the labyrinthine structures of an ancient civilization on the ground, he is apt to become entangled in the details and be unable to see the picture as a whole. Aerial photographs now make it possible to see the shape and scope of entire cities and civilizations of the prehistoric past.

I shall describe here how we used these two new aids to investigate the early civilizations of northern Peru, where Spanish explorers found the home of the fabulous Incas when they first came to South America in the 16th century.

Let us first sketch in what was known about ancient coastal Peru before we began our study. For at least 3,000 years before Europeans discovered them, American Indians who had settled in Peru had been building civilizations of higher and higher complexity. The North Coast of Peru is a 400-mile strip of coast, bounded on the west by the Pacific Ocean and on the east by the bleak, steep foothills of the Andes. It is a narrow ribbon of desert crossed at intervals by small rivers that flow from the hills into the Pacific. The peoples of ancient Peru lived in these river-valley oases, and the small valleys are crowded with the remains of their civilizations.

The earliest permanent settlements in the area were small fishing villages; they were in existence by 1500 B.C. or earlier. By about 800 B.C. a new people had come into the region, presumably from the highlands, and introduced an agricultural economy, based on the staples maize and yuca. This phase of the region's civilization is called Chavín. We do not know how long it lasted, but it had practically disappeared by the year A.D. 1, and during the next 1,000 years or so a number of different local cultures developed in the individual valleys. Toward the end of this period one of these cultures, called Mochica because it is believed to have originated in the valley of the Moche River, expanded and conquered much of the region. But about A.D. 1000 it in turn was overthrown by an aggressive culture from the south known as Tiahuanacoid. That occupation was short-lived. The next 200 to 300 years of Peru's history, known as the "middle period," is obscure. By about 1300, however, the picture again becomes clear: under a dynasty called the Chimu the people of the Moche Valley once more conquered the coastal lands. The Chimu empire attained splendid heights, but by 1470 it was subdued by a new invasion from the south, this time by the redoubtable Incas. The Inca occupation of the region lasted until the arrival of Pizarro in 1532.

In short, the chief phases in the chronology of Peru's North Coast were the early fishing settlements, the Chavín period of the first truly agricultural communities, the development of local cultures, the emergence of the Mochica as the dominant culture, a time of invasion and conflict lasting several hundred years, unification of the entire region by the Chimu empire and finally conquest by the Incas.

IN 1948 I was called to organize an Institute of Anthropology at the University of Trujillo, the provincial capital city in the center of this region. The Peruvian authorities gave me *carte blanche* to do as I pleased, provided that my work shed more light on Peru's past. I came to the conclusion that we should take stock of the total picture before burying our noses too deeply in any one excavation. Most of what was known about the sequence of Peru's civilizations had been constructed from stratigraphic studies of pottery types. We

FROM THE GROUND Galindo, a Chimu ruin near the Moche River, is hard to find. Until it was located on aerial photographs (*see opposite page*) it was unknown to archaeologists or to some people who lived nearby.

FROM THE AIR Galindo is the ruin of a teeming city. At the top of the page is the large aerial photograph on which the ruin was discovered; at the bottom is an en-largement made from the same negative. The low ramp in the photograph on the opposite page is in the large rectangular structure at upper right in the enlargement.

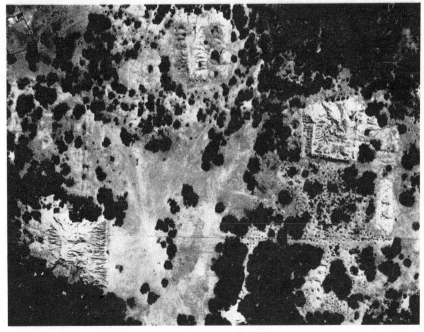

BATAN GRANDE was occupied during Chimu times but was built earlier. The photograph at the bottom is an enlargement of the one at the top. The small pits at the lower right of the enlargement were dug by grave robbers.

undertook to make a large-scale survey of the ancient settlements, temples, towns and cities with the aim of determining to what phase each belonged and placing them all in the chronological framework. Fortunately the blueprints from which this broad-scale history might be read were already in existence. Peru had an Aerial Photographic Service which had photographed or was in the process of photographing all but one of the valleys in the North Coast region.

The first phase of the survey—a reading of these photographs to locate all possible ruins in 11 coastal valleys of the North Coast—was carried out in Lima, where the photographs were kept, by Paul Kosok, chairman of the history department of Long Island University, and his son Michael. They were in Peru to study prehistoric irrigation in the very region in which we were interested. For several months the Kosoks, father and son, labored day and night over the photographs until their patience and eyesight were well-nigh exhausted. They examined thousands of prints and wherever they found what looked like walls, buildings or other signs of an ancient community they located the site with the aid of a map and ordered enlargements of the photographs. The work took great patience and skill, but it was richly rewarded; when they had finished, they brought me enlarged photographs of a tremendous number of large ruins, most of which had not been known to archaeologists before.

WITH the photographs in hand, I set out with a field crew in the jeep, which the University had provided, to find the sites and examine the ruins at closer range. Our expedition blazed a trail of many miles of jeep tracks through dense forests, across rock-strewn river beds, along old canal bottoms and over barren wastes of desert. The aerial photographs helped us to avoid most of the natural obstacles, but we had trouble with man-made ones. One of these hazards was bulls (raised for bullfighting) that were pastured near some of the ruins. Another was the numerous craterlike holes dug by "huaqueros," Peru's time-honored grave robbers, who have left few ancient ruins uninvestigated. We found also, to our surprise, that farmers had turned some of the old ruins to their own use. In some places they utilized ancient pyramids as observation towers for watching the progress of crops in the surrounding fields. Occasionally we discovered that a pyramid which had stood for 1,000 years without major alterations had been provided in the 20th century with a circular ramp for the ascent of horse or automobile.

It was surprising how seldom the aerial photographs betrayed us into visiting something that was not a ruin. To be sure, some of the ruins were not

CAJAMARQUILLA, a huge ruin near Lima on the central coast of Peru, was inhabited as late as the Inca conquest. It sheltered some tens of thousands of people. Although the many walled structures of the city appear to be separated by streets, they are not; the people probably moved about by walking on top of the walls.

as impressive on the ground as they were from the air. We were somewhat disappointed, for example, when we reached one ruin in the Lambayeque Valley which the photograph had indicated to be of enormous extent. Its main pyramid proved to be gutted, little was left of its ancient walls and some of the old lines that showed in the photograph were virtually invisible on the ground.

On the other hand, in many places we were very pleasantly surprised to find the structures much more magnificent on the ground than they had seemed in the photographs. One of these was a ruin, previously unknown, in the Nepena Valley. This site, called Punkuri Alto, showed only as a vague outline in the aerial photograph. It stood on a hilltop, and the ruins of its adobe buildings blended with the bare rock on which it

was reared. But when we reached it in our jeep, we found an impressive, palace-like building with terraced platforms and a series of corridors leading to upper rooms. We were delighted to discover the remains of a geometric frieze lining one of the corridors.

Among our problems was the fact that it was sometimes not easy to distinguish ruins from farms in the aerial photographs. The farmers of modern Peru have unintentionally camouflaged some of the old ruins by using well-built ancient walls to mark off sections of their fields. Their newer fences and boundary walls often merge with the walls of the old compounds.

WE WERE struck by the fact that often one might ride to within a few hundred feet of truly huge ruins and

still be unaware of them. This is partly due to the fact that many of the ancient hillside towns were built on the leveled terraces of the hill, either of adobe or of stone and rubble from the same hill, and few of them had walls high enough to cast large shadows until late afternoon. Thus they were often hard to pick out from the natural hillside, and were also difficult to photograph. Only in late afternoon do Peruvian coastal ruins become photogenic.

Perhaps the most striking case of a large hidden city is the one named Galindo. The main highway to the north highlands in Peru today passes close by these ruins, and the site is within 20 miles of Trujillo. Yet no archaeologist had ever before laid eyes on this ancient town, which runs for about five miles beside the highway. It is effectively blocked

PHOTOGRAPH OF EL PURGATORIO, a massive ruin on the Leche River, shows some structures in sharp outline and others as shapeless masses. The elevated structure at the upper left is some 1,200 feet long.

from view by a high fence that borders the highway, and it is also screened off by vegetation, so that the ruin is visible only from one rise in the road, and then only if the observer knows it is there.

After I had shown slides of Galindo before a class of students in the University of Trujillo, one of the girls came up after class to inquire where this town really was. It turned out she had lived within 10 minutes' walk of the ruin all her life and had never heard of it!

B Y the time we had finished our reconnaissance, we were able to answer some of the questions we had set out to study. We defined the geographical extent of the Mochica culture and of the later Tiahuanacoid conquest, located the main provincial capitals of the Chimu empire and mapped the locations of the Inca garrisons on the North Coast. We were also able to determine that three main cultures had fought for control of the region during the confused "middle period," and to identify these cultures.

In addition, our reconnaissance yielded some information on a more interesting and important matter—the origin of the first cities in America. The Mochicas and their contemporaries did not build cities, although they did construct some of the largest pyramids in South America. Their typical capital consisted of several large adobe pyramids grouped around a central plaza. Only a limited group of priests, chiefs and artisans lived in these ceremonial centers; the rest of the population dwelt in the countryside. True cities did not arrive until several hundred years later, when the Chimus erected their magnificent metropolis called Chan Chan. The Chimus were the first civilization in the Western Hemisphere to cross the threshold of urbanization.

The towns of the "middle period," between the fall of the Mochicas and the rise of the Chimus, represent the be-

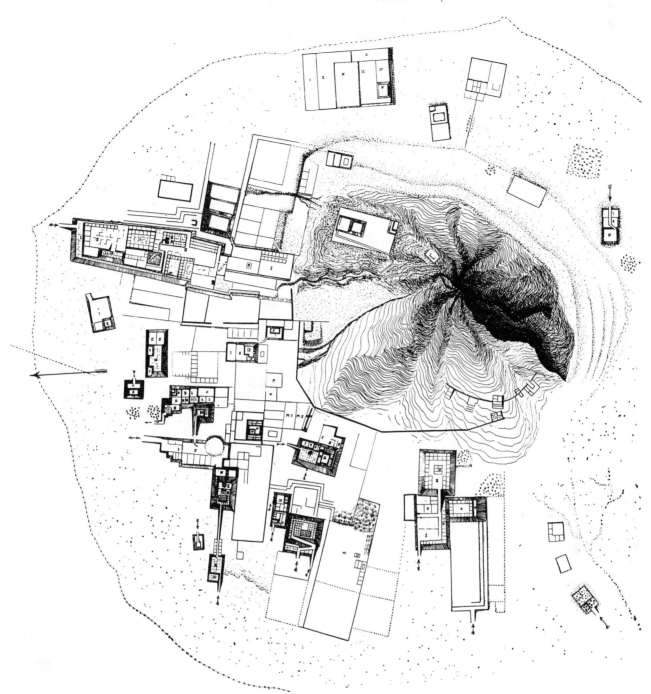

DRAWING OF EL PURGATORIO is a partial reconstruction based on ground surveys and the aerial photograph on the opposite page. The elevated structures of El Purgatorio were built with an eye to defense.

ginnings of city life. And here in coastal Peru we had an unusual opportunity to study how cities began, for the sites of the towns and of the metropolises that came later stand side by side, whereas in the Old World the former are buried beneath the latter. Thus from the data revealed by the aerial photographs we could work out the origin and development of city life in more detail in Peru than anywhere else in the world.

On the basis of these photographs and first-hand reconnaissance at the sites we have been able to draw ground plans of some of the town sites. One of these is

illustrated in the photograph and drawing above. This town, called El Purgatorio, is built around a large natural hill in the center of the well-watered plain of the Leche Valley. The main buildings, dating from the "middle period," are clustered at the north end. These large pyramids with numerous room divisions are transitional building types between the solid pyramids of the earlier Mochica period and the later truly urban compounds, in which all the building space was given to rooms. It is likely that they were palaces housing several families of the ruling class, along with servants and

craftsmen. At the southern and southwestern sides of the ruin are remains of what appear to be old pyramid complexes.

Until the last decade the quantity, size and complexity of ancient Peruvian towns and cities could only be guessed at. Aerial photography has made it possible for us to comprehend them for the first time in their large-scale significance. Let us hope that the sandy mantle that has covered them for centuries will be lifted soon to reveal the internal functioning of these thriving metropolises of prehistoric Peru.

17

The Prehistoric Ground Drawings of Peru

by William H. Isbell
October 1978

They look so much as if they were intended to be viewed from the air that they have stimulated much vivid speculation. The archaeological evidence indicates who made them and perhaps also why they were made

In the coastal deserts of Peru are the remains of ancient irrigation systems that held a particular fascination for Paul Kosok of Long Island University, a student of pre-Columbian South America. Some 40 years ago, while he was mapping what he took to be shallow irrigation ditches leading away from tributaries of the Rio Grande on the south coast, Kosok encountered something quite unexpected. In the valley of one such tributary, the Rio Nazca, he came on the giant image of a bird, more than 100 feet long, silhouetted as though it was meant to be viewed from above.

Irrigation ditches seldom if ever form pictures of animals. Kosok inquired among his Peruvian colleagues and learned that many even larger "dirt drawings" of a geometric nature had been noted in the same area. They included long lines (usually called "roads"), zigzags, trapezoids and spirals. Kosok's discovery of a seminaturalistic dirt drawing, however, was a surprise.

Among those who had studied the geometric figures was Toribio Mejía Xesspe of the National University of San Marcos. In a paper published in 1938 he had argued that the ground drawings of the Nazca area were unrelated to irrigation and must have served some ceremonial function in pre-Columbian times. Reconnaissance continued. A huge spider was the next seminaturalistic ground drawing to be added to the list, and others soon followed. Today the total number of such figures exceeds 30.

Before Kosok left Peru in 1941 he speculated that the "roads," at least, might represent ancient astronomical sight lines. He made this suggestion as a possibility worth investigating to Maria Reiche, a German-trained student of mathematics and astronomy who lived in Lima. She has been studying the ground drawings ever since.

What can archaeology and its related disciplines do to explain an odd phenomenon such as the Peruvian ground drawings? Three questions that seem difficult to answer arise immediately: When were the drawings made? Who made them? Why did they make them? In the years since Kosok brought these curiosities to the attention of the general public the first two of the questions have been answered beyond doubt. As for the third question, a number of reasonable conjectures can be proposed. Here I shall review the steps that have led both to the answers and to the conjectures.

The south coast of Peru consists of a range of low hills that runs generally from north to south. Between this coastal rise of land and the foothills of the Andes to the east lies a long lowland basin. For thousands of years the runoff from the higher ground to the west and east carried erosion products into the basin. Most of the eroded material is fine light-colored soil. Occasional flash floods also carried in larger erosion products: stones ranging in size from tiny pebbles to boulders.

Where the Rio Nazca runs down from the foothills to join the Rio Grande these thousands of years of erosional filling have created a wide and level plain. The strong south winds that blew across the plain carried away much of the dusty surface soil, leaving behind a "desert pavement" of pebbles and boulders. In the early morning the stones were damp with dew, but for the rest of the day they were exposed to the hot desert sun. As a result the stones oxidized until their color became a dark red brown.

This change in color actually reduced the amount of wind erosion in the desert. The south wind still blows today, but as the damp stones dry and get hot in the sun their radiation helps to maintain a surface layer of hot air that serves as a buffer against the wind. As for rain erosion, rainfall is so rare along the south coast of Peru that its erosive effects have been negligible for at least 3,000 years.

The geological circumstances that have produced hundreds of square miles of natural blackboard in southern Peru are nowhere seen better than in the plateau above the valley of the entrenched Rio Nazca: an area about 30 miles long and 15 miles wide known as the Pampa Colorada (the Red Plain). Here if one picks up one of the red brown stones, the light soil that lies under it is exposed to view. Pick up a row of rocks and a light-colored line appears. That is how the ground drawings were made: by selective displacement of the desert pavement.

Natural blackboards are well known to archaeologists in areas other than Peru. In southern Britain, where a thin dark soil overlies formations of chalk, the ancient inhabitants selectively exposed the chalk to form, among other images, the great "white horse" effigies of Wiltshire and Kent. Desert pavement was also removed to form figures in the deserts of southern California, as surveys by Dean R. Snow of the State University of New York at Albany have shown. Indeed, if wind and water erosion were as slight in other desert areas of the world as they are on the south coast of Peru, the total number of ground drawings known today might be substantially greater. However that may be, all such figures present a challenge. How can one determine when the work was done?

DESERT "BLACKBOARD" of the ground drawings, the Pampa Colorada near Nazca, appears in the aerial photograph on the opposite page. A variety of drawings are visible. Roadlike lines run in different directions. The broader cleared areas are trapezoidal in outline. A typical spiral appears at the left center. An animal effigy, perhaps a lizard, appears at the bottom right.

The prehistoric pottery found at grave sites in southern Peru, such as the great mortuary center at Cahuachi, is so distinctive in decoration that it has been given the name Nazca, after the modern city and the river valley where many examples of these wares have been unearthed. The Nazca wares were made from about 200 B.C. to about A.D. 600. Students of Andean archaeology call this span in the prehistory of Peru the Early Intermediate Period.

Some Nazca pots are effigies: they are made in the shape of animals and human beings. Others are painted with animal figures: fish, a trophy-bearing killer whale, seabirds, hummingbirds, reptiles, monkeys and llamas. When it was learned that a similar repertory of seminaturalistic animal figures was to be found among the ground drawings of the Pampa Colorada, it was hard to avoid the conclusion that the same prehistoric population was responsible for both creations.

WEST COAST OF SOUTH AMERICA is dominated by the steeply rising Andes. In Peru the foothills of the great mountain range reduce the coastal plain to a narrow strip of desert made fertile only where rivers carry highland rains down to the Pacific. Rain along the coast of southern Peru is almost nonexistent.

This evidence, however, was only iconographic; a more direct kind of evidence was soon forthcoming. A limited amount of broken pottery is to be found on the Pampa Colorada. Since the area is too arid for settlement, it seems reasonable to conclude that the potsherds must have been left by temporary visitors to the desert: casual travelers, traders, pilgrims (if the ground drawings were ritual ones) or work gangs (if the making of the ground drawings was an organized effort). In the early 1970's Gerald S. Hawkins of the Smithsonian Astrophysical Observatory collected a number of sherds from the Pampa Colorada and asked Gordon R. Willey of Harvard University and John H. Rowe of the University of California at Berkeley to identify them. Willey and Rowe found that 85 percent of the sherds were Nazca wares. The remaining 15 percent were wares of a subsequent period: the interval between A.D. 900 and 1400. At about the same time Rodger Ravines of the National Cultural Institute of Peru made a collection of sherds from sites on the periphery of the Pampa Colorada; they proved to be exclusively Nazca wares. The peripheral sites give the appearance of being temporary shelters; perhaps they were camps for work gangs.

This evidence, a positive identification of users of Nazca pottery as visitors to the ground drawings, taken together with the presence of the same animal figures in both mediums, settled once and for all the question of who had so artfully disturbed the desert pavement of the Pampa Colorada. The fact remains that the interval between 200 B.C. and A.D. 600 is almost a millennium. Might it be possible to find more precisely when during the Early Intermediate Period such activity took place? Precise dating of this kind became possible after World War II with the development of carbon-14 analysis. Some of the long lines laid out on the Pampa Colorada terminate where a wood stake was driven into the ground. In 1953 W. Duncan Strong of Columbia University collected a sample from such a stake for carbon-14 analysis. The analysis showed that the wood was from a tree that had been cut down in A.D. 525 (±80), very late in the Early Intermediate Period. To be sure, the finding can at best only suggest when the long line associated with this particular stake was laid out (and perhaps not even that if one considers that the stake might be the second, the third or the 30th replacement of the original one). Nevertheless, the carbon-14 date falls within the limits of Nazca times and therefore lends weight to the other evidence.

Now that the questions "Who?" and "When?" are answered, it is time to consider the question "Why?" Again archaeology and its related disciplines,

ethnology in particular, offer useful clues. For example, it may seem peculiar that any population would invest a significant amount of energy in constructing displays that are best seen from the air rather than from the ground. Indeed, the people who made the chalk figures in Britain did so on hillsides where they are clearly visible. On the other hand, parallels to the Nazca displays do exist. Among the ambitious earthworks raised by the Hopewell cultists of pre-Columbian North America are a number of figures that would certainly be less readily recognized from the ground than from the air. The great serpent mound in Ohio is an outstanding example. The same is true of the California desert figures documented by Snow. Since this feature of the Nazca ground drawings is not unique, it would seem unnecessary to suppose the drawings were made to be viewed from the air, even if one could imagine how it was done.

What about the cost in energy that had to be paid to shift stones and create a ground drawing? Here again archaeology offers a clue. Elsewhere in Peru during the Early Intermediate Period the local farming populations were engaged in work-gang labor of staggering proportions. For example, the largest prehistoric pyramid in Peru is located in the valley of the Rio Moche. An enormous temple platform, the Huaca del Sol, called for the manufacture of 140 million adobe bricks. Studies of the construction methods and of the bricks themselves indicate that the work was done by crews of unskilled laborers. Each crew, probably composed of men recruited from a single region, manufactured its own bricks, transported them to the construction site and there built one or more of the columns of brick that make up the pyramid. Each crew's work is still identifiable by the distinctive marks on different batches of brick.

The pyramidal structures and other monumental buildings of the Early Intermediate Period in northern and central Peru evidently represent the apogee of a pre-Columbian period of Andean ceremonial architecture. Some temple platforms are also found along the south coast of Peru, but they are modest compared with the massive adobe edifices raised to the north. By the same token ground drawings were laid out at desert sites along the north and central coast of Peru, but they are modest by Nazca standards.

Those who are not familiar with the ground drawings may find it hard to compare the effort involved in their creation with the effort involved in making and laying bricks. The reason is that the discussion so far has been confined largely to the animal effigies. In terms of the tonnage of stone shifted the animal portrayals represent only a fraction of the total energy input. For example, an animal may be sketched out by a single continuous line. Many of the lines, however, originate at a distant trapezoid or rectangle and then return to it.

The geometric figure that provides the point of origin may be more than a kilometer long. The same figure may also be the point of origin for a series of zigzags or for a single line that runs straight across the desert eight kilometers or more before terminating at a stake or a heap of stones. Only if one were to measure the effort required to duplicate a representative ground drawing today would it be possible to estimate the total prehistoric investment of labor at the Pampa Colorada in any but the most general way. It nonetheless seems reasonable to suppose the ground-drawing efforts in the Nazca area represent an energy investment roughly comparable to that which created the monumental adobe structures to the north.

Whether or not the two efforts were equal in scale, both seem to have fulfilled similar economic functions. These functions are related to the drafting of community labor for public works. The nationwide controls exercised by the Incas at the time of Pizarro's conquest of Peru are well known. It is less well known that the earliest of the Incas' imperial predecessors had a similarly centralized regime. Whereas the Incas' capital was at Cuzco, that of the earlier empire was at Huari.

Provincial administrative centers, all linked to Huari, collected and stored large quantities of foodstuff and goods produced in the rural hinterland. If there were local or regional variations in agricultural or cottage-industry productivity, the overall economy was balanced by adding to the centralized stores or by exchanges among the provincial centers. Such economic uniformity enabled the population of prehistoric Peru to expand and then to stabilize at a level higher than that in the preceding period of regional autonomy.

Such was far from the case during the Early Intermediate Period. That some kind of control was exercised over community labor is apparent in the construction of the great adobe temple platforms. There is no evidence, however, that the people of the period built administrative structures or storage facilities such as were characteristic of the imperial regimes of Huari and Cuzco. This suggests that each region was subject to local economic fluctuations and directly related population changes.

Consider the effect of such fluctuations. A series of good agricultural years in a region would have led, in the absence of any local control mechanism, to a population increase. Thereafter a series of bad years would have been disastrous for the larger population. The way to avoid this kind of response to economic fluctuations is to keep the

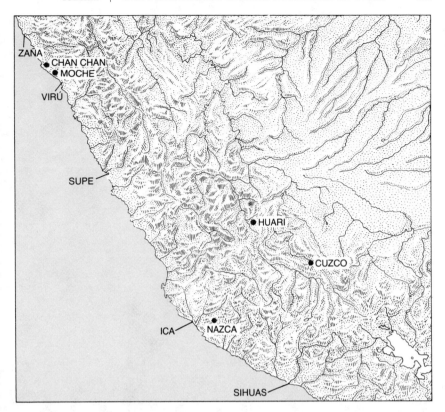

GROUND DRAWINGS have been located in the coastal deserts of Peru from as far north as the Virú valley to as far south as the Sihuas valley. They are found in the vicinity of Supe, Lima and Ica and have been reported but not confirmed in the Zaña valley. They are commonest in the vicinity of Nazca, where ancient graves have been found to contain distinctive pottery.

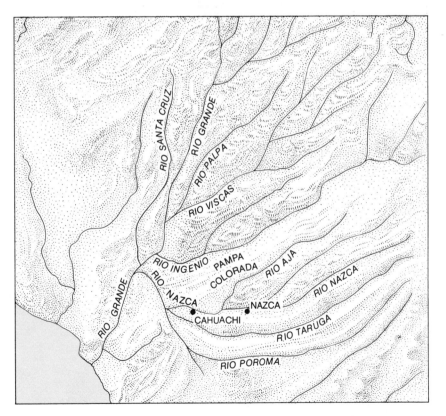

DESERT PLATEAU north of the Rio Nazca, the Pampa Colorada, is 30 miles long and 15 miles wide. It has the greatest concentration of ground drawings in Peru. The nearby ruins of Cahuachi, a mortuary site of the Peruvian Early Intermediate Period (200 B.C.–A.D. 600), is one of the numerous sources of the Nazca-style pottery that is indigenous to this part of Peru.

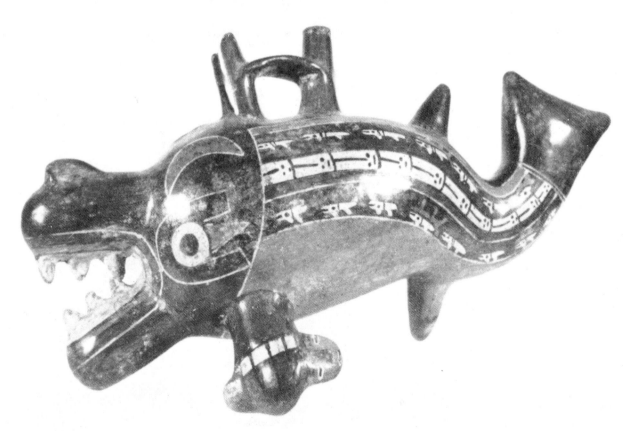

KILLER WHALE is the subject of this ground drawing on the Pampa Colorada (*top*). The circular object seen to dangle below the jaw of the whale is a human head, a war trophy that is regularly depicted in Peruvian pottery designs and other decorations of the pre-Columbian period. The effigy pot (*bottom*) also depicts a killer whale, complete with a trophy head. The effigy was unearthed near the Pampa Colorada; it was made during the Early Intermediate Period of Peruvian prehistory. It appears here courtesy of Wilfredo Loayza.

surplus of the good years from fueling an increase in population. An artificial leveling of the economy will inhibit population growth, holding the total below the one that taxes the maximum carrying capacity of the regional economy.

How might this leveling be achieved? One way is to cultivate a common concern with ceremonial activities that call for a large investment of labor. In Nazca times the kinds of centralized food storage characteristic of the Huari and Cuzco regimes would not have existed, and surpluses would have been dispersed not on a provincial and state level but on a local or even familial one. If an autonomous region suffered bad years, drawing on such decentralized stores would help to tide it over. If, on the other hand, the region enjoyed good years, the accumulated private stores could be tapped to provide support for local work gangs engaged in ceremonial activities such as building temple platforms or laying out ground drawings. In either event the population would remain relatively stable.

Seen in this light the basic function (or, if one prefers the terminology of Darwinian evolution, the selective advantage) of laying out ground drawings has nothing to do with whether they were viewed from the ground or from above, or for that matter with whether they were viewed at all. The function lies in the fact that societies with a cultural mechanism for investing unpredictable surpluses in ceremonial activities have a selective advantage over societies lacking such a mechanism. They regulate their population, and societies that do not are doomed to cycles of "boom" and "bust."

Were the leaders of these regional societies in the Early Intermediate Period of Peruvian prehistory consciously aware of such complex concepts as the allocation of surplus resources to prevent an excess of population? Whether or not they were aware of them makes little difference; those who had such a system eventually replaced their neighbors, and the successful ceremonial behavior was thereby perpetuated. At the conscious level such continuity may have been based on a decision-making process no more profound than the argument that "this is the way we have always done it."

Much human behavior is based on this kind of "custom," a simple following of behavior patterns that have been successful in the past. In nonliterate societies the information on such behavior is often codified as ritual to ensure that it is conveyed to future generations. A pertinent example is contained in the study of a modern but barely literate Peruvian highland village by my wife, Billie Jean Isbell of Cornell University.

Her research has revealed that these farming families depend for their economic independence on a strategy of cultivating a variety of crops at different elevations. The villagers have a specific name for each crop zone. The distinction between the zones has been symbolized by the construction of a chapel at the boundary of each one. The annual harvest ritual involves a series of visits to the chapels and the harvesting of a sample of the produce grown in each zone. A cross is taken from each chapel and is decorated with the harvested plants. All the crosses are then brought to the village and presented to the village priest.

Even if a young villager fails to learn how to farm from his family and his village elders, the message of this annual ritual could scarcely be overlooked:

PERUVIAN SCHOLAR Maria Reiche (*left*) demonstrates the surveying methods she has used for more than 30 years in recording Nazca ground drawings. Her audience is Patricia J. Knobloch of the State University of New York at Binghamton, a visiting archaeologist. The rocks that form the "desert pavement" at the Pampa Colorada range in size from pebbles to boulders.

ZIGZAG PATTERN on the Pampa Colorada was formed, as were all the ground figures, by selectively removing the rocks that cover the desert floor, thereby revealing the lighter-colored earth under them. Here some of the shifted rocks were piled up at the bends of the figure.

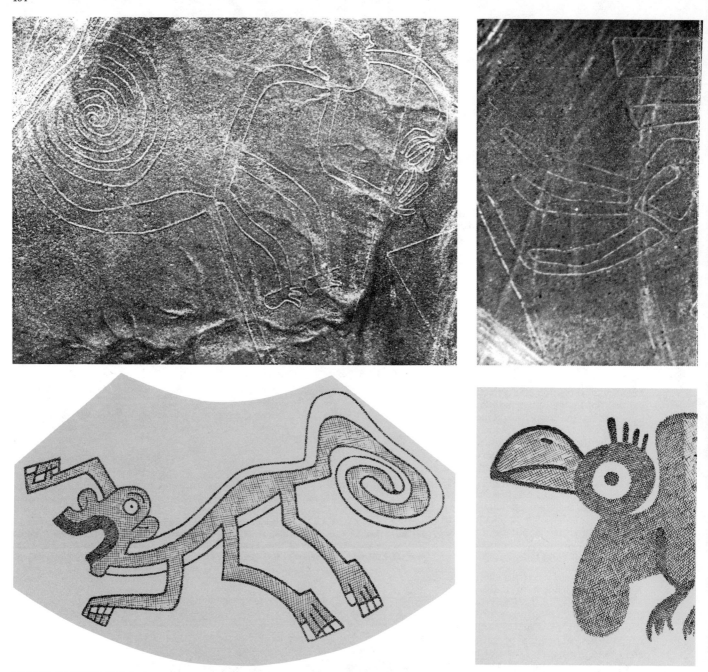

THREE GROUND FIGURES (*top*) are compared with portrayals of the same animals that appear on Nazca pottery (*bottom*). At left is a stylized monkey with a much exaggerated tail. The drawing of a monkey appears on a double-spout pot photographed by Loayza. The bird figure at center may represent a frigate bird; these birds have a conspicuous throat pouch. The drawing of a similar bird figure ap-

"Here are the sections that divide the earth. Here are the crops that are grown in each section. It pleases God (and the priest) that all these crops are grown every year." Conscious recognition of the economic advantages of mixed farming may not even exist among the villagers, but the pattern of behavior that the ritual symbolically reinforces helps to protect its practitioners from the danger of single-crop failure and the social disruption that accompanies dependence on wage labor.

R. Tom Zuidema of the University of Illinois has reconstructed similar rituals observed by the people of Cuzco when the city was the capital of the Inca empire. At that time imaginary lines radiated in all directions from Cuzco. The lines were imaginary in that they were unmarked, but the orientation of each line was indicated by a series of shrines. Every day of the year a different kin group among the city dwellers worshiped at a different shrine; in effect the floor of the valley of Cuzco had been mapped out in an annual ritual calendar. Information about the agricultural cycle, social obligations, military activities and many other topics was thereby symbolically communicated to the people of Cuzco. The fact that the Incas felt a concern for this kind of informative mapping is demonstrated by the ground plan of the capital itself. The Incas called Cuzco "the puma" and its inhabitants "members of the body of the puma." The city was laid out in the shape of a puma, although the animal form was somewhat distorted by the fact that it had to conform to the topography of the valley.

I have suggested that the ground drawings at Nazca were primarily a product of social mechanisms for regulating the balance between resources and population. Zuidema's findings on the

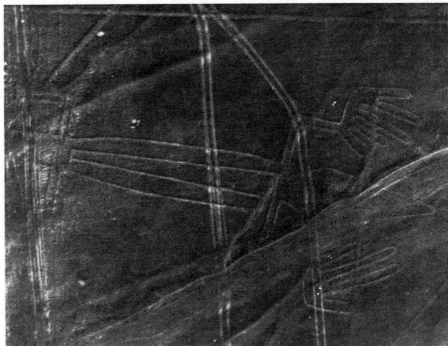

pears on a Nazca pot in the collection of the Putnam Museum in Davenport, Iowa. The lizardlike figure at the right has a long tail that does not appear in this aerial photograph, but its hind legs were not executed with the same detail as its forelegs. The drawing of a similar lizard appears on a Nazca pot in the collection of the Robert H. Lowie Museum of Anthropology at University of California at Berkeley.

symbolic ground-mapping practices of the Incas (who eventually succeeded to authority over the Nazca region) and Billie Jean Isbell's documentation of agricultural ritual among the highland Indians of Peru today suggest that the Nazca ground drawings also contained certain symbolic information, mapped on the ground for successive generations to observe, recognize and memorize.

What were these mapped messages? As Reiche has pointed out for many years, certain of the Pampa Colorada lines mark the position of the sun at the summer and winter solstices and certain other lines also appear to have calendri-cal significance. A computerized analysis of line orientation conducted by Hawkins, although it failed to demonstrate that a majority of the lines have astronomical significance, showed that twice as many of them were oriented with respect to annual solar and lunar extremes than would be expected on the basis of chance.

Both studies indicate that at least some of the Nazca ground drawings have calendrical potential. The mapping of calendrical data on the ground, if it was combined with ritual observations, could have communicated not only information of agricultural signifi-cance but also other kinds of information useful to a complex but preliterate society faced with a pressing need to store the knowledge acquired from generations of experience.

To return to the questions I raised at the outset: Can archaeology and related disciplines determine when the ground drawings of the Pampa Colorada were made, who made them and why? It seems clear that the answers to the first two questions are that most if not all of the drawings are the work of the same people who shaped and painted the lovely pottery of Nazca in the period between 200 B.C. and A.D. 600. The graves of this prehistoric farming people and the ruined towns and villages where they once lived both lie near the drawings.

As for the question why, it also seems clear that the making of the drawings, like the building of the enormous adobe-brick structures to the north, served to regulate population increases related to changes in the available energy. It is one thing, of course, to recognize the function served by energy investments of this regulatory kind and quite another to gain an understanding of the tangible form the investment takes. I nonetheless find it a credible hypothesis that the ground drawings reflect the general need by the various preliterate societies of Peru to record or, perhaps more accurately, to store significant information about how their system worked.

The storage of inventories by means of the well-known Peruvian string-and-knot system of enumeration, the quipu, was evidently a practice adopted early in the prehistory of the Andes. Calendrical data, particularly when their use calls for the cross-check of actual astronomical observation, might be impractical or impossible to store by means of quipus. I suggest that such kinds of information were symbolically coded and recorded in the most durable medium available: the surface of the earth itself.

If the Pampa Colorada ground drawings were the only ones in Peru, such a hypothesis might carry little weight. Actually ground drawings have been found in many other places. A rectangular figure 60 meters long and 30 meters wide and including geometric "decorations" has been mapped in an area above the Sihuas valley south of Nazca. "Road" lines are present in the Ica valley just north of Nazca, in the vicinity of Lima still farther to the north, north of Lima in the Virú valley near the monumental Huaca del Sol and reportedly in the Zaña valley 180 kilometers north of Virú. In the Supe valley between Lima and Virú, Alberto Carbajāl, Carlos Williams and I recently photographed previously unreported lines, geometric figures, chains of spirals and a ground drawing of a human face 43 meters wide. Low-altitude aerial photography and ground surveys of other Peruvian desert-pavement areas might reveal many more figures. It is plain that energy was invested in the production of ground drawings even in parts of Peru where the major community-labor investment was in the construction of adobe platforms and other monumental works. The ground drawings along the north and central coast may be modest by Nazca standards, but they demonstrate that such figures were not exclusively a south-coast phenomenon.

In the centuries following the Early Intermediate Period the energy investment in temple platforms continued but on a far smaller and less impressive scale. The same appears to be true of the ground figures. Evidently the emerging state authority centered at Huari saw to it that the main community effort was redirected into the construction of administrative buildings, storage facilities, fortifications and what seem to have been manufacturing centers. Regional autonomy gave way to centralized authority, setting the stage for the eventual rise of the Inca empire. One can logically expect that the earlier practice of regional data storage and retrieval, written on the earth and vested in local ritual, then slowly ceased to be.

Pre-Columbian Ridged Fields

by James J. Parsons and William M. Denevan
July 1967

*In four areas of tropical lowland in South America
there are huge arrays of ancient earthworks. Many
of them are ridges put up to farm land subject to
seasonal flooding*

In South America thousands of square miles of tropical lowlands are submerged in shallow floodwaters for weeks or months during the rainy season and are parched by drought during the dry season. Covered either with savanna grasses or with forest, these poorly drained river floodplains have generally been considered unfit for agriculture since the Spanish Conquest. When they are exploited at all, it is usually as cattle range. In the open savanna the grass is renewed by annual burning; in some wooded areas today the trees are being cleared to make way for planted pasture.

Recently the surprising discovery has been made that areas in several such regions were once intensively farmed. The pre-Columbian farmers had a specialized system of agriculture that physically reshaped large parts of the South American continent. Aerial reconnaissance and surface exploration have now located the intricate earthworks required by this system in the tropical lowlands of four widely separated regions: eastern Bolivia, western Ecuador, northern Colombia and coastal Surinam (Dutch Guiana). Similar earthworks are said to exist in other parts of the continent, but such reports have not yet been substantiated. Here we shall describe the earthworks in the four areas that have been identified and mapped thus far, review what is known about prehistoric earthmoving for agricultural purposes elsewhere in the Americas (both lowland and highland) and then examine the implications of these early works with respect to the rise of civilization in the New World.

Except for two brief references in early chronicles, the first mention of agricultural earthworks in South America was made in the 1900's by the Swedish ethnographer Erland Nordenskiöld, in connection with his studies in the Llanos de Mojos (Plains of Mojos) of northeastern Bolivia. Located in the heart of the South American continent, between the Andes and the Brazilian highlands, most of the Mojos plains area is less than 800 feet above sea level. Bounded by the Beni and Mamoré rivers, these broad lowlands are a sea of grass in which occasional islands of forest mark the higher, better-drained ground; indeed, the vegetation is locally known as *pampa-isla*. Here for as much as seven months of the year floods cover the grasslands with a sheet of water ranging in depth from a few inches to several feet.

Faced with a hostile environment of this kind people everywhere usually adapt their lives to the circumstances; a commonplace example in areas subject to flooding is the building of houses on stilts. The modern cattle ranchers of the Llanos de Mojos do much the same: they simply select high ground for building sites. The pre-Columbian inhabitants of the area chose instead to modify the landscape. They raised mounds, causeways and serried ridges for their crops, all of which stood high enough to surmount the floodwaters. To this day the wet savannas are crisscrossed with narrow causeways that connect the natural islands of high ground. The causeways are as much as seven miles long; their total length in the Llanos de Mojos, as measured on aerial photographs, exceeds 1,000 miles. Also visible in the area are many artificial mounds that served as sites for burials, for houses and even for small villages.

The agricultural earthworks in the area cover at least 50,000 acres. They are of three kinds. West of the town of Trinidad the prevailing pattern is narrow, closely spaced ridges. South of Lake Rogoaguado the ridges are much larger: as much as 80 feet wide and 1,000 feet long. In other areas there are rows of small circular mounds six to eight feet in diameter. Whatever their form, most of the earthworks are less than two feet high. Originally they were doubtless high enough to stand above the average flood level.

In 1908 and 1909 Nordenskiöld excavated several burial mounds east of the Mamoré River that were associated with some of the Mojos causeways. Within the mounds he found fragments of elaborately decorated pottery, which he attributed to the ancestors of the region's Arawak Indians. This work of half a century ago is the only serious archaeology that has been undertaken in the area. Early Jesuit accounts of the region imply that the socioeconomic development of the Indians was advanced enough to enable them to construct the kinds of earthworks found there, but such literature, some of which is quite detailed, makes no mention of any agricultural ridges. Indeed, the extent of the ridges was not realized until 1960, when swamp buggies engaged in petroleum exploration encountered seemingly endless ridges near the town of Trinidad. Thereafter the ridge system was examined on aerial photographs. Here in Bolivia, however, the lack of archaeological investigation makes it impossible to determine exactly when the ridges and other earthworks were raised.

Another ridged area is in northern Colombia some 150 miles inland from the Caribbean coast. There the waters of the San Jorge and Cauca rivers join with those of the Magdalena in a great interior basin that is less than 80 feet above sea level. Known as the Mompos

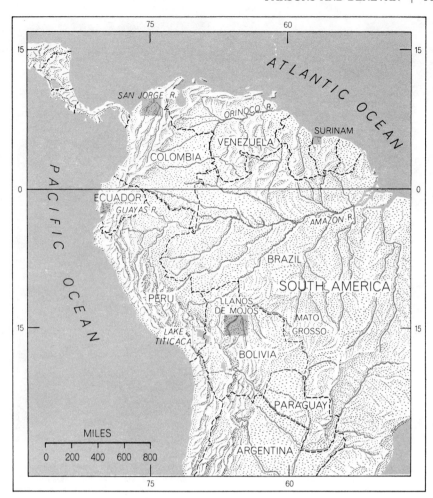

FOUR REGIONS in the tropical lowlands of South America (*color*) have pre-Columbian earthworks built so that lands subject to seasonal flood and drought could be utilized for farming. Similar earthworks were also built in the Andean highlands at Lake Titicaca.

second type short ridges are arrayed in a checkerboard pattern. In the third type the ridges are in clusters, generally parallel but unoriented with respect to the higher ground of the levees. Averaging about 20 feet in width, the ridges vary in length from a few feet to almost a mile; the ditches between them are in some places wider than the ridges and in some places narrower. The majority of the ridges are two to three feet high; a few are nearly five feet. Most of the San Jorge fields have been invaded by forest since they were abandoned. Where the trees have been cleared and the area has been planted with pasture grass the ancient ridge system gives the landscape a distinctive corrugated appearance.

A third ridged area is immediately north and east of the airport for Guayaquil in Ecuador. To the east of the Guayas River, opposite Guayaquil and just north of the town of Durán, an extensive system of parallel ridges is visible that looks almost exactly like the ones at San Jorge and Mojos. Another area of earthworks lies some 15 miles north of Guayaquil, in the lowlands between the Babahoyo and Daule rivers, where rectangular mounds predominate. These relics of pre-Columbian agriculture in Ecuador seem not to have been recognized for what they are until we observed them in 1966. We might not have noticed them ourselves if it had not been for our familiarity with the earthworks of Bolivia and Colombia.

The ridged fields of the Guayaquil area cover substantially less ground than those of San Jorge and Mojos; the floodplain and swampland they occupy probably total some 10,000 acres. The system of ridges near Durán is currently being cleared of second-growth forest and sharecroppers are planting it mainly with rice and maize. Rice seedlings are transplanted from seedbeds into the ditches, the soil of which is heavier than that of the better-drained ridges. The ridges, which are 30 to 40 feet wide and as much as two miles long, are being planted with maize, squash, beans, sugarcane and cotton.

As in Bolivia and Colombia, serious archaeological investigation that could identify the peoples who raised the Guayaquil earthworks has yet to be undertaken. The Guayas floodplains are known to have been occupied from about A.D. 500 to the time of the Spanish Conquest by a people of the Milagro culture, noted for its elaborate work in gold. The low-lying countryside is dot-

Depression, this seasonally flooded alluvial plain is covered with a constantly changing complex of lakes and swamps. When it is not covered with water, it is a rich reserve of pasturage for Colombia's two leading beef-producing provinces, Córdoba and Bolívar.

Since the Spaniards entered the region in the 16th century the western part of the Mompos Depression has also been famous for its Indian mounds and their content of gold. Neither the early settlers nor today's *colonos*, however, seem to have been aware that some 80,-000 acres along the San Jorge are covered by a pre-Columbian ridged-field system.

The San Jorge ridges, like those of the Llanos de Mojos, are not easily perceived on the ground. From a dugout

canoe, a common means of travel in the area, they are virtually invisible. The local people are aware of the ridges but few recognize them as man-made features. From the air the ridges are clearly distinguishable [*see illustration on page 198*]. When the Mompos Depression is partly inundated, slight differences in relief are emphasized and the ridge pattern is sharply outlined by the floodwaters. Moreover, both before and after the rains the color of the grass reflects the difference between the dry ridge crests and the damp ditches between them; for several weeks the pattern is clearly painted in tan and green.

The San Jorge fields are of three kinds. In one type the ridges are on the natural levees of old stream channels and are perpendicular to the channels. In the

ANCIENT EARTHWORKS visible in the aerial photograph of the San Jorge River area in Colombia on the opposite page are evident where the forest still stands and where trees have been cleared for pasture (*upper left*). In pre-Columbian times the inhabitants of this seasonally flooded river lowland built such ridged fields over an area of some 80,000 acres.

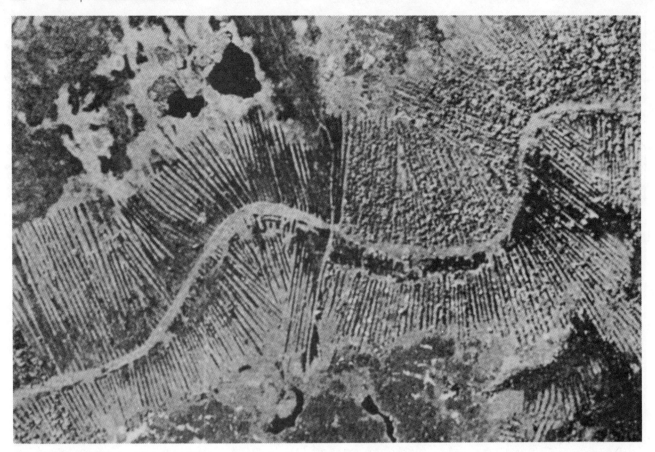

RIDGED FIELDS in Colombia, built on the natural levees that adjoin abandoned stream channels, are usually oriented perpendicularly to the course of the stream. The height of the ridges seen in this aerial photograph is from two to five feet above the ground.

ted with thousands of *tolas,* or artificial mounds, built by the Milagro people for burial places and house sites. Some of the *tolas* appear to be associated with ridge systems and others with the rectangular earthworks. It is possible that the same culture made both. Only investigation can prove or disprove the association.

The coast of Surinam, the site of our fourth example of ridged-field agriculture, is a low-lying plain consisting of a series of ancient beaches running parallel to the present shoreline. Between these fossil beaches are swampy strips of clayey soil that support savanna vegetation. At a number of places along the coast ridged fields have been noted in these grassy swamps. The most extensive system of ridges is associated with an artificial mound known as Hertenrits, which is about 800 feet in diameter and rises six to seven feet above the level of the surrounding swamp. Hertenrits is three miles from the coast between Nieuw Nickerie and Caroní, in the middle of a long-uninhabited savanna belt that is now being reclaimed as part of a government rice-growing project. The

mound is being investigated by the Dutch archaeologist D. C. Geyskes and the Dutch pollen analyst D. M. Laeyendecker-Roosenburg.

The Hertenrits ridges are short—perhaps three times as long as they are wide—and haphazardly arrayed. Some stand alone; others are clumped together like sausages in a pan. The aerial photographs indicate that the ridges rise two to three feet and that in many places they support vegetation distinctly different from that of the surrounding savanna.

Analysis of pollen contained in peat taken from the Hertenrits mound and from an adjacent swamp indicates that the mound was raised not long after A.D. 700. At that time the sea had encroached on the area; the evidence for the encroachment is a marked increase in the abundance of mangrove pollen in the samples. The Dutch investigators suggest that, in order to continue living in the area under these conditions, the local people were obliged to build the mound as a village site and presumably also to make ridges for their crops. They calculate that the mound was occupied until at least A.D. 900 and probably later.

The pollens identified at Hertenrits do not include those of any cultivated plants such as maize. Although the evidence is admittedly negative, this fact suggests that the ridges were devoted to growing manioc, a plant that rarely flowers and is propagated not by seed but by stem cuttings. Manioc was a staple crop in much of tropical South America at the time of the Spanish Conquest, and it is still widely grown today. The cuttings are usually planted at the start of the rainy season and require good drainage. More than most crops, manioc would call for artificially raised ground in areas subject to flooding. It is probable that not only here but also in Bolivia, Colombia and Ecuador the peoples who made mile after mile of ridges were growers of manioc. It seems possible, although it is by no means proved, that the oldest earthworks in some of these areas may date back to a period before maize had arrived from Middle America.

In the absence of archaeological investigation making possible carbon-14 dating or other age determinations, one can only speculate on the antiquity of most of these early agricultural works. The ridged-field system in the Mompos

Depression of Colombia appears to be associated with the Indian mounds there, and the mounds seem to have been more or less continuously occupied for a long time before the Spaniards arrived. A hundred miles or so to the north, near the Caribbean coast, there are mounds of shells that have been dated by the carbon-14 method. These dates range from 800 B.C. at Momil to about 3000 B.C. at Puerto Hormiga, making the latter the oldest-known site in the New World where pottery is found. There is no evidence that the San Jorge fields are equally old, but it is interesting that some of the shell mounds occupy a similar ecological niche, being located on the margin of seasonally flooded lands.

One possible means of determining the age of the San Jorge earthworks arises from the fact that there the ridge pattern is often oriented at right angles to old stream channels. A reconstruction of the district's history of sedimentation might provide a key to the question of age. Many of the ridges appear to be related to the oldest and longest-abandoned channels, which are now choked with water hyacinths when they contain any water at all.

Although many other lowland regions of tropical South America have terrain suited to ridged-field agriculture, our investigations up to now have produced concrete evidence of their existence only in the four areas described here. Nonetheless, promising conditions for the discovery of similar earthworks exist over huge areas: the Orinoco delta, Marajó Island at the mouth of the Amazon, the Pantanal region of the western Mato Grosso in Brazil and the broad llanos of Venezuela and Colombia.

South of the old colonial city of Barinas in the Venezuelan llanos a complex of man-made causeways as much as six feet high, 20 feet wide and three miles long has been described by the Venezuelan archaeologist J. M. Cruxent. Both in Bolivia and Surinam similar causeways, possibly used as footpaths during periods of flooding, are associated with ridged fields. Our inspection of the available aerial photographs of the grassy Venezuelan plains has failed to reveal any ancient agricultural earthworks, but the area deserves more intensive examination. The 16th-century Spanish chronicler Juan de Castellanos, writing of the plains country, mentions "old cultivation ridges" (*labranzas viejas camellones*), an indication that the agricultural areas of this kind he had seen or heard about had been abandoned at the time of his ob-

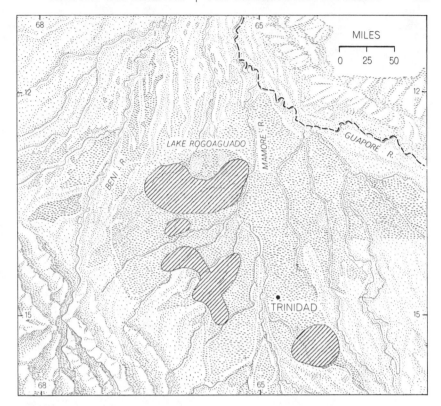

MOJOS GRASSLANDS of northeastern Bolivia have earthworks of several kinds in the indicated areas. These include causeways, settlement mounds and 50,000 acres of ridged fields.

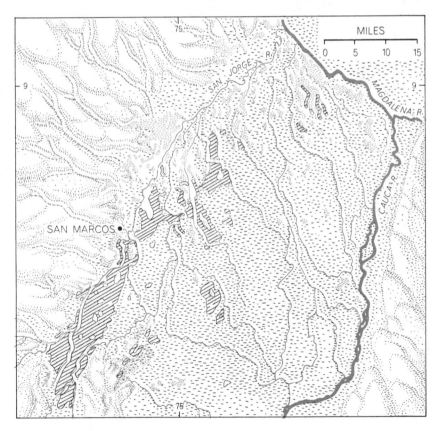

MOMPOS DEPRESSION is the alluvial plain in Colombia where seasonally flooded ridged fields are found. Fields near San Marcos are shown on the preceding page and on page 198.

CAUSEWAY in the level, seasonally flooded Mojos savanna of Bolivia runs among a series of ancient ridged fields made more prominent by the play of the late-afternoon shadows.

servations. Yet some 200 years later the author of *Orinoco Ilustrado*, Father José Gumilla, clearly described the continuing use of ridged fields. "In poorly drained sites," he wrote, the Indians "without burning the grass...lift the earth from ditches on either side, mixing the grass with the earth and then planting their maize, manioc and other root crops, along with pimento."

Father Gumilla does not say exactly where he observed this practice. It could have been anywhere in the llanos of Colombia or Venezuela, but visible remnants of this farming system must still persist. Bush pilots, if they are on the lookout for such ridges, may find them on the lower floodplains of such major tributaries of the Orinoco as the Apure, the Arauca and the Meta.

Several parallels to the ridged fields of the tropical lowlands are found in the highlands of South and Central America. It seems likely that the earth-moving practices in both environments were related in function, if not always in form. One of the closest approximations in both form and function are the ridged fields recently discovered along the western shore of Lake Titicaca, at an altitude of 12,000 feet in the Andes. These fields, covering some 200,000 acres, are found over a distance of more than 160 miles, from north of Lake Arapa in Peru to the Straits of Tiquina in Bolivia. Today the ditches are encrusted with alkali and the ridges are highly saline, so that cultivation is usually impossible. The fields still serve as grazing land, however, particularly during the dry season. At that time the upland pastures are parched and brown, but the high water table along the shore of the lake serves to keep the grass among the ancient earthworks green.

The Titicaca ridges are from 15 to 40 feet wide and range up to hundreds of feet in length. The height from ditch bottom to ridge crest is usually three to four feet. Most of the ridged fields are on the poorly drained margin of the lake plain and are subject to flooding in years of high water. The fields form checkerboard or ladder-like patterns or are irregular; their resemblance to the ridged fields in the Mojos area nearby in lowland Bolivia is striking.

Another form of agricultural earthworks in the Andean highlands consists of narrower parallel ridges, often built on sloping ground and running straight downhill rather than across the slope. Some of these ridge systems are old but others are new. Called *huachos*

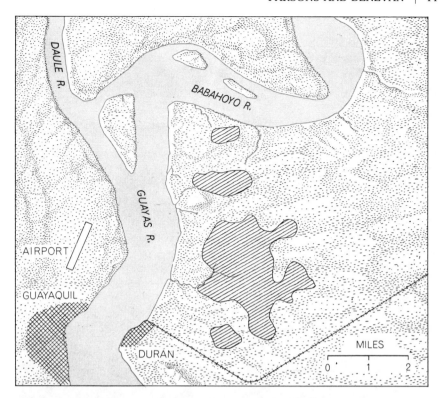

RIVER JUNCTURE near Guayaquil airport in Ecuador is area with ridged fields. To the north are found broader agricultural platforms (*see top illustration on page 204*).

in Peru and Bolivia, they help to aerate heavy sod, to channel excess water from parts of a slope and to improve drainage on slopes so gentle that they are subject to waterlogging. In Colombia's central mountains, where old second-growth forest is being cleared to establish coffee plantations and pasture, the ancient ridge systems are so abundant that the hillsides in places give the appearance of having been combed. These pre-Columbian ridges are five to six feet wide, as much as twice the width of the *huachos* that are built today.

Huachos are usually confined to hillsides but are also found on level plains. Near Like Titicaca, for example, recently dug *huachos* can be found overlying the pre-Columbian ridge systems. Above 10,000 feet in the central Andes *huachos* are planted mainly with potatoes. To the north in the Colombian Andes, where the earthworks have been raised at much lower altitudes, they are used to grow maize, manioc and the white carrot-like root known as *arracacha*.

The well-known chinampas, or artificial islands, of the Valley of Mexico have some characteristics in common with the various drainage-promoting earthworks that are found in South America. Although many chinampas were built up in shallow lake waters, others served to convert swampy ground into useful fields. Still others were evidently formed on lake margins subject to seasonal flooding. At Xochimilco, the classic chinampas site [see the article "The Chinampas of Mexico," by Michael D. Coe, beginning on page 119], the planting areas are quite large. They are squares 100 yards or more on a side, surrounded by navigable canals edged with alders and willows. In the poorly drained basin at the headwaters of the Balsas River in the nearby state of Tlaxcala another example of artificial-island agriculture is found; it is apparently a variation on the Valley of Mexico pattern.

Raised fields built to avoid the hazards of floodplain agriculture are not confined to Latin America. Henry Schoolcraft, a pioneer ethnographer who worked in the U.S. Middle West in the middle of the 19th century, described agricultural earthworks or "planting beds" in valley bottoms extending from the vicinity of Fort Wayne, Ind., to the St. Joseph, Kalamazoo and Grand rivers in Michigan. Parallel ridges were laid out in rectangles with "paths" between them; some were as much as 300 acres in extent. Similar tracts existed in Illinois, Wisconsin and Missouri. Observing that the contemporary Indian inhabitants of the region cultivated maize only by "hilling," Schoolcraft concluded that the ridged fields were the work of an earlier culture, perhaps the then little-known Mound Builders. The possibility of some link between these garden farmers of the Mississippi valley and the ridged-field farmers of Latin America invites further study, particularly by those who are reluctant to accept the idea that similar environmental adaptations are independently invented again and again.

Putting together all our evidence concerning pre-Columbian agriculture in the seasonally flooded lowlands of tropical South America, we find that remarkably little is known other than what can be deduced from studying the ridged fields themselves. In the absence of any but the scantiest of early accounts, the means used to build the earthworks, the crops raised on them and the ways in which the crops were fertilized and rotated remain matters for speculation. It is especially difficult to attempt a projection of the number of people who could have supported themselves on the produce of the ridged fields, although some useful insights can be gained by examining the populations of areas where similar agricultural systems are used today.

Before considering this question it is only fair to mention several explanations of the earthworks that deny them any agricultural function, or at least rule out the role of improving drainage. Some observers have suggested that they might be fortifications, others that they might be the remnants of sluice-mining systems. They have been called fishponds, irrigation channels or enclosures for the culture of freshwater mussels. They have even been declared to be the result of natural sedimentation processes and not the works of man at all. The last is the easiest of the alternative claims to disprove. The evidence of the aerial photographs—in particular the variety of intermingled patterns they reveal—makes it clear that man is responsible for the raised ground. The tremendous extent of the works may seem to present a puzzle. What we know from the construction of contemporary chinampas in Mexico and from gardening practices in New Guinea indicates, however, that simple digging sticks and wooden spades are the only tools needed for similar earth-moving projects today.

What are the advantages that floodplain rivers and their associated swamps offer as a habitat for a settled people? For one thing, the rich protein resources of such an environment would have allowed a settled way of life even before the development of agriculture. In the tropical lowlands of South America the rivers, swamps and even the flooded grasslands harbor abundant

ANCIENT ECUADORIAN FIELDS are being cleared of trees and cultivated by local sharecroppers today. Between the 30-foot-wide platforms the damp ditches (*darker areas*) are used for rice. Maize and other staples are planted on the higher and drier platforms.

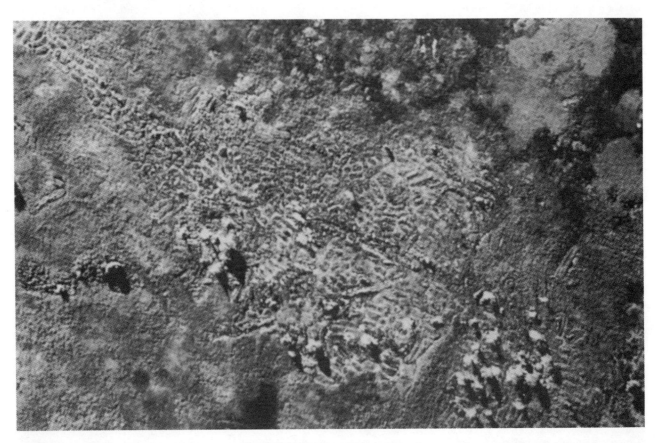

SWAMPY SAVANNA near the coast of Surinam has numerous examples of raised fields. The clusters of sausage-shaped ridges in the vertical aerial photograph are near a large, man-made earthwork, known as Hertenrits, that was put up soon after A.D. 700.

fishes, turtles (both land and water), iguanas, manatees and large rodents such as capybaras, pacas and agoutis. There is also a large and diverse population of waterfowl. Even after farming had become an established way of life, tropical agriculturists whose main food was a starchy root crop such as manioc would have valued the animal protein available in this environment.

A dual economy of this kind—ridged-field agriculture supplemented by hunting and fishing—should have been able to support far larger populations than the ones that scratch a living from the tropical forests today. Estimates of population density based on the extent of the ridged fields, however, are risky. For one thing, we do not know what fraction of the fields in a given area were under cultivation at any one time. The fields along the San Jorge River in Colombia, if they were all cultivated at the same time, could have supported as many as 400 people per square mile. In 1690 the Llanos de Mojos of Bolivia had a population of about 100,000 Indians. A century earlier, before the first contacts with Europeans resulted in deadly epidemics of Old World diseases, the population very likely numbered several hundred thousand. There is no reason to believe it was any smaller when the pre-Columbian ridged fields were under cultivation.

New archaeological evidence and new analyses of historical records attest to the existence of a surprisingly large aboriginal population in many parts of tropical South America. Both the extent of the seasonally flooded tropical farming areas and the evidence for a massive human effort that they provide suggest that the early lowland cultures had achieved a highly complex adjustment to their environment. The direction of flow of early cultural influences between the highlands and the lowlands of South America is a matter of continuing controversy. Those students of the question who contend that major cultural elements moved upstream from the lowlands of the Amazon, Orinoco and Magdalena regions into the Andean highlands in the past 2,000 or 3,000 years may find their arguments supported by the evidence for a complex, socially stratified lowland culture in pre-Columbian South America presented here. It is certain that future archaeological studies of South America's tropical lowlands and the complex ecological relations worked out by the region's early farmers should contribute much toward a more precise reconstruction of New World culture history.

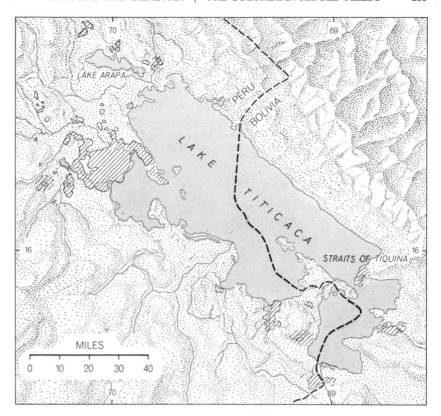

EXTENSIVE ARRAY of ridged fields lies in the Andean highlands on the poorly drained western shore of Lake Titicaca. Spread over 160 miles, the fields cover 200,000 acres.

TITICACA RIDGES, three to four feet high, are white with the accumulated salt that makes farming difficult today. When the photograph was made, the ditches were filled with water.

INDEX